Healing Dreams

Healing Dreams

Exploring the Dreams That Can Transform Your Life

Marc Ian Barasch

Riverhead Books

a member of Penguin Putnam Inc.

New York

2000

RIVERHEAD BOOKS
a member of
Penguin Putnam Inc.
375 Hudson Street
New York, NY 10014

The author gratefully acknowledges permission to quote
from the following:
"Last Night" by Antonio Machado, from *Times
Alone: Poems of Antonio Machado,* translated by Robert
Bly, and published by Wesleyan University Press, 1983.
Reprinted by permission.
"Burnt Norton" by T. S. Eliot, from *Four Quartets,*
copyright 1936 by Harcourt, Inc., renewed by T. S.
Eliot. Reprinted by permission of Harcourt, Inc.
"Little Gidding" by T. S. Eliot, from *Four Quartets,*
copyright 1942 by T. S. Eliot, renewed 1970 by Esme
Valerie Eliot. Reprinted by permission of Harcourt, Inc.

Library of Congress Cataloging-in-Publication Data

Barasch, Marc.
    Healing dreams : exploring the dreams that can
transform your life / Marc Ian Barasch.
        p.   cm.
    Includes bibliographical references.
    ISBN 1-57322-167-8
        1. Dreams.   2. Spiritual healing.   I. Title.
    BF1099.S76 B37   2000   00-030501
    154.6'32—dc21

Printed in the United States of America

10 9 8 7 6 5 4 3 2 1

This book is printed on acid-free paper. ∞

Book design by Chris Welch

Acknowledgments

Thanks to Ned Leavitt, who kept his cool and kept his hat on; Amy Hertz, who kept the ball rolling; and Chris Knutsen, who picked it up and ran with it.

Thanks to pillars of strength: Norman and Gloria Barasch, Mimi and Peter Buckley, Maryse Elias, Alan Menken, Neva Newman, John and Margo Steiner. And angels of mercy: Mary Benjamin, Bruce Fetzer, Tom Gherardi, Bob Kaplan, Ginny Jordan, Brugh Joy, Cynthia Lazaroff and Karl Kugel, Richard Peddie, Anna Sandor, John Solomon, Robin Temple, David and Laura Lea Tressemer, Merle Worth. And for timely assistance, to the Authors League Fund.

To heartful healers: Dwight McKee, Julie Nowick, Rhonda Akin and Aiko Kyle, Mark Renneker, Zoe Zimmerman. And intrepid helpers: Chris Cutbirth-Davidson, Kellee Elkins, Jane Kagon, and Ellery Smith.

To friends indeed: Marilyn Auer, Christine Brotherson, Michael Chender, the Clan Barasch (Leah, Latha, Doug, Lynne, Katie, Nicholas), Kelly Bulkeley, Jeff Cohn, Raven Dana, Roz Dauber, Jayne Gackenbach, Mark Gerzon, Peter Goldfarb, Dan and Tara Goleman, Annie Gottlieb, Bill Gray, Jeannie Halbert, Sarah Harman, Derek Hart, Norman Heumann, Andrew Heyward, Caryle Hirshberg, Peter Ingersoll, Catharine Ingram, Helen Jensen, Dave Kawecki, Karen Koffler, the Reverend Karl Kopp, Karen Littman, Gaetano and Ayelit Maida, Diane Markrow, Ron Masa, Caroline Myss, Susan Noel, John and Emma Purdie, Tom Rautenberg, Franc and Carina Roddam, Steve Roth, Dora Ruffner, Tami Simon, Tasha Sparks, Laura Uhls, Eve Wallace, Stanley Weiser.

And to dreamers everywhere.

Author's Note: Some names and identifying characteristics have been changed to protect privacy. Some dream narratives have been paraphrased or compressed for the sake of coherence.

To Neva,
who kept the faith

Contents

Last Night

Last night, as I was sleeping,
I dreamt—marvellous error!—
that a spring was breaking
out in my heart.
I said: along which secret aqueduct,
Oh water, are you coming to me,
water of a new life
that I have never drunk?

Last night, as I was sleeping,
I dreamt—marvellous error!—
that I had a beehive
here inside my heart.
And the golden bees
were making white combs
and sweet honey
from my old failures.

Last night, as I was sleeping,
I dreamt—marvellous error!—
that a fiery sun was giving
light inside my heart.
It was fiery because I felt
warmth as from a hearth,
and sun because it gave light
and brought tears to my eyes.

Last night, as I slept,
I dreamt—marvellous error!—
that it was God I had
here inside my heart.

—*Antonio Machado,*
    translated by Robert Bly

Introduction

I've dreamt in my life dreams that have stayed with me ever after, and changed my ideas; they've gone through and through me, like wine through water, and altered the colour of my mind.

—*Emily Brontë*

Fifteen years ago, I was abducted—there is no other word for it—into the realm of the Dream. It occurred without precedent or preamble: one day I was going about my business, with its usual mix of high goals and low concerns; the next, I was cast away in a far country from which I've never quite returned.

Before I knew that there are dreams and there are *dreams,* I treated them as most people do: as nocturnal reshufflings of the mental deck; as fantasy and wish fulfillment; as psychic leftovers, those emotional coffee grounds and crumpled-up impulses toward sex and violence the mind ditches nightly down some inner Disposall.

But suddenly my dreams, usually hazy and easily dismissed, acquired a jolting, Technicolor realism. They gleamed with mysteries both opaque and insistent, their meaning tantalizingly beyond my grasp. "*Weird* dream!"

my girlfriend remarked one morning as I washed up, shipwrecked, on wakeful shores, another traveler's tale on my lips. "No," I'd murmured, struggling to describe it. "A *vision*." I would awaken, stunned, from visits to places of near-hallucinatory intensity, where the sky was translucent sapphire, the grass dew-dipped emerald, and discarnate voices tore the air like thunderclaps. The dream characters I encountered were so vivid and alive, the landscapes so cinematic, that my waking world seemed paltry and limited by comparison.

The dreams were mostly ominous. In one, a maniac heralded as the "Greatest Mass Murderer in the History of Mankind" had "escaped from a cell" and was chasing me with an ax to decapitate me. In another, Death peered through my basement window, his gaunt face glowing like phosphorous beneath his hood, coolly casing the joint. Necks were a puzzling leitmotiv: six long needles were stuck in my "neck-brain" by a circle of primitive tribesmen; a "World War II bullet" was lodged in my neck, and a kindly Chinese surgeon removed it; or I was crawling through a tunnel full of crumbling bones in a Mayan "necropolis" ("neck-cropolis?" I had asked myself, mindful of dreams' incorrigible punning, but could make no further sense of it).

I would go to my job as a magazine editor still enveloped in their aura, soldiering through the day, as if all-night creep shows at the inner drive-in were the norm. But after one terrifying dream—torturers had hung an iron pot filled with red-hot coals beneath my chin, and I woke up screaming, the odor of searing flesh in my nostrils—I couldn't ignore them any longer. I was sure that something inside me had gone drastically wrong. Each successive dream had spelled it out more explicitly until, although the word was never uttered, it glared down at me from a neon marquee: cancer.

I made an appointment to see a doctor and blurted out my fears in a rush, embarrassed the only symptoms I could offer were a fistful of nightmares. Skeptical, he pressed and prodded my neck, informing me he felt nothing out of the ordinary. He suggested, not unsympathetically, that I was suffering from job-related stress. It was true enough: after a frenetic year spent revamping a homespun new-age journal into a slick national monthly, my work life remained a treadmill, its dial stuck permanently at a dead run. Before I left the doctor, I awkwardly asked if there were a bodily organ that might fit my dream's peculiar image of a "neck-brain." "Maybe the thyroid gland," he offered dubiously. But the blood test he ordered showed my hormone levels were perfectly normal.

The nightmares continued, flooding in as if a hellish levee had burst. I badgered the doctor for a more complete workup. This time, palpating my neck, he detected a hard lump beneath his fingers—a thyroid nodule. Tests were ordered. I dutifully swallowed a few pellets containing tiny amounts of radioactive iodine—the thyroid sucks up iodine like a sponge, which, I was told, would "light up" the normal cells in contrast to any abnormal ones. The absorption pattern on the diagnostic film showed a dark suspicious mass that the doctor assured me was almost certainly benign. But some weeks later, I felt a grim twinge of vindication when a needle biopsy confirmed what my dreams had hinted—it was a cancerous malignancy.

I took a sabbatical from my job. My days filled with a procession of friends, relatives, colleagues, and medical experts, each bearing conflicting advice, all urging me to brush my dreams aside. I could scarcely blame them. But I felt doubly a pariah, self-exiled from the inner world by my own incomprehension, regarded querulously by those around me for putting too much stock in it. I drove people to distraction trying to explain how these dreams were different—deeper, wider, higher, more *real*—but they seemed not to know what I was talking about. The doctors came to regard me with condescension and barely concealed irritation. My friends thought I was going a little crazy. The metaphysical world was breaking over the real one like a tsunami, inundating it with a significance I could not fathom.

One evening before falling asleep, I scribbled, in some desperation, a formal request in the dream notebook I'd started to keep: *What is the direction of a cure?* That night, I had a startling vision: *under the ground a white, snakelike worm is turning in upon itself in a perfect spiral. When its head reaches the center, blinding rays of light shoot out, and a voice solemnly intones: "You have been living on the outer shell of your being—The Way Out Is the Way In!"*

The image was as repulsive as a moldering grave ("The worms crawl in, the worms crawl out," goes the childhood singsong). I would come to understand only much later that this was a picture of the spiraling inner journey, of the archetypal descent that leads to wholeness. But at the time, if I sought anything from my dreams, it was specifics: I wanted oncological status reports, with symbols as clear as the meteorological symbols on a TV weather map. Instead, here were these mysterious hieroglyphs. It added insult to injury. The medical quest—finding the most accurate diagnosis, the best doctor, the ultimate cure—was tough enough. Now, just as I needed to stay outwardly focused, my dreams became a centripetal force, pulling me deeper within. In the weeks and months that followed, the conflict became ever more maddening. In the end, I chose surgery, as much, I'm convinced, to still my dreams as to save my life.

The rigors of the thyroid operation (an excision my dreams had prefigured as a guillotining, a ritual sacrifice) were more traumatic than I had anticipated. My cure left me wounded in body and spirit. I was unable and finally unwilling to step back on the merry-go-round of ambition. My pursuit of the brass ring had led me to the proverbial edge of the abyss. Driven by a journalist's curiosity and a need to feel less alone, I spent a decade interviewing hundreds of patients and doctors, plunging into the literatures of medicine and mythology, seeking new compass points for the healing process, and for my own soul.

I eventually published two books on the mind-body connection and found myself in a career as a quasi-medical expert. But even after years of conscientious probing, I was haunted by a mystery. What had been the source of the torrent of images that had threatened to submerge me even as I struggled for my life?

I had always been, in an unreflective way, a Freudian when it came to dream analysis. Dreams were elaborate concealments of the sex-and-power-hungry id: rip away the mask, and there, invariably, would be the glowering features of our instinctual being. A dream, whether horripilating, ecstatic, or just plain baffling, had predictable mechanisms, a symbolism amenable to categorical analysis. Yet my dreams had made me feel utterly out of my depth. They had almost mystically anticipated events.

(Had it been pure coincidence I'd dreamed that a Chinese surgeon took a "bullet" from my neck, and months later, a real Chinese surgeon—a Dr. Wang, the country's premier thyroid specialist and the spitting image of my dream doctor—had operated to remove my tumor?) They had galvanized me to act, almost against my will. How could dreams, evanescent wisps of the night, gather the force of a Kansas tornado barreling toward Oz? What kind of dreams *were* these?

The Never-Ending Story

Going over my old journals recently, I was surprised to find, as if stumbling upon a message in a bottle, a dream I'd jotted down months before I knew I was ill. At the time, it seemed nonsensical: *I am flying on the back of a dinosaur that is ravaging a city from above. Its face looks like a cocker spaniel with snow on its nose. Then my nine-year-old daughter (who is somehow also my sister) and I are sailing a boat that is being blown out of control by a great wind. Then I'm sick, and trying to get to a plane.*

Though these images had been unusually vivid—I felt vertigo as I clung to the creature's back, the wind blasting in my face—their meaning eluded me. My sister had died of leukemia almost ten years before, at the age of twenty-two: perhaps her presence in my dream reflected my lingering grief, or signaled some irrational anxiety that my daughter, Leah, might suffer her same fate. I put it out of my mind shortly after I woke up.

The next evening, Leah and I went out to get some ice cream, then decided to pass by the local theater. I noticed a poster for a new children's movie called *The Never-Ending Story* in the lobby. It depicted a snow-white flying dragon whose goofy, canine-looking features were those of the snow-covered spaniel of my dream. Leah clamored to see it. Now curious, I bought two tickets.

The film begins with a boy named Sebastian bolting awake from a nightmare. An imaginative child having trouble in school, he is admonished at the breakfast table by his father to stop "daydreaming" and get his head "down out of the clouds." Instead, Sebastian sneaks off to play hooky. He wanders into a bookstore, where the proprietor hands him an ancient book embossed with mystic symbols, entitled *The Never-Ending Story.*

Hiding in an abandoned school storeroom, the boy is quickly entranced by this tale of a faerie land threatened by a malevolent force called the Nothing, which manifests as an all-powerful wind. The story has the hallmarks of a standard quest: a boy hero and a friendly dragon set out to save a princess whose kingdom is being destroyed while she wastes away from a mysterious disease. But as Sebastian reads on, he finds that the curtain between the book's fantasy world and his real life is becoming unnervingly gauzy. When a violent storm arises in the book, real rain and lightning suddenly crash through his own window. And when the boy hero in the story gazes into a magical mirror to "face his true self," he sees instead the face of . . . *Sebastian!*

"This is going too far," Sebastian shouts in a panic, hurling the enchanted volume across the room. But fiction and real life continue inexorably to merge. Returning to his reading, he eavesdrops on the characters as they explain that it is he himself who must rescue the princess (a beautiful blond girl who, I was startled to note, bore an uncanny resemblance to my late sister). The princess explains that her realm, called Fantasia, is dying because people no longer cherish their own dreams. Sebastian can cure her, and defeat the Nothing, only by giving life to his imagination. The climax of the film is the boy's acceptance of the imaginary world as a reality. After saving the day, he triumphantly returns to his own world on the dragon's back, swooping down city streets to terrorize some bug-eyed schoolyard bullies as the theme music swells, "Dream a dream, and what you see will be."

Though I'd been surprised at the time that elements in the film had been foreshadowed the night before, I chalked it up to one of those down-the-rabbit-hole coincidences. But renting the video recently to refresh my memory, I was astonished to see how the movie filled in the blanks in my dream like a jigsaw puzzle piece. It seemed the film had contained a pointed message: my dreams were real, and I—just like the little princess and my sister—had my own deadly, all-devouring Nothing to confront.

This interplay between the dreamworld and the real one was at odds with my understanding of how dreams worked. I remembered from my college psychology texts there were various schools of dream interpretation, although seldom on speaking terms with one another. There were what might be called the symbolists, who took dream elements as representations of hidden meanings that could be decoded by a skilled interpreter. On the other hand were the phenomenologists, who said there was nothing hidden behind the curtain—dreams were dress rehearsals of new ways of being and doing, experiences that could in themselves lead to personal growth. And then there were physiological reductionists, who insisted dreams were mere neural discharges, "noisy signals sent up from the brainstem"[1] that created random images. Dr. David Foulkes, a leading proponent of this now resurgent viewpoint, has written: "The reason why dreamers can't understand what their dreams mean is that they don't mean anything." The dream, he has suggested, *has* no "message"; moreover, "if we persist in searching for one, we're in the angel-counting business."[2]

But I had been forced into the angel-counting business by default. I began to wonder what other treasures lay hidden in my dream notebooks. Paging through them was like finding an infantryman's field diary, scrawled fast and furious in battle with little hope it would ever be read. In the years that followed, I was drawn deeper into the study, word by word and image by image, of this personal apocrypha—truly a book of secrets. As complex new meanings unveiled themselves, I realized how much I had failed to see, and how meager had been the analytic tools at my disposal. It was as if I'd been trying to disassemble a fine watch with a hammer, photograph the Grand Canyon through a pinhole camera, or facet a rough diamond with a pocketknife.

The Starfish

Among the bizarre dreams that accompanied my illness, one stands out for its marvelous peculiarities, not least of which was a final meaning that would unfold, rather spectacularly, only years later. The dream landed in my life a week after my diagnosis. Looking back, it surprises me how half-hearted my attempts were to answer its riddle. But perhaps it was understandable. My doctor had pronounced the dread word "cancer" as sonorously as a judge at sentencing. I was spooked and disoriented, running from macrobiotic healers to endocrinologists, reluctant to pause lest death catch my heel. But years later, through new eyes, I saw that a dream I had taken to be a psychological refuse heap was a rich archaeological site, awaiting only excavation:

> *I am standing on a residential street watching a private plane, a Cessna, blow up in midair. The cockpit falls from the sky into a blond Western boy's backyard, then bounces onto the front lawn of a "tinkerer." I am amazed to see that a "sacred intelligent starfish" has survived the crash. It's barely alive, but the tinkerer is already working on it, gently placing it in a bath of salt water to help it heal itself. Suddenly the boy in whose yard it had first landed comes to claim it. We reluctantly hand it over, though I see he doesn't have a clue how to care for it. I watch in horror as the boy removes it from its water. It immediately starts drying out, turning into "dried cod" and then, in his clumsy hands, crumbling irreparably apart. I am inconsolable at the loss, shocked to see a magnificent creature so heedlessly destroyed.*

When I awoke, I had seized on the images as medically significant. A "private plane," I thought, was a metaphor for the body, the soul's personal vehicle. Perhaps the pilot's cockpit, where the controls are, stood for the head and neck area, and the starfish for my thyroid gland, a self-regulating, "intelligent" source of sacred life energy.

If these first images were a sort of anatomical schematic, there were also images of treatment. The blond boy seemed to represent my Western doctors. I *had* first landed in their yard—had gone to them to be diagnosed—and was deciding, with no small ambivalence, to surrender my body to their care, though still hoping against hope for a more natural remedy.

This would have seemed a straightforward enough interpretation. But the next day, my daughter cajoled me to take her to the Boston Science Museum, which we happened to pass on the way back from school. No sooner had we wandered into the marine exhibit than an eager young staffer in charge of that day's demonstration thrust a living starfish into my hand, loudly proclaiming its unusual trait: "It can regenerate!" Later that day, a friend who makes public television documentaries stopped by, mentioning that he had just returned from Nevada, where he had been hired to "shoot an airplane explosion"—a Federal Aviation Administration test to ascertain the role of "fuel misting" in air crashes. (In an engine, fuel is mixed with air in the carburetor—a device to which my doctors had often compared the thyroid, which regulates the body's "mix" of metabolic energy.)

Poring over the dream's text in my notebook, it was as if a clear picture was finally emerging from some slow-developing photographic emulsion. I could still recall the contempt I'd felt for the dream "tinkerer," my impatience with his slowness and simplemindedness in the face of a dire emergency. My pocket dictionary defines *tinker* as "to work in a bungling way; to make clumsy, unsuccessful attempts to mend or repair something." But now, consulting my big *Webster's*, I was surprised to learn that this connotation of amateur and ineffectual fussing is not the word's original meaning. Harking back to an earlier time, a *tinker* is defined as "a mender of metal kettles, pans, and the like, usually going from house to house; a jack of all trades." A tinker, then, is a kind of healer—-he makes house calls, like an old-fashioned doctor; he patiently repairs vessels used to prepare food, the body's fuel.

But such menders are generally disdained in our throwaway society. They would be unwelcome in a surgery ward specializing in radical excisions. I also devalued them in my own psyche. The attitudes of the two dream characters, the patient tinker and the impulsive, aggressive boy, mirrored two sides of my personality, which were often at war. The starfish, too, was a creature of contradictions. A hybrid animal, a creature both of the heavens and the ocean, it suggested a balance I was trying, mostly without success, to strike in my life: to be a star in the media firmament, yet remain in my own watery, private depths. The image also suggested a dangerous psychological inflation—the starfish was "flying too high"; it was a "fish out of water," existing on its own aloof "private plane" of existence.

The specificity of the word *Cessna* remained irksome. The name did not seem to be a play on words. The brand of plane favored by drug smugglers, I had thought it might express my anxiety about being "addicted" to a pharmaceutical replacement hormone following my surgery. It wasn't until five years later that the dream's last puzzle piece slipped unexpectedly into place. I had moved back to Boulder, Colorado, where I was leasing a sprawling suburban house with a few friends. One day, it was my turn to walk the ten blocks to our landlord's to drop off the rent. Just as I was heading out with the envelope, my roommate stopped me. "You can't go over there," she said. "The street's cordoned off. A plane just crashed into a yard two houses from where she lives." It was April first. I looked at her quizzically. "No," she said, "I'm not kidding. It was a little Cessna."

The pilot and passenger, she explained, had been killed. The only injury on the ground was an older man who spent Sundays tinkering with vintage cars. A piece of the plane had fallen on his garage. Had I gone over there a few hours earlier, as I had planned, I would have been a firsthand witness to the uncanny dream spectacle of a Cessna plummeting from the sky right before my eyes.

I did a little research into the case—which Boulder authorities told the local paper was the "most bizarre" they'd ever seen—discovering odd resonances to the situation I'd found myself in five years earlier. The passenger turned out to be a man convinced he had a fatal brain cancer (a common variety of which is astrocytoma, named for its starlike shape). Investigators had labeled him a "doctor shopper" who went from physician to physician seeking diagnosis, which would have well characterized me at the time of my dream. After writing farewell letters to friends and relatives, the man had rented the plane with the intention of committing suicide.

Once airborne, he had attacked the pilot, causing the plane to crash. Ironically, a subsequent coroner's autopsy revealed no evidence of cancer: the passenger's certainty that he had the direst medical condition was misplaced.[3] I was reminded of the morbid letters I had written to friends, convinced I'd been facing imminent death, learning only later that my cancer was a slower-growing, less virulent type.

What were the odds I would be, five years after my dream, within a few blocks of a Cessna falling into the yard of a tinker? Here was clear indication that the imaginal realm could intrude into "real" life. I began to wonder if every dream theory I'd heard was, if not wrong, at least radically incomplete. Perhaps a dream had to be analyzed not just as a series of metaphors but as a collection of stories, radiating out in many directions like starfish arms—stories that could sometimes burst the confines of time and space.

My starfish dream became a model of how to think in a multidimensional way about interpreting a "big" dream—for its stories address many issues simultaneously. One story concerned vital *personal issues:* it said I was a fish out of water, trying to be a star, headed for a crash. The characters represented different aspects of myself: the starfish, rarified and vulnerable (its many arms also suggesting the potential and perils of doing many things at once); the tinkerer, the embodiment of care and patience; the rough boy, a classic *shadow figure* representing undesirable traits—arrogance, disdain, and impulsiveness—that I needed to face up to.

But another "story" was a *warning,* in this case a medical cautionary tale: be wary of treatment by the impetuous "young science" of Western medicine. The fate of the starfish would, in a sense, later overtake me. The operation months later had felt crude, even barbarous. I, too, would crumble apart after losing something that seemed precious and irreplaceable. The dream also put forth, as such dreams usually do, an alternative approach to a problem—in this case, to help the affected organ in its own milieu (which early physiologists called "nourishing the terrain"). I was shown a creature that was the very spirit of the affected organ, and told of its capacity for self-healing (the thyroid is one of the few organs that, like the liver, is capable of tissue regeneration). The dream juxtaposed the prevailing medical attitude of the body-as-machine with the ancient idea that the body's organs are sacred, living creatures. (In Taoist medicine, for example, the lungs were said to be inhabited by a white tiger, the heart by a red bird, the spleen by a phoenix.)

The dream also had distinctly *sexual* overtones Freud would have found familiar: in a crude pun, the starfish was in the "*cock*pit"; later, it turns into "cod" (according to my dictionary, an archaic term for the scrotum), which "dried out" in contrast to the starfish's moist Eros. (Indeed, my love life, subsumed by work, was perishing.) The twinned Freudian theme of aggression is also implicit in the word *cockpit*—a place where cockfights are staged between male birds—suggesting, when I reflected on it, my competitive relationship with my father.

Yet another of these brachiating story lines was a *social* commentary. It suggested we have forgotten the value of people like the old tinker, who gently restores what is broken. It furnished a critique of society in general, and of the institution of medicine specifically, which has too often forsaken the "tinkerer" approach in favor of fast-paced, aggressive "heroic intervention." Another part of the dream's social message had to do with my own professional milieu: working in a fast-paced business, I tended to value quick, sharp, extroverted colleagues over slower-paced, less forceful, more inward ones. The dream was applying a corrective, suggesting I might need to reverse those values. Indeed, it was my fast-track friends who most quickly ran the other way when my crisis hit, and the "slow" ones who caringly stayed behind.

Another of the dream's multiple stories is *archetypal*. If it were being told as a myth, it might go something like this: Starfish, possessor of the sacred power of restoring wounds, falls to earth from heaven. He finds a mortal ally, who performs a sort of baptism—in my dream the starfish had been placed in what looked like a combination birdbath and baptismal font—but he is betrayed and finally sacrificed. There are hints of the tale of Icarus, who flew too high and crashed, or pop mythologies like *E.T.* and *The Man Who Fell to Earth,* in which a vulnerable alien with strange powers crash-lands on our world, finds a sympathetic protector, but ultimately falls prey to short-sighted authorities. (Both films feature a motif of clumsy and destructive medical treatment.) To ascribe a mythic dimension to a dream may seem overblown. But in myths, we may discern our own life story writ large; uncover patterns and belief systems that, once understood, may be changed; find perspective on our individual concerns as reflections of eternal human themes.

Then the tale jumped the boundaries of the page entirely. The dream amplified its impact through *synchronicity,* barging into my life. Against all odds, the next day an actual starfish, wet and gently stirring, was placed in the palm of my hand. Through a direct encounter with my dream creature, I was initiated into a relationship with a sort of totem animal—one capable of self-healing, and so a palpable harbinger of my inner resources.

Finally, five years later, a *precognition*—through the crashing Cessna—was revealed, forcing me to give serious consideration to the mystical belief that linear time is an illusion, that we are not the purely earthbound creatures we think we are but are also starfish of a sort, plying a sea of past, present, and future.

To this day, the dream remains a *Rashomon*-like story, where many versions can be told of the same event, each bearing a fresh truth. It is this approach that will characterize this book—to suggest not just a method of interpretation but a way of seeing.

The Call of the Dream

Can we really believe in our dreams? Is it so that, as *The Never-Ending Story*'s chirpy theme song insists, "what you dream will be"? We tend to deride the source of our dreams as "just our imagination," as a never-never land without any practical value.

Though our national lexicon is rife with expressions like "Believe in your dreams" (generally meaning one's ego ambitions, which dreams love to puncture), few of us follow our nightly fantasias. Our dreams are left, like Rapunzel, to spin out their tales in a tower, their long golden hair not quite brushing the ground. We seem to suffer, the radical psychiatrist R. D. Laing once told me, from a sort of collective "psychophobia, a fear of the deeper contents of our own minds." Our horror films teem with cautionary tales about what happens to those who delve into the phantasmagoria of the psyche. Taking dreams seriously *can* be dangerous business—was not the Son of Sam killer also a visionary?[4] We're not sure how safe it is to gaze too deeply within, let alone act on what we may find there.

If we consider heeding the directives of our dreams, we may easily wind up in Hamlet's metaphysical dilemma, which the novelist John Gardner once described as whether to follow "higher law in an uncertain universe . . . on the say-so of a ghost." Hamlet's choice leads to murder and mayhem. Yet the price for ignoring the inner world is also steep: "The tragedy of Hamlet," noted the writer Laurens van der Post, "was precisely that he always found a reason for not obeying the readiness of his own spirit."

I've puzzled over my dreams, cherished them and run from them, and when I couldn't figure them out, saved them as one would a loose bolt in a junk drawer, wondering if it might someday prove valuable. But to take dreams seriously—enough to act on them, to live by them—is potentially subversive. Dreams smash down the barricades: they admit all, proscribe nothing, view life through a different moral aperture. They do not always flatter us. They are a mirror of human imperfectibility, held before the face of our most burnished ambitions. They may scare us: a nightmare is a concrescence of our most private terrors. But even a purely exhilarating dream, a flight to the heavens astride a winged horse, stirs a different sort of unease—that we may harbor an unrealized greatness, a potential that, if we dared fulfill it, would bring an end to ordinary life.

These days, I try to listen to my dreams, even for critical decisions, though such a provisional reliance on phantasms may mark me for a fool. I can't help but see life binocularly, through night eyes as well as day sight, and this changes everything—my relationships to others, to myself, to reality in general. Some dreams, I think, *are* a form of reality. These don't seem "dreamy" in the normal sense of the word, denoting things indistinct, wispy, and dissipative. To the contrary, they make the everyday seem more evanescent. They suggest it is the ship of waking life that yaws and drifts, lacking the rudder of the infinite. The closer I look, the more my dreams seem to insist upon the same spiritual onus: *You must live truthfully. Right now. And always.*

In an era where everything is being mapped—every geographic feature from the highest heavens to the sea bottom, every physical object from distant supernovae to the last glinting speck of the human genome—dreams remain, by their very nature, terra incognita. They push at the edge of our limitations, urging us toward the wild boundarylands of the possible.

What Is a
Healing Dream?

Defining the Indefinable

> I have had a most rare vision. I have had a dream, past the wit of man to
> say what dream it was: man is but an ass, if he go about to expound this
> dream. . . . The eye of man hath not heard, the ear of man hath not seen,
> man's hand is not able to taste, his tongue to conceive, nor his heart to re-
> port, what my dream was.
>
> —*Bottom, in Shakespeare's* A Midsummer Night's Dream

M ost of us have had (or, inevitably, will have) at least one dream
in our lives that stops us in our tracks. Such dreams tell us that
we're not who we think we are. They reveal dimensions of experience beyond the everyday. They may shock us, console us, arouse us,
or repulse us. But they take their place alongside our most memorable life
events because they're so vivid and emblematic. Some are like parables, setting off sharp detonations of insight; others are like gripping mystery tales;
still others are like mythic dramas, or horror stories, or even uproarious
jokes. In our journey from childhood to age, we may count them on one
hand. Yet once they have flared in the soul, they constellate there, emitting
a steady, pulsarlike radiance.

The number of people I have discovered grappling with these powerful
inner experiences has astounded me. In a time when the individual psyche

is increasingly colonized by mass culture, when media images seem ever more intent on replacing dreams wholesale, here is an unvoiced parallel existence dreamers sometimes do not share with even their loved ones.

People often describe such striking dreams in a self-devised lexicon: "deep" dreams; "vibrational" dreams; "strong" dreams; "flash" dreams; "TV" dreams (a South African priestess); "lucky-feeling dreams" (a dog breeder in Quebec); "true"dreams (a Salish Indian healer in Oregon). A folk artist named Sultan Rogers, famous for his fancifully erotic woodcarvings, refers to his most powerful dreams as "futures," so filled are they with the urgency to be manifest in the world. (He makes a point of carving them immediately upon waking, while the sensuous images are still fresh.) Yet many I spoke with displayed a genuine reticence about discussing their dreams, as if exposing them to daylight might stunt some final germination still to come. Famed Jungian analyst Marion Woodman declined to share a dream she believed helped heal her of a serious physical illness, because, she told me, "I cannot let others into my holy of holies." Some said they feared the professional consequences of being seen as overly attentive to dreams. "I'm in the midst of putting together a multimillion-dollar deal based on a dream I had ten years ago," one man confided. His vision had become the polestar of his life. "But it wouldn't do," he said, "for my partners to think I'm relying on invisible consultants."

In the fifteen years since I began my exploration, a nascent field of research has arisen, along with a host of terms—*impactful, transformative, titanic, transcendent*—to differentiate big dreams from ordinary ones. I have coined the term *Healing Dreams,* because they seem to have a singular intensity of purpose: to lead us to embrace the contradictions between flesh and spirit, self and other, shadow and light in the name of wholeness. The very word for "dream" in Hebrew—*chalom*—derives from the verb meaning "to be made healthy or strong."[1] With remarkable consistency, such dreams tell us that we live on the merest outer shell of our potential, and that the light we seek can be found in the darkness of a yet-unknown portion of our being.

Jung labeled them numinous (from the Latin *numen,* meaning "divine command"), but often just used the succinct shorthand, *big.* While most dreams, he wrote, were "nightly fragments of fantasy," thinly veiled commentaries on "the affairs of the everyday," these significant dreams were associated with major life passages, deep relationship issues, and spiritual turning points.[2]

Many cultures have had a terminology for such dreams of surpassing power. The Greek New Testament seems to contain more words for inner experience than Eskimos have for snow: *onar* (a vision seen in sleep as opposed to waking); *enypnion* (a vision seen in sleep that comes by surprise); *horama* (which could refer to visions of the night, sleeping visions, or waking visions); *horasis* (a supernatural vision); *optasia* (a supernatural vision that implies the Deity revealing Himself); and so on. By and large the English language has been impoverished of a working vocabulary; we have little at hand beyond *dream* and *nightmare*. Given our cultural paucity, it can be a struggle to define these signal occurrences.

"How do you know when you've had a special dream?" I once asked a Choctaw Indian acquaintance named Preston. A humorous man with rubbery features—his role in his tribe, he told me, was as a "backwards person," a trickster and comedian—he grew uncharacteristically serious at my question.

"These vision dreams are things that you follow," he said. "Things that you do. They show you a situation that needs to be taken care of, and a way to turn it around."

"But *how* do you know?" I pressed him.

"It's the way you feel. That kind of dream wakes you up very suddenlike. Maybe you wake up really, really happy." He looked at me, eyebrow cocked. "Or maybe you wake up with your bed so soaking wet you'da thought you'd peed on yourself!"

His ribald comment points to a universally reported attribute of Healing Dreams—what we might call ontological weight, the heft and immediacy of lived experience. Remarks from various dreamers return often to a common theme of "realer than real." They often comment on the acuity of the senses—taste, touch, sight, smell, and hearing. I, too, can recall awakening with my ears still ringing from a dream gunshot, or waking up momentarily blinded by a dream's burst of light.

There is often a depth of emotion that beggars normal waking life. The sixteenth-century rabbi and physician Solomon Almoli wrote: "If one dreams of powerful fantasy images that cause him to be excited or to feel anger or fear during the dream itself, this is a true dream; but if the images are insipid and arouse no strong feelings, the dream is not true."[3] Such dreams are filled not with simple anxiety, but terror; not mere pleasantness, but heart-bursting joy. People report waking up on tear-soaked pillows, or laughing in delight. (The Bantu people of Africa have a specific term for the latter—*bilita mpatshi*, or blissful dreaming.[4])

Healing Dreams are analogous to ancient Greek theater, where actors in colorful, oversized costumes presented stories contrived to put an audience through the emotional wringer; to make it feel, viscerally, the heroes' agonies and ecstasies. Indeed, some Healing Dreams feature larger-than-life settings and personages—palatial buildings, sweeping landscapes, beings of supernatural goodness or terrible malignancy. Healing Dreams seem designed to produce a catharsis, to lead their "audience" to a metanoia, a change of heart.

Like drama, such dreams often have an unusually coherent narrative structure. Islamic dream texts refer to the ordinary dream as *azgha*—literally, "handful of dried grass and weeds," signifying a lack of arrangement—in contrast to the more coherent messages of *ahkam* ("genuine inspiration from the Deity, warning from a protecting power, or revelation of coming events"[5]). The Healing Dream's storytelling tends to be more artful, often containing a rich array of literary or cinematic devices—subplots, secondary characters, sudden reversals and surprise endings, flashbacks and flashforwards, adumbration, even voice-over narration and background music.

Healing Dreams often involve a sense of the uncanny or paranormal. Within the dream, one may find one has special powers to telekinetically move objects; receive information as if via telepathy; levitate; transform oneself into other creatures; visit heavens or hells. Dreamers report of out-of-body experiences; actual events foreseen; talking with the departed; having a near-identical dream to that of a friend or loved one; and other strange synchronicities. Healing Dreams hum with so much energy that, like a spark from a Van de Graaf generator, they seem to leap the gap between the visible and invisible worlds.

In such dreams, symbols tend to be extraordinarily multilayered—exaggerated cases of what Freud referred to as "overdetermination," where an image seems to be "chosen" by the unconscious for its multiplicity of associations. Language itself reveals a dense richness. A key dream word may yield half a dozen definitions, each with a different or even opposing nuance. There is often a powerful aesthetic component—such dreams may depict dances and rituals, music and song, poetry, photos, paintings, and other art forms. There is frequently a collective dimension—the dream seems to transcend the dreamer's personal concerns, reaching into the affairs of family, clan, community, or the world at large.

Such dreams also have a peculiar persistence. People report waking up with the images still before their eyes. The dream lingers in memory long after common ones fade. New meanings emerge over time. One lives, as it were, into the dream. "The *find-out,*" the Native American sage Lame Deer told one researcher, "has taken me all my life."

Most important, Healing Dreams, if heeded, can be transformational—creating new attitudes toward ourselves and others, magnifying our spiritual understanding, deepening the feeling side of life, producing changes in careers and relationships, even affecting society itself. After a Healing Dream, one may never be the same again.

Entering the Realm

To fathom such dreams, to dive into their depths, is to find ourselves under a pressure of many atmospheres. If we bob too quickly to the explanatory surface, we will get the bends. Yet if we remain too long beneath the ocean of the unconscious, we risk the psychological equivalent of that intoxicated confusion divers call "rapture of the deep." If we take dreams naively—either assuming "I made it up in the first place, so I can easily explain it" or, conversely, believing one is receiving infallible dictations from higher powers—what might otherwise heal us could harm us.

Jung cautioned that a relationship with the unconscious can flourish "only when the conscious mind fulfills its task to the very limit."[6] He himself described occasions when he was plunged precipitously into the realm of big dreams. He was notably unsentimental about the rigors of the experience: "Unpopular, ambiguous, and dangerous," he wrote, "it is a voyage of discovery to the other pole of the world." During what he called his "confrontation with the unconscious"—a period beginning in 1913, after a traumatic break with Freud—he was inundated with dreams and visions he was unable to trace back to his own personal history. Afflicted by a "mass of doubts," he withdrew from the world to his house on the shores of Lake Zurich, resolving to explore the depths of the psyche. There he felt himself becoming "a blank page whirling about in the winds of the spirit," often fearing he would be "driven out of my wits."[7]

On one occasion, Jung had a dire vision of a monstrous tide of blood flowing across Europe, bearing untold numbers of corpses. Fearing that the macabre flood symbolized his own onrushing psychosis, he decided all that was left was to keep an exact record of the experience—then, at least, his demise might make a contribution to science. Scant months after his vision, the sanguinary tide of World War I engulfed the continent. "Shocked and horrified at the news as he was," writes biographer Barbara Hannah, "he was completely and for always relieved of his fears about his own sanity, for he then recognized the vision for what it was: a singularly clear premonition."[8] Over time his inward journeying, at once perilous and revelatory, led him to a breakthrough insight, which he called "the objectivity of the psyche." The images of the unconscious were not just fragments of memory or symbols of repressed inner drives, he decided, but had their own mysterious life ("like animals in a forest"[9]) and would speak if we learned to listen.

Several years ago, when I was traveling in southern Germany, I impulsively got on a train bound for Zurich. I wanted to visit Jung's old house by the lake, not so much to sightsee but to make pilgrimage. Learning that his aged son, Franz, still lived there, I called from a pay phone and was surprised when he invited me to drop over. As I approached the stately home, I felt a small thrill to see, carved over the door, Jung's famous shibboleth, a

Latin saying that translates, "Invoked or not invoked, the god will enter." It is a viewpoint at once optimistic and a little unnerving.

Franz Jung, with his pouched eyes and enigmatic half-smile, was at eighty-six a dead ringer for the cover picture on his father's spiritual auto-biography, *Memories, Dreams, Reflections*. He led me upstairs and gestured to a worn, overstuffed chair in "C.G.'s" library. As we sat surrounded by the great psychologist's own copies of Cicero's *De Divinatione* and fraying leather editions of Goethe, he asked bluntly why I had come. When I told him I was still struggling to understand my own big dreams, he responded with delight: "I see we will not waste our visit!"

He abruptly rose, saying he had something he thought would interest me—"since you want to sniff around"—and after a few minutes of rummaging, strode in with a book bound in red leather. My heart leaped: the *Red Book*! That legendary, profusely self-illustrated folio from Jung's period of inspiration and near madness, long banned from publication by his heirs, was about to be placed in my hands. No, Franz told me, that work remained "locked in the family vault." This was Franz's one remaining copy of *Seven Sermons to the Dead,* a beautifully crafted limited edition his father had printed for friends.

Its dense, Gothic, almost heraldic lettering seemed well suited to its provenance as epiphany. The book had been written on an occasion Jung had suddenly sensed "a peculiar atmosphere," as if his house were "crammed full of spirits." One night Franz, then age nine, had a disturbing dream of an angel and a devil battling in midair over the figure of a fisherman. He drew it in crayon and ran into his father's study to show him. The next day, a Sunday, Jung had begun writing his *VII Sermones ad Mortuos*. It poured out in a matter of days, a strange, incantatory work that attempted to re-solve "pairs of opposites"—good and evil, beauty and ugliness, the one and the many—into a single "fullness of Divine Being." Jung had slyly credited the work to a first-century heretic, Basilides of Alexandria, concealing his own authorship for years. On the one hand, it was a self-protective ges-ture—doctors of the fledgling science of the mind were not supposed to be outright visionaries. On the other, it was his way of honoring a text he felt was not properly his but had been retrieved from the otherworld.[10]

I paged through it, relying on my rusty high school German to decipher a few of its portentous phrases. Here was a vision of wholeness stripped of piety, in which the dead return from Jerusalem empty-handed and line the walls clamoring, "We want to know about God!" Much of the book is an invocation to a forgotten deity named Abraxas—"the god whom it is difficult to know . . . the unlikely likely one who is powerful in the realm of unreality"—who, from the description, might justly be called the god of Healing Dreams. "His power is the very greatest," the text comments tellingly, "because man does not perceive it at all."[11] Franz and I sat silently as the afternoon sun turned the room golden and spun dust into motes of light, feeling the walls breathe in this place where once, it seemed, some ancient veil had parted.

Dreams and Divinity

Though Jung's experiences were highly dramatic—his critics would say self-dramatizing—Healing Dreams often have an otherworldly aura. They tend to sound spiritual themes rather than purely psychological ones; to address not only our personal situation, but also the human condition. It is startling to encounter a force that, despite our best efforts to limit ourselves, will not resign itself to our smallness. A Healing Dream may have many of the qualities we traditionally associate with divinity: omniscience, omnipresence, truth, and compassion (most often of the tough-love variety!). Properly attended to, they do "God's work," making us more skeptical of our vanities, more attuned to the transcendent, less fearful of the unknown.

Some would say that the Healing Dream is simply presenting back, in exotic form, our own intelligence. We are talking to ourselves; where *else* would it come from? But I am persuaded that, in such dreams, the fingerprints of something beyond the egocentric "I" are unmistakable. The sixteenth-century churchman Benedict Pererius, in his book *De Magia*, decreed that while most dreams are "groundless, empty of all rational basis" (he compares them to the visions of the drunk and the madman[12]), some are divine messages. Such divine dreams, he wrote, are "given distinctly and explicitly." But Pererius was forced to acknowledge that even these can be "obscure and perplexing," offering the explanation that this is God's way of impelling the dreamer to consult "no others but holy men" for understanding.[13]

One of the great services rendered by Sigmund Freud, surely a twentieth-century wise man, was his stalwart insistence that *all* dreams—even the kind Pererius termed "jumbled, confused, and bizarre"—were meaningful. Severing dream interpretation from religious dogma, Freud attacked the lingering view that dreams with grotesque or "sinful" images were nonsense or worse. To the contrary, he said, the dreams we find most repellent are the very skeleton keys to self-revelation, and even a commonplace dream, passionately inspected, is a "royal road" to the unconscious.

Healing Dreams needn't deal exclusively with some higher plane of existence. Our most vital dreams, the ones that spiritually mature us, may be more often mortifying than exalted; they play out at the level of blood and muck, lack and deformity. They confront us with a vision of wholeness beyond hearts and flowers. Spirituality, after all, is not existential Prozac. The psyche can be fiendish, puckish, imperious, tender, faithful, pestilential—whatever rivets our attention to the inner task at hand.

Few forces in life present, with an equal sense of inevitability, the bare-knuckle facts of who we are, and the demands of what we might become. Healing Dreams are what Hindus call *satyagraha*—soul force, truth medicine. They thrust upon us realities obscured by our propensity to smooth things over, to sell ourselves short, to split the difference between what we know deep down and what we prefer to think. Such dreams disturb us because of their utter refusal to pander to our fondest notions of ourselves. Is it any wonder they are so often labeled pointless fantasy?

The Dream Uses You

Many people wonder why they should bother with their dreams at all. A common answer is that they will help us with our lives, and this is certainly true. Even the most extraordinary dream, properly investigated, will have much to say about bread-and-butter issues like work, love, and health. But the Healing Dream is less a defender of our waking goals—material achievement, perfect romance, a modest niche in history—than an advocate-general for the soul, whose aims may lay athwart those of the ego. It is often uninterested in the self-enhancement stratagems we mistake for progress. "It's vulgarizing to say that we can use dreams as tools—like shovels!—to get ahead, or be more assertive, like a kid who prays his little sister will drop dead so he can have her candy," a dreamworker once told me with some passion. "It's more like"—and here he seemed to fluoresce with certainty—"the dream uses *you*."

Such dreams "use" us only if we are willing to dwell for a time within their ambiguities without resolving them. The Jungian psychologist Robert Johnson tells of the time he had a dreamlike vision of a "spirit man" with burning orange fire coursing through his veins. The man plunged to the bottom of an indigo lake, but the fire was miraculously unquenched. Then the spirit man took Johnson by the hand and flew him to a great nebula coruscating like a diamond at the center of the universe. Standing on the very threshold of divine majesty, before vast, dazzling whorls of light eternal, Johnson tugged at the man's sleeve and asked impatiently, "This is fine, but *what is it good for?*"

"The spirit man looked at me," wrote Johnson, "in disgust: 'It isn't good for *anything*.' " Still, Johnson wondered for a long while afterward how his experience might tangibly change his life. Then he had a key insight: *He would never know.* "This magnificent power," he wrote "is transmuted into small things, day-to-day behavior, attitudes, the choices that we make in the ordinariness of daily human life."[14]

Johnson's experience emphasizes that, contrary to a slew of popular works (starting with the dream manuals of the early Egyptians), there may be no surefire, direct method to utilize the power of dreams. We may be astonished by a bolt of lightning, but that doesn't mean we can harness it to flash down upon the grill to cook our steak. Healing Dreams offer few outright prescriptions. They often require us to live our questions rather than furnish instant answers.

How, then, should we see a Healing Dream? We might think of it as a window that enlarges our perspective, freeing us of a certain tunnel vision. It frames our daily concerns in a context beyond the confines of our room. The view from this dream window opens onto what we have thought the exclusive province of mystics and philosophers—conundrums like the meaning of the sacred, the problem of evil, the nature of time, the quest for a true calling, the mysteries of death and love—making these issues intimately our own.

Or we might see the dream as a worthy opponent. It is often said that spiritual work is an *opus contra naturam,* going against the grain of what seems natural, normal, or even good. The unconscious is not just the repository of beauty and light, or the issuer of benign, firm-handed guidance, but the home of the trickster. The dream figure that bears the denied powers of the self often appears sinister and antithetical. Yet he may also be our secret ally: in spiritual life, what is merely pleasant can become the ego's friction-free way of sliding by without learning much of anything. By rubbing us the wrong way, the Healing Dream kindles an inner heat, forcing us to include our obstacles and adversaries in our process of growth.

We might regard a Healing Dream as a work of art, something that evokes a feeling of meaningfulness that cannot be put into words. Like the glowing Vermeer painting of a simple woman with a pitcher, it is the extraordinary thing that sheds light on the ordinary. Like art, dreams create a shift in perspective in the very act of beholding them. Seeing things in a way we have not seen before—taking the stance of the appreciator rather than the analyst—changes us, as suggested by the remark by the phenomenologist Merleau-Ponty: "Rather than seeing the painting, I see according to or with it."[15]

Healing Dreams might be conceived as visits to an otherworld with its own geography and inhabitants. From this perspective, we are explorers visiting a foreign land whose citizens have customs, beliefs, and language that are not entirely familiar. Dream images thus are experienced in their own right, not just as self-fabricated symbols. Through this sort of living encounter, dreams become the proverbial travel that broadens the mind.

Or we might regard the Healing Dream as a wise teacher, one who instructs us in the most personal way—embarrassingly so, for she knows our forbidden desires and deepest fears, our secret hopes and unexpressed gifts. This teacher tells us stories about ourselves, about our relationships to others, about our place in the larger schema. This approach may require a humility the ego finds discomforting. Jung told one dreamer: "Look here, the best way to deal with a dream is to think of yourself as a sort of ignorant child, ignorant youth, and to come to the two-million-year-old man or to the old mother of days and ask, 'Now, what do you think of me?'"

What *does* the dream think? Or is a Healing Dream itself more a question posed to *us*? If so, the most reasonable-seeming answer is often the wrong one. Such dreams play by rules that confound the waking mind. But at the heart of Healing Dreams are certain consistent, if challenging, attitudes. Before we set out to understand the big dream, it would be helpful to consider some of the principles and perspectives that will recur on the journey:

- *Nonself:* Dreams show us we are not who we think we are: "We walk through ourselves," wrote James Joyce, "meeting robbers, ghosts, giants, old men, young men, wives, widows, brothers-in-love."[16] Dreams de-center us from our everyday identity, pushing us toward a richer multiplicity of being. Thus in dreams we may be startled to find, as one dream researcher puts it, that we are "a woman and not a man, a dog not a person, a child not an adult . . . [even] two people at once."[17] As Alice in Wonderland says: "I know who I *was* this morning, but since then I have changed several times." What Healing Dreams attempt to cure is nothing less than the ego's point of view— that habitual "I" that clings to rigid certainties of what "I want," "I fear," "I hate," "I love." What is sometimes called the ego-self or the "I" figure in our dreams may be a mere side character, reacting or observing but not in control of events. We may experience the diminution of what in waking life we most prize in ourselves, and the elevation of what we find belittling. One sign of a healthy personality is the ability to acknowledge other selfhoods and inhabit other skins.

- *Nonsense:* From the ego's standpoint, dream logic is an oxymoron. It is a sure bet that whatever we deem most ridiculous upon waking is the fulcrum point of what the dream wants to tell us. Indeed, when we find ourselves disparaging an image as meaningless, it is a signal to retrieve it from the scrap heap and place it on the table. Like a magician, the dream may confuse us through misdirection, but only because we are paying too much attention to the right hand and not enough to the left. Like a fool in the court of a king, dreams use absurdity to tell the truth when none else dare; but the king must realize the joke is on him in order to get the punch line.

- *Balance:* A Healing Dream often comes to redress imbalance—something in the personality is askew, awry, not right (or perhaps, *too* right). If we have become inflated, it cuts us back down to human scale; if we wander in a dark vale, lost, it suddenly illumines the mountaintop. The psyche, Jung suggests, "is a self-regulating system that maintains its equilibrium just as the body does. Every process that goes too far immediately and inevitably calls forth compensations."[18] The quickest way to the heart of a dream is to ask what one-sided conscious attitude it is trying to offset.

- *Reversal of value.* In dreams, our fixed reference points—our opinions, values, and judgments—may be revealed as mere tricks of perspective. What the conscious mind believes to be a precious gem may be a beach pebble to the spirit, while what it tosses aside may be the pearl of great price. Alice, on her journey through Wonderland's dreamscape, first drinks a potion that makes her large, and she weeps in misery. Then when another elixir makes her shrink, she finds herself literally drowning in her own tears. A few small tears, usually a matter of little import, suddenly become a matter of life or death—as indeed they may be to the dreaming soul.

- *Wholeness:* Healing Dreams point to the relatedness of all things, reveling in the union of opposites. They show us a vision of the divine that encompasses both growth and decay, horror and delight. We may crave a world of either/or, but the Dream says, *Both/and.* We build a wall between our social persona and our inner selves; the Dream bids us, *Demolish it.* We wish to believe we're separate from one another, but the Dream insists, *We are in this together.* We believe time to be a one-way river, flowing from past to present to future, yet the Dream reveals, *All three times at once.* We wish to be virtuous and free of taint, but the Dream insists, *The dark and the light are braided and bound.*

Stone Soup

If I had to sum up these principles, I might simply say, first impressions are deceiving. What a dream says and what it means are often two different things. In this light, conscientious dreamwork is its own reward. As I was wondering how to illustrate these ideas, I coincidentally received a phone call from Christine, a friend whom I hadn't heard from for months. She was upset. For weeks, she told me, she had been plagued by a series of relentless nightmares, each a variation on the same theme: she had lost everything. Sometimes she would be standing in rubble, her clothes in tatters, the earth leveled by some disaster. Or she'd find herself utterly bereft, in an empty house. She would wake trembling, suffused with, as she put it, a sense of "total nothing, nothing, nothing."

The night before she called me, there had been an awful culmination: *I dream everything has finally been taken from me. I possess absolutely nothing—no clothing, no food, no love. I'm standing naked, though oddly I don't feel destitute. I'm really hungry, but all I have is a bowl filled with stones and water. I say in deep, final resignation, Well, I guess I'm just going to have to make stone soup!* Christine had no idea what she could have meant by this and awoke "feeling desolate all over."

I couldn't help myself. I burst out laughing. "What's so funny?" she asked.

"Don't tell me," I said, "you don't know the story of stone soup?" Apparently she'd never heard the famous folktale.

"*What* story?" she replied, a bit indignant. I promised to tell her once she'd caught me up with her life.

I knew that Christine, an L.A. art curator turned social worker, had a few years before gone back to the small Pennsylvania town where she'd grown up. Now in her forties, she had begun working with disturbed adolescents, recently founding a therapeutic community for girls who were wards of the state, many with severe mental disorders and histories of prolonged abuse. These were the "throwaway kids" of the TV newsmagazine shows. One girl had been dragged through twenty-seven foster homes before she'd reached her teens.

But Christine adored her work. Kind, competent, idealistic, a Buddhist by persuasion, she had thrown herself wholeheartedly into the business of reclaiming lives. But lately, she told me, the grind of administration, the emotional neediness of the girls, the ceaseless cycles of financial meltdowns and emergency fund-raising, had started to drain her dry. She felt she couldn't struggle another step on what was looking more and more like a road to nowhere.

To top it off, Christine—lissome, smart, and sophisticated—had finally found, from the limited local pool of eligible bachelors, a great boyfriend. But on the day she introduced him to her best friend, she knew it was over: "I saw in a flash *they* were meant for each other." Christine, a woman of formidable intuitive gifts, sighs: "There was nothing to do but give him away." She'd just gotten a card from her friend inviting her to the wedding. Christine felt bleak and cold and alone. She'd given so much away in her life, there was nothing left over for herself.

I asked her to tell me more about her dream. The image of a bowl of stones, she said, particularly dismayed her. What could be more stark, lifeless, and unforgiving? Our colloquialisms say it all: heart of stone; stone-faced; stone-cold. Sink like a stone, as if it were the very material of defeat and inexorable gravity. Seeds cast upon stony ground, says the Bible, can never grow.

When I asked her to describe the stones in her dream, however, she told me they reminded her of the round, smooth kind used in ikebana, the traditional Japanese art of flower arranging.

"And the bowl?"

"It's a low, flat-sided dish. Well, actually, it's an ikebana bowl."

Her tone was one of surprise, as if she were noticing these details for the first time. What, I inquired, did ikebana mean to her? "It's the artful arrangement of natural elements in their environment," she promptly offered. "It's awake and mindful, the opposite of haphazard and unconscious."

"And what about the water?" I prodded. "What's it like, where's it coming from?"

There was a pause as she mentally reentered the space of her dream. "Fresh, crystal clear, bubbling, just pouring over the stones from somewhere outside."

She laughed now, a little astonished. Her disconsolate nightmare was being revealed, in a startling reversal, as a font of beauty and possibility. She was having the "aha" well known to dreamworkers, when something clicks and there is a sudden burst of insight.

"Okay," she said quizzically. "What's going on here? What *is* stone soup?"

I began to recite the tale, hazily recalling it from childhood: There once was an old woman so poor she had nothing but the clothes on her back and a battered cook pot. One afternoon, her feet aching mercilessly, her stomach a shrunken knot, she stopped by the side of the road. Not knowing what else to do, she filled her pot with water from a nearby stream and kindled a fire. When the pot began to boil, she laughed to herself and, delirious with hunger, threw in a round stone she found at her feet. "There, now at least I've got something to cook."

A man passed by. "What are you making?"

"Stone soup," she muttered, then, struck with a sudden inspiration, added, "Old family recipe. Best you've ever tasted."

"What's in it?" he asks her.

"Can't tell you. But it all starts with a secret ingredient. A certain magic stone."

The man was intrigued. "If I wait here, can I have some?"

"Well," the old woman told him, making an elaborate show of sampling a taste, "it's not quite perfect yet. Needs a little salt, to adjust the seasoning." As it happened, the man had some salt tied in a cloth napkin in his coat pocket, which he gladly supplied. Then a farm wife happened by, lugging a bulky sack of potatoes. "What's cooking?" she sang out. "Stone soup," answered the woman. "Recipe passed on from my grandmother, who got it from her *great*-grandmother." The old woman dipped in a spoon, clacking tongue on palate. "Good, but it wants thickening." The farm wife was glad to pitch in, also unburdening herself of some juicy family gossip as the old woman stirred.

And on it went. A butcher passed by in a stained apron, some lamb shanks he hadn't managed to sell at market slung on a pole across his shoulders. He, too, inquired about the soup and was told it was nearly ready. But perhaps—? In a few minutes, the soup had some meat on its bones.

Now a wonderful smell arose, attracting more passersby.

"What, you're not using celery?" asked one. "Here, have some of mine, fresh from the garden. . . ."

Finally, the soup was served. An improbable feast was doled out to each person in the crowd, and all declared it the best soup they'd ever tasted. But though they begged her for the recipe, the old woman only smiled and said, "You have to start with a secret ingredient, a certain magic stone."

I didn't need to belabor the point. Stone soup, Christine realized, was the very recipe she had used to create her center for troubled girls, starting from scratch, but acting for all the world as if she were cooking something up, finding that resources appeared almost magically out of nowhere. Oddly enough, she said, the past week had been just like that. She'd described her community to a board member of a national health-care corporation, and he had been inspired to step in to see how he could help. A woman had appeared in response to an ad in the local paper, an RN administrator and fellow Buddhist whose qualifications precisely complemented her own. Her stone soup had been already getting richer with fresh ingredients. Her ikebana arrangement, made with found elements from her own backyard, was becoming more artful. Only from her ego's myopic vantage point had everything seemed to be going wrong.

The dream metaphor, the more we thought about it, seemed to surround her. Were not her children her adamant stones? In alchemy, the *lapis philosophorum* ("stone of the wise") is said to be "the stone the builders reject," cast aside by masons because it doesn't fit. What better symbol could there be for her "throwaway kids"? Yet within each she had glimpsed the magic of the human soul—the philosopher's stone, unrecognized and disdained, which is the basis for all transformation. The children *were* her ikebana, the implausible miracle of flowers blooming up from bare rock.

Christine's weeks of nonstop nightmares had been akin to that phase the alchemists called the *nigredo*, "the blackening," when the material to be transformed becomes foul and dark. But it is the darkness that prepares us for the dawn, and emptiness hollows us to receive the elixir of grace.

Indeed, her dream had been littered with clues of the new world gestating in the darkness, filled with the aroma of stone soup cooking right beneath her nose. Just the mood of the dream was a tip-off to its meaning. The fact that Christine was bereft but "didn't feel destitute" was an indication that not all was as it seemed. And while her ego self found her nakedness shameful, it is once we stand naked that life comes toward us with unexpected bounty; for we finally are without armor, arms wide in supplication. As Christine and I talked, even the word *stone* revealed itself not as desolate but rather as a noble material: things destined for posterity are carved in stone; firm decisions are cast in it. A stonemason builds slowly and methodically for the ages, very much in the manner Christine was proceeding, building her center from the ground up.

I asked her to call me in a few weeks, certain that her stone soup would continue to thicken. When I next heard from her, her voice was filled with enthusiasm, a striking contrast to her previous wan, hopeless tone. She had gone to a bookstore, she told me, to look for a copy of "Stone Soup." Unable to find it in the children's section, her eye fell on a book in general nonfiction titled *Stone Soup for the World*. Its subtitle was *A Handbook for Humanitarians*, the slogan on the cover, "What One Person Can Do."

"My head turned so fast I heard my neck snap!" She opened the book to its foreword, and there, as if written personally for her, was an essay on at-risk children. Back home, leafing through the pages, she discovered a wealth of inspiration and practical help—international connections through Web sites and E-mail, links, guidance, directions. "I'm starting to think the dream *sent* it to me," she said.

A Healing Dream seems to demand its own being in the world. It wants to be seen and heard. Tribal cultures say something is lost if we don't take our dreams seriously enough to embody them—that we ignore them at the peril of our souls, if not our lives. As one Mexican Huichol shaman noted: "If a person doesn't believe in his dreams, he might say, 'It's only a dream; it's not real.' . . . Little by little, if one doesn't do what a dream has directed, one won't be able to dream well anymore. That's why so many people don't know how to dream. But if a person believes in the dream and follows the directions once the [shaman] explains it, then the gods will send more dreams of this type, because the person has proven that he believes."[19]

In such societies, a powerful dream is often followed by action (anthropologists refer to this as the "performative" aspect of dreaming). A dream may bestow a gift of power to be shared with the community, or a new rite revealed by a dream spirit will be incorporated into ceremonial life. The world as dreamed and the world as lived cross-pollinate each other.[20] A South African woman in a shantytown told me: "When you are in a crisis, your ancestors call you in a dream. You can't ignore it, because it will just keep coming back. It works inside you. It forces you. It is not an ordinary dream, but one which says, *This is true;* it just says, *Do it!*"

Christine has taken her dream as a call to action. She had considered purchasing a sixty-seven-acre parcel of bare land to create a center for at-risk children. Visiting it again, she regained her inspiration at the sight of the stream that runs through the property. "Even in this drought, there's fresh, clear water trickling over the stones." She pauses, realizing her dream has again made itself visible. She has no idea how she will afford it, but has started making plans for an "earth-friendly facility, harmonious with the land." She's contacted a cousin, a landscape architect just back from Hong Kong, who has agreed to help her. Through her *Stone Soup* handbook, she's gotten in touch with a Swedish expert in the cleanup of environmental toxins. Her life suddenly seems not an empty house but a larder well stocked with ingredients. The world seems itself to be a gigantic cauldron in which stone soup could be prepared by (and for) everyone.

"I feel like the dream is with me," Christine says, "reverberating, giving me a heightened awareness of things." She has started telling people about it, finding it touches a chord in her listeners. The dream has become an invisible organizing principle, exerting a palpable field effect on those who come near it. Her project is acquiring a magnetism, the force of spell, the allure of a dream becoming real.

The Healing Dream Speaks for Itself

A Healing Dream can never be completely "interpreted" or fully understood. Its soup pot is a bottomless well. But work—what the alchemists referred to as operations (*operatio*)—must be performed on the basic material (*prima materia*) for transformation to occur. The nourishment of the dreamworld is a reciprocal affair: we provide for it, and it provides for us. It is not raw experience that makes life worth living (or a dream worth having) but the depth and nuance we bring to it. We must offer our own ingredients: as in all things, we receive what we give.

Stone soup, in fact, is a wonderful metaphor for the Healing Dream and how to work with it. The dream is the stone (the *lapis philosophorum* itself), dropped into the water of the psyche. It becomes a robust meal through our conscious offerings, by what we add to the pot. Dream soup combines disparate elements into a whole. It needs time to simmer before it's ready to be consumed. It gathers people together, preferring the mealtime atmosphere of slow, circuitous talk over workaday, get-to-the-point communication. It becomes even more nourishing when we invite others to contribute their ingredients. Many dream groups practice a ritual: One member tells a dream. Then others around the circle offer their insights, always prefacing their remarks with "If this were my dream . . ." so as not to impose on the actual dreamer's inner process. The group is enjoined not to try to "get anywhere" with the dream. The more we try to use the dream to get something, the thinner and more tasteless it will seem, and the fewer will gather at the table. Stone soup says: This is *our* dream. Nourish it, and it will feed us forever.

A Healing Dream does not work only for the benefit of its dreamer. Christine's stone soup has also apportioned gifts of understanding to me at the moment I most needed them. For we embark on a quest to explore some fundamental questions: How do dreams "work," what do we do with them, what do they want of us? I have often quailed before the profundity of the topic. Through Christine's timely call, it was as if the Healing Dream were deigning to share some of its secrets.

Deciding that I wanted to explore Christine's ikebana association further, I made a quick foray to an Internet site. I learned that the art first appeared six hundred years ago as a Buddhist flower offering to the dead. This seems appropriate—Healing Dreams often come to us when an outworn attitude is dying, heralding the bloom of the new. I also learned that ikebana arrangements always contain three stems, representing heaven, earth, and man. This also fits nicely, for the Healing Dream bridges what's above and below our threshold of awareness, linking this to the earthly human struggle of transformation. (In dreamwork, one should always be mindful of these three stems—the dimension of the transcendent, the shadow world underneath, and the realm of daily life.)

Ikebana eventually became a secular form, reaching its peak during the Edo period in the form called *nageire,* meaning "thrown-in style." I recognize this concept as similar to the Greek root of the word *symbol*— *symballein,* meaning "to throw together." Here the dream is telling us to regard its arrangement of elements as ikebana, where everything has been artfully placed, although so as to seem as deceptively haphazard as nature appears to us. (In stone soup terms, although dreams are in crucial ways raw and require our cooking, they are in some mysterious way *already* cooked. They are, as it were, the cooked presented in a perfect simulacrum of the raw.)

Christine's dream—the Healing Dream incarnate—has told me everything I need to know about itself in a simple and elegant arrangement of images that only appears accidental. It has made its own ikebana, and I am in awe of its art.

The Way of the Healing Dream

We live in a practical era, one that stresses the productive usage of things. Yet Healing Dreams are not easily reduced to the utilitarian. Although they may offer practical revelation, they have more in common with the realm of art, poetry, and music, where what you do with an experience is not the overriding issue. Such dreams open up a gap in the ordinary, allowing something new, and often indefinable, to enter our lives. We can work with our dreams, "unpack" them, analyze them, learn from them. But it is their residue of mystery that gives them enduring power, making them touchstones we return to again and again.

When we take our dreams seriously, their images and feelings subtly begin to alter our waking lives. Meaning seeps in through a kind of osmosis. We begin to glimpse the principle that connects each to all. Any sincere attention (and commitment) to our dreams renders us spiritually combustible. What was once inert now strikes sparks.

Healing Dreams seem to *want* something of us, and often will not let go until they receive it. But few of us pay them serious mind. Their images dissipate into air, dissolve like snowflakes on water. We dive back into the slipstream of our dailiness with something akin to relief. We sense that if we were to draw too near, the gravitational field of dreams might perturb, forever, the fixed orbit of our lives.

For this reason, I've chosen to focus as much as possible on those dreams that won't allow themselves to be tossed aside; the ones that yank off the bedclothes, spook us, amaze us, drag us below, lift us above, damn us, save us—in terms so strong, in presence so palpable, we simply can't ignore them. *These* dreams refuse to go quietly, for they mean to change us utterly. If we look into their depths, we may behold a unique destiny struggling from its chrysalis, and watch, astonished and not a little afraid, as our unsuspected selfhood unfolds a new, wetly glistening wing.

What Does the Dream Want?

Interpretations, Appreciations, and Enactments

I am sunlight, slicing the dark.
Who made this night?
                    —*Rumi*

I t is hard to know how to approach what the writer Jorge Luis Borges called "the incoherent and vertiginous matter dreams are made of."[1] We want clarity, yet dreams seem to prefer obscurity. They play hide-and-seek with meaning. Why do they not come out and just tell us what they want to say? Why not speak in blunt prose instead of allusive poetry?

We often speak of a dream in terms of a mystery, something to be solved by sifting through clues and gathering evidence. Dreams *are* puzzle boxes, jam-packed with symbols and puns, tricky testimony, and narrative twists. A certain amount of detective work is required if we're to make sense of these marvelous contrivances. But we also must remember that "making sense" is not always paramount. Healing Dreams want us to *stop* making sense; not just to crack the case, but to *enter* the mystery.

The word *mystery* comes from the Greek *myein,* "to shut the eyes." To shut the eyes is to withdraw from the outer world and open to the inner senses, to offer the hidden world a screen on which to project itself. It is pithy instruction for dreamwork. We must first meet the dream on its own terms. Another root was *mystes,* meaning initiation into the sacred rites. Just as Greek seekers of the Eleusis were required to symbolically drink of the river Lethe (a word meaning both "forgetfulness" and "sleep") before being admitted, we're asked to leave the logic of the day world at the threshold of our work on a dream.

Sometimes we are not meant to solve the mystery, at least not right away. Rather *it* means to solve *us. Solve* comes from the Latin *solvere,* "to loosen, release, or free." It is the same root as in the word *solution*—a dissolving of individual ingredients into a greater whole. In dreams our narrow selfhood is loosened; the ego experiences itself as an element in something larger. In dreamwork, too, we must first allow ourselves to dissolve back into the dream, allowing its images to wash over us. We are being confronted with an ancient, urgent question: not merely what does the dream mean but what does the dream *want?*

Many dreamers I interviewed wondered if meaning itself were not beclouding the point. "My 'big' dreams," one told me, "are more like taking Communion in church. You don't interpret them. They're like blessings from a higher intelligence. They're still in my nervous system thirty years later." A church pastor concurred: "My dreams present information that can't be transcribed. It's the sort of wisdom that's given all of a piece, as a body of knowing." Another compared them, more earthily, to "my first orgasm, such deep feeling I walked around rosy-cheeked for months."

Some "big dreamers" have even taken issue with the central psychoanalytic tenet that dreams are a code to decipher; that they have both an apparent surface meaning ("manifest" content) and a covert "latent" one that can only be revealed by rigorous analysis. It was Freud who promulgated this dichotomy, enumerating a set of mechanisms—"condensation," "displacement," "reversal," "archaization," "distortion," "overdetermination," and "wish fulfillment"—by which dreams disguise their meaning. Freud insisted that symbols arise from repressed mental contents we cannot consciously acknowledge. Dream images are the packing crates, as it were, in which forbidden truths are smuggled through the customs office he called the superego, and analysis a way to pry them open for inspection. The most spiritual-seeming dreams, in this view, are only the end products of the sublimation of sexual and aggressive urges. Freud would have objected to the notion that the goods being smuggled were the sometimes radiant, sometimes dark contraband of the soul.

Freud's single-minded championing of the "sexual theory" against all alternate schemata cast a long shadow over the very art of dream interpretation. His contention that the dream is merely a guise, to be forensically stripped away, created what one researcher calls a lingering "climate of suspicion" about dream images themselves. His dogmatism is on display, in full feather, in this passage from *The Interpretation of Dreams.*

> All elongated objects, such as sticks, tree-trunks and umbrellas (the opening of these last being comparable to an erection) may stand for the male organ. . . . Boxes, cases, chests, cupboards, and ovens represent the uterus. . . . Rooms in dreams are usually women. . . . Many landscapes in dreams, especially any containing bridges or wooded hills, may clearly be recognized as descriptions of the genitals.[2]

Still, the value of Freud's epochal studies remains incalculable. The fact that he undertook to rigorously analyze dreams at all was extraordinary. Western science had long suffered from a sort of dream amnesia. Victorian doctors had dismissed dreams as "froth," with one nineteenth-century theorist proposing that dreams were only stray "chips from the workshop of the mind."[3] Freud was a new Prometheus, shedding light upon a darkened landscape.

Freud had enlisted Carl Jung, a brilliant young Swiss analyst, to help him dispel what he viewed as centuries of encrusted superstition. In one letter to his heir designate, he expressed his delight that they were setting out together to "conquer mythology," unaware that the obverse would soon come to pass. Jung had already begun to treat the dream less as a libidinal rebus than as a labyrinth leading to humanity's "collective unconscious." If Freud saw a snake as a phallic symbol, Jung was interested in its

mythic heritage as a creature associated with wisdom and healing. He crit-
icized Freud for treating symbols as "nothing but signs and abbreviations,"
suggesting they were more like living things that could be creatively approached and engaged. If Freud believed symbols were a dream's way of
concealing the truth, Jung believed they were more an attempt to *reveal* it.
"The dream is a natural occurrence," Jung wrote. "There is no earthly reason we should assume it is a crafty device to lead us astray."

History has judged each man's founding work to be an admixture of
brilliant insight and misconception, of objective study and personal folly, a
legacy their successors still contend with. A therapist once remarked to me
that it was a shame there were only these two lights to illuminate the vast
region of experience occupied by dreams. But this is hardly true. The
world's indigenous peoples possess a treasure trove of dream knowledge,
though the opinion endures among many Western psychiatrists that tribal
peoples do not understand how to interpret their own dreams—indeed,
naively believe them to be real occurrences. But non-Western cultures
have long been aware of the subtleties of dream life. Here, for example, is
the eleventh-century Tibetan hermit-saint Milarepa describing dreams in
terms remarkably like Freudian "day residues": "Mental activity in the
daytime creates a latent form of habitual thought which again transforms
itself at night into various delusory visions sensed by the semi-conscious-
ness. This is called the deceptive and magic-like Bardo of Dream."[4]

Once, while on a book tour in Washington state, I had a long conversation with a healer from the local Salish Indian tribe about dreaming.
"Most dreams are just to empty out stuff in your mind," she informed me.
"When I was a kid, I asked my elders, 'How come if you play Monopoly
before you go to sleep, you have a dream like you're playing it in reverse?'
They said, 'Well, that's your mind throwing out the trash, starting with
what's laying on top of the pile.' What causes people to go crazy, they said,
is trying to hold on to the garbage, the unnecessary stuff." (Her description oddly tallies with the views of those neuroscientists who declare
dreams to be "a form of 'neural dumping' that clears semantic memory
stores of all excess information from the previous day."[5])

However, my Indian friend contrasted her "garbage dreams" with her "true" dreams, which she said influenced her profoundly. True dreams pertained to events in the spiritual universe, relationships with loved ones, or the collective concerns of her people. The psychoanalytic idea that one's dreams pertain solely to the intricacies of one's own personality is a viewpoint indigenous peoples find almost laughable.

Jung made it a point to seek out Hopi Indian elders and African shamans to learn their opinions on the subject. Those conversations contributed to his conclusion that our minds contain not only our own personal unconscious, but a deeper stratum of universal motifs. He said, a bit disingenuously, that his theory was "really quite simple. Our mind has its history, just as our body has its history. We do not need to think that there is anything mystical about it."

But the mind unavoidably turns to things mystical when confronted by such purported phenomena. How, for example, are the contents of what Jung called the "storehouse of relics and memories of the past" transmitted from one generation to the next? He seems to suggest that such collective images are contained within a nonmaterial sphere of awareness. For the past fifty years, researchers have used many labels to describe such a sphere, hoping to explain cognitive functions that shouldn't by rights exist: "clairvoyant reality" (Lawrence LeShan); nonlocality (David Bohm); One Mind (Erwin Schrödinger); Totality (Carl Jung); mind-at-large (Aldous Huxley); "morphogenetic fields" (Rupert Sheldrake).

Sheldrake uses the analogy of a TV set: just as the source of the scenes depicted on TV cannot be found in the tubes and wiring of the box, our dream images aren't literally inside our neurons. Rather, the equipment (our brain) acts as a receiving device for images, an invisible field of information that continues to exist even if the "set" is junked.

Whatever name or concept one applies, there is pure mystery in how Healing Dreams seem to draw upon unfamiliar myths and icons, know the archaic meanings of words, even display images of the future and the thoughts of distant minds. While these almost occult elements should not overshadow the need for careful, humbling psychological work, it is also no use hiding our heads in the sand, pretending such phenomena don't exist. With such dreams, any single interpretive strategy is inadequate. To expect conventional theory to entirely suffice would be akin to playing by the rules of checkers when the Healing Dream is playing four-dimensional chess.

Manners of Interpretation

In light of this, we might speak not so much of a fixed interpretive method but of a path, an art—even an etiquette, for we are meeting an unknown person. Though it is tempting to add, "and that person is you," this would be too glib. Though it *is* best to look at dreams first as commentary on one's everyday personal concerns, anyone who approaches a Healing Dream honestly cannot fail to note its persistent intimations of a not-you, a beyond-you, a you-plus.

We might imagine a dance between waking awareness and dream reality, where we are learning new steps with an unfamiliar partner. It is a pas de deux that alternates leading and following. We're engaged not just in the interpretation of dreams but an interpenetration, a back-and-forth dialogue between conscious and unconscious. Still, we inevitably come back to the task of making sense. While it is true that interpretation can, if we are not careful, insulate us from direct experience—can, in effect, sidetrack us from what is being demanded of us by our inner lives—without it, we are lost.

This requires true patience. Our dreams do not yield themselves instantly upon request, or dance to our tune. They move at their own pace, ripen in their own time; they may deign to reveal just so much and no more. Jung counseled against a frontal attack of analysis in favor of a more elliptical approach. His key technique was what he called amplification—a process of taking an image and turning it over in one's hand like a faceted gem, watching how it catches the light. He compared it to the method of a philologist trying to understand a foreign lexicon: "For instance, in the case of a very rare word you have never come across before, you would try to find parallel text passages, parallel applications . . . the context, the tissue that word or image is embedded in."

Care is taken to always return back to the image (rather than pursuing a linear chain of associations that might lead us further away from it). If, for example, we dreamed of a wheeling flock of birds, an association with the classic movie *The Birds* could be apropos—but not to then proceed via the director Alfred Hitchcock to portly, balding Uncle Phil. Rather, we might think of aspects of birds in general (migration, say, or nesting); or in specific (were they cheerful bluebirds, or woebegone crows?); or simply feel what is evoked by the image, and see where those feelings lead us.

In the Talmud-based tradition of Jewish dream interpretation, a single dream is said to have at least twenty-four possible meanings. In the case of a Healing Dream, the use of multiple methods to understand a dream is almost required. I will suggest a few such strategies here in broad strokes, giving each a somewhat arbitrary label. In fact, these can be thought of as different modes of retelling the same dream, part of the recipe for making stone soup.

A Structural Approach

We can look at the notion of structure on several levels. The soul itself seems to have a kind of architecture whose blueprint may vary from person to person and from culture to culture, but whose basic floor plan, as it were, remains remarkably similar. Thus, certain figures recur in our dreams in various guises—so-called archetypes like the "wise old man" and the "eternal child," or basic psychological stances like "the victim" or "the rescuer." Though new characters and situations are always appearing, they often fit into a pattern of conflicts and affinities that remains relatively constant in our lives, and in human life in general.

Archetypes, like snowflakes, might be seen as natural occurrences, formed according to basic principles—in this case, our emotions (love, hate); primal relationships (mother, friend); our body and its organs; innate linguistic operations (subject, object); and our tendency to process events into narrative structures. Our human heart and mind, though entirely unique, respond to conditions of the world in ways that are strikingly consistent.

There is also a structural approach to looking at a dream image, focusing on both its form and its function. Dreamworkers often suggest taking the stance of someone from another planet, inquiring about each element of a dream as if it were entirely foreign: What is this? What does it do? What is it used for? According to this mode of inquiry, if we dream about, say, a wagon, we would be less concerned with the little red wagon featured in a childhood trauma at Grandma's than with what a wagon *does*— it carries heavy loads, for example, or transports people to new frontiers. We might then ask ourselves what burdens we are carrying, or what pioneering efforts we are trying to make in our lives.

An analogous approach can be found in an ancient Greek dream book, Artemidorus's *Oneirocritica,* which explains that a dream of drinking vinegar presages a sour family quarrel ("because of the contraction of the mouth"); or that dreaming of "vegetables that give off a smell after they are eaten as, for example . . . cut leeks," means that "secrets will be revealed, and signals hatred for one's associates."[6] (Vegetables that broadcast their odors are offensive to others.) In this approach, we do not, for example, proceed from leek to "leak" but try to stay with the actual image and see what it can tell us directly.

I might illustrate this interpretive technique using a garden-variety dream I had recently, which contains a few simple images: *Leah (my daughter) has put an ad in the paper to sell a dark wood acoustic guitar. No, I tell her, that's the good one. Sell this cheaper, light-colored one instead.* In a structural approach, I would first look at a guitar as something one plays (perhaps suggesting a need for more playfulness in my life); as a thing that makes music (a deep soul pleasure I tend to neglect); or as an instrument made from an organic material, whose sounds are produced by resonance rather than electricity—an invitation to a more natural, intimate, "unplugged" life. I could see an ad as a way to get rid of something unwanted (in this case the "dark side" of myself, which the dream suggests is actually more valuable and should be kept); and my daughter, my offspring, as a child-part of myself I need to better understand.

A Literary Approach

A rather simplistic example of the associational method I will refer to as literary can be found in a Twelfth Dynasty Egyptian dream book from 2000 B.C.: a dream of "seeing a large cat" is said to mean "a good harvest is coming to the dreamer"; the image of "uncovering the backside" means (in a reference researchers trace to an ancient Egyptian pun) the dreamer will be an orphan![7] This sort of standardized meaning, relying on purely symbolic interpreting, can be found in dream dictionaries still published to this day.

But a dream can be a literary product of startling subtlety, building suspense, tangling its characters in subplots, all created, as if by a master author, to spring an exquisitely set trap of revelation. The plasticity of language— semantic back flips, neologisms, and other linguistic legerdemain—can be nothing short of breathtaking. Dreams do not mince words, neither do they waste them. As in all good literature, everything is there for a reason. The notion that language is embedded in our very perception is on full display in dreams, where the objects we take to be real are revealed upon waking to be symbols and metaphors. (If, in our dream, we run into a brick wall, our head hurts; it is usually not until we wake up that we get the literary pun.)

These layers of meaning may not be revealed until we commit a dream to paper. To track the literary dimension of dreaming, many people find that an ongoing journal becomes a primary act of fidelity. In dreams, as in literature, the slogan "No truth but in specifics" amply applies. Vocabulary counts. *Spelling* counts. Talking to nearly a hundred dreamers over the course of my research, I have been amazed how many have, entirely on their own, inscribed the texts of untold numbers of dreams in their diaries and then struggled, often in solitude, to coax out their hidden truths.

In Lakota culture, important dreams are shared with others by using a special coded speech called *hanbloglaka,* or "relating visions." Similarly, dream journals reveal the dream's own code—it "dictates" itself in special wording that conveys ever-shifting layers of meaning. When we write out our dreams, we find that language itself behaves in almost magical ways. The Sufi-influenced writer Peter Lamborn Wilson has noted that dream-writing always shows signs of being "infected with the unconscious."

One symptom is the preference of dreams for "spillover words"—a term coined by Chuang Tzu to describe "the highest form of language possible," words that "reveal a surplus of meaning," that "contain more than they contain." (Freud referred to this as overdetermination.) A dimension of creative play emerges from the dream text, which becomes more than a chronicle, as alive and ever shifting as poetry. I have found that using a dictionary for dream amplification—I prefer the massive, ever-revelatory *OED,* with its meticulous documentation of antecedents and obscure meanings—shows the almost shocking extent to which a dream "chooses" an enriched linguistic palette where simpler words might have done. The night before I began writing this section, for example, I had a dream so fragmentary it was only a word. However, as if I were too near-sighted to make it out, this one word seemed to oscillate between three, which I woke up with on my tongue: *Orison. Origen. Horizon.*

Upon awakening, I had an uncharacteristic urge to plant myself at my correspondence desk and pay a long-languishing stack of bills—always an odious chore—after which I was relieved to get to work on this infinitesmal dream, which I suspected was offering itself as an exemplar. I first looked up *orison,* confirming, as I had vaguely remembered, that it was a prayer or supplication. I *had* been supplicating the dream gods to, as it were, bless my undertaking and guide my hand in this crucial chapter. (I was also amused, given my morning's check-writing, to note the dictionary's example of usage was a line from Milton: "Their orisons, each morning *duly paid.*")

The meaning of *horizon* seems common enough. But I have found that when a dream highlights a particular word, it means us to pay close attention. Precise definitions and original roots often reveal unsuspected nuances of meaning. I'd always taken the horizon as a symbol of limitless potential—as in "new horizons." But I was surprised to discover that the literal translation of the Greek word *horizon* meant "the bounding circle; to bound, limit." The dreamworld was reminding me, even as I wrote a section—indeed, a book—I wished could say all and be all, that the circle of knowledge is finite. Yet a circle's roundness also signifies wholeness and completion. It marks off what is inside from what is outside; its circumference cradles the interior life. The word also contains the meaning of horizontal—flat, level—reminding me to not allow the transcendent dimension of Healing Dreams to blind me to the plane of ordinary life.

Origen proved the most challenging of the three word variants, though it complemented and extended the others' meaning. Vaguely recollecting a figure by that name in the early Church, I found an encyclopedia entry that gave me a wealth of biographical material. Origen, born in second-century Alexandria, was a prolific writer of some eight hundred works, yet was renowned for refusing money for his teaching. (I was reminded of this less voluntary aspect of my own career during my "orisons" to my creditors.) Origen's specialty was the very theme of this section: he devised a multi-tiered system of scriptural analysis in which he advocated interpreting the Bible on three different levels—literal, ethical, and allegorical. In his day, Origen was considered unorthodox to the point of heresy, since he attempted to blend pagan philosophy with Christian theology—much as, it occurred to me, my approach to Healing Dreams attempts to combine religion, psychology, and shamanism. I was also to learn that Origen was a man who took asceticism so far that he castrated himself in the name of purity. Thinking about this, I was struck by the realization that I, too, had been living an overly ascetic life, unplugging the phone, skipping meals, locking myself in alone for days with my books and papers, pacing my cell unkempt as an anchorite. (Dream memo to myself: Do *not* live the life of Origen!) Here, in three small, deft strokes worthy of a master calligrapher, the dream had sketched a robust commentary on my life.

Dreams often present their own parallel—even contrarian—story line, reminding us of unattended emotional issues. My aforementioned "two guitars" dream, for example, was freighted with personal history: I had bought my daughter, Leah, two guitars on different childhood birthdays, one dark, one light, neither of which she ever learned to play. She'd beautifully decorated their cases, though, proving what I'd resisted acknowledging—her artistic talents ran to the visual arts, like her mother, and she would never share my passion for playing music. The guitars still sit in my garage. I've often thought of selling the dark one (jet black with a white pick guard, an Elvis special) but feel too sentimental, as yet unwilling on some lost-cause level to admit defeat.

Or to take another literary tack on the same dream, a guitar is notoriously shaped like a woman. Am I trying to come to terms with the dark and light aspects of the feminine—something that I, like many men, have often struggled with? A bit of a stretch, perhaps, but this possibility is amplified by my daughter's name: Jungians often see the biblical Leah (dark) and Rachel (light) as two aspects of the same feminine psyche.

Leah's name also reminds me that the theme of the Bible story is that of a father trying to "sell" his daughter(s) in marriage in a kind of two-for-one deal (the "light" Rachel being the fair and favored). At the time, "my" Leah had just begun her first serious long-term relationship, evoking any number of feelings. Could my child actually get married someday? I wondered. Will I have to "give her away"? In many cultures, a bride represents, for the father, a complicated financial transaction, involving analogies to advertising, buying, and selling. Could the image of selling the guitar be the dream's invitation to face my anxiety about having, with great finality, to give up my image of Leah as my little girl? Although she wishes to sell the guitar, to relinquish outgrown vestiges of her childhood, I try to stop her—I'm not ready. If I cared to pursue it further, I would no doubt uncover more unresolved family "emotional business."

Dream Appreciation

The minute parsing of dream meaning can be revelatory. At the same time, if we are not careful, it can become another way of killing the image, like a lepidopterist mounting a butterfly on a trophy board rather than marveling at its living presence. It is a convention in psychology to talk of "dream mechanisms," but the psyche is not a steam engine or a computer. We are investigating an ecosystem, not the innards of a device. What I am referring to as the appreciative mode of dreamwork involves a vivifying encounter with the imaginal realm. Here the images not only stand for something, they exist in their own right. Instead of labeling and sorting them, extracting their meaning and discarding them, one enters openhanded into their world.

Jung used a technique he called active imagination to participate in a dream's living presence. He describes his discovery of this method in his autobiography. While sitting at his desk one day, trying to come to grips with his own intractable fears he abruptly had the sensation of letting himself inwardly "drop" to a deeper level of imagination. He felt himself plunge down, "as if the ground literally gave way beneath my feet," eventually landing in a dark cave where he encountered various mythological creatures, personages, and symbols—dwarves, glowing red crystals, enormous black scarabs. Repeating the exercise over a period of weeks, he found he could induce a state between waking and dreaming in which he could converse with dream figures and vividly experience an imaginal world. Jung wrote in a typical passage: "I caught sight of two figures, an old man with a white beard and a beautiful young girl. I summoned up my courage and approached them as though they were real people, and listened attentively to what they told me."[8] Anyone who practices this sort of exercise will find that such "beings" may offer radically divergent opinions from those of the conscious self, along with a wisdom one did not know one possessed. (There are dangers, as well. It is not unknown for people to get lost in these fantasized realms, finding that they take over more and more of their own consciousness—one reason these exercises are sometimes best conducted with a skilled guide.)

Healing Dreams have such an authoritative feel—their presentation as deliberate, exacting, and inalienable as the director's cut of a film—that the dreamer's first challenge is simply accepting them as they are. Psychologist Mary Watkins counsels against imposing a burdensome conscious structure upon a spontaneous creation: "Try to take the image as a given and as completed," she writes, "rather than a play which you, as ego, must rework and finish."[9] This, she adds, counters "ego's attempts to consume the image as the bird would the spider."

This act of appreciating is in the spirit of what the poet Keats once characterized as "being in uncertainties, Mysteries, doubts, without any irritable grasping after fact and reason." We take the position of opening ourselves to the dream without unsheathing the sword of interpretation. I have often found myself returning to certain images I have allowed to live, gratified that they still retain the power to inwardly move me, and have not been "analyzed to death."

Indeed, a hallmark of this mode of living encounter is an upwelling of feeling, for here we are seeking the emotional, not the intellectual, center of the dream, that place where wordless transformative energies pool and stir. Sometimes an image arouses a full-fledged mood state—a catch in the throat, a gut feeling, the sudden pounding of our hearts in "irrational" fear or "wild" passion. Then we know that the imaginal creatures, which are intimately connected with the body, are hungering to be part of our lives.

Another aspect of appreciating a dream involves sharing it with others. When we work on a dream alone, we tend to repress those aspects we don't want to see. To encounter a dream in the company of others helps us see what we would otherwise gloss over. The Jungian analyst Marie-Louise von Franz writes, "Dreams generally point to our blind spot. They never tell us what we already know. . . . The trouble with interpreting your own dreams is that you can't see your own back."[10] We require companionship with others who have become sensitized to the imaginal dimension, for we may see more through their eyes than we see through our own.

If we open our hearts as well as our minds to the dream, then its entire world—and by analogy, our "real" world, too—is revealed as a living plenitude. The simplicity of an open gaze is itself transformative. Then life willingly bears us beyond our habitual viewpoint, showing us where faith sleeps in a mustard seed, and a cosmos really does glimmer in a grain of sand.

Enactment

Another mode of dreamwork concerns what might be called the objective component. Many traditional cultures insist that the dream requires a place in waking reality. Bob Randal, a sixty-three-year-old Australian aborigine from the arid Northern Territory, told me one day, "When you say 'dream,' it may not mean the same thing *we* mean." What *do* you mean? I asked him. He stroked mahogany-colored fingers through his frizzy white beard. "Y'see, mate," he finally said, genially, "us people, we don't just see a dream as something that just happens at night. It happens *all the time*." Our Western notion of dreaming as alien to waking life is seen as a patently false dichotomy.

A true dream cannot, such people say, be bottled up without expression. Choctaw Indian Preston Scott told me: "A vision is telling you as an individual to do things a certain way. You can run and tell it to one interpreter or another, but the dream will still mean the same. You gotta *test* it."

There are many ways to "test" the dream. The simplest is telling it to the person you dreamed about. When I had my dream about my daughter and her "two guitars," I decided to call her in New York. I had felt hesitant, but was startled when she informed me her new boyfriend had that very week put an ad in the paper to sell two acoustic guitars—one dark, one light. She had never even mentioned to me that he played music. She also mentioned she was about to go to the wedding—a second marriage—of her boyfriend's father, where the entire family, including five siblings, would inevitably size her up. She asked what I thought she should wear—there was a sense of "selling herself" to the clan. Seven months later came an even more extraordinary confirmation. While visiting home for Christmas, Leah made a surprise announcement: she and her boyfriend had become engaged to be married. It was a happy occasion, but I felt fortunate that my dream, by alerting me to a possiblity I hadn't considered, had helped cushion the shock (which, as father of the bride, included paying for a large ceremony!).

When a Plains Indian would have a powerful dream, he would bring it out into the world. He might teach others its songs of healing, paint a shield, or perform a ritual dance. Many people I spoke to devised their own not dissimilar ways to bring their dream into the world. A strange aura surrounds any symbolic enactment of a dream. Anyone who tries this, even if just to make a crude drawing in crayon, will feel the energy of two worlds bumping up against each other.

For example, I'm passionate about playing the guitar but sometimes have a dark feeling when it silently beckons me from its stand. I think of it as an aging adolescent indulgence; I should be working; the neighbors will complain. But the morning of my "two guitars" dream, I strapped it on before I got dressed, put on an Otis Spann CD, and ripped through the lowdown Chicago blues for an ecstatic hour. I felt invigorated and liberated. I was struck anew how forcefully a dream image can speak to us. Something is visiting us, in all the ambivalence and mystery the word evokes—a visitation. This visitor proposes novel arrangements and, sometimes, radical departures. All may not go according to plan from ego's point of view, but the dream, which answers to a higher authority, has other mandates to fulfill.

Meetings with Remarkable Animals

Dreams and beasts are two keys
by which we find out the secrets of our own nature.
—*Ralph Waldo Emerson*

There is no category that so clearly illustrates the extraordinary, sometimes overwhelming living presence dreams can acquire than the encounter with the Animal. Such dreams begin as early as childhood and appear sporadically throughout life.

When we meet a dream animal, we are encountering our own soul (*anima*).[11] This anima, as the word suggests, is intimately connected to our corporeal existence, with its bodily instincts and primeval processes. But the animal, for indigenous peoples, was also a repository of higher qualities—

specific kinds of intelligence, attributes of character and personality, subtle feeling, secret knowledge of the world, even outright divinity. I have been struck, in my own experiences and in those of others, by how ineffably real these encounters with dream animals are—and how profoundly affecting. They are initiations into the true habitation of our world.

In the book *Writers Dreaming*, Alan Gurganus remembers a dream experience he had as a child, a vision of a living world pulsing with magic:

> I had a dream when I was about eight years old that was one of those dreams that's so real you're sure that it's happening. You can't quite believe that you've imagined it because all the details are in place. I was in my knotty pine bedroom in my maple bed with the quilts pulled up over me—the history of the locomotive across my bed quilt—and I heard a sound in a black walnut tree right outside my window. It was a kind of shuddering, tinsely, rustling sound. I leaned out of my bed and looked and I saw the tail of an enormous beautiful bird, probably forty feet long from head to toe. It had a kind of peacock tail and the feathers were as big across as palm boughs. It was the most ravishing thing I'd ever seen. It was all the colors. All those rich blues and greens and purples and reds that you see in a peacock, but it was a huge, seemingly mythological bird that had somehow come to rest in our tree outside my room.

The young Alan felt faced with a dilemma. In his dream, he wanted to alert his family so they could witness the sight and confirm its reality. But if he got up to run fetch them, he worried, the noise might scare the bird away. He made the decision to just sit and appreciate it. "And so I got an extra fifteen minutes with this extraordinary creature which was preening itself." Those minutes, that choice to abide a while with the transcendent, changed his life. The lesson, he says, was that rather than seeking outward affirmation of an experience, "my responsibility as an artist and a dreamer and the keeper of the tree was to notice as thoroughly as I could. To drink it all in because I knew that I would never see this magical creature again, and that the very act of trying to prove it meant that I lost it. Saving it meant being alone with it in the moment and drinking it in forever."[12]

I have had my fair share of dream-animal encounters. Animals have moved back and forth across the threshold of my dreams, sometimes in stealth, sometimes with heart-stopping clatter. Just when I thought I could read them as well-crafted allegories or symbols, they have melted away, camouflaging themselves in the underbrush or exploding toward me in a blur of motion. They have rarely stood still in my analytical crosshairs. I've often been unsure that they represent *anything*, only that they are irreducibly, mysteriously alive.

Over the course of the last decade, I have encountered an astonishing menagerie: white wolves and black crabs; polar bears and fuzzy caterpillars; a small black elephant and a miniature tyrannosaurus rex; moray eels and shiny black carpenter ants; bees and boars. I've dreamed of animals of jungle and forest and water and air; everyday animals and mythical animals; animals extinct and endangered. I have encountered them in their own habitat or, disconcertingly, intruding into mine—on my street, in my house, under my bed. They may be metaphors, but they are distinctly self-possessed. They have little in common with Disney creatures, or domesticated pets, or dusty, bored-to-tears zoo animals; they are a bestiary of real creatures that seem to cohabit my skin. I feel I am contending with natural beings with their own desires. I don't know yet what they want, much less what they might "mean." Their growling, snuffling, prowling presence makes me profoundly uneasy, but I can't shake the sense I must learn something from them, even as their naked voracity keeps me on my toes. On one level, perhaps,. they have represented my cancer, itself a fierce, wild, hungering creature with its own agenda, aloof from my ego's best-laid plans—but this is also a fair description of my soul.

The animal is that part of our being that remains enfolded in the natural order no matter how high the spirit soars. They call us back to the earth, and to earthiness, to our at-homeness in our bodies. Our dream animals crave intimacy, dynamic concourse; they offer us communion with powers high and low; they make clear, in visions of the night, that they consider us ever and always their own.

My friend Demetrios is a man who has allowed himself to be guided by his own inner directives. A conscientious objector during the Vietnam

War, he had for five years performed alternative service with the families of men in maximum-security prisons: Soledad, Folsom, San Quentin. He started a company to create participatory environmental events, including annual coastal cleanups still observed around the country. He became a sculptor, traveling the world to collaborate with artists in other countries on the monumental works he envisioned.

Then he moved into the woods above Santa Cruz. Not long after he settled in, he received an unforgettable visitation. He dreamed he was in a remote mountain meadow, under a starry night sky, sitting on a couch set up as an observation point for "spirit wolves." Movement flickered at the edge of the meadow, as shadowy forms multiplied into a pack. Then suddenly one wolf was behind him. He heard its deep, heavy breathing and sat motionless, waiting to see what it would do. It pushed him with its nose, then walked in front of him, a magnificent two-hundred-pound alpha wolf with exquisite silver-and-black markings. Demetrios wrote a moving narrative of this imaginal encounter:

> *There is very focused and inquisitive intelligence in the wolf's eyes. He begins to bump me again with his nose, wanting me to touch him. I slowly reach up my hands and begin to scratch his head, carefully controlling my actions so as not to scare him off. My scratching evolves into stroking as I begin to outline his beautiful facial features with my hands. He is very responsive to my touch and demonstrates acceptance and affection at my caresses. I put my arms around him and begin to hug him in close. For a moment I feel fear, as I remember that this is a predator who could do me very serious damage if he turns aggressive. But I let that thought pass and trust the integrity I feel from the animal I now am holding in my arms.*

This strange dream courtship with the great beast continued. It stared into his eyes, then turned and sprayed him, as if marking him with his scent. Controlling his revulsion, Demetrios allowed the initiation to proceed, eventually becoming one with the pack. He says he still feels the powerful "presence" of the alpha wolf occasionally—once it seemed to show up and sit beside him during a grueling business negotiation that required a lupine strength and cunning.

(I was fascinated, not long after Demetrios sent me his dream, to come across the following Native American account: "When the Absarokee warrior Hunts to Die was wounded in battle with an arrow in the hip, he had a vision of a buffalo bull singing sacred songs and spraying water over him. As a result of this vision, he was healed and awakened just as he was being prepared for burial by his relatives."[13] Here, as in Demetrios's dream, the animal confers a graphic blessing, a renewal of vital force, an act of communion and affirmation of kinship.)

My friend Ginny confided to me one day that she's had repeated dreams about a lynx. "I didn't know what animal it was at first," she said, still sounding a little bemused, "but I was able to look it up in a nature book because it had these distinctive tufted ears. It said to me, 'I'm so glad we've finally come together.' " She had no idea what it meant. She has since had some sixty dreams of this animal. Though she wondered what I'd think, she told me, "It's as real to me as you are. In one dream, it seemed to break through the glass door in my bedroom—and I woke up and *saw* it, looked into its eyes. I reached out, and was shocked to feel fur."

Later in the evolution of her "relationship," she said, the lynx would "walk through my dream, as if it were only a stage—as if *it* was a different order of reality than a mere dream. Now it's like it's accompanying me in my life. I see it as close to my own personality. It's small, refined, loves to be alone; its ear tufts are like sensitive antennae, picking up the subtleties." I looked at her with new eyes: with her lithe, compact frame, alert gaze, and sharp nose, she *does* resemble her totem animal.

Psychologist James Hillman suggests dream animals give benediction to our inherent personality; are a way to know ourselves without applying the judgments that too often paint our almost instinctual traits as pathological. He makes a lovely suggestion about how to incorporate our dream animals, even those—as is often the case—we are repelled by:

Let's say you have a quick and clever side to your personality. You sometimes lie, you tend to shoplift . . . you have such a sharp nose that people are shy of doing business with you for fear of being outfoxed. Then you dream of a fox! Now that fox isn't merely an image of your shadow problem, your

propensity to stealth. That fox also gives an archetypal backing to your be-
havioral traits, placing them more deeply in the nature of things. The fox
comes into your dream as a kind of teacher, a doctor animal who knows lots
more than you do about these traits of yours and that's a blessing. Instead of
a symptom or a character disorder, you now have a fox to live with, and you
need to keep an eye on each other.[14]

I can attest that this feels true—the animals in a dream seem so real in
their appearance and behavior, one cannot help but relate to them as fellow
beings. And once they have entered our lives, they come ever closer.
Ginny's lynxes have shown up almost at her doorstep. A decade after her
dreams first began, Colorado's Division of Wildlife announced an attempt
to reintroduce a viable lynx population for the first time in nearly half a
century. The local papers are suddenly full of lynx lore and lynx tales: lynx
lovers in tie-dye T-shirts facing off with developers bulldozing new ski
runs in prime habitat; blustering local politicians versus bespectacled biol-
ogists ("Jinxed Lynx" read one headline). Ginny has become something
of a lynx-activist, trying to help a creature that first thrived only in her
dreams to regain its place in a world that has nearly allowed it to perish.

For dream animals not only confer power but convey a poignant
fragility. An Israeli dreamer told me, "I had a vivid dream about three baby
elephants that has haunted me for thirty years. Their skin is patchy, as if
they were sick. All I remember is how my heart went out to them. Five
years of Freudian treatment, then in Jungian analysis four times a week,
and I still don't understand this dream. I think I will, eventually. "

Are these visitations pleas from our dying evolutionary companions to
notice them, cherish them, love and even fear them while they are yet alive
and can be saved from extinction—before they haunt our dreams as
ghosts?

We have always learned from the animals, say indigenous tribes. In some
traditions, animals created the world. They were our first tutors about how
the world works and how to survive in it. They are beheld as totems, fa-
miliars, carriers of one's "bush soul." In many cultures, they are referred to
as four-legged "people" with their own "nations." Perhaps this is why

animals so often appear in our dreams as filled with clear, albeit nonhuman, intelligence. Unlike their plight in the waking world—domesticated, eaten, hunted to extinction, or, worse, perishing wholesale as a footnote to progress—these dream animals are at once ancestral and coeval. They accompany us, as mentors and brethren, trying to tell us, in our dreams, that our fate is bound to theirs.

Naturam expellas furca tamen usque recurret, reads a Latin proverb: "You can throw out Nature with a pitchfork, but she'll always come back." We pollute the environment and find ourselves in the midst of a cancer epidemic traceable in large part to the same pollution; our bodies become new habitats for displaced predators. "Do we believe," asks a recent ad for Friends of the Earth, "that we no longer need Nature?"

We might also ask: Do we believe we no longer need our dreams? Just as animals vanish like smoke when we no longer honor them, so might those inner beings that carry our potentials for growth and depth, for earthiness and transcendence, for authentic sorrow and true joy. By and large, we do not believe our dreams as did the ancients, let alone act upon them. The failure to respect the messages emanating from within lead to even worse depradations—against ourselves, against others, against the living planet itself. Our dreams bring parts of our ourselves—and the world—alive. To forsake them, ignore them, or interpret them away is to limit our aliveness, cramp the soul, constrict the heart. If we wish to encounter, understand, and finally embody our dreams, we must first sincerely bid them welcome.

The Dream of
the Body

Inner Journeys of
Health and Illness

On a journey, ill,
and over fields all withered, dreams
go wandering still.

—Bashō

I once appeared on a television show whose producer decided to drama-
tize the dreams that had led to my diagnosis of cancer. He tracked down
my doctor, who told of his skepticism when, ten years before, I had appeared in his office, affrighted with nightmares. "He didn't look sick," Dr.
Jekowski told the camera. "He had no physical symptoms. I didn't see any
point looking for a needle in a haystack because of a few bad dreams." The
doctor confessed his lingering bafflement: "How could someone know
about a small, localized tumor that was not secreting any substances that
would make him feel different?" What *had* made me feel different, and
what had kept me returning to his office until the tumor was finally diagnosed, was the unprecedented clarity and emotional pitch of my dreams.
They had so ratcheted up my feelings of terror and despair that I was

forced to respond, for I had never felt anything of such intensity in waking life.

The TV show also included a segment in which a medical sleep specialist was interviewed about his technique for "curing" nightmares. "First we change the original dream," the therapist explained, "and then we rehearse a new one." One of his patients recalled a long-tormenting, repetitive dream: "I'm in a log cabin on a cot with a blanket over me, and something comes under the covers. It's coming up to kill me. I start screaming and yelling and kicking and hitting, and then I wake up." The doctor urged his patient to "rescript" the dream's ending to a "more positive and comfortable version." She obligingly imagines the "thing under the blanket" as "just my dog Missy, coming up to cuddle with me." The patient said this image made her feel "warm, so when I get scared in a dream it's okay, because I saw it was only my dog, and I love my dog." Added her doctor, with a note of satisfaction, "She'll repeat this whenever she has a disturbing dream." Concluded the sonorous narrator, "If we have the courage to face up to our nightmares, we can control and eliminate them."

Who would begrudge this tormented woman a peaceful night's sleep? But I felt like shouting at the screen: What really *was* under those covers? It could have been a long-covered-up anxiety; an urgent warning; a lover or a personal demon. We will never know—now it is a dog.

Had I followed this sanitized "control and elimination" strategy to deal with my own disturbing images, I might not be alive today. I'd chosen to act upon what theorists call a prodromal dream—one that anticipates a medical problem not yet clinically detected. Freud, among others, took note of this "diagnostic power of dreams," remarking that it was hardly mysterious that a person with a disease of the lungs would dream of suffocation, or someone with a digestive problem of food. He believed that such images arise from subliminal physiological cues amplified in sleep, citing the philosopher J. Volkelt, who suggested that "in dreams due to headaches, the top of the head is represented by the ceiling of a room covered with disgusting, toad-like spiders. . . . The breathing lung will be symbolically represented by a blazing furnace, with flames roaring with a sound like the passage of air," and so on.[1]

But the situation is often more complicated. Even in a fairly straight-forward dream of the type Volkelt describes, some dreamwork may be required to ferret out the real state of affairs. A woman I'll call Ellen had been diagnosed with benign fibroid tumors. She dreamed: *I am on an old-fashioned plane that's waiting on the runway. There's a woman outside the window trying to warn me about something. She is frantic, banging on the window, but I'm not paying attention. The plane begins to taxi and the woman runs alongside. A handle of the plane catches on the woman's overall strap, forcing her to run faster and faster to keep up, trying desperately to get my attention. She is sure she'll have to lose her feet in this effort to warn me—she imagines the bottom of her legs with just exposed bone—but this is nothing compared to the danger if this plane takes off.*

The dream woke her up in shock, though the terrible urgency seemed disproportionate to her current health problems. She had been told the fi-broids were not serious. True, she had been concerned about a mild condition of numbness in her toes, diagnosed as a "peripheral neuropathy." Perhaps, she thought, the dream was reflecting her anxiety about her feet. A therapist might have chosen to focus on relieving her anxiety or to probe if she felt she was "losing her footing" in life or was "unable to keep up" on the job.

But the dream had been so horrifying, its imagery so clear, Ellen knew it was something far more urgent. Deciding the plane was the key image, she did an active imagination exercise in which she herself "became" the plane. What ensued was a kind of Little Airplane That Could soliloquy: "I am just trying to do my job, but this woman running alongside me desperately wants me to stop. She must know something I don't know, I have to take inventory. Oh, I'm really out of balance. Someone has loaded me wrong, I don't have just luggage in me—I feel as if I have something huge inside my belly, like an army vehicle—something way too big for me to carry. I can't take off with it in there. It has to be removed!"

Her dreamwork convinced her to get a second opinion about her fi-broids. The original diagnosis turned out to be incorrect—she had cancer. She wrote me, "When it was suggested I should have an operation to remove the whole thing, I knew (*knew!*) this was the right thing and scheduled it right away." The operation was a success; luckily, the cancer hadn't spread and was still completely contained in the "belly of the plane." Says Ellen: "I shudder to think if I had hesitated, or tried some lesser form of treatment, or just ignored my symptoms."

Such occurrences still go largely unrecognized, unrecorded, unconsecrated by physicians. Years ago, I was buttonholed at a conference by a psychologist who told me I was the only verified case he had found "in the literature" of a medically confirmed diagnostic dream. But I've since seen enough instances to feel assured it is more commonplace. It's often struck me what a detriment it is to medicine that prodromal dreams are considered such oddities. Patients are rarely asked about their dreams nor do doctors routinely monitor their own, though this has been counseled since the dawn of the profession.

Hippocrates, the father of Western medicine, spoke often of the medical value of dreams, and anecdotal reports date back to Galen, the master surgeon of ancient Rome. (Galen relates the story of a man who dreamed that a second shinbone had been made for him out of solid rock, and whose lower leg thereafter became paralyzed.[2]) There have been various modern attempts to systematize the use of dreams in diagnosis. In a massive 1967 work, the Russian psychiatrist Vasily Kasatkin catalogued more than ten thousand dreams from twelve hundred patients suffering a range of disorders, from tooth infections to brain tumors. He noted that changes in dream content often preceded clinical diagnoses, and that illness seemed to enhance dream recall. The images were most often nightmarish, showing scenes of war, fire or battles, bloody raw meat, corpses, graves, dirt, garbage, muddy water, and spoiled food, usually accompanied by feelings of terror and alarm. The dreams tended to change, becoming more unpleasant or less so depending on the progress or regress of the disease. Kasatkin has even stated his hopes of developing an "early warning system" based on specific images—repeated dreams of a chest wound symbolizing impending heart attack, for example, or of stomach wounds indicating liver or kidney disease.[3]

No interpretive task is more dicey, more fraught with peril and promise, than depending on dreams in a health crisis. Here, when our lives may be at stake, dreams persist in their gnomic, symbolic utterance. But sometimes dreams get fed up with the bobbing and weaving of metaphor, opting for a gloves-off punch in the eye. In this example, drawn from the dream journals of a patient named Mark Pelgrin, it almost seems as if the dream were arguing the case for its own truthfulness: *I dreamed that I had cancer, that I woke up, and that the dream was then verified by my having to go to the doctors to assure me it wasn't a dream. This happened twice.*

This was soon followed by yet another dream: *I am in a doctor's office and he is taking various tests on my ear. Finally I get the news and break it to [my wife]. She is not too disturbed because the doctor said I would die sometime around fifty. This would give me six or eight years in which to live. . . . Then I wake up in my dream and try to verify this as a dream.*

Pelgrin was diagnosed with pancreatic cancer, to which he succumbed not quite eight years later. (Were the "tests on his ear" to make sure he "heard the news," and lived as fully as he could during the time he had?)

I spoke with two women who'd had similarly direct dreams, albeit with more curative outcomes. The first, a head nurse in a Canadian hospital, heard an authoritative voice in her dream telling her she had breast and uterine cancer. She told her doctor about her dream and was grateful to be sent for a pelvic exam and mammogram "instead of to a psychiatrist." The dream's diagnosis was confirmed, and she had a successful operation. The dreams then ceased. A second woman related the following dream: *A friend who had died of cancer and I are making a soup. Then she starts putting crabs in the kettle, which isn't an ingredient we'd agreed on. Crabs are cancer, I think to myself.* "I was worried enough to tell my analyst," she told me, "but he said I wasn't 'the cancer type.' Still, for the next six months, I found myself repeatedly writing in my journal, 'You *have* to take care of yourself. There are difficult times ahead.' Sure enough, I found a lump in my breast— cancer—and I needed a mastectomy. But it wasn't a great shock. My unconscious had prepared me." Such dreams may have little power to ward off the inevitable, but being braced for the onset of illness may itself lead to a more timely intervention or a favorable outcome.

A few medical pioneers are trying to revive this neglected line of inquiry. Robin Royston, M.D., the staff psychiatrist at Ticehurst House

Hospital in East Sussex, England, began collecting prodromal dreams in earnest after one odd instance he'd encountered in his practice: A patient had come to him with a terrifying dream in which a black panther had attacked him and sunk its claws into his back "between my shoulder blades just to the left of my spine." Royston was nonplussed when the man later developed a melanoma (*melanos* means "black") in precisely that spot.

After he wrote up the case for the London *Times,* Dr. Royston was deluged with letters from dozens of patients eager to recount their own similar cases. After accumulating some two hundred fifty instances, he concluded that they are more common than is generally thought. Many cases might be explained, he surmised, by the immune system signaling the brain about a subliminally perceived change in the body's condition. But others seemed weirdly predictive, even precognitive, sometimes providing more accurate information than the most sophisticated medical tests. "These are not ordinary dreams," he noted, "but big dreams, archetypal dreams, so laden with powerful emotional affect that the dreamer is forced to take them most seriously."

Dr. Royston recounted for me a fascinating case from his files that exhibits all the art and device of Healing Dreams: A fifty-seven-year-old woman named Nancy had an extraordinarily vivid and disturbing dream on two successive nights in March of 1985. In her dream, she was walking on a campus crowded with students (not an unusual circumstance, as she was then a graduate student). Suddenly she was pushed from behind, a stunning blow she felt "through my chest," which knocked her over a fence to the ground below. She got up only to be struck down again. Anticipating a third blow, she whirled around to face her attacker. She was disconcerted to see a strange hooded figure: *I knock him to the ground, sit on him and punch him in the face with my fist. Then the hood falls off, and I see it is myself! I continue to punch the figure in the face and in the chest, shouting "Bad Nancy! Bad Nancy!"* She felt depressed for days. When she told a friend about the dream, she burst into tears.

Five months after this violent inner event, Nancy discovered a lump in her left breast. A biopsy was scheduled. At home, cleaning her closet to distract herself before the procedure, she came across a cartoon she'd once clipped of a woman with a shovel standing in deep snowdrift, captioned "I'm invincible!" On it, Nancy had jotted a list of the things she had to accomplish that semester. "The thought popped into mind I might have one more thing to conquer. I was going to write 'cancer,' but then found myself starting to write 'malignancy.'" She felt a jolt of recognition from head to toe. *Mali* means "bad," she thought. She had been shouting at the dream figure: "Bad Nancy. Mali Nancy. Malignancy." Shortly thereafter, the tumor was diagnosed as malignant, and she had a lumpectomy.

Her dream has many layers of meaning. There is an amazing factual bombshell (though on a delayed fuse) that only detonates upon solving a word-puzzle. The dream also makes a metaphoric statement about the nature of cancer as a sort of evil twin of one's normal physiology—the "bad" cells have her own face. There are graphic clues about psychological traits some researchers have linked to a vulnerability to cancer—a deep sense of self-criticism (Bad Nancy), coupled, as is often the case, with a compensatory "I'm invincible," can-do persona. (The cartoon shows a person who, even when she's in deep trouble, can't admit it: she's "snowing herself.")

Four years later, Nancy noticed another lump, which two successive oncologists diagnosed as a benign cyst, telling her she need not be unduly alarmed. Around this time, a powerful dream awakened her:

> *In an open village square, a crowd has gathered around listening to a hooded figure preach on some subject I don't seem to understand. I push through the crowd to the front and begin arguing with the figure, shouting, "I don't understand." He ignores me. I am so angry I take my boot and kick a mound of white crusted snow that is between us. I make a hole in the crust, and out comes a slurry of white and black rabbits in a greenish, syruplike fluid! Everyone reacts with horror.*

The next day, Nancy contacted a surgeon and insisted on a biopsy, which revealed that the fluid in the "benign" cyst contained both live and dead cancer cells. After diagnosis, she elected to have a double mastectomy. Dr. Royston noted: "The dream had used all her symbols: the snowbank from the earlier cartoon, and the hooded figure from the first dream—

which was now a male figure, no longer herself, perhaps implying a worse malignancy. And the rabbits symbolized something that could breed very rapidly. Having already seen a demonstration of her dreams' accuracy, she opted for the most aggressive treatment."

Still, such dream prognosis is, Royston adds, "a difficult area. Some people may have a dramatic and awful dream about a physical problem, and nothing ever happens. Even the predictive dreams only make sense once the illness has happened, and they realize in retrospect what the dream was talking about." Referring to Vasily Kasatkin's large-scale study, he conjectures, "There may be a time when we have gathered enough data to get closer to being able to do some useful diagnosis and prediction. But at this point, any set way of interpretation is useless."

As well, to try to reduce such a dream to a single, fixed diagnosis may be to miss its other hidden meanings. I have found that the course of an entire health crisis may be told through dreams, heralding its imminent arrival, providing descriptions of disease processes, bulletins and updates, comments on decisions made, guidance, and repeating themes.

Intriguingly, the Healing Dream—if we trouble to decipher it—tells a parallel story of illness from the psyche's standpoint. The previous dream, for example, equates "Bad Nancy" with malignancy, suggesting that the dreamer's negative self-image—her "beating herself up"—also needs healing attention. A therapist once told me of a patient who dreamed: *I find a lump in my breast the size of a golfball. I ask myself, How could I not have felt this before?* When they explored the dream, the woman mentioned how angry it had made her when her husband came in from a night out carousing with his golfing buddies. The habit was emblematic of their marriage. She indeed found something—not just beneath the surface of her skin, but of her life—that she now marveled at "not having felt before."

When we are ill, our reasonable goal is to get better; but dreams seem to insist, over and over, that it is not enough to cure attenuations of limbs and maladies of organs. *Become well to what purpose?* they inquire sharply, persistently. *To what end?* The Dreamweaver often seems to care as much, or more, for our spiritual growth as our physical survival. We wish to be free of ailment, but the dream adds a contrapuntal line: that illness is also a *call*, although from what, and to where, may be unclear.

Once, for example, I had what seemed to be an illness-related dream in which I was part of the *Star Trek* crew on a voyage into the unknown:

> *We discover artifacts of an interstellar civilization that died out thousands of years ago, but not before it achieved one great, unprecedented technological triumph: It had learned to freeze Time by supercooling molecules in jars until their motion— indeed, all chronology—stopped. We discover an impossibly ancient cache of these jars aboard the drifting, lifeless vessel. But they've thawed slightly, and I see that Time has started up again. One squarish jar is crowded with sproutlike growth. I'm exhilarated: even after millennia-long stasis, the life force is unstoppable, ever springing up unbidden. As I'm waking, I think of an old pop song, "Time in a Bottle." A poignant verse springs to mind: "There never seems to be enough time, to do the things you want to do, once you find them."*

At the time, I was feeling this sentiment only too acutely. I'd had cancer, which in a sinister and paramount sense, is a disease of time. Its "natural history" is to just keep growing, filling the container of the body with a profusion of useless cells. The dream had clear overtones of individual promise cut tragically short, and a warning of the dangers of thinking one could freeze time and make growth stand still. (In fact, tumor biopsies are called "frozen sections.")

A few days later, I found myself driving past a cutting-edge art gallery I'd been hearing about, and decided to stop in. The theme of the exhibit turned out to be the Mexican Day of the Dead, and skeletons grinned from every corner. In the midst of this grimacing death was one artifact that was undeniably alive: a painting where a glass jar filled with profusely sprouting sunflower seeds had been mounted in the middle of a frame. The title, repeated around the work's edge for emphasis, was *Fear of Growth*.

I gazed at it for long minutes, feeling I had walked into my dream. I rolled the double entendre over in my mind like a Zen koan. On the one hand, the plants seemed to be ominously outgrowing their container and would soon die back, unable to penetrate their self-enclosed boundary. It made me ponder the ways that I was afraid of growing, and the notion that emotional blockage, in some schools of thought, is contributory to disease. But this image's flowering of life was inspiring. Sprouts of a flower that follows the light of the sun seemed a healing image.

Whether we are sick in soul or physically ill, Healing Dreams may show us a vision of wholeness at a time when we feel most imprisoned, trapped, mortal. This might fall under the banner of compensation, the psyche's innate drive for balance, but a powerful vision of health can itself have the force of a self-fulfilling prophecy.

A friend named Ruth, who worked as a nurse counselor in the hospices of the British healthcare system, once had a cancer patient who was a gardener by avocation. He was tormented that, in his early forties with two young children, he'd been given a four-week prognosis with only palliative treatment.

"He was very closed and introverted, not used to talking about himself, stiff upper lip and all," says Ruth. "He told me he'd never recalled a single dream in his life!" Ruth taught him imaginative exercises, and encouraged the man, "a very concrete 'thinking type,'" to try drawing and painting. One night, he had a luminous dream about a geranium. "These plants usually have three or four little flowerheads on a long stem, but his looked more like a daisy, with a terrific profusion of petals. In this dream, this flower was saying, 'I want you to collect my seed so we can continue.'"

When Ruth asked what the dream meant, the man replied, "That I still have time to go. The soil, my immune system, looks undernourished, but here, growing out of this diseased earth is a contradiction, a magnificent flower. The dream is telling me, 'Don't stop believing.'" The man surpassed his weeks-only prognosis and lived for the better part of a year, during which time he resolved many inner conflicts and took an international trip he'd longed for all his life. "He *didn't* stop," Ruth recalls, "and remained very, very well until just days before he died." The man had accepted a message of hope proffered by a single numinous flower.

Other times, a Healing Dream's invitation to live is almost a command performance. A patient I'll call Sarah—a forty-three-year-old with a loving husband and three young sons—was diagnosed with terminal cancer, with rapidly growing tumors in her liver and lungs. "My oncologist," she remembers, "practically sang my funeral dirge."

Sarah began preparing. She calculated the ages her children would be at her death, imagining divvying up her jewelry among her boys ("Maybe they'd have daughters someday"). She made photo albums for her kids to document their lives together, lest she be forgotten. Then she had a dream— "a real humdinger," she told me. It began with a poignant deathbed scene: "My eight-year-old gives me his Baby Bear he's cuddled since birth, my middle son gives me his good-luck rock and his old dirty Hackey Sack ball. My husband gently kisses my cheek." She bids a tearful farewell to her sorrowing family. As they slowly walk out, she feels her eyelids closing, her heartbeat waning. Her dream diary reads:

> *My chest stops rising and falling as I take my last breath. Patiently I wait for a bright ray of light to beam down and carry my tired soul heavenward. Angels, where are they? Elijah? I wait. Nothing. And then I see, walking toward me, hands outstretched, Albert Schweitzer, Eleanor Roosevelt . . . Harry Chapin . . . Jim Henson. Beckoning, calling my name. Rin Tin Tin . . . Lassies one, two, and three all panting my name. But then—Nixon . . . Lenin . . . Stalin . . . Mussolini . . . Hitler—Hitler? This is getting really ugly! Aren't we supposed to go to different places?*
>
> *"No guarantees!" a booming voice shouts from above.*
>
> *Suddenly a pain pierces my body like a train thundering through at full speed. I scream out "No!" Cells in my body begin to explode. Cancer cells burst in my lungs and liver, imploding, and healthy cells snatch them up, absorbing them like blobs of mercury eating their own kind.*
>
> *My eyelids seem to fly open and I throw off the covers with a scream: "Forget it!" Dragging a bed sheet that has attached itself to me, I run down the corridor to the nurse's station wailing like a banshee: "Where are my children? I want my children!"*
>
> *A nurse scolds that I'm a bad patient and orders me back to bed, waggling a long, crooked finger in my face. But I'm nasty, defiant, in control. "I'm the boss now," I tell her. Instantly my husband appears at my side. My children are back and so is my oncologist.*

"Your CT scan is clean," he tells me. "Your tumors are gone."

"Well, just as I thought," I huff, and march back to my room to pack my suitcase.

She woke up startled to find "it was only a dream, and I'm still stuck in reality." But the dream had rudely disturbed her fantasy of a gentle exit, cutting like a trumpet blast through the sentimental violins of her final scene. Sarah's dream contained many classic features of Healing Dreams: the graphic images of biological processes—here, cancer cells being exploded (the actual method used by natural killer cells), their remains gobbled up (the clean-up role of macrophages); the "booming voice," a typical representation of greater forces in a dream, insisting there are no cosmic warranties; the priceless bits of sardonic humor—of Lassie the Good and Hitler the Evil marching side by side.

Healing Dreams often feature such "big" people—religious figures, pop idols, portraits come alive from history books, as if the titanic scale of the struggle against death must be acknowledged. In seeking wholeness, we become players on a mythological stage.

In Sarah's "I'm the boss" dream rebellion, leaping from her deathbed trailing her own burial shroud, she assumed more power and control, a turning point often seen in cases of remarkable recovery. The dream encouraged her to be more assertive in waking life. She soon started to take on a new identity better adapted for a fight against cancer than Patient Saintly Mom. Win or lose, her dream had told her, it was better to fight on. The afterglow of its power and mystery, its fear and exhilaration, furnished her with enough borrowed courage to undertake a journey not in keeping with meek acquiescence to imminent mortality. Sarah has recently decided to go to Budapest for an experimental immunotherapy, and her family has rearranged itself to accommodate her. She feels, she tells me, as if her dream is still guiding her in her journey, reminding her she has nothing to lose by trying.

Dreams of Guidance: Crossing the Waters

It was told me in a dream
That I should do this
And I would recover.
—*Algonquin healing song*

When Dr. Brugh Joy strides out with a friendly wave to greet me on the porch of his house in the low, scrubby Colorado hills just south of the Wyoming border, his appearance startles me. His shaved head gives him the ascetic look of a chemotherapy patient, or a Zen sensei. In fact, he's something of both—a former cancer patient, and the informal preceptor of a far-flung community that formed in the two decades since the publication of his healing classic, *Joy's Way.* After a powerful spiritual awakening in his early thirties, he had hung up his stethoscope, becoming an early prototype of today's ubiquitous doctor guru. He freely admits that in his heyday, his tendency to harp on the ecstasies of the spirit—"God as the Great Good, all love and no darkness"—had drowned out the earthier, darker tonalities of the spiritual path.

But that was before a series of calamitous nightmares precipitated what he calls his "spiritual fall." In one nightmare, he saw "a devouring, merciless tyrannosaurus rex in an ancient religious meeting tent, whose thrashing tail formed a twisting, spiral image on the canvas floor. I felt stark terror, knowing no one could survive such a creature." He dreamed of black tornadoes and monstrous tidal waves.

At the time, however, his own life seemed on an even keel. He wondered if the dream's enormity heralded some natural disaster: "For two years, I'd watch CNN every morning thinking I was going to be shown some huge outer event equal to these titanic inner catastrophes I'd 'witnessed.'" Then, in 1993, Dr. Joy, who'd been immersed in new-age doings for decades, received a disturbing phone call. "It was a woman psychic I trusted, who said, 'You have a mass at the head of the pancreas.' And I knew *that* was what I'd been expecting."

He asked his doctor to do a CT scan, which revealed a cancer in the area the woman had intuited. The only possibility, he realized from his own medical training, was a typically futile, "god-awful surgery" called a Whipple procedure. He decided to withdraw for ten days to meditate. His retreat culminated in a powerful dream:

> *I am in a Jeep being driven across the ocean by a kind of rustic, sandy-haired guy. An invisible force field holds up the car and parts the water, allowing us to drive through. It is a long, difficult, circuitous route that requires a great deal of concentration. This force field is transparent. I see a column of water and air suspended, and think, Ah, that's how the spiritual and the physical operate together.*

The dream, with its biblical resonance of God parting the waters for the Israelites, came the night before he was to meet a highly recommended surgeon. "When I met him, lo and behold, I recognized him as the driver of the Jeep, sandy hair and all! When he saw my scans, he told me it didn't look good. He described how he'd have to cut into me layer by layer, and if he got down far enough and still found disease, well, that was it. Ninety-nine of a hundred pancreatic cancer patients die no matter what is done." Plunging in, Brugh told the man his dream.

"Did we get across the water?" the surgeon asked gravely.

"Yes. And you're going to get me through this."

Brugh's dream left him no doubt about proceeding, although the six-hour surgery was "amazingly difficult from a technical standpoint. Only that dream allowed me to go under anesthesia, knowing I had to be the passenger, someone else was doing the driving, and I might die on the operating table. It was a *consolamentum*—it showed me that something would survive, in life or after death." He adds, with a poet's panache: "The dream made the operating theater a sacred place of blood sacrifice, of the conjoining of flesh and soul." He had new faith in his survival: he had witnessed in his dream the power of the connection between body and spirit.

Indeed, it has often been suggested that the imaginal realm is the meeting ground between the physiological and the spiritual. In 1932, a colleague of Jung's wrote: "The world of images is attuned to blind organic happenings. . . . Though these appear psychologically as images, they work physiologically." Does this imply that Healing Dreams can actually affect the physical healing process?

To believe too literally in the power of dreams to heal the body could be dangerous. The ancient Greek writer Aelius Aristides, in his book *Sacred Tales,* relates one man's dream in one of the sanctuaries of the healing god Asklepius: The god told him that "it was necessary to remove my bones and put in nerves, for the existing ones had failed." A literal interpretation, in a period of history when, as one writer notes, "the cure of illness was frequently associated with potent fantasies of violent dismemberment and reintegration,"[4] would have been disastrous. But in the reported dream, the god also told the patient, "in consolation and instruction, not directly to knock out the bones and cut out the existing nerves, but that there needed to be, as it were, a certain change of these existing ones."[5] It is a wonderful ancient example of looking first to dreams for inner transformation, not an exact prescription.

This is not to say that instructions of the gods were never directly heeded. Galen, the father of surgery, was twice in his sleep admonished by the gods to cut the artery between his forefinger and thumb. This he did, and claimed in his great work, *Venesection,* that the treatment had freed him of a continual pain in the area of his liver.[6] Many a tribal shaman claims to have learned the medicinal uses of specific plants through dreams. Yet there are also disturbing instances of people following their dreams with naive literalism to this day. (A recent Associated Press item from China reported, "Lurid crimes of superstition have cropped up in the state media: An aluminum factory worker reportedly dug up more than one hundred graves after being told in a dream that handling bones would cure his chronic heart palpitations."[7])

Still, occasional accounts have appeared throughout history of physical healings resulting from dreams. Perhaps the most famous one occurred in Italy near the end of the thirteenth century, when a zealous young priest of the order of Servites fell ill with a painful cancer of the foot. He bore his trials without a murmur and, when it was decided that amputation should be performed, spent the night before the operation in prayer. He then sank into a light slumber from which, claim contemporary reports, he awoke completely cured. He lived to the age of eighty, and later became known as St. Peregrinus, the patron saint of cancer patients.

It seems clear that dreams can produce strong physical sensations that persist even upon awakening. Pioneering psychologist Frederic Meyers cites the case of a patient named Albert, who was prone to somnambulistic "fugues." Albert remarked, "Every time I dream that I have been bitten or beaten, I suffer all day in the part attacked."[8] Dream researcher Jayne Gackenbach cites a pilot study at the University of Texas Southwestern Medical School in which subjects who characteristically had "lucid dreams" were instructed to visualize an increase in cancer-destroying natural killer (NK) cells in their blood during dreaming. Normally, NK cell levels drop during sleep. But drawing blood throughout the night, researchers found that cell levels in several subjects unexpectedly rose to waking levels following periods of lucidity.[9]

Gackenbach cites two intriguing anecdotal cases. In one, a construction worker in Tennessee had injured his arm so badly during an arm-wrestling match he was unable to work. He suggested to himself before falling asleep that his arm be healed. "I recall a man in my dream state twisting and poking around on my elbow," he reported, "and it hurt." The dream figure explained that he was healing him, and upon awakening, the man discovered his right arm was tingling as if it had gone to sleep. When the tingling dissipated, the pain was gone, and his arm, he claimed, was "as good as new."[10] Another lucid dreamer with a badly sprained ankle reported a dream in which "I reached for my ankle with my dream hands, which caused me to tumble in my dream. As I held my ankle I felt a vibration similar to electricity. Amazed, I decided to throw lightning bolts around in my dream. . . . I awoke with next to no pain in my swollen ankle and was able to walk on it with considerable ease."[11]

Lucid-dream researcher E. W. Kellog has reported at least one case where someone claimed to have been healed by a "warm, buzzing, electric" sensation in a dream. He also showed me a fascinating account he received from a woman who had gone to bed one night barely able to walk from the pain of six plantar warts on her feet, each about one centimeter across. Here, abbreviated, is the lucid dream she had that night:

> *I am walking through what appears to be a museum. I see small lamps attached to the walls, illuminating alcoves where religious objects sit on display. I realize that while I have visited museums like this, this one appears more like a movie set. I think of my feet because they are hurting as I walk. I sit down on a wooden cube. Then I remember I can heal my feet. A ball of white light I had been visualizing before sleep appears around my hands. I put my hands on my right foot, and the light enters it, glowing golden from within. I hold it there for several seconds, then move to the left foot. Same process. It seems amazing and terrifying. The feeling is so intense that I wake up with my heart pounding.*

The next morning, the woman was surprised to feel no pain upon walking. She checked her warts and discovered they had uniformly turned black overnight. All fell off within ten days.[12]

The psychosomatic disappearance of warts is a well-known medical phenomenon. But what to make of occasional reports, like that of St. Peregrinus, of healing from significant disease associated with a vivid dream? Dr. Larry Dossey cites in a recent book a letter he received from a thirty-six-year-old man diagnosed with an inoperable brain tumor in 1994. Chemotherapy was not an option. He had received the maximum dosage of radiation. Not knowing where else to turn, he obtained holy water from Lourdes, which he rubbed in his scalp daily while supplicating Mary to heal him. An MRI showed some shrinkage of the mass. A year and half after his diagnosis, he reported a "very unusual dream" of an ineffably simple encounter: A plainly dressed woman "about my age" named Mary said to him, "Jeff, be happy." What was extraordinary about the dream, he says, was the "the incredible love I felt from this woman. It was the most unusual feeling I have ever had. It was not a sexual love, but one that resembles a mother's love for her child. I did not believe it was possible to feel such deep love and warmth. . . . The dream and the sensations associated with it lingered for several days. I could not think of anything else." When the man went to a scheduled MRI three days later, he wrote Dossey, "The tumor had virtually disappeared."[13]

Such anecdotal reports take us to the far edge of Healing Dreams. Even after my years of research into medically well-documented cases of remarkable recovery, the most honest assessment is that I scarcely know what to make of them. Medical science has, however, amply confirmed the physiological power of emotion, and Healing Dreams often feature emotional states of unprecedented intensity. Leaving aside theological aspects of "miracle" cases, we might speculate that in dreams the mind-body connection is more direct, more able to slip past the routinizations of waking thought. Perhaps the currents of the psyche become, as it were, more "hot-wired" to the engines of the body during dreaming.

The most plentiful claims of dream cures come down to us from the ancient cult of Asklepius. The Greeks believed that if an ill person slept in one of the god's temples, he could awaken from a divinely inspired dream physically healed. What was required was a vision of unmistakable meaning, which they termed the "effective dream" or simply the "healing dream." The actual cure might be accomplished, for example, through a dream of a dog, a snake, or Asklepius himself. In the latter case, the healing would be instantaneous. Indeed, the first "case studies" of miraculous healing were carved by grateful beneficiaries on the temple walls of Epidaurus and Cos. (A sample: "Alecetes of Alicos, blind, dreamed Asklepius opened his eyes with his fingers. The next day he could see.")

If he had lived a few thousand years ago, a man I'll call Thomas might have commissioned a similar plaque. Thomas, who walked up to me after a lecture I gave to the staff of a southwestern hospital, had been a lawyer and instructor in civil procedures when he had suddenly fallen into a coma. A quizzical, slow-talking man in his late fifties, his account of what happened to him one day in October 1972 is as matter-of-fact as his tragedy is opaque: "I'd gone to bed on a Friday night, but at noon Saturday my dad still couldn't wake me up," he says mildly. Neither could his mother when she got home from work later that day, nor his police officer brother. Paramedics were summoned who, unable to rouse him, rushed him to the hospital. By Sunday night, as far as his doctor was concerned, it was all over but the last rites. "He told my mother to go home, and call him later with the name of which mortuary to send the body to."

But his mother refused to let him die. She insisted on home care for her mysteriously vegetating son, whose inert body still retained the ability to breathe unassisted by a respirator. Thomas lay in bed, fed through a tube, his true whereabouts unknown. "I was just unconscious," he explains in a tone that is almost embarrassed. "Three years later, I was *still* unconscious." Then one day, as he recalls, "A man came to the foot of my bed. And he said, 'Get up, Thomas, I have need of you.' So I got up! I walked into the living room and my mother screamed. So did my dad.

"I just asked them, 'Where'd that neighbor go?' because that's who I thought it was. He didn't have on a beard, or a robe or a halo, and he certainly didn't have wings."

Thomas's bewildered parents explained that no one had been in his room.

"I spent three weeks afterward searching for that man, sitting on a bench in the middle of town, waiting to spot him in the crowd, because I couldn't believe he wasn't real. If I had to describe him," he says with a wry smile, "I'd say he looked like Alan Ladd, who played the hero in *Shane*. I didn't see him as a religious *anything*."

Thomas says he was disoriented for a while, unable to comprehend that three years had passed. "I couldn't believe you'd elected that peanut farmer Carter as president of the United States. I thought that was more unbelievable than what happened to me!"

A friend of Thomas's at the hospital tells me he still has cognitive deficits and perceptual problems, lingering aftereffects of his peculiar ordeal. Whatever great force woke Thomas, it couldn't abrogate all laws of physiology. After a long, slow recovery, he decided to attend divinity school. Though he'd had a strong religious background ("a couple years of seminary before law school, but I didn't feel called") and is well aware of the contemporary rage for angels, he's reluctant to affix any labels to his Lazarus-like resurrection. He was simply struck, he says, by the man's cryptic words, "I have need of you," remembering this as "something Jesus says to his disciples in a Bible passage."

Thomas is now a chaplain specializing in deathbed counseling. "I deal with any issues that need to be reconciled," he explains in his slow, sincere way. "A father hasn't talked to his children in years. A brother or sister who haven't spoken in decades because they're still on the outs about some old argument. I try to get them to at least make one last effort, rather than having them go to death with it hanging over them." He smiles slightly. It's the smile of someone who *knows* something but can't put it into words.

What happened to Thomas? Did he have a dream? See an apparition? Experience a vision? Given the imprecision of our language for altered states, the terms seem nearly interchangeable. All we know is that something—some force of wholeness—intruded upon his brokenness. Whether this actually caused his awakening, or whether his physiology had slowly, imperceptibly been healing until it broke all at once through his coma, or whether physiological and psychical events abruptly synchronized is a mystery as deep as his healing itself.

Dream Doctors

I was introduced to Thomas by one of the hospital's doctor administrators, who appeared to have no problem with a man who put such stock in Healing Dreams making rounds to his patients. I've met a small number of such medical practitioners—doctors and nurses who will admit, often only off the record, that dreams have a place in their practice. A number of them could be called "wounded healers" who had profound dream encounters during their own health crises.[14]

Dr. Julie Carpenter, a handsome, almost relentlessly upbeat woman in her late forties, is an unabashed product of the spiritual ferment of the 1960s. She studied yoga with Swami Satchidananda and philosophy at Stanford before becoming what used to be known, in the preholistic medicine days, as the "hip doc" of my town. A top-drawer pediatrician, she was willing, unusual back then, to supervise home births.

"When I delivered babies," she tells me, "I used to have striking dreams all the time." Once a family was adamant about delivering their baby at home. Julie, however, had a vivid dream that the infant would be stillborn. She pleaded with them to consider hospital birth, and the family finally opted for the medical setting. "It was a good thing," she remembers. "The baby's heartbeat suddenly dropped to forty during delivery. I had to pull him out with forceps. He would have died at home. He's grown into a wonderful young man."

It could have been coincidence, she realizes. But it kept happening, not always with such a happy outcome. Julie had delivered the baby of an older couple, and everything had proceeded normally. She'd noticed him sleeping peacefully in his mother's arms a few months later at an outdoor auction—looking, she thought, a little wan, but so did everyone on that cold December day in the Rockies. A few nights later, though, she had a dream that woke her with a start. She had seen the baby in a car with its parents, when suddenly it *vomited up its heart*. She still looks distressed at the horrible, unbidden image. Not long after, she got a desolate phone call from the parents, telling her the baby had died of sudden infant death syndrome. "They'd been driving home on a lonely road during this bitter cold spell, and their car had suddenly stalled out. When a farmer came by and picked them up, they discovered the baby was dead."

The farmer and his wife had coincidentally also lost an infant child and were able to calm the parents' wild grief and escort them to the hospital. Julie was so deeply affected by her dream that she disputed the SIDS diagnosis and insisted on an autopsy. It revealed that the baby, in fact, had died of a heart defect. She sometimes wonders what would have happened if she had somehow acted on her dream. Could it have led to a more timely diagnosis of the condition? "They now do heart transplants for this. But in those days, there was no really good procedure. Children's Hospital would have tried surgery, and the baby would've died anyway, but only after a lot of terrible suffering."

Julie did act on a dream once, which saved her own life. At an age when biannual mammograms are a standard medical recommendation, she, the consummate woman's doctor, had put off having one. "I didn't want to expose myself to radiation for no good reason. I took the arrogant position that I ate well, lived well, exercised, and had no family history of cancer— why bother?

"But then I had a brief, vivid dream that I was walking down the hospital hall to get a mammogram. I work in hospitals, so that was nothing very unusual, but the image just wouldn't leave me. I called to schedule a scan. Half an hour later—they'd had a sudden cancellation and got me in right away—they found a tiny cancer lesion, less than a centimeter. Three weeks later, I had the operation, and my lymph nodes showed positive. If I hadn't done it right when the dream 'told' me to, I wouldn't be here." She points upward, then to her heart, and shrugs. " I give the Great Spirit, the collective unconscious, whatever, full credit. It made me realize that we live in the lap of the Other."

As a result of her experiences, Julie makes a point of honoring her patients' inner diagnoses almost as much as her medical algorithms. "If someone has a strong dream that I can't find a regular explanation for, I'll respond in some way. If it turns out there's nothing going on medically, then we look for another meaning."

Her approach harks back to earlier times, when the Healing Dream was an indispensable instrument in the physician's kitbag. (The sixteenth-century theologian Benedict Pererius wrote in his tract *De Magia,* "Dreams which indicate good or bad states of the body . . . are observed and exploited to full advantage by physicians."[15]) Their use in medicine today is haphazard, if not downright disreputable. Though physicians who include dreams in their practice are considered oddities, a quiet, professional underground continues to explore this unmarked territory. After experiencing her own series of life-changing dreams, Katharine O'Connell, a Santa Cruz, California, nurse-practitioner, not only has incorporated dreamwork into her practice but also has given seminars at several medical schools to teach young doctors dreamwork techniques.

Like Dr. Carpenter, O'Connell has noticed that startlingly accurate dreams occur during pregnancy. She even goes one step further: these dreams, she believes, can be used to actively guide the process itself. She cites the case of an anxious, pregnant, thirty-nine-year-old preschool teacher named Joan, whose obstetrician had referred her after she had miscarried four times.

Joan, who was married to a professional football player, had had the same nightmare before each miscarriage. In her dream, she was a member of an all-women's football team dressed in white uniforms. The object of the game was to go nine yards (clearly, the "whole nine yards" of a nine-month pregnancy). But every time Joan ran with the ball in her dream, she would fumble it at the four-and-a-half-yard line. At this point, the game would stop, and her uniform would turn an alarming bright red, the color of fresh blood. And in fact, most of her miscarriages had occurred around the fourth month.

Nurse O'Connell remembers Joan gasping aloud when she first walked into her office. "She said, 'My God, you're wearing the same outfit the coach in my dream wore last night!'" It turned out that Joan had had her usual dream, only this time everyone was wearing emerald green uniforms, and there was a new coach with an unusual blue necklace. "Sure enough, the day she first came in, I was wearing an emerald green outfit and a one-of-a-kind, deep blue lapis lazuli necklace. We knew there was some synchronicity here, an indication something wonderful might happen."

Joan's dream continued to progress throughout her pregnancy, but not according to the recurrent pattern. As the dreaded four-and-a-half-month mark neared, the football team got a new female assistant coach who wore an M.D.'s white medical coat. In her dream, this new coach told her, "You need to sit by the sidelines for the rest of the game." Joan made an appointment to see her obstetrician, who counseled nearly complete inactivity and bedrest. At six months, Joan had a dream in which she was sitting on the bench and the doctor-coach told her, "This game will end at eight and a half."

"That week," says Nurse O'Connell, "at her regularly scheduled appointment, Joan's ob-gyn told her, 'You're going to have elective C-section at eight and a half months.' Not long after, Joan dreamed she was sitting in the bleachers, with her team around her, holding a healthy baby girl." The dream came to pass. The baby was delivered by a young woman doctor whom Joan instantly and delightedly recognized as the white-clad "coach" from her dream.

Nurse O'Connell has devised her own working theory of how dreams offer their healing wisdom: "First there's a 'presentation stage,' where you're shown the problem, symptom, or challenge. Later, there's an 'information-gathering' stage, where the dreams reveal more about the illness, and give clues to its healing. Then, after months or even years, there's a 'processing stage' in which images of a helpful individual or group often appear. Then finally, dreams offer some resolution of the problem." Such healing journeys proceed most effectively, she's observed, when physician and patient collaborate in this feedback loop between dreams and reality.

Gladys McGarey, an M.D. in family medicine, has spent a good part of her life attuned to the invisible realm of dreams. Born and raised in India, she was influenced by Hindu philosophy and by missionary parents who "knew the importance of prayer and the action of spirit." When as a young woman she encountered the work of Edgar Cayce, the famed psychic known as the "Sleeping Prophet," she became deeply involved in dreamwork.

Seven years after she'd begun her formal studies, she had her own terrifying dream. She had previously noticed a little nodule on her thyroid but assumed, as is usually the case, that it was benign. In her dream, however, she caught a huge black widow spider in a jar. It escaped, and she grabbed the back of its head, whereupon it turned around and delivered a poisonous bite to her finger.

"The pain was so severe," she reported, "that it wakened me." Then she went back to sleep and dreamed: *I am in a restaurant, and someone sitting beside me is cutting up dream books and throwing them away. Then a minister I know sits down, and we decide the spider dream has something to do with the nodule in my neck.*

She immediately went on retreat, started a thirty-day water fast, meditated deeply, and continually consulted her dreams. She still has a meticulous dream diary chronicling the gradual increase in positive images: her childhood house (a frequent symbol for the body) being fixed up and newly furnished, successful operations, and the like. When she emerged, she claims, the tumor was gone. Since it was never biopsied, we cannot know if her tumor was malignant. What is startling, perhaps, is the degree to which she resolved to follow her Healing Dream.

Dreamwork is now an integral part of her practice. When patients bring her dreams, she writes them in their charts as part of their medical records. When she's concerned about a patient, she invariably "asks" to dream about him. "Then I make the best possible conscious decision, then ask God if it's right. If don't get a dream saying differently in a week, I figure the first intuition was right. If you're barreling down the freeway with a good set of directions, you don't look for unmarked turnoffs."

She describes a seventy-two-year-old patient who'd had a shoulder removed for osteosarcoma and then developed lung cancer. He'd been given only weeks to live. Then he had a striking dream: He was pinned to the ground with four large wooden pegs that were "the four powers of earth," which prevented him from getting up. *Fine,* the man enigmatically declared in his dream, *then I'll use the twelve powers of the mind!* He woke up with a start, not sure what he'd meant. But, Gladys says with a laugh, "The man went to Colorado, got twelve white turkeys, and said, 'You're my white cells.' He fed them grasshoppers, and said, 'These are my cancer cells.' The next Christmas, after exceeding his prognosis, he died of pneumonia. When they looked at his lungs, they were clear."

Gladys has delivered a fair number of babies—a notably unpredictable business—trusting in dreams to prepare her for the unexpected. She recalls a patient in labor who said, "This is going to be a C-section." Gladys urged her to stop worrying—all indications showed hers would be an exceptionally routine delivery. But the patient was insistent. The night before, she'd dreamed that her old teddy bear had a baby in its stomach and needed to be "unzipped" to get it out. She showed Gladys where the "zipper" was located. A few hours later, she did require a cesarean, and Gladys, prepared, wound up making an incision just where the patient's dream had indicated.

Her account brought to mind a story told to me by an Australian aboriginal man. Before his daughter was born, he'd had a dream in which he was told her name. He had written it in his diary: Itimathangawa. "*Iti* means 'small,' " he explained to me. "*Thanga* means 'honey-ant.' And *wa* means 'mother.' But I didn't know why the dream frightened me so.

"Seven months later, my wife went in for a checkup and the doctors said that she had toxemia—that she and the child were fighting, poisoning each other. They said to me, you will either have a mother without a baby, or a baby without a mother. No way, I told them. I know different. I didn't tell them I knew from my dream! In the end, they did a cesarean. My daughter was very small and premature, but now she's a great, healthy twenty-one-year-old."

His eyes crinkled in mirth as he explained, "See, the way you get honey ants is, you have to cut into Mother Earth to scoop them out. So what the dream meant was, mother had to be broken open to get this very small child, see?"

Nature and Dream Body

The man's experience points out a common theme in Healing Dreams—the equation of events inside the body with events in the natural world. A cancer, for example, might be represented as a landscape swarming with insect plague, or by a lava-spewing volcano, as if the disruption of our physiology is experienced at some deep level as the natural world itself sinking into chaos. Perhaps it is, for what could be more grounded in nature than our bodies? "What happens to the earth, happens to us" is the view of all indigenous peoples. It should be no surprise that in dreams of illness, Nature is depicted rudely barging into the house or the city (how we feel when disease invades our precincts), or conversely, man-made things are shown impinging upon the natural (representing, perhaps, what epidemiologists call "diseases of civilization").

A woman named Wendy dreamed of a "very loud toad, eating live spiders and larvae," that followed her into the back of a store. Then she dreamed of a town whose beautiful lake "has shells floating on the surface; I realize I should check for pollution." Finally, she dreamed: *I see a black man who works alone on a sewer line in New York City. There are two frogs near the opening, a very large one and a baby one. I tell him how great it is you can see so much life in New York but that frogs are very sensitive.* Not long after her first dream, she went in for a checkup and discovered she had two fibroid tumors, one of which had actually begun to protrude. She had a successful operation. But her dream led her to ask herself what had caused the fibroids? Frogs are regarded by scientists as sensitive barometers of environmental health, our planet's equivalent of the canary in the coal mine. Could it be her illness had been not just some imbalance in her own system but a sign of pollution in the ecosystem itself? (One current theory of why fibroids are so rampant—some forty percent of American women—is the prevalence in the water and soil of dioxin, a xenoestrogen affecting estrogen-mediated tumors, making its way up the food chain.)

Wendy's subsequent dreams often featured other creatures of water—a symbol Jung believed represented "the feminine," as well as the watery depths of the unconscious itself. The following dreams, drawn from three different cancer patients, seem almost to insist that disease involves an unavoidable confrontation with the unconscious, with an unknown life lying beneath the surface of awareness. A woman named Demaris, for example, one night heard an "inner voice" telling her to get a mammogram. She is married to an acupuncturist, and Western medicine is not her remedy of first resort. But breast cancer runs rampant in her family, and after a little deliberation, she made a doctor's appointment. A few days before she went in, she had what she described to me as a "tremendous" dream:

A strong young man is fishing in a huge canal. His father, gentle and strong, with blue eyes and graying hair, tells me, "I'm worried my son will catch something too big." Then we see in the sky the hugest fish, its color an unearthly yellow-green fluorescence, pulling a long line with the boy attached at its end by a harness. It's literally dragging the boy through the sky. Then the fish dives into the water, and the boy is submerged underwater for a long time. I'm wondering if he'll drown. Then back into the sky he's pulled as the fish leaps up again. We're helpless. The fish is one hundred percent in charge. In the end, the fish hovers over the land and sets the boy gently down. The boy unbuckles the harness, and the fish flies off. I say, 'He's had the ride of his life.' I see his eyes are brighter blue, and though shaken, he only has a slight bump on his head.

Her dream—a kind of *Moby-Dick* with a happier ending—showed her, she says, "that I could trust my own healing journey and where it was about to take me." Demaris was successfully operated on for her cancer. She associated the luminous fish with "Christ consciousness," and its color with "transformation." The dream had seemed to her an initiatory voyage, as if her soul itself had burst its bounds, leaving its natural abode to fly through the sky, leaving her no doubt about its primal power.

The cancer patient Mark Pelgrin recounted a powerful dream:

I find myself camping with some mysterious woman figure. A man comes up to us with a very big fish for dinner. We go over to his camp with him, and this enormous fish, a kind of Leviathan of a golden trout eight feet long, is stretched out on a pole. The fish is not dead yet, for its mouth is gasping for air. As it dies, I can see it is in great pain. It shudders. I feel for it, but realize now that I am to be one of the eaters of the fish. It is food we need, this woman figure and I.[16]

He, too, interprets the fish—which, unlike Demaris, he finally devours—as a Christian motif, but also a way of partaking of "the great undifferentiated body of nature" and "the irrational side, the side that lay close to the unconscious." He incorporates the fish, which has died on a sort of crucifix, into himself, almost as a Eucharist, a feast of spiritual need.

Gail, a forty-two-year-old art therapist, had what she called "a really major wake-up dream" while recuperating from a grueling but successful treatment for breast cancer.

I dream I am fishing in the dark. The water is shimmering in the moonlight. I put a worm on the hook, proud I'm not too squeamish, and cast my line out again. A little fish takes the bait; but then I see a flash of gold and silver, and am delighted to watch a really large fish swallow the little one. I reel it in and grab the big fish to take it off the hook. Then, shocked that I am really touching it, I throw the fish up into the air and it lands onto the rocks up an embankment behind me. And I look more closely at it and see that its eyes are wide open and really round, and its mouth is gaping, unable to breathe. It is so beautiful, this luminous, yellow-and-white-speckled fish against the absolutely black rock, gasping for air. And I panic—what do I do now? Should I watch it die? I am feeling very queasy and also this deep emotion of compassion. I pick it up again and fling it back in the water, where it swims away.

Gail felt "the waters were myself. I reached down inside and found something that at first was small, then was a bigger thing, which frightened me. I felt I had to separate myself from it, toss it onto the shore, but then, finding it so beautiful, I had to reintegrate it by tossing it back into the water." She sighs. "All of this is still a mystery. "

Her journal entry immediately following her dream gives a picture of life lived, at least for a time, at the behest of the unconscious, beneath the surface of any pragmatic goals: "I want to give in, and surrender," she wrote, "wallow in myself, be content to think or not think, just be me with the sunlight streaming in the window, the cars going by on the street outside, the birds chirping and fluttering at the feeder. Can this be a way to live? It makes me happy. I've been excused from productive, working, purposeful life. But am I avoiding something? Avoiding what? I'm looking at what it means to be Being."

It is almost as if these three patients had torn a page from the same book of mythology. It is the sort of thing that led Jung, inexorably, to his theory of the archetypes—that each of us carries a collective inheritance of images and stories, as much a part of our psyche as the brain's innate capacity for grammar. In each case, the dream insists that disease is not only a physical malfunction but also a luminous (albeit often terrifying) journey into the dark, undiscovered waters of the self. The dreamers had accidentally "hooked a big one," and it turned out to be much more than they bargained for—more terrifying, yet weirdly beautiful.

In each dream, the fish were literally "too big to handle." These forces of the psyche reveal their secret existence to us, but they are not under our control. Nor can they live indefinitely in the air and daylight of the waking world. Their natural place is in the deeps, where sometimes they pull us down with them. Landed, the fish gasps for air; beneath the water, it is the dreamer who cannot breathe. Conscious and unconscious: neither can exist solely in the other's world; yet without intercourse, they are radically incomplete. Their mutual revelation is fraught with risk and potential. It is a striking metaphor for the dynamic wholeness at the heart of healing.

Gail said she was looking at what it meant *to be Being*. Even in the face of death, dreams are a sharp spur to enlarge our life even as its circumference contracts.

I have come to trust my dreams almost as much as X rays, CT scans, ultrasounds, blood tests, and palpations. They diagnose my body, take the pulse of my soul. I have tracked them as climatologists track vagaries of wind and current to discern patterns in diverse, seemingly unrelated phenomena. What is my own long-range forecast? What do my dreams portend, forbode, promise? What do they *want,* these night visions that wrap their arms around my personal predicament and our collective one, an embrace that seems to call for both dancing and weeping? A few friends have chided me for being self-mythologizing. I let them bring me up short, grateful, sometimes, to be pulled from my own deeps. But I can't convince myself that our journey, the arduousness and audacity of it, does not require an even greater mythos: In the end, it may be for want of myths that we perish, and only through courage to live them that we become truly whole.

Chapter 4

Dreams of Personal Calling

Healing Our Life Path

> A people who do not dream never attain to inner sincerity, for only in his dreams is a man really himself. Only for his dreams is a man responsible— his actions are what he must do. Actions are a bastard race to which a man has not given his full paternity.
>
> —*John Butler Yeats (in a letter to his son William)*

What would happen if we followed the call of a Healing Dream? Would things fall apart, the center no longer hold? Or would life wax fuller, our inner and outer selves mirroring each other more faithfully that we'd ever dared imagine? Would our trajectory have more loft, our fate more consequence? Or would we crash to earth, having too readily trusted our waxen wings to the sun? What does a life that honors the dream *look* like?

Career consultants say they have never heard so many people yearning for meaningful vocation—for a life's labor that satisfies both head and heart, that custom-fits inner being to outer circumstance. But it can be difficult to tease out the thread of true calling from lives woven by necessity or default. We chart a course, only to discover we have drifted by invisible increments from where we first aimed our sextant. But if in waking life we are actors on a social stage, delimited by norms, expectations, and personal history, in dreams we reenter the realm of our full potential. Here our spiritual challenge remains alive. We may find to our amazement (and dismay) that the yearnings of some greater Self can no longer be placated with token gestures or halfway measures. Even if we've forgotten our dreams, our dreams remember us well. They rap on the window at night, drawing us from the comfort of our abodes, or bide their time, keepers of the flame, awaiting the right moment to ignite the soul and set our life ablaze.

Healing Dreams in Childhood

In Native American tradition, a child's dreams can reveal his destiny. They are divinations of his basic nature, hints about his future role in the community. At the age of nine, the Oglala Sioux medicine man Black Elk dreamed he flew to a high peak in the Black Hills. There he met powerful ancestral totems, like the thunderbird, which initiated him into the sacred mysteries and charged him to one day lead his people. Janet, a Salish Indian acquaintance living outside Seattle, told me that in her tribe, children's dreams are routinely sifted for clues to their calling. "They're taken seriously, always," she said emphatically. "Nobody makes fun of them." Relatives watch their own dreams for key insights into the child's soul.

Janet says she had "a strong imagination" as a child. When she was seven years old, she was taken from her mother's home to live with her biological father, whom she remembers "was an alcoholic—a mean drunk. He made me sleep in one of those government cribs with iron bars. One night, when I cried because no one would help me comb my long hair, he took a pair of scissors and cut it all off." Many miles from home, she went to bed heartsick.

"That night I had a dream so vivid I remember it to this day: *I am in my bed and I am flying through the sky. There are four spirit beings, one on each corner of my bed, taking me someplace. I get scared because I can feel the wind in my face; but they keep telling me, Don't be afraid, we're not going to hurt you. And then I come back, and I'm not afraid anymore.*

After that dream, Janet says, "I decided, no matter what, I was going home." A few days later, she secretly packed her suitcase, pretending she was using it to play house, but instead lugged it up to the highway. She stuck out her thumb every time a car with a woman at the wheel approached, but none stopped to pick her up.

She kept walking, dragging the heavy suitcase all day until, lost and exhausted, she stopped to hide in the tall grass by a house where some children were playing. Spotting her, the children called their mother, who turned out by coincidence to be Janet's great-aunt. After a weeklong family council, a beloved grandmother offered to take her in. "So it was kind of weird; that dream was the trigger point in my life. From then on, if I didn't like the way things were, I'd get inner guidance about what to do, and I'd do it."

In our culture, children are rarely told of the value of dreams. Their parents themselves may not know it. The dream has little place at the breakfast table or, for that matter, in most theories of child development. Psychology postulates that our childhood waking experience forms the basis for our personalities, with dreams mere reflections or barometers. But this is not a universal view. As one anthropologist has noted, "When we think autobiographically we only include events that have occurred when awake; the Ojibwa include remembering events that have occurred in dreams. And far from being of subordinate importance, such experiences are for them often of more vital importance than the events of daily waking life."[1]

I have been startled how often people have reported to me some unforgettable visitation in early childhood that acted as a lodestone, exerting a magnetic pull on the rest of their lives. Around the age of six, I had a repetitive dream that so awed me I didn't tell anyone for twenty-five years. In it, my world—*the* world—is literally coming apart:

> *The air is charged with trillions of lit-up, whirling particles. I realize the earth is being destroyed, and I must run to a special meeting place in the woods. I arrive at a clearing, in the middle of which sits a large flying saucer. The next thing I know, I am aboard it, in the company of a group of strangers. The atmosphere is somber, elegiac. We gaze out a window in silence, sharing a communal sadness. I*

wonder why none of my friends or family are there, yet I know that I belong with
these people—as if we've been selected. As the ship begins to pull away, I can see
the earth is undergoing an unimaginable catastrophe, its continents cracking in
upheaval. My mind stretches to breaking, unable to take in a tragedy so gigantic.

My parents had never taken me to a sci-fi movie. In my young life, there
was no divorce, abuse, alcoholism, or poverty to escape from. We lived in
the placid suburbs of New York, and though my upbringing was emotionally trying, it could not entirely account for this titanic dream. It
seemed to establish within me a secret bastion of knowledge no adult I
knew would comprehend. It wasn't until my late twenties that I began to
realize the extent to which it had shaped my life. This subliminal sense of
urgency to "save the world" had been a touchstone for my life decisions.
The dream had been a background hum so constant I barely noticed it, yet
I knew it had contributed to my later interest in radical politics and environmental activism, had given me that feeling of "being in this world but
not of it" that eventually led me to Buddhism. I've tried to dismiss it as
overheated childhood imaginings, fueled by early cold-war bomb paranoia. But the dream's inexpressible realness had lodged it in my mind long
after most actual childhood events had faded.

I have found others who remember similar dreams that charged them
with a distinctly unchildlike sense of responsibility for the world. Michael,
born twenty years later than I, remembers having the only recurring
dream of his life when he was seven:

The world is being messed up, big-time. Two big countries are marshaling their
forces, atomic explosions are already happening far away. I and a bunch of other
kids, from my age ranging to young teenagers, have secretly constructed this whole
underground complex—you get there by a tree elevator a hundred feet under-
ground. We have control panels, viewing screens for taking in intelligence. We're
very well protected. I am kind of the leader, but everyone is working together.

"The striking thing for me," he says, "was how vividly colored and real
it seemed. I remember the brilliant blue on the computer screen. Three

nights in a row, the identical dream! There was a strong sense that we children were more intelligent than the so-called adults, who were acting like children—that *they* were insane, and we were more cognizant of how we needed to act."

"Big" dreams of early childhood may contain a surprising number of adult themes. They may go against the grain of the prevailing culture, grant new autonomy in the face of social authority, provide contact with some guiding power, or produce insights—often of a quasi-religious nature—that overturn received doctrine. The dream researcher Harry Hunt reports the following dreams, experienced on successive nights by a seven-year-old boy born and raised in Italy:

1. In church. God tells him that his grandmother has died because he did not attend church. [The dreamer] walks toward the coffin, swinging a crucifix menacingly and insisting that she must become alive again or he will kill God. Suddenly she sits up in her coffin.
2. The devil is by the water fountain in the town square attempting to carry away his cousin. He attacks the devil and strangles him, holding him under the flowing fountain water.
3. He is in church. The statue of St. Anthony is holding the Baby Jesus. St. Anthony offers Jesus to the dreamer to hold, who says, "But I don't even go to church." Still, St. Anthony smilingly offers Jesus until the boy awakes in the cold sweat that ended each of these dreams and imprinted them as critical life experiences.[2]

Here is a complex, unorthodox version of spirituality—more like an episode of God-wrestling—including a forced baptism of the devil and a holy blessing unmediated by church authority or catechism. It is a dream brimming with spiritual paradox. A number of people have told me about childhood Healing Dreams so precocious that thereafter they felt a sense of "otherness" in their family surroundings. Dr. Brugh Joy, for example, had a "wondrous dream" when he was nine that shaped his adult life:

I am running home to tell my mother that Christ has come and I am going to follow him. It is a beautiful, sunlit day. I enter what is our home in the dream— a pure, white adobe building, rectangular in shape, with a large wooden plank front door and wooden plank floors. With all the excitement and wonder a nine-year-old boy can express, I make this announcement and beg my mother, my twin brother, and my older brother to follow, but they are not interested in what I have to say. I realize that I will leave home alone and follow this great Being.

When he awoke, he was overwhelmed with both ecstasy and profound grief. He told no one of the dream. Though it gave him a "rich, warm feeling" whenever he recalled it, it felt "too foreign. The adobe house was nothing like any of our homes had been," Dr. Joy recalled, "and neither I nor my family were religious in the traditional sense. The dream had to wait thirty years before I could appreciate how prophetic it had been."[3] Though he went on to pursue a medical career, his childhood calling secretly informed his work, leading him to finally pursue a more explicitly spiritual vocation.

Childhood callings are not unknown in the history of the Church. In 1825, nine-year-old Giovanni Bosco, a violent child prone to resolving schoolyard arguments with a well-placed punch, dreamed of a "shining man in white" who instructed him to use kindness to win over his playmates. Then "a woman in a garment of light" showed him a scene in which wild animals turned into lambs, telling him it would be his "field of activity" to do the same for "my children." Bosco later founded his own Salesian order, whose task is to care for homeless children.[4]

Jung, famously, had a childhood dream infused with a different sort of religious mystery, melding forces of goodness and menace, sensuality and transcendence. The dream, which occurred when he was three or four, was to preoccupy him all his life:

Playing in the meadow, he discovers stone steps leading to an underground passageway. With trepidation, he descends to find a doorway hung with a rich green brocaded curtain. Curiously he parts it, and sees to his astonishment a thirty-foot chamber with an arched ceiling of hewn stone. A red carpet runs to a low plat-

form on which stands a magnificent golden throne worthy of a fairy tale king. But sitting upon it is a thick, towering trunk of flesh topped by a round, faceless head, with a single eye fixed and staring upward. Above the head was an aura of brightness.

The image remained with him throughout his youth, a "subterranean God not to be named." Jung, a minister's son, was later in his career to recognize this as a "ritual phallus." He was mystified by "how exceedingly unchild-like, how sophisticated and oversophisticated" an icon could have entered his mind. He wondered:

Who brought the Above and Below together, and laid the foundation for everything that was to fill the second half of my life? . . . Through this childhood dream I was initiated into the secrets of the earth. What happened then was a kind of burial in the earth, and many years were to pass before I came out again. Today I know that it happened in order to bring the greatest possible amount of light into the darkness.[5]

Throughout his youth, Jung never spoke of the dream image to anyone. He treated what he called his "original revelation" as "a secret I must never betray." Yet it remained an interior foothold when religious teachings were, as he put it, "pumped into" him, enabling him to tell himself, "But it is not so certain as all that." This sense of inner authority conferred by a childhood dream formed a template for his entire life work.

I was surprised when, as I was discussing my fascination with Jung's dream with my friend Franc, a British film director, he offered that he once had a similar experience—only he seemed to be awake! Franc grew up in a small village in the north of England, in an area where his family had lived since A.D. 712. The town adjoined a valley that had once contained a settlement sacked by the Danes. The area had been thoroughly plundered by grave robbers throughout the eighteenth century, but children could still discover arrowheads and sword fragments dating back hundreds of years.

When he was eight, he and his brother were crossing the valley when a torrential summer rain struck. They ran across the meadow looking for shelter. "Normally we never forded the stream, but there were trees on the other side. We waded across to get under them, but they weren't much protection.

"Suddenly I looked down and saw a little tunnel, about two feet above the water level, near a disused ancient mill. We crawled down the tunnel and came to a strange old room we'd never seen before. And there, sitting in the middle of it, was a golden harp! I have a clear memory of waiting for the rain to go and playing this harp. What I don't know to this day is whether I went into some kind of dream or trance, or if it was really there. A week later, I went back to look, but I couldn't find the tunnel. I've asked my brother over the years, and he has a vague recollection of seeing it, too."

Franc, who prides himself on what he calls a "near-photographic memory" of incidents going back to when he was two years old ("I remember the day I got my first hobby horse"), remains baffled. "The golden harp" has been an image he has rolled over in his mind throughout his life, like a personal Grail. He was intrigued to later read about the German mystic Heisenberger, who as a child claimed to have seen a golden chalice and, fueled by his vision, grew up to be a charismatic cult leader. "I have no plans to take over the world," Franc jokes. " But I look back on this experience as a mystical awakening. I saw something golden, of remarkable beauty, a gift that came especially to me and almost seemed to open some new faculty in my brain."

To this day, he says, he attributes his "intuitive powers" to this early vision. "Ideas come fully formed out of nowhere. I know things without having to be told them. I can see a devious agenda coming at me in a millionth of a second. It's been useful when I've found myself in dangerous situations, such as when I was a documentary filmmaker working in some violent part of the world. I somehow relate that kind of thing to the golden gift I was shown. I don't usually speak about it because it sounds like madness and conceit."

Sometimes these formative dreams—dreams that create early self-awareness and individuation—are without words or images. A middle-aged woman named Susan still clearly remembers a dream she had when she was eight. "It didn't have any particular content, just feelings of emptiness, terror, helplessness, a sense of my mortality. What was I doing here on earth? Who was I? I was nothing, a speck, my life impermanent—a midlife crisis at eight! I remember this feeling of the ground opening up under me, and everything I knew suddenly being null and void.

"I went to my mother, and asked, 'What do you do when you have a very frightening dream?' And she said, 'Think of something nice, like Christmas trees.' I had a very mature and disturbing insight at that moment. I thought, 'What a stupid woman,' because she had given such a completely inadequate answer. She was my main source of love, but from that point on, I started to psychologically detach from her. The dream was definitely a wake-up call that there was more to me than just my physcial body living in this house in England. In retrospect, I wonder if I haven't spent my life traveling, moving around, doing different things, keeping my eyes and ears open, just to find out what that dream meant."

Daniel Quinn, author of the novel *Ishmael*—a strange, compelling saga in which an intelligent ape laments humanity's betrayal of nature—recalls a dream he had in the spring of 1941, at age six. In his dream, he was trudging home in the dead of night, past silent, dark houses and their sleeping occupants, only to find his path blocked by a fallen tree trunk. A "great black beetle" scurried up from it. Quinn, who as a child was terrified of insects, feared it would blame him for the ruin of its tree home. Instead, the beetle, which emanated an aura of adult authority, spoke reassuringly to him "in his mind." The beetle said emphatically, "'You don't really belong here at all, do you? You don't feel much at home in these streets, in these houses, in this world." Quinn still remembers the sensation in his dream of tears stinging his eyes at this "great revelation." When the beetle added, "The thing is, you're not needed here," the boy felt speechless with grief.

But the beetle informed him he was needed "very badly" somewhere else, and gestured toward a forest, where a deer grazed in a moonlit glade. The beetle explained that they, the creatures of the wood, "need to tell you the secret of our lives," and that he, Daniel, must help, even though it would mean almost becoming one of them. He understood this was something that would happen in the future, but he didn't want to wait: "The forest was there now, a step away, and I was entirely ready to give up my life to be in the company of these creatures, who needed me and wanted to share their secrets with me. I turned and stepped off the sidewalk, and was instantly awake. Instantly awake—and utterly heartbroken, sobbing uncontrollably," because, as he told his uncomprehending mother, "it was so *beautiful.*"[6]

Quinn says that from that time onward, "I accepted this six-year-old's dream as a description of my destiny." His experience highlights a common aspect of dreams of calling—an emphasis on personal responsibility. What the dreamer is shown, he is now charged to accomplish. Such dreams are similar—I would argue, nearly identical—to what recent psychological research labels "personal event memories," those pivotal moments that shape our lives and become key elements in our personal autobiography. (One category of such memories, an "originating event," is defined as a momentous happening to which people "trace the beginning of a life path, or the birth of enduring beliefs and attitudes."[7]) In light of this research, the implications of Healing Dreams for our present theories of childhood personality development are profound. Here are dreams that are not mere responses to circumstance, but shapers of new attitudes and actions, catalysts of psychological patterns that persist into adulthood.

Dreams of calling, even in childhood, can be solemn and preternaturally morbid, containing startling philosophic themes. The novelist Anne Rice dreamed as a child: *I saw a woman who appeared to be made completely out of marble. She was walking on the street. . . . Somebody said, "That is your regis grandmother."* Rice had no idea what the word meant. She had never seen it in print—she is not sure she then knew how to read. She learned only as an adult that it is a word applied to a university professor. "When a dream is that intense, when it's that otherworldly, it's a little frightening," Rice says. "It's almost as if you saw into some other realm. You saw something that had to do with heritage or lineage that went beyond what you could see with rational eyes."[8]

She thought of the dream repeatedly when she was writing *The Queen of the Damned,* a book that features ancient, wise immortals who resemble moving alabaster. The childhood vision formed the basis of her core adult beliefs: "I fear the pure idea. These elders, and this dream figure were too detached from the flesh. The sense of menace, perhaps, came from that. It was too divorced from what we are." Rice, who has written erotica under several pseudonyms, says, "My writing, the whole thrust of it, has been to say, 'Listen to the lessons of the flesh.'"

A graduate student named Jan reports a pivotal dream with a similar flavor. At the age of seven, she recalls being angry at a Catholic elementary school teacher whose description of the soul, it seemed to her even then, was too superficial. Soon afterward, Jan had an unforgettable dream: *She was to undergo a surgery to have her soul removed.* She was frightened—this was, she says, "not like having your tonsils out." She was first taken to an observation room outside the surgical suite to witness this strange operation through a one-way mirror. She saw an older man lying on a metal table, seemingly anesthetized and covered in a surgical sheet. Then *there was a loud noise . . . a lot of wind. Almost like what you'd experience if you opened the door on a plane, a big sucking sound. The instant I heard the noise, his body shrunk down, and his head blew up like a big balloon. I was terrified, because this was going to happen to me.*[9]

The image from her dream—which touched upon spiritual issues like the relationship of the spirit to the body and the terrible consequences of "loss of soul"—has spontaneously recurred throughout her life. She did not realize until after she had written her doctoral dissertation on women's eating disorders—an analysis of Western culture's mechanical attitudes toward the body, under the rubric "The Bodiless Head"—how this dream had directly inspired her work. Jan's dream clearly displays a pattern in childhood Healing Dreams: a child is given a vision of life from a source of greater wisdom not available from family, school, or church; she is given to understand that prevailing attitudes may be stunningly wrong; and she is left with an unarticulated compulsion to change them.

Such dreams, at whatever age, do not necessarily result in immediate transformation but force a precocious recognition of other realities, setting life's course by different compass points. They become catalysts for new behaviors and attitudes that ripen over a lifetime. Black Elk's great vision didn't begin to actualize itself until nine years had passed, during which time he had mentioned it to no one. There are cases of twenty or thirty years going by before a shaman becomes convinced that a childhood vision really came from the spirits and begins to use the songs and "medicine" with which he was entrusted.[10]

Heeding the Call

Conversely, a Healing Dream may resurrect a key childhood event in the context of adult destiny. When television actress Martha del Grande was nine, a terrible ice storm smashed down the power lines in her hometown near the Kentucky border and brought her a cherished interlude: uninterrupted time with her adored, eccentric grandmother, whose house was reliably heated by several fireplaces.

"Nobody liked my grandmother," Martha remembers. "She was a family outcast, but she was my lifelong savior. Her home was my sanctuary. She had this sense of detachment from the world, but she also lived with a spirit of compassion. She fought segregation and defended the black folks in town. She got a kick out of little things, gardening, playing cards, making bacon and eggs for breakfast with such zest, you'd love them, too. You'd go, 'My God, I'm having bacon and eggs!'"

The night of the ice storm, her grandmother set up a folding bed near the fireplace, tossing a Kleenex she found lying on it into the fire. In the morning, panic-stricken, she remembered she'd hidden a big diamond ring in the wad of tissue. Martha spent hours sifting through to find the now cindery stone. A jeweler later split it in two and made two rings, one of which her grandmother bequeathed to her in her will. After her grandmother's death at 106, Martha had the diamond set alongside an emerald her husband had given her. The ring, symbolizing both her marriage and the most beloved person in her family, became her prized possession.

Then, when she was fifty-four, she dreamed:

My husband Louie and I are walking around Toronto on holiday. He suggests we go to a restaurant we used to eat in, and the owners come out and say they have something for me. They give me a jewel box, and in it is my grandmother's diamond ring. I cry from happiness. But they tell me, "We've had this ring for five years and you haven't come for it—how can you say it's valuable to you?"

I say, "I didn't know it was gone!"

The woman says angrily, "You'd better take care of it, because you could lose it."

I asked Louie whether I should wear it, or put it in my purse for safekeeping. He says the purse. Then he says he doesn't like the restaurant we're in, so we go to another one. But when the next restaurant owner comes out to greet us, I realize, my God, I've left the purse with the ring behind! "How could you do that?" the owner demands. "Lose your most prized possession!"

When I tell him, "I can get it back," he says, "No, you'll never have it again, you lost your chance." And as the dream dissipates, I wake up bereft, saying over and over, "But I will, I will, I will!"

Martha says she rarely recalls her dreams, but this one was "so vivid, so real, I remembered every detail." She was being forcefully told, it seemed to her, that she was "on the brink of losing something vital," but she didn't know what—"maybe some core part of my soul, the seed of my spirit." She felt that she, like the diamond thrown in the fire, was "losing my shine, my awe and wonder."

She didn't discuss the dream with her husband, who she was sure would be bored by it. "I felt it was so crucial I could only share it with other dreamers, or it would really turn to ashes." One friend told her the loss of the ring symbolized a loss of affection in her marriage. Another suggested it was the loss of her own capacity to love, represented by her grandmother. Others thought it was a loss of trust in herself—in the dream she was too dependent, letting her husband make the decisions. But Martha felt the dream was "like a yardstick that has no numbers. I wasn't ready to put any fixed markings on it. I sensed in my spirit what it meant—that my greatest gifts as a young person, of joy and wonderment, had gotten ground away without my knowing; that I was on the road to being a bitter, negative old woman. The dream was a signpost, a beacon. It was like a kernel that gradually becomes this living, growing thing."

Shortly after her dream, she decided to move out of the far suburbs and back into the city to be near her grandchildren. She told her husband that she wasn't ending the marriage, but she couldn't live there any longer. As she settled into her new life, it became clearer to her, she says, that being near her grandchildren was "something I was put on earth to do." She's learned to enjoy her daughter and son-in-law "moment to moment, whereas before it was predicated on what they did and achieved. All you can do for another human being is love them." Her previous career as an award-winning Canadian television star looks, in retrospect, hollow.

Martha's dream of a ring—an object symbolizing the unbroken circle of spiritual fidelity—oddly echoes that of John Newton, the eighteenth-century composer of "Amazing Grace," who had been a slave trader until a Healing Dream transformed his life. Newton dreamed he was on night watch on the deck of his ship in the Venice harbor. An unknown person brought him a ring, making him promise to keep it at all costs. If he preserved it, he was told, happiness and success would be his; if he lost it, dire misfortune would follow.

He accepted the terms, certain he could carry them out. But soon a second unknown person appeared, chiding him for believing a ring could produce such effects and urging him to throw it away. "At first I was shocked at the proposal; but his insinuations prevailed," he later wrote in his autobiography. "I plucked it off my finger and dropped it over the ship's side."

The effects were instantaneous and ghastly:

A terrible fire burst from a range of mountains. . . . I perceived, too late, my folly; and my tempter with an air of insult informed me that all the mercy God had in reserve for me was comprised in that ring which I had willfully thrown away. I understood that I must now go with him to the burning mountains, and that all the flames I saw were kindled upon my account. I trembled, and was in a great agony.

In the midst of Newton's hopelessness, a third man appeared and, hearing his confession, asked if he thought he would be wiser if he had the ring again. Before he could answer, this "unexpected friend" dove into the water and returned with the ring. The fires in the mountains were instantly extinguished. When Newton approached his benefactor for the ring, however, the man refused, saying that he would take it for safekeeping, making it available when needed.

The dream haunted him for days, making it impossible for him to go about his business. But, as the "friend" had intimated, Newton soon forgot, and for several years went on as he had before. Then, he wrote, "a time came when I found myself in circumstances very nearly resembling those suggested by this extraordinary dream," in which he was being seduced into taking part in "a most complicated crime." It was then, on his "day of distress," that the dream arose again in his mind, and he had a sense that God was restoring the ring as a symbol of devotion to the most High. Newton later joined the ministry, the words of his famous hymn testimony to his vivid dream experience of being "once lost, now found."

The insistent, unforgettable summons to a sacred vocation through a dream is well known in the literature of all religions. The word *vocation* derives from the Latin *vocare*, "to call," reflecting the ancient world's belief that one is summoned to one's true work by a divine voice in a dream or a vision. It is sometimes the role of Healing Dreams to insist upon the pursuit not of the ego's ambitions, but those things that render all others fool's gold. It is hard to overestimate the extent to which such dreams seem obsessed with the perils and promise of the human soul.

The Business of Dreams

Ah, these good, efficient, healthy-minded people, they always remind me
of those optimistic tadpoles who bask in a puddle in the sun, in the
shallowest of waters, crowding together and amiably wriggling

their tails, totally unaware that the next morning the puddle
will have dried up and left them stranded.

—*Carl Jung*

The calling to live and work with fidelity to our inner dictates may be more pandemic than is generally acknowledged, even if it is left to our private dreams to bear witness. I know a young woman who sometimes spends hours each day working with her prolific dreams. A former official in the Department of Energy, she might seem to be literally dreaming her life away. But why *shouldn't* she so honor her dreams? What would our lives—our very civilization—be like if we considered dreamwork as valuable as our vaunted "productivity"? Perhaps incorporating our dreams into our individual and collective lives would be the ounce of prevention worth a pound of cure, the navigational reading that ensured we were heading true north, not sailing off the edge of the world.

My Choctaw friend Preston, whose dreams have directed him throughout his life, says: "You always have a choice. If you have a big dream and *don't* want to follow it, well, then, you can leave it alone. But that's when you start to go blind. You go into the dark world. You make the same circle again and again, the same routine day in and day out. If you follow your dream, humbly, that is where your real life begins."

Jung once had a patient, a businessman, who was troubled by a series of powerful dreams. Though Jung urged him to follow their bidding, the man told him there were too many urgent things to attend to. Jung had only shaken his head: "Poor man, he doesn't realize his dreams *are* his 'urgent business.'" The logic of our business in the world does not sway a dream, which remains stubbornly fixed upon deeper values.

I was recently queried by an executive headhunter about a job opening at a national magazine. I had once met the magazine's founder, who had spent our entire lunch holding forth on his favorite topic—himself. He had a reputation as a difficult boss, and I hadn't worked for anyone for a long time. But my friends were urging me to take it—I needed the money, the subject matter was worthwhile; even if I had to kowtow a little, how bad could it be? That night, however, I dreamed, *I'm offered a lucrative "ser-*

vice contract" as a *"gigolo sex slave" in front of the whole community. I agonize for a moment, then shout* No! I woke up with my pulse pounding. Though I had been on the verge of calling the recruiter back, I realized I could not take the next step.

Instead, during the same period, I poured my energies into a music-and-poetry performance I'd been asked to do for a healing conference that New Year's—a "gig" I had very nearly turned down. Though I'd been a professional musician in my early twenties, I felt too rusty. I was embarrassed at the thought of getting up on stage to do a piece of "performance art," singing with my barely listenable voice. But during the days I was deliberating on the invitation, I remembered a wonderful dream I'd had five years previous: *I'm at a lectern about to give a talk on the future of medicine in front of an audience of health professionals. I get up and shock everyone by belting out an a cappella version of "Rockin' Robin."* I'd awakened jubilant, with a sense of subversive mischief and bubbling delight. The memory, still vivid, clinched my decision. The mixed-media presentation went well. I was asked to play the New Year's dance, and that night found myself on a stage—behind a built-in lectern—belting out a set of rock 'n' roll tunes before an appreciative crowd of mostly medical professionals. I made sure to lead off with "Rockin' Robin," which I'd memorized just in case. The enactment of this dream, with its pure whimsy, was amazingly vivifying. Months later, I can still call up the thrill of playing and the addictive endorphin rush of the applause. I'm mulling over offers for a repeat performance. The dream still seems to be leading me toward new work about which I'm both dubious and excited.

The entire experience was in marked contrast to my days as a magazine editor. Then, I had lived in a state of almost overwhelming cognitive dissonance between my dreams and my life. I had attained a hard-won perch—running a spiritually oriented national magazine that was, I thought, the precise place I belonged in life. But the round-the-clock schedule was taking a horrendous toll on my health and my family. I wondered if the magazine wasn't purveying a kind of junk-food for the soul. The owners' own questionable business practices made the articles we ran on "ethical investment" seem a sham.

But I'd managed to avert my eyes. Somehow, I told myself, no matter how treacherous the footing, good would come of it all. While I was busy nurturing my illusions, my nightmares were dispensing cold doses of reality. I recall one morning waking from an awful dream:

> *I'm being tortured on the edge of a cliff, hung from a rope that swings out over a deep chasm. When the rope swings over solid ground, my naked back is cruelly flailed. When it sways over the abyss, there is a brief respite. But to truly escape, I would have to let go of the rope and plummet to my death. It is a version of the Pit and the Pendulum. Finally, unable to stand it a moment longer, I let go and, pinwheeling through the air, land with a thump on the mummified corpse of a "bog man."*

When I awoke, I recalled an article about how the preserved bodies of Neolithic Celts were occasionally still discovered in the peat bogs of Ireland. That day, I looked up the piece, which described unearthing the body of a man presumed to be a priest, his skin like tanned leather, a strangulation cord wrapped around his neck. He had a peaceful expression on his face, and had been strewn with flowers. Anthropologists surmised he had offered himself willingly in midlife to the gods of the harvest. Was *this* what I was doing—making a pointless sacrifice for some misguided notion of the common good?

That "at the end of my rope" dream was followed by a succession of nightmare scenarios rife with conflicts between good and evil, the spiritual and the material:

- *I'm fighting evil from my office, a cramped space in a hollow tree. Then I find, in a frozen pond by a fortress at the ocean's edge, an ancient scabbard, encrusted in stone, its silver trim still gleaming.*
- *My guru gives me a "Book of Days" that predicts my life span, embroidered with mystic symbols and set with semiprecious stones. I show him the magazine I'm editing, and he laughs, amused and dismissive: "I didn't realize you were still doing that stuff!"*
- *I have an audience with the pope. He is utterly bemused by my bulky appointment book, which has a little kit of miniature office supplies in it.*

• *A black van marked "U Pay Association" is following me, harsh music blaring. It has a red interior, from which snipers are trying to shoot me. No one will believe me. Then, the logo of the magazine has been redesigned so that each letter is a statue of Isis, but I'm not supposed to know about it.*

Looking at these dreams, I'm amazed I was able to ignore their common themes: work became so empty, my office is a hollow tree, and my sword of righteousness a fossil; the disdain of spiritual preceptors for what I have taken to be my high-minded work; the implication that my "book of days" is finite, I should not waste precious time, and a day of reckoning was drawing high.

Before a year was up, the magazine *Camelot* I had tried to create had been dismantled; the idealistic, carefully assembled staff had quit or was fired. I had been forced out, and found myself in a battle for my life. The quest, it seemed, had come to naught. It felt like a death, though I didn't realize that at the time that I had been freed to pursue an unknown calling. Only much later, delving into my dream's reference to "Isis," did I discover she was the goddess of healing, a subject that was to occupy me professionally for the next fifteen years. (In myth, she resurrected the dismembered Osiris, god of the underworld, and so was a restorer of the unconscious life.)

It is not easy to listen to our dreams when they call for wrenching change. Sometimes we are predisposed to heed their clamor that we live with inner consistency and assume our unique place in the world. Other times, the shock wave hits with such stunning force that we are borne along as flotsam, as was Saul of Tarsus, whose vision on the road to Damascus transformed him into St. Paul.

My friend Jeff, by no means a saint, once had his own bolt from the blue. Jeff is a practical, earthy man who claims he almost never remembers his dreams. One of the world's foremost whitewater rafting guides, he learned in the Army Rangers to survive by foraging in the harshest wilderness. His many and varied knee operations are the consequence of over a hundred paratroop jumps. For years, he had been a successful commercial real estate developer, always able to close the big ones, dating a string of models, jetting off to Europe on a whim. But one night, he says, "a voice came to me, so real that it woke me up. It just said, in this wordless imperative tone, 'If you live this way one more year, you'll be dead.'"

The dream had come just after he had cashed out a huge deal, "flipping" a piece of undeveloped land after holding it only three months and clearing a clean, cool million. Most people would have brushed off the dream as uneasy conscience at easy money and kept ploughing the fertile field. But Jeff, a former lymphoma patient, couldn't shake the feeling he was being outnegotiated by forces beyond his control. The dream had come in November. In December, he told his colleagues he was packing up and quitting the business. He needed time to rethink his life, he informed his shocked staffers; he didn't know when he'd be back. He left the country on a personal pilgrimage, wending his way to Bali, New Zealand, Sumatra, and Borneo, biking through Europe, then wandering down to Africa, where he "messed around for a while in Okakavanga." A stint in Argentina was followed by an expedition to Antarctica. Finally, he returned home.

Today Jeff lives in humbler circumstances, a small, slightly run-down rural cabin. His shelves are packed with spiritual self-improvement tapes and dog-eared Joseph Campbell books, bulging planning folders and stacks of FedEx envelopes. It is a base camp for his new aspiration—to start a holistic television channel. Spending what's left of his real estate savings, schmoozing his old contacts, making new connections in the world of show business financing, relentless yet ever philosophical, Jeff says he's at peace with himself. If the ship comes in, it was meant to happen. If not, that was meant to happen, too. A man once distracted by dozens of options, he has developed the peculiar quality of all good executives: he makes the person he is with feel he has his total attention. He has learned, he says, that the small things count as much as the big stuff—sometimes more.

Another businessman, call him Philip, told me a similar story of how a single dream had led him to a change in his professional life. In his dream, Philip recalled: *I am standing nude in front of a mirror in a fitness workout room. I have a "golden-boy" physique, but it is somehow artificial looking. And I have a tiny penis. Then, in an adjacent room, I see in the mirror not the young macho man I'd expected but a homely, thin man of about fifty. Then I hear a tremendous thun-*

derclap, which wakes me up. The sound had been so immediate, Philip had jumped out of bed and run to the window to see if it were raining, but the sun was shining brightly.

Still in the grip of his experience, he decided to take a walk down to the local bookstore. As he idly browsed the shelves, his eye fell on a book that startled him. There, on the cover, was a picture of the "homely man" from his dream—it was the Trappist monk Thomas Merton. Philip purchased the book and hungrily devoured its contents. It began a life-long pursuit of spiritual study. Not long thereafter, Philip changed careers, leaving his thriving business to become a student of theology. His unexpectedly winding path eventually led him to a job with a national charity. A few years ago, Philip recalls, he came across a remark in Merton's writings that brought him up short: "It was a passage about Zen where Merton explains that the experience of *satori* is often accompanied by the sound of a thunderclap!"

Here, again, we see the principle of compensation in action: the ego is stunned by a dream that cuts it down to size (in Philip's case, right down to the emblem of his virility). His reflection is "homely," for to come back to ourselves, to a humanity stripped of props and trappings, *is* to finally come home again. Whereas in professional life, our "fitness" is often gauged by money, power, and prestige—our "image"—in dreams we stand naked before the mirror of our soul.

From Job to Calling

To leave a livelihood can be a fearsome thing, a leap into an unknown void. Sometimes our dreams insist on a complete change of venue. Other times they tell us we belong right where we are—it is our approach to our vocation that needs radical change. In this case, we are being asked to make our work sacred, to anoint a hollow place with our own heart's blood. Analyst M. L. von Franz was treating a painter famous for the photography-like precision of his style. The man had a violent distaste for abstract modernism, which he deemed destructive to the very ideal of art. But he was haunted by repetitive dreams that told him to paint in bright colors instead of his usual dark palette, and worse, to render abstraction rather than literal images of the outer world. Von Franz reports that soon after the man began to obey his dreams and changed his artistic style, one of the physical symptoms that had brought him to analysis, sexual impotence, vanished. In bringing suppressed parts of his imaginative being to his work, he enlivened his relationship not only with his muse (it might be said he had discovered the potency of pure creative expression) but also with his flesh-and-blood partner.

I found a similar case of transformation in situ, of a change in approach rather than career, in an essay detailing the case of a woman called Alice. Alice's lifelong passion was helping others. When she was young, she had brought home strays, both animal and human, giving away money to anyone who tugged persistently enough at her sleeve or her heartstrings. Predictably, her saintly attitude had its shadow side: she was compulsively drawn to "desperate, needy men." She chose a career in human services and set out "ferociously trying to learn every skill thoroughly, to be the best quality helper I could be."

But as she was completing her training, she had a stunning, pivotal dream:

It is a foggy night. I am standing near an old post office. I am driven by a great urgency to mail a package of letters which contain crucial information. These letters, in fact, are going to save the entire world of all the unnecessary pain and suffering that people endure. I am terrified that this most important mission on earth will be intercepted.

At last I mail them. Then I anxiously run down an alley looking for a safe place to hide. I see a man walking slowly toward me. I am terrified he will find out about the letters. He calmly approaches me and tells me that he thinks what I had been contemplating has been very brash.

Now I get up my bravado, cockily informing him that it was too late—I had already mailed the letters. But in a very nonpunitive tone, he suggests that I don't understand the consequences of my actions. With mounting defensiveness, I maintain that I certainly do—I am saving the world. The man challenges me, protesting that it is just for the purpose of growth that we go through pain. Reflecting on this, I suddenly get what he is trying to say. I go through a complete about-face. I

am convinced that it is essential to our evolution that we live through our suffer-
ing. I am struck by the realization I have been totally wrong to try to short-circuit
that process for people. Now I am desperate to get those letters back into my pos-
session. As I run up the alley to the post office, I experience myself surrealistically
rise off the ground, as if I am running on air.[11]

Alice awoke in a panic. "As I lay in my bed, my body still felt very light, as if I were still running on air. I tried to catch myself from falling! I had to defy a compulsion to run out the door and find that post office."

Alice's dream stayed with her for months afterward, "as graphically vivid as when I first dreamed it." Hers was a classic Healing Dream, with a novelistic plot that begins in self-ignorance and leads to catharsis and revelation. People in her life began to notice a change. A teacher praised her shift from mere sympathy toward her clients to real empathy. Relatives noted she wasn't bringing home any more social strays. She began dating an older man who was emotionally and financially self-sufficient. Alice began to question if she hadn't been harming people by her overbearing need to rescue them. She was starting to respect, as she put it, "the power people have to play out what they need to grow."

Whenever she feels the temptation to "take over" someone's life, the intense anxiety she felt in the dream returns. The sensation has become a red flag. She says she feels more grounded in her work with felons in an alternative-sentencing program. "I tell them that if things don't work out, I will write up revocation papers for them to return to prison. That attitude is effective. Because I don't *have* to have the program work for these people, I actually have the highest success rate in the state."

Alice's dream remains vivid to her two decades later. "I still remember precise details—color, clothing, architecture. I can still feel the wet mist on my face, remember the worry that my makeup would run. I have never had such a powerfully clear or detailed dream before or since."[12] Healing Dreams change our lives not merely by showing and telling but by making us viscerally *feel* the truth, unbuffered by the ego's "wiggle room." Here Alice has experienced a viewpoint she could not have conceived of before, for the brightest light may create blind spots. The purpose of her Healing

Dream was a sort of vocational alchemy—a reorientation of a ordinary pursuit into sacred calling, harmonizing personal with universal, transmuting private neuroses into collective nourishment.

Her story has much in common with that of Dr. Marty Sullivan, a leading cardiologist at Duke University. I'd met Marty at a dinner party sponsored by a Midwestern medical school. A charming man abrim with self-confidence, he took me aside when he heard I was writing about dreams. "I have some doozies to tell you," he said, "but not here." He gestured to our companions, an assortment of conservative faculty. Marty, too, was once an obdurate pillar of orthodoxy, and proud of it. A spokesman for his profession, he characterized himself as "a former true believer in the biomedical model. I didn't think, for instance, that a depressed patient should ever be given psychotherapy, since it was a purely biochemical disorder." But ten years ago, he had what he calls "my conversion experience." His life, which had seemed a perfectly tuned engine, began to knock, sputter, and fail. He found himself in constant skirmishes with his academic colleagues. His marriage became a disaster area. "I was unhappy in *everything*," he recalls. He fled to a rented house for a three-month professional sabbatical.

Overcoming his prior skepticism, he chose a psychotherapist at random from the Yellow Pages, taking the woman aback by introducing himself with a simple, "I am so *fucked.*" When she suggested he begin keeping a dream journal, he promptly and with characteristic efficiency bought one the same day. That very evening, he had "a nightmare I'll never forget as long as I live," shocking him awake a scant hour after he'd gone to sleep: *I'm in a whorehouse in New Orleans, on the top floor. There's no one but me, going from room to room searching desperately for something I've lost. I get to the last room, exhausted and panicky, and look in mirror. I'm horrified to see myself bleeding from my ears and eyes, like a leukemia patient with no platelets.*

Working with his therapist, he realized: "Here I am, on top, a paragon of doctors, searching for a vital something in a place where people sell themselves for money. It's an institution where you're not going to get what you really want—love, relationship, caring. You're paying for some-

thing inauthentic, valuing people only as bodies. And while you're searching for something outside of yourself, you're bleeding to death inside."

The dream stunned him. It seemed to symbolize all that had gone
wrong with his life, his relationships, and, especially, the profession he'd
once loved. It was the beginning, he says, of "a hundred-and-eighty-
degree turnaround" in his medical practice, from being "a hostile, arrogant
cardiologist" to an aspiring healer. Shortly after his first titanic dream, another came, which presaged an extraordinary process of change: *I see the
cocoon of a caterpillar on a tree limb. A light pulses down from above and hits the
cocoon. I'm overwhelmed with an incredible feeling of peace and harmony I've never
experienced in a waking state. Then I hear a booming voice that says: "I will lead
you in dreams."*

Since then, Marty has been instructed by dreams in what he feels is a
progressive course, as if enrolled in a personalized reeducation program.
His dreams, he claims, "are beyond my conscious ability to generate. The
concepts, the imagery, feel like they're wholly 'other.' I don't ask for them.
They just come." They have overturned much of what he once thought
he knew, and have helped him integrate his new understanding into his actual practice. He tells me one by way of example:

> *I'm in a psychiatry clinic, and they tell me my patient's arrived. I go out and
> there's an older guy, a downtrodden street person, a veteran's-hospital type, angry
> and upset. He starts a diatribe, and after five minutes, gets up and leaves. I think
> to myself I just can't help him. Then the nurse says the patient is back, but now
> he's an adolescent girl. I say, okay, now I can help you, but she looks at me and
> feigns a seizure disorder, and again, I walk away, saying I can't do anything. The
> nurse tells me to go back into the room, and there's the same patient yet again,
> only now he's a baby. I pick this baby up and feel an incredibly strong sense of
> love and connection. And I think: This is the level where all healing occurs. Until
> you get down deep enough, you're not really doing healing at all.*

There are few patients now in whom he cannot perceive this child
within, in whom he cannot find that seed, which, if nurtured, makes even
miracles possible. It is this inner knowing, he says, that has made the doc-

tor a healer. Marty continues to dream, each time feeling his understanding has been strengthened and reinforced. In another recent dream, *people come to me to have their wounds ministered, but instead of emitting sanguinous fluid, it is Grand Marnier!* "It shows me even our ailments contain the sweetness of living." The heart, his area of specialty, is no longer just a biological pump, but now an organ that circulates life's intoxicating nectar. His inner guidance has led him to begin the painstaking work of establishing a new mind-body clinic in conjunction with his medical center. In recent dreams, he's begun to see "a retreat place for doctors, where they could get a perspective that transcends medical technology."

His dream calling sometimes clashes with the rush of technological innovation that characterizes his profession. Dreams may force us into conflict with a world that spins ever faster. The endless flood of new artifacts and technologies threatens to overspill into the spaces dream and myth once occupied. The Buddha predicted that a Dark Age would arise when people's thoughts became so torrentially fast, overlapping one upon the other, that there would be little room for inner stillness. Perhaps this is why Healing Dreams so often place an emphasis on replenishment and preservation over innovation. A lawyer in Santa Barbara, for example, dreamed repeatedly of a crumbling cathedral in a square in a small Mexican town. He was puzzled. He knew he had a grandmother somewhere in Mexico who had stayed on when the rest of the family had emigrated north. They had long since drifted out of touch. After seeing a local therapist, the man went to visit an aunt to ask about the lost grandmother. Gleaning the name of the village she had lived in, he decided to take time off from his job to make a pilgrimage. When he arrived, he discovered that his grandmother was a community leader in a local movement to keep the town's beloved church from being condemned to make way for a new housing development. He spent six months donating all his financial and legal resources to ensure the church's preservation. He is now helping to rebuild the church, restoring the soul of the town to its once central place, a task that has by increments become his life's work.[13]

As our inner and outer places of sanctuary are encroached upon, it is not surprising that people's dreams lead them not forward toward the shiny and new but back to the heartfelt and handmade. Russell Lockhart, an influential Jungian analyst, is a man who allows himself to be guided by dreams. As we sat in his office, a cozy space decorated with an assortment of ethnic statuary and cherished bric-a-brac, he shared a simple, memorable dream he'd had in Scotland after a late evening of talking and drinking with a local poet: *I am operating a large old nineteenth-century handpress, printing a book called* Moonstone.

It immediately reminded him of an early boyhood interest in printing, when he and a friend, as a grade-school hobby, printed their own magazine on a toy printing press. His first paying job had been in a print shop, and he used to work for free in the college printing facility just to be near the smell of ink and the clattering old equipment.

Russell's childhood magazine, *The Tech Observer* ("We had stories about the stars and the moon and astronomy and bugs and stuff") began his lifelong fascination with applied science. "Some time ago," he told me, "I had one of those 'voice' dreams, in which someone uttered the words, 'God is in the computer.' I didn't take this to mean God is a computer, or that a computer is God, but that the psyche and our rapidfire technological advances have to somehow find a meeting ground."

He pondered why after so many years the image of a handpress would recur so forcefully, summoning up such deep feeling. "I decided it was not about what a printing press might mean symbolically, but rather, what happens if I really *get myself a printing press?* What happens if I set out to actually *make a book?*" Poking around, Lockhart eventually located a fire-damaged nineteenth-century handpress at the Cincinnati Museum of Science and Industry, bought it for a bargain price, and set about learning to make books on it. "It sometimes seems peculiar to me," he admits, "wanting to publish on handmade paper according to this painstaking old craft." But he is convinced that he—and even, in some small way, the world—is intangibly being changed by his new avocation. A few years later, after a learning curve that was not without bumps, a book he published won the prize for best letterpress book in the Northwest. "All of the books so far have been poetry," he notes, "but I still have the book called *Moonstone* to make!"

Some dreams are a summons to a larger destiny—a so-called higher calling—while others bind us to life's subtler weavings. Contrary to what society tells us—that we must, at some point, put away our dreams—those same dreams tell us it is never too late to hear a new calling and to follow where it leads. Socrates recounts in the *Phaedo* how a dream convinced him to create songs during his last days in prison: "The same dream came to me sometimes in one form, and sometimes in another, but always saying the same or nearly the same words: 'Set to work and make music.'" Socrates, as uncertain as anyone about the meaning of his dreams, had first assumed he was simply being encouraged to continue his study of philosophy, "the noblest and best of music," to the very end. It couldn't be that a new direction was being demanded of him at such a late date; surely he was being encouraged on his accustomed route, the way "a competitor in a race is bidden by the spectators to run when he is already running." But thinking on it further, Socrates made the breakthrough of all who honor the dream—he concluded he was being urged from the rutted track to take the road less traveled. The dream, he became certain, was demanding a new flowering of poetry and song. In prison, awaiting death, he decided "in obedience to the dream" to "compose a few verses before I departed."[14]

"We are the hollow men," wrote T. S. Eliot. "Between the idea and the reality . . . falls the shadow." We have not necessarily lost our dreams, the poet suggests, but our organic connection to them, and thus our ability to act upon them. If we fail to give our dreams a place in our life, our existence may become a wraithlike affair. Healing Dreams are not career counselors, telling us how to repackage our assets for success. They speak for the innermost when no else will. They do not calculate the shortest distance between two points but suggest that we take the long way home. Though we often content ourselves with having to maintain different faces—one for the job, one with our families; one for society, one for the heart—Healing Dreams want to make visible the pattern that connects; they tempt us to bring forth what is most passionate and profound within us, for our own sake, and for a world that is yet parched for the soul's true music.

Chapter 5

Dreaming Together

Love's Deeps, Destinies, and Disarrays

But in my dream . . .
We swim in tandem and go up and up
The river, the identical river called Mine
And we enter together. No one's alone.

—Anne Sexton

Adream, we are told, is a purely subjective affair, the outcome of forces contending within the psyche. If we dream of someone else, it is because he or she is a symbol of some interior push and pull, a self-palpation of our emotional pulse. (The dream, wrote Freud, "has nothing to communicate to anyone else . . . and is for that reason totally uninteresting to other people.") But the testimony of dreamers the world over belies this limiting view. They say our appearances in each other's dreams can be personal—that our dreams may not be entirely our own. How might we see our closest relationships in light of what Healing Dreams seem to show: that our connections with spouses and lovers, friends and enemies, parents and children extend into our most private inner spaces?

Early in her pregnancy, my vivacious, redheaded sister-in-law dreamed of a baby girl born with a full head of flaming hair.

"I'm looking for my mother," announced the dream child.

"*I'm* your mother," Lynne said delightedly, grabbing a lock of her own hair and waggling it. "See? I even have a name for you!"

"I have my own name," the child said firmly, then recited a haunting lilt of syllables that Lynne could not, despite her best efforts, remember when she awoke. She found the dream child, with its emphatic intelligence and serene autonomy, an enigma—she had not seemed at all like a figment of imagination.

Depth psychology might regard such a dream as an example of the "wise child archetype"—as in myths where the hero is born with hair and teeth, declaring his purpose upon quitting the womb. But in some cultures such dreams during pregnancy are seen as visitations, a first spiritual meeting between parent and child, as well as a clue to the child's future character.[1] (And indeed, my redheaded niece, Katie, now age six, is precocious, willful, affectionate, utterly self-possessed.) A friend who has been a midwife in Bali writes: "The 'spirit' child appears to his or her father in dreams before conception. 'Bring me to my mother' is most often its message." The message of the dream child is the paradox at the heart of family: *Yes, we are connected, flesh and blood and spirit, but I am my own person.*

Such events mark the very beginning of an ineffable bond between loved ones that can persist for a lifetime. Dr. Medard Boss, one of the few orthodox psychiatrists to write about this phenomenon (which one researcher calls "symbiotic dreaming") describes a young man in his training analysis who became delirious with pneumonia. The man was convinced that his mother, who lived in very remote rural area, was there with him, and he begged her to place a cool hand on his forehead. The next morning his mother called, having dreamed that her son had been lying in bed, feverish, asking constantly to be cooled. Three years later, the same young man broke his right thigh on his way to the office. The following day, he received another call from his mother, who had dreamed he was in a hospital bed with his right leg bandaged from top to bottom. Writes Boss: "These two telephone calls were and remain the only long distance calls that his mother had been able to afford *throughout her life.* If she had not been completely convinced of the reality of these dreams, she would no doubt, on grounds of economy, have made neither of them."²

Psychologist Edward Taub-Bynum coined the term "shared family dreamscape" to denote how "each family member's dream life can reflect the dream life of every other family member." Such interconnectedness does not require clairvoyance, of course. Our dreams are ever mapping and remapping the geography of relationship, like survey teams getting the lay of the land from different vantage points.

In Healing Dreams, we dream of each other, to each other, even for each other. My sister-in-law once had a vivid dream that she felt didn't have much to do with her. She finally concluded that she had dreamed, by proxy, on my behalf:

> *The whole family—me and Doug, Marc, their parents, my brother and my parents—are sleeping in the same room. Marc is on the chaise but can't sleep. He pulls the shade up, and light comes in the room. He smiles, looking out the window with a thoughtful expression. My mother gets really furious at him: Goddamn it! Can't you tell everyone here is trying to sleep!*
>
> *Marc briefly looks horrified, but then a few minutes later, he just yanks the shade up again. It is the crack of dawn, that auspicious moment when the light's just starting to come up. I think, He's just defying the whole group, not getting the message, making everyone irritated. But he looks so happy and peaceful.*

Her dream came at a time when she was just beginning to get a picture of how I, the seldom-seen brother to her husband, living in the mountains thousands of miles away, fit in the family portrait. I have often been the odd person out, the one at cross-purposes to family consensus, who tries, sometimes clumsily, to let in some light and "wake everybody up." The dream was useful for her, but also helpful for me, giving me more insight into my role in the family system and creating a bond of shared perception and empathy with my new relative.

The Unbroken Circle

Perhaps, in the end, there are no dreams intrinsically more healing than those that demonstrate that our separation is an illusion; that we are part of a living web that extends beyond our own skin and skull. No matter what turmoil we go through with our families, it seems that our ties—sometimes to our chagrin—are nonnegotiable. On some subliminal level, in the very coursing of the blood, we seem to "track" our loved ones through life. My own dreams about my parents, grandparents, children, ex-wife, lovers, and close friends have been so striking that I no longer hesitate to phone them upon awakening from a significant dream. More often than not, it turns out there is a good reason.

For some, this dream tracking of family is a more matter-of-fact occurrence. A seventy-four-year-old grandmother told me she learned to watch her dreams for news of loved ones from *her* grandfather, the scion of a nineteenth-century pioneer family who was, she avers, "the first white boy born in Ukiah, California." Her grandfather would often dream about family back East, particularly in matters of health. "He would see them all together in a rowboat. If it tipped over, it meant trouble. If he was able to save someone, he would find out later they'd been very ill but had recovered. And if he couldn't save them, he would later get a letter that they had died."

Such dreams often contain specific cues that telegraph that they bear news. One woman told me she knows to pay particular attention when she dreams about someone three times in a row.[3] An Australian aboriginal man told me about daydreams in which sensations in different parts of his body indicate which blood relative is ailing: "Right leg is grandfather," he said, slapping it fondly. "Knee is uncle. Breast is mother. Brother is right shoulder, sister is left shoulder." Such perceptions, he claims, were unfailingly accurate, and he would never hesitate to follow up on them.

The Dutch psychiatrist and political scientist Joost Merloo coined the term "hidden communion" to describe these "heteropsychic" connections between people. His certainty on the subject came from his own wrenching experience. In 1943, Merloo was on a troopship bound from New York to England. He awoke one night from a vivid dream in which he had heard his brothers calling for help. His anxiety was so powerful that he left his bunk to hunt through the dark and crowded hold for materials to write it down, convinced it meant they had fallen into Nazi hands. Two years later, in liberated Holland, he located records confirming that on the date of his dream, Nazi soldiers had entered the institution where his two neurologically damaged brothers were housed and, after brutalizing them, had flung them into mobile death wagons to be gassed.

Dr. Merloo concluded that we each live in a sea of "unconscious and unobtrusive interaction" with our intimates. This, he conjectured, may even be a hidden source of our ego defenses. "We have thick skins," he wrote, to "continually ward off" the thoughts and feelings of others, which moment to moment "bombard us." Merloo's clinical findings suggest that such communications take place "under less pleasant conflict situations," in times of distress or danger: because people are "afraid to give up their illusion of autonomy,"[4] it takes the battering ram of emergency to punch through the hard shell of separation.

After the war, Merloo had had another vivid dream about his dead brothers: *I am trying to find room in my bombed-out house for medical consultations. To make space, I eject my brothers from their former playroom by beating them pitilessly.*[5] That morning, a long-awaited letter arrived from the Netherlands Red Cross. In it were the official details of his brothers' gruesome deaths. What intrigued Merloo was that, apart from heralding the arrival of the letter, his dream also contained psychological material that needed to be healed—specifically his "confusing, ambivalent" attitude toward his brothers. He *had* felt a childishly murderous hostility toward them when he was growing up, and these memories and the fact that he had escaped their terrible fate caused him recurrent feelings of guilt. He categorizes the "telepathic communication" about their deaths on the ship, and the dream coinciding with the Red Cross report, as "anxiety-allaying wish fulfillment: 'It is not I who wish to beat my brothers, but the Nazis. *They* killed them.'" Merloo fearlessly touches upon the dark currents that run through all families. While we strive for harmony, our dreams often reveal a parallel story, a shadowy underbelly that paranormal dreams may vividly high-light.

What might be called "objective" aspects of the dream are thus inter-woven with psychological content. When Freud later in life entertained the possibility of telepathic dreaming, he took pains to illustrate that even seemingly clairvoyant material, once analyzed, yielded the same Oedipal themes, wish fufillment, repression, and other mechanisms as normal dreams. He advised treating what he called "the telepathic message" as a dream element no different from "any other external or internal stimulus, like a disturbing noise in the street or an insistent organic sensation in the sleeper's own body."[6]

People do tend to take a gee-whiz attitude toward paranormal dreams—the classic "I hadn't spoken to or even thought about Renee for years, then last night I dreamed of her, and today she called"—and then leave it at that. But closer examination would reveal a mine (if not a minefield) of mutual emotional history. A single Healing Dream may display, as if on a radar screen, the entire family gestalt. Even the clearest "clairvoyant" dream often contains distortions having everything to do with underlying inter-personal issues. To tell another person about their guest appearance in a dream can have catalytic effects.

I was reminded of this recently when I orchestrated an informal exper-iment, asking a few dozen people to incubate a dream on my behalf. (This "dream helper" ritual is treated in detail in the following chapter.) It sur-prised me that my father, who claims he rarely dreams vividly (and then, never about me), had the most striking dream: *Marc tells me he's living at 116 Village Avenue. I say, My God, that's the apartment over the store my father once owned! The door to Marc's room was closed. I open it and see him surrounded by books stacked on the floor, which he gestures to, saying, "I have to read them all."*

My father was surprised that his attempt to dream about me, skeptically undertaken, had actually "worked." The pile of books was easily ex-plained—I was in the thick of a writing deadline. He had gotten an accu-rate dream picture of my chaotic office, dominated by a tower of dog-eared volumes rising from the floor, all of which I had compulsively decided I had to read. I asked him for his associations about his father's apartment. "It was over the big clothing store that we used to own," he informed me, "until my father made some bad investments and went bankrupt." He added, with a catch in his voice, "It was a family catastrophe I never got over.

"Why in the world would I have dreamed such a thing?" my father demanded. Now it was my turn to be taken aback, for I had been keeping a secret from my family: I was on the edge of bankruptcy as a result of my own bad investment decisions. Now virtually penniless, I had contacted a bankruptcy attorney and had begun drawing up papers, but had not been able to bring myself to tell my parents.

After hesitating a moment, I realized I had to confess my quandary. I could not morally leave my father to fret about his dream after I had, in effect, invited him to open the door to my psyche and walk in. When I told him the truth, he was dumbstruck. The silence lengthened; I'd knocked the wind out of him.

The revelation of what has been concealed from one another is a frequent feature of such dreams. Merloo has written: "A telepathic dream is often a cry for help, or a breaking through a formerly existent communicative inhibition, as if the sender wants to say: 'I have been silent for such a long time, now finally you have to know what I have been hiding from you!'"[7]

In this instance, the breaking of silence went both ways: To my surprise, with my dire straits as an impetus, the story of my father's own childhood, often alluded to but never spelled out, now poured forth in a torrent. "We had a *big* clothing store," he told me. "My father went bankrupt because my mother, who could barely write her own name, decided she was above selling clothes to common folk. She decided there was more money to be made building houses. But my father's real estate partners cheated him of everything. Then the Depression hit. We found ourselves living with no heat, no food, no clothes, cardboard in our shoes. We'd live anywhere we could get the first six months rent free, then move on to the next place."

I was awed by these revelations, whose analogues were uncomfortably clear in my own life. I had been juggling introductory six-month credit cards for years to support my writing habit, moving on to the next "teaser" offers the minute the rates shot up. My father's history seemed to explain the atmosphere of both entitlement and defeat that I'd always sensed permeating our family. More, it shed new light on the dynamics of our persistently troubled relationship. My father could be charming, caring, and funny but also domineering, volatile, and hypercritical. I had grown up in his shadow, fearing his outbursts, feeling hopelessly defective. Despite our best intentions, we were still fighting the running skirmishes of our respective and common pasts. Now as my father, caught up in the rush of dream-sparked emotion, unveiled his own childhood horrors, I felt new compassion stir.

"My mother told me she once jumped off a low roof to try to 'get rid of me,'" he said in a choked voice. "Threw herself down the stairs to try to abort me. She'd wanted a girl, so she used to put my hair in curls and make me wear a dress. She called my older brother, who had infantile paralysis, 'the Cripple'—or just *schmutz,* dirt. My brother revenged himself by physically tormenting me, my personal Torquemada, finding every way to humiliate me." I listened to this outpouring not a little astonished. How could I have been so blind—my father, who made me feel so small, had himself been diminished by his own family.

Our dream exchange had a surprisingly tangible result. My father, now knowing my predicament, offered me a personal loan that pulled me back from the financial brink. The effects of our dream sharing have rippled through my life, not only enabling me to climb back onto solid ground but also making it possible to consider moving back to New York, where my entire family, from my daughter to brother to parents, now lives. Looking back, I am astonished at how a single dream has begun to heal generations of family karma.

Generational continuity seems to be an imperative to the dreaming soul, which is ever intent upon the connections of each to all. I have heard several Healing Dreams, where a person dreamed of a "lost" relative they were never supposed to know about—a birth parent, or a sibling given away for adoption—without whose link the family chain is incomplete.

I met a striking example in a South African sculptor named Percy Ndithembile Konqobe. I met Percy in a Johannesburg hotel coffee shop in

1996, when the euphoria over the peaceful overthrow of apartheid had given way to raw anxiety. The city was in the midst of an unprecedented crime wave. Office buildings were bannered with "For Lease" signs as nervous white businessmen made way for an uncertain new order.

Percy, though, was optimistic. A big man whose broad face glows with goodwill, he received his initiation into the world of the dream while serving time in prison on robbery charges. It was during a time, he said, laughing a bit ruefully, when even a thief might imagine himself to be a minor hero of the Struggle. "I thought," he said, "I was hitting the government by taking the cash."

One night, in his cell, he'd had an overwhelming dream. He saw an open book that spoke to him, uttering a phrase he can still repeat verbatim: "'I am the pot of all life and knowledge.'" As it happened, Percy's aged cellmate was a healer and mystic, a *sangoma*. He smiled when Percy told him the dream, informing him that it meant he was being called by his ancestors. Percy just laughed at him. But weeks later, in another dream, Percy had a vivid vision of his mother's naked body directly in front of him. He awoke horrified. In Africa, he explained, this is a great taboo, and it filled him with unnamable disgust. But again, the old man elucidated, "the more ugly the dream, the more information it contains. Seeing your mother naked means there will no longer be any secrets from you, and all that is hidden will be revealed."

The dreams, which Percy calls "talking dreams"—"I can *feel* them talking to me," he says—continued for months. One night, he dreamed the stark image of a pile of prison shoes, socks, trousers, shirts, jerseys and caps. The old man, who in a teasing biblical reference had nicknamed him Joseph, informed him: "It means a lot of prisoners will be released by Pharaoh, and you will be among them." This was 1966, the fifth anniversary of the founding of the South African Republic. Shortly after the dream, President Verwoerd declared a limited amnesty, and Percy was among the lucky ones freed from bondage.

Vowing never again to be involved in crime, he set out to become a *sangoma*. There were many dreams he did not understand, but he remembered the old man's teachings. "He said, 'A dream is like your hand, it has two sides. If you can't understand what you see, turn it on the other side and see what is written there. Ask it, Are you fake, or are you genuine?'"

Percy's synopsis of African dreamwork techniques were in many ways identical to current Western methods, especially that of active imagination: "Dreams are like a medicine we don't want to take, even though it is best for us," he told me in a confident, booming voice that made the diners next to us swivel their heads. "After a big dream, you must talk to it. You can't do this *during* the dream. You have to bring the dream back to you. You ask the dream in a sacred place what it wants, let it turn itself over and over. When you figure it out, it's like putting a car in the right gear— you feel a click."

As skilled as he was becoming in the ways of true dreaming, it took Percy time to get up the courage to ask his mother about a dream he'd been having since childhood. In his dream, he would be trying to climb a mountain but would slip down before reaching the top. But now, he told her, a new element had appeared:

> *There is an old man pushing a bicycle up the hill, as if it had a flat. The two of us go up, and when I reach the top, I am alone. But there is a beautiful railroad on top of the mountain. I think, I'll follow this track until I reach a station, then I'll know where I am. I see a bright light behind, like yellowish red sunrise, so I know I am going west. Then I hear voices: "The road to success is in Kafkat, in a place called Goshen." I look back, and see seven male shadows. I turn to them, and they entreat me to go to this place.*

He had awakened at four in the morning in a sweat, unable to go back to sleep. He already suspected what the dream might mean. "I told my mother, 'The other children have left. You have only me, the firstborn, and my brother, the last of your five. I will always take care of you. But you must tell me the truth. Who is my real father?' She broke down and confessed to me, 'Your father was in Kafkat, Goshen, but he died in 1939.'

"I knew this couldn't be true," Percy told me," because in my dream, I saw him alive. So I traveled to that place and I found him. He said he had dreamed about me just a week before, and was calling out to me!"

In traditional societies, the link with the ancestors is a defining aspect of identity. Yet I have talked to Westerners who have had nearly identical experiences. One psychologist, for example, had a repetitive dream of a man who looked like a sea captain announcing, "I am your grandfather." After trying unsuccessfully to work through the dream using conventional methods, he decided to tell his mother about it. He was amazed when she tearfully confessed a deep family secret: His grandmother had had an affair with a sailor, and she was the offspring of the illicit union. She gave him a frayed picture of his unknown grandfather—a picture that uncannily matched his vision—along with the man's old navy dog tags. After many months of research, he told me, he finally located his "lost" family in Colorado. Though his grandfather had died, he felt a great sense of completion when he visited the man's grave, and delights in the long-lost relatives his dream restored to him.

If we return to our central question—what does the dream want?—we would have to say it wants these primal connections. It wants us to know ourselves not as solitary dots moving from past to future but as strands in a web of ancestry (in Australian aboriginal lore, a *Dreaming* is a term for an ancestor), as players, even minor ones, in the great serial drama of human generations. The Healing Dream reminds us that some relationships, in an era of broken families and romantic angst, are well-nigh indissoluble.

Dreams of Romantic Destiny

Healing Dreams seem to survey the entire panorama of our personal connections, sometimes addressing our familial past, other times our romantic destiny, always telling the story behind the story. It is not uncommon for a dream at the outset of a relationship to prefigure its course—revealing the spiritual purpose of coming together, the emotional dynamics that will become themes, even the denouement, whether a crash-and-burn parting or eternal wedded bond. The dream often highlights what is overlooked in the soft-focus first blush of love. It may point us, insistently, toward someone who appears entirely unsuitable, or away from someone who seems the perfect match. If we are receptive, we may have to question our first impressions of who is our Mr. Right or Ms. Wrong.

Michelle seemed an unlikely candidate for an extraordinary dream of romantic destiny. Born in a mountain farming community in Colorado, she'd opted to attend college an hour away, then worked as a nurse in the hospital she was born in. She'd married and divorced, never moving far from home. Her self-enclosed, almost circular life path was nonetheless fulfilling. She was passionate about holistic medicine, particularly Chinese acupuncture, and adored her specialty in elder care. In other ways, her life was almost metronomically predictable—until the strange dreams began. She'd had this special kind of dream a few times before in her life—"teach-type" dreams, she called them, "strong" dreams. But nothing like these: night after night, the same scene would vividly unfold: *I am on a cruise ship. There's a group of people and I'm instructing them in something. On the periphery of my dream is a man, though he's not on the ship. He has a brother, and I am going to marry one of them.*

She was baffled. She'd never lived near the ocean, let alone been on a ship. When she'd visited the San Diego pier once as a child, the big boats had frightened her. But the dreams continued unabated, at least one a week for the next six months. Sometimes she would be on shore watching the great ship depart. Other times, she'd be running across the dock to catch it, or strolling the upperdeck promenade, or wandering below where the big motors thrummed and churned. The dreams were indecipherable. "I'd just wake up in the morning, and say to myself, 'Well, I was on that cruise again!' and leave it at that." She told no one.

One of Michelle's favorite patients was a feisty nonagenarian named Irene, an inveterate traveler and a font of stories from her globehopping days. From the moment they met, they hit it off famously. Their friendship had bloomed, then faded as Michelle's nursing duties grew ever more time-consuming. Their visits tapered off to once a month, then every two months.

One day, when Michelle arranged to stop in, Irene greeted her with an array of cruise ship brochures spread out on her end table.

"Irene, you're going on a cruise!" Michelle had exclaimed.

"I've been waiting for you all summer," Irene shot back. "I've been around the world seven times. This is my last trip. I need a nurse. You're going with me!"

Michelle was nonplussed. She'd never told Irene her dreams. Now, as they spilled out, Irene became as immovable as a monolith. She insisted she wouldn't even go unless the cruise line allowed Michelle to hold shipboard classes in Chinese medicine. Dubious, but with another of her dream's puzzle parts sliding into place, Michelle decided that if Irene managed the impossible, that would be the clincher.

"Somehow she worked it out," Michelle recalls, laughing. "She got the Princess Line to actually *hire* me for their annual Arthritis Cruise. They decided it would be good to have an acupuncture instructor. So now I had no choice."

She had to tell her other patients she would be away for a while, particularly one woman with cancer whom she had been helping with her injections. Michelle mentioned that they were going to St. Croix. "I have a son who lives there! " the woman exclaimed, and insisted on prearranging for him to show them the sights. When the cruise ship docked at dawn a few weeks later, the young man met them at the gangplank. "The minute I saw John, I was overcome," recalls Michelle. "The first words that popped out my mouth when we met were, 'I'm going to have a child.' I blushed and got completely flustered." It was a supremely awkward moment. She had no idea why she'd utter such an absurdity on meeting a total stranger. It was as if she'd fallen abruptly into a trance. But somehow John had been hit by the same lightning bolt—what the French call a coup de foudre. "He's since told me that he would have normally turned tail and run, but the minute he saw me, though he'd vowed eternal bachelorhood and no kids, he knew he'd marry me."

As they had talked in the compressed span of her visit, she was amazed at the correspondences. "I had told my friends that I would never marry again. And if I did, just to make it impossibly exacting, he had to have a blond ponytail, and my type A negative blood, so the baby wouldn't suffer from incompatibility. *And* he had to remember his dreams." John was custom designed. His dog tags from his Navy days said he was A-negative; he had just prior to her arrival decided to grow his long blond hair into a ponytail; and he was an avid dreamer. Two weeks after she left, he packed up and moved to Colorado to court her. A few months later, they were married.

Michelle is adamant that she would never have agreed to go on the cruise had she not already rehearsed the voyage so many times in her dreams. Even the theme of the dream-man's brother would later play out in real life—within a few weeks of their wedding, John's younger brother got married. The enactment of a Healing Dream often affects, almost magically, other aspects of life—Michelle, the archetypal landlubber, has found a new calling, a side business giving health classes on cruise ships.

John and Michelle might well be said to be a dream couple. "We talk about our dreams first thing in the morning, before we're fully awake, so they can't slip back into their hidey-holes." Their dreams lead them to "our little secrets and passions, our dark sides, our sexual history: it's like marriage therapy in bed." John often dreams about his new life, what it means to have left the islands to settle in the Rocky Mountains: *Three eagles pluck this huge oak tree out of the ground, roots and all, and they set it down at a beautiful crater lake.* He recently had a strange dream that his head turned to wood, cracked open, and out ran a beautiful American Indian woman. John, taciturn and introverted, woke up in tears. A stoic ex–military man, whose ancestors were Union army men who settled Fort Pitt and "went out hunting Indians," he is now studying tai chi with a female martial artist. The dream, he and Christine agree, represents a new, tenuous revelation of his feminine side, another step in their dream journey together.

One of the glorious hopes of romantic union is that the undeveloped parts of our being will blossom. Beyond the vision of couplehood, laughter, passion, and family is the dimly sensed possibility of a *hierosgamos,* a sacred marriage that brings each person to his or her highest spiritual potential. We come to each other, says the Healing Dream, not just in the name of love, but transformation.

Rita, a medical lecturer, was working in her cottage in Devon, England, one afternoon when she suddenly felt overwhelmed by sleep. "Or at least," she says, "I thought I was asleep, but there was a man standing there talking to me. I could see every detail, could hear his voice. We had a great conversation. I knew this was a very important person to me—I just didn't know who."

When she woke up, he vanished. Stunned, but not knowing how to wrap her arms around the vision, she mothballed its memory. A few years later, Dan, an American psychiatrist and healing researcher, was invited to make a presentation to her medical group. When they met, she says, "My breath just whooshed from my lungs! I was instantly transported back to this dream. He was identical—same face, haircut, build. The only difference was that the dream man was wearing a colored waistcoat of pinks and reds and yellows, and Dan was dressed rather conventionally."

Shocked and off guard, she refrained from telling him about her dream. Why? I asked her. She grimaced: "Well, I didn't *like* him at all. I basically had to have dinner with him, and I remember feeling, I'll just be so glad when this man *leaves!*" Still, the two corresponded for a year. He invited her to a professional meeting in London, and she offered to make space in her cottage—"a swap, like a bed-and-breakfast"—when he next came through. She was going out with someone else and hadn't ever considered Dan a candidate for romance. When months later he arrived at her door, she had planned to simply show him how to work the stove and the TV and head out the door. But he stopped her, apologizing, telling her they needed to talk. He was feeling, he said, a close connection with her that was mystifying, disturbing, exciting. The conversation continued long into the night, and, Rita says coyly, "something shifted." It was still six months before they owned up to a growing mutual certainty they were meant to be together, and a year before she told him about her dream.

By literally stepping out of her dream, Dan forced Rita to wrestle with every aspect of her life. Divorced, she had determined to avoid getting romantically entangled for the forseeable future. "But something whispered to me, 'You'd better change your mind.'" Before she met Dan, she had been a well-known lecturer "with a respectable reputation, considered to be of sound mind." But she'd also been, she says, "a closet healer" who kept her intuitive talents on the back burner. Dan, who had produced a detailed, two-volume academic study of purported psychic healers, changed all that. "He forced me to come out," she says simply. "He'd say, 'You're seeing more than you're saying.' He's a noodge. I think he's in my life so I don't need to be ashamed of the intuitions that first tempted me into the healing arts. Our meeting was life-changing from the get-go. We've had our ups and downs and crises, but the voice inside me hasn't wavered: 'This is the man you have to be with to serve your purpose in this life.' "

When Rita first had her dream vision, she thought it perhaps symbolized a masculine aspect of her personality rather than the man who would later become her husband. "I wondered: 'Is my animus so nice? Usually, it's horrible!' " This Jungian term for what is thought to be a woman's "inner male" suggests the dichotomy at the heart of relationship. Jung believed, as did many ancient traditions, that the nature of every human being is dual, that we each contain a contrasexual essence (for men a female soul, or anima). Dreams are windows into this exciting, threatening territory, revealing how the unconscious bears the imprint of the other sex's way of being, compensation for the lopsidedness of our dominant side.

Jung had a tendency to fall into gender stereotypes—the feminine as receptive/emotional versus the masculine as active/rational, as Eros versus Logos. But his primary thrust was to show how our partner outwardly carries a submerged component of our being, and so is intrinsically our teacher, pointing to undeveloped potentials within. The dream's romantic pedagogy in this regard is not always gentle: "In both its positive and its negative aspects," Jung wrote, "the anima-animus relationship is always full of 'animosity.' "[8] Inevitably, we project not only our wholeness but our incompleteness upon each other. Romance's magic, the boons it confers and balms it applies, cannot instantly cure our inner wounds. In relationship, dreams often sound the counterpoint to bliss, the dissonant flatted fifth that jars us from a superficial harmony, insistent that we gain a fuller knowing of each other—and of ourselves.

Love, after all, is a word that sails over a Sargasso of meaning: it is not only cherishing, passion, loyalty, and nurturing; it is also jealousy, betrayal, rage, and mistrust. Though we seek through our lover the fulfillment of our fondest fantasies, secretly hoping for paradise without tears, couples' dreams reveal that even the most wondrous fairy tale may be undergirded by a subterranean story. Sometimes a negative dream image of the beloved may symbolize a denied aspect of ourselves; other times, it may reveal a darker side to them we cannot yet bring ourselves to acknowledge.

A woman I'll call Sally Anne told me that when she first met Bob, he was Prince Charming incarnate—a handsome captain of industry, with mansions scattered around the world, impeccably generous and exquisitely considerate, a dream come true. But one night she had a peculiar night-mare: *Bob is at the window asking to be let into my house. He is dressed in a Santa Claus costume; in fact, I think he is Santa Claus. But as I'm letting him in, his hat, which had obscured his face, falls off, and I see that he is really Rasputin.* She awoke in horror but could not understand why the dream had depicted her gift-bearing lover as the villainous, debauched manipulator of the last Russian czarina.

What was the dream trying to tell her about herself? she wondered. About Bob? Baffled, she chose to ignore it, and the courtship culminated in a spectacular wedding. Though she gradually came to see that her new husband had a penchant for control, it seemed a small price to pay for a ba-sically fortunate union. But a year into her marriage, she began to experi-ence odd health symptoms. She was feeling weak, dizzy. Her hair began to fall out in clumps. She developed peculiar skin rashes. After going to spe-cialist after specialist, she was finally diagnosed with heavy metal poison-ing. What unfolded was a horror story of gothic proportions: as it turned out, her husband, a mining executive, was a deeply disturbed man who had been slowly, secretly *poisoning* her. Her dream of Rasputin had been a red alert; the jolly bearer of boons turned out to be a charming sociopath. (Under the circumstances, the dream's choice of the figure of Rasputin was weirdly apropos: perhaps the most famous historical incident of his life was the attempt of the czar's courtiers to murder him by lacing a gift of sweet cakes and wine with poison.)

Sally Anne quickly divorced Bob, though her years of subsequent law-suits amounted to naught. He was so powerful as to be untouchable; like Rasputin, he had behind him the power of a throne, albeit a corporate one. Glad to have escaped with her life, she has often thought of her dream over the ensuing years, and how readily she brushed it aside. The healing potion distilled by dreams can be a bitter medicine against which we close our lips, preferring our lovesickness.

When the Dream Is Over

Sally Anne's strange case was one for a police detective, not a marriage counselor. Though her dream warning was shockingly literal, its morbid imagery was not unusual. Healing Dreams often speak about relationship in the symbolic language of life and death—from the soul's point of view, the stakes are nothing less. When we join together to make a new life, some part of our old self dies in sacrifice to union. On the other side, nearly half of Americans will experience a dissolution of their marriages, an event that can feel akin to dying. (I spoke to one woman who dreamed of her divorce as quaffing a fatal cup of hemlock, and another who dreamed of her breakup as a comet smashing into the earth, destroying all humanity.)

Sometimes a dream image carries such weight that the entire equation of relationship shifts as if in the twinkling of an eye. Sue first met her boyfriend, Allen, in college, beginning a relationship that had lasted eight years. A fiercely independent woman who went on to do social work at a psychiatric hospital in London's tough-as-nails East End, Sue at first didn't take seriously Allen's suggestions that they marry. But one February evening, he formally proposed and "to my surprise and his delight, I said yes."

Almost immediately she was possessed by profound ambivalence. As Allen's mother began making guest lists for the wedding, Sue remembers "not wanting to discuss it, not being enthusiastic, backpedaling. The message that got back to his mom as Allen and I were coming up to visit was: '*Don't* talk weddings to Sue.'"

The wedding planning proceeded inexorably. The couple went to Scotland to visit her parents. A few weeks later, her mother called to fret about the choice of wedding cake. "That's the moment it began to click," Sue recalls. "Like, Why am I worrying about the number of layers on my cake? How about how I *feel,* and what I want? But my unease was still beneath the surface. I went through all the motions. We chose a church, talked to the minister, picked a date."

Then, in June, after a big family banquet in a fancy London hotel celebrating the engagement, Sue had a dream. "I'm not good at remembering dreams," she told me, "but this one is still as clear as day": *I am ascending the Pyramid of the Moon outside Mexico City, which I had actually once visited. I am being escorted up the steps in my wedding dress. My feet feel like lead. There is a sense I'm about to be sacrificed. I am filled with dread, panic, and helplessness. I wake up feeling an incredible sense of relief that this is only a dream.*

A therapist might plausibly have suggested that Sue's was a typical anxiety dream, premarital jitters on the threshold of a momentous transition. But the dream had been so vivid, she awoke knowing that she couldn't go through with it. She called off the wedding the same day. Although her fiancé was startled, she was surprised and relieved when he accepted it without recrimination or tears, as if he, too, had been harboring doubts he had been afraid to voice. They have remained good friends ever since.

The extraordinary dream brought a conviction to the fore: "I've got things to do with my life. And it's not about being a wife, settling down, and having children." Sue has since had several satisfying relationships, "but from that point onward, I was on my own journey. That's been my driving force." How, I asked her, did she find the courage to make such an abrupt about-face? All she could say was, "The dream was so absolutely *real,* the feeling of impending doom so terrifying, the relief so huge that I had not been sacrificed." She looked pensive, then brightened: "Something informed me, and I just followed it in an uninformed way!"

Her remark echoes what many say who opt to heed a Healing Dream. The dreamer is told something of enormous import, by whom or what she scarcely knows. She opts to proceed by turning toward the light, be it warm sunshine or a searing illumination, because in the end there seems little alternative.

Another woman I spoke with, a forty-five-year-old computer programmer whom I'll call Deborah, also reached the end of relationship's road through what she calls "the most memorable dream I've ever had." In her dream, she is on an ascent, but her journey is into the mountains:

Suddenly it starts to snow. I find myself getting disoriented. I recall that there was some woman hiker who had gotten lost here not long ago, and they had never found her. As it starts to get dark, panic sets in. I come to an abandoned cabin in the woods and I go in for shelter, but stumble and fall through a hole in the floor. My big backpack keeps me from wriggling free—I'm trapped. The snow and wind howl outside. Suddenly, to my horror, I realize that I was that woman hiker who had gotten lost!

Then I remember my backpack has all these things like dishes and silverware, which I thought I needed for this hike. I realize that without the weight and bulk of this stuff, I could escape the hole I'm stuck in. But now I'm going to die here with all these stupid domestic items I couldn't leave behind.

At the time, Deborah was mired in a deeply unhappy union of nine years. The dream, a proverbial wake-up call, was ruthless in its urgency: it did not end in her escaping but left her facing senseless, unnecessary death, freighted with the same domestic items that had once comforted her with their orderly familiarity. Healing Dreams know we are creatures of habit. In the sometimes numbing regularity of our lives, we rationalize away our pain. It is left to the dream to provide feedback—to amplify the low, near-inaudible hum of chronic unhappiness into an acute screech of anguish.

Deborah credits her chilling dream with helping her to leave her marriage and begin the new life she had been afraid to even contemplate. "Before, I thought I'd never be able to pay my mortgage and raise my children alone, that I needed the material security my marriage provided. The dream said it wasn't so much that I was trapped, but that I was trapping myself."

Dreams of Betrayal

Dreams have an almost eerie ability to ferret out the secret weaknesses of the bond of relationship. Deep in the heart of a seemingly stable marriage runs an underground river, ferrying impermissible perceptions that only dreams can bring to light. My writer friend Felicia had always been a vivid dreamer, sometimes remembering three or four dreams a night. But she had never thought to turn toward them for guidance until midway through her marriage, when she had a dream that "knocked at the door, hard, and said, 'You need to get real.' "

She was researching a biography in New Orleans, a city whose street crime, a friend pointed out one day, was particularly violent. That night Felicia dreamed:

> *I am walking down a street that is strange to me. Two men grab me from behind, pinioning both my arms, and pull me back into an alley. They mean to murder me. They take my wedding ring from my finger and another ring I'd been given by the woman I was writing about and drop them both down my throat! As I wake, I am choking on these rings.*

"It had the atmosphere," she says, "of a terrible tragedy." The next day, as she was walking in the French Quarter, she realized she was on the same street as in her dream—the same shops, the same apartment balconies with plants dripping from their ornate railings. She walked warily, without incident, but now the dream seemed more compelling. "I understood it to mean my work could damage my marriage," says Kelly, "which turned out to be prescient. My husband didn't like the time or the direction it was taking." The dream continued to haunt her. "I kept looking back and finding new interpretations, feeling there was more it was trying to tell me." Not long afterward she was diagnosed with thyroid cancer in her throat.

As the marriage worsened, other disturbing dreams would wake her up: *My husband is driving the car and I am a passenger. He lets loose with an uncharacteristically mean remark, and when he turns his face toward me, I see he's been transformed into a deranged monster.* It disturbed her so much she told him about it. "He thought I was loony putting such stock in dreams. I agreed; he was nothing like that creature. But to my shock, a few months later, as the marriage deteriorated, he became this kind of enraged person."

Then her dreams began to reveal another hidden dimension of their relationship: They showed her husband having an affair. "I saw him with a woman with long brown hair. In the dream, I knew she worked with him. Then one day he introduced me to a woman from his office, and it was *her!* I recognized her immediately. I told him my dream and asked him point-blank, 'Is this something we need to talk about?' "

Her husband denied that they were sleeping together. The more he refused to talk, the more trapped and immobilized she felt. Felicia's was not an atypical situation—one person in the relationship is paying attention to dreams; the other wishes to avoid the festering issues they reveal. In one dream, *We are in bed, facing head to toe, and I am all wrapped up in the sheets like a mummy. He gets up and walks away, and I am left tied up, constricted, while he was free.*

"At our twelfth-anniversary dinner," she says, "he admitted he was in love with his co-worker, and had decided to leave me and marry her."

Some relationships end with an explosive bang, others with a quiet whimper; some by the slow cooling of affection, others in a firestorm of betrayal. But the infidelity is always a shock to the spirit, the razing of an entire edifice of mutual trust. The ground we stand on cracks open, and a chasm swallows our heart. In the surreal light of revelation, cognitive dissonance reigns. Our loving boyfriend or girlfriend or husband or wife is not the person we thought. We wonder what we *can* believe to be true. Was he really at work that night? Was she really out comforting a distraught friend? Every commonplace is defamiliarized. What, now, *cannot* be questioned? And yet on some level, we already know. We know it in our marrow. We have known it in our dreams.

In a series of experiments on "anomalous communication" in the 1960s, New York's Maimonides Dream Research Laboratory quietly and with little fanfare demolished the notion of privacy of thought. A subject was wired to monitoring equipment so that he could be awakened whenever he showed the rapid eye movements (REMs) characteristic of dreaming. Through the night, in a separate room down the hall, a psychologist sat gazing intently at a randomly selected fine-art print. Independent judges compared the sleeping man's dream reports with a varied assortment of art prints, including the target, looking for a match. Elements of the target painting were observed to show up in the sleeper's dreams two out of three times, making the odds of mere coincidence vanishingly small.

In one trial, for example, the "sender" spent the night gazing at *Downpour at Shono* by the Japanese artist Hiroshige, which depicts people caught in a rainstorm. The sleeper reported dreaming of "an Oriental man with an umbrella." Another subject dreamed *I am buying tickets to a boxing match at Madison Square Garden,* while through the night a psychologist in a distant room was concentrating on a painting of a boxing match. In yet another instance, a researcher focused on Edgar Degas's painting, *School of the Dance,* featuring young ballerinas. The sleeper, a male psychoanalyst, dreamed successively, "I was in a class made up of maybe half a dozen people. . . . At different times, different people would get up for some sort of recitation or contribution. . . . It felt like a school. . . . There was one little girl who was trying to dance with me."[9]

Though the participants were not even friends, and most subjects joined the experiment for just a single night, the exquisite permeability of dreams even among virtual strangers was revealed. How much more so, then, between marriage partners, where, the psychoanalyst Merloo noted, a "state of hypersensitivity towards hidden thoughts can be reached." The implications of the Maimonides experiments are exhilarating and dismaying: like a paparazzo snapping a candid shot from ambush, the secret life of someone we love can be revealed in a flash. Our partner may unexpectedly "see" directly into our inmost heart, dream about our longings and fears, our acts of omission and commission. On the plus side, it is a demonstration that sharing our lives with another person connects us to them in a way that transcends time and space, a phenomenon to which many husbands, wives, and lovers can attest.

In his 1926 novel *Dream Story* (*Träumnovelle*), the Viennese writer

Arthur Schnitzler tells the tale of a doctor and family man who allows himself to be drawn into a web of erotic deceit. One night, telling his wife that he has to attend a dying patient, he instead slips out to a sinister sexual debauch at an isolated mansion, where he must dress in a fancy costume and use a purloined password—"Denmark"—to gain admittance. But he is exposed by the masked revelers as an uninvited intruder, only escaping with his life when a beautiful woman offers herself in sacrifice to save him.

The doctor flees home, guilt-ridden but relieved to have returned from his secret misadventure intact, and unsuspected by his wife. As he slips quietly into bed, he sees that his wife is tossing and turning in the grip of a powerful nightmare. When she wakes, he listens in astonishment as she describes her strange dream. In it, *she is looking for her wedding dress and sees instead "fancy costumes" hanging in her closet. Then she finds herself at an orgy, feeling a "sensation of terror, shame and anger much more intense than anything I had ever felt when awake." She sees her husband, dressed in a marvelous outfit of gold and silver, seized and about to be put to death, when a beautiful young queen offers her own life in exchange. She sees that the queen is a woman her husband once described watching naked on a beach in Denmark.*

The doctor is stunned. He finally confesses all, as his wife listens in silence. Finally he asks her what they should do:

> She smiled, and after a minute, replied: "I think we ought to be grateful that we have come unharmed out of all our adventures, whether they were real or only a dream."
>
> "And no dream," he said with a slight sigh, "is entirely a dream."
>
> "Now I suppose we are awake," she said, "for a long time to come."[10]

This clever story, with its haunting feeling of a dream-within-a-dream, was the basis of director Stanley Kubrick's final film, *Eyes Wide Shut*. Though the movie was panned as a clumsy adaptation, I had been riveted by it: I knew, from personal experience, how deeply true it was.

At the very beginning of my relationship with Carolyn (a pseudonym), the night before I was to leave on a business trip, she'd told me a vivid dream: *We find an isolated island that had a beautiful climate and a perfect balance of flora and fauna. But you want to try an experiment. You order several crates to be shipped, and when you open them out leap dozens of unruly monkeys who scamper off into the underbrush.* "You were excited," she told me, "but I felt a sense of dread." In her dream, she had feared that these wild, impulsive creatures would overbreed and destroy the paradisical ecosystem.

On our way to the airport a week later, we had a terrible fight. Carolyn threw down the luggage she'd been helping me carry in the middle of the lobby and stalked off. I'd boarded the plane in a huff, wondering how much longer our fledgling relationship could last. That night, at a Hollywood party, I met a statuesque younger woman. The proverbial spark jumped between us. We had dinner a few nights later, and after several glasses of wine, she asked me to drive her home. We fell into each other's arms. Afterward, I was consumed with a darkening guilt. I had violated Carolyn's trust—had impulsively unleashed my "monkey business" into an Eden still innocent of betrayal. To compound my sense of remorse, the next morning, on the phone, Carolyn told me a vivid dream that had woken her that night: *I am taking a bath, and suddenly the warm, comforting, clear water turns jet black. I feel shocked and horror-struck.* She'd awakened certain it had something to do with me—with us. I had bitten my tongue and kept my silence—it had just been a harmless one-night stand. I wouldn't do it again.

I had brushed over my tracks, crafted my alibi, uttered my white lies. I would hang tough for a few days, and any lingering suspicion would blow over. What she didn't know couldn't hurt her. But I couldn't banish from my mind the idea that on some level Carolyn *did* know. Her dream continued to disturb her—she mentioned it several times—and her sincere bafflement shamed me. Though I'd chalked up my misdeed to the shakiness of our relationship and a night of out-of-hand high spirits, I couldn't bear the thought that I was causing her to mistrust her own inner promptings. I finally broached the subject and confessed all. It occasioned a traumatic, tear-flooded evening, and months of estrangement. The incident left aching scars we had to work hard to heal.

Her dream made me challenge any morally slippery notions of relationship on a need-to-know basis. It seemed that thoughts and feelings, deeds visible or covert, had wings to fly to those with whom we are deeply bound. Carolyn's dreams, in that sense, were speaking to both of us. They have led us to try to practice a rigorous mutual truthtelling. We have made a point of sharing our dreams, come what may.

I once dreamed: *Carolyn has found a new lover who looks like me and has had a slew of fascinating experiences all over the world. But he is less erratic than I am and can offer her more stability. Carolyn declares she is taking a hiatus from our relationship to be with him, and I feel bereft.* The next evening, as we ate dinner in a Chinese restaurant, I mentioned the dream. She told me she had that day coincidentally bumped into an old lover on the street after not having seen him for years. He had regaled her with exciting stories of his travels—he'd been to India and Nepal, rafted the Amazon, and now was on his way to Paris. He had even suggested she come along with him, offering to buy her a ticket on the spot.

I, too, had traveled to India and Brazil, but had little interest in Paris, which Carolyn had always wanted to visit. I quailed a little at her retelling, and she relished my discomfort before reassuring me, "No sale. He didn't interest me at all." When I told her my dream from the previous night, she added that he *did* strongly resemble me in height and weight and features, adding teasingly, "And his eyes are just as blue." As we continued to talk, she spoke of the yearning she sometimes felt to meet someone with my sense of adventure but who also fulfilled her needs for domesticity. The discussion was painful bordering on excruciating, but the sharing of the dream had freed us to talk frankly about our needs, disappointments, and hopes. (A year later, we did find a way, on the cheap, to spend a week in Paris.)

Caring is a web so sensitive that even the brush of a mayfly's wing can be felt as a subtle vibration. We cannot have it both ways, say our dreams: it is by love that our lives are woven together, because of love that the delicate strands thrum. There are no secrets, dreams tell us, especially from the heart.

These are not easy times for relationships, when all the rules are in flux and affections seem subject to a kind of quid pro quo: am I getting as much as

I'm giving? Am I growing or shrinking? Is my partner the wind beneath my wings or a downdraft? A sixtyish woman named Alma had rarely thought to ask such a question. She had been with her husband for thirty-three years, though the marriage sometimes seemed to offer little more than lifelong emotional tenure. One night she had a terrible dream:

> *I see two birds of prey, falcons I think, male and female. The male is inside the house, strutting back and forth. He will not allow the female bird to come in. Every time she tries to cross threshold, he ruffles his wings. I watch as the female bird outside finally dies. Then like fast-forwarding a videotape, like flowers blooming in time lapse I watch as she first falls over, her bodily fluids running onto the patio, her feathers blowing away, until nothing is lying there but bones!*[11]

Alma awoke horrified. She realized she was the female bird, her husband the strutting male. She wondered out loud if it meant one of them was soon going to die. Realizing she needed help, she decided to share her dream in a writing workshop run by a deacon in her church. "No one's going to die," he told her, "but something is going to happen within."

With his guidance, she began to see the dream as a parable about her stagnant relationship, the dying bird a dire version of till-death-do-us-part. "Paul has his door shut," she explained, "and you don't get inside that man. He doesn't share, doesn't talk." Her husband had so long been closed off to her, she realized, that some part of her was dying of despair. She admitted to herself that she often wondered "if I can get through another day. Can I live this way a moment longer?" One night she got down on her knees in her living room and wept, praying to God: "Give me a sign, show me where to go, what to do!"

She went to bed that night and had a second unforgettable dream:

> *Paul knows I am very upset and am going to leave him. He says to just come and look at our dining room table, which is now overladen with gifts and flowers and candy. I looked at all the knicknacks, and I say, "There's nothing there I want, nothing that will make me stay." He says, "Then come back and look at*

this one last gift, and if you can look at this, you can leave." And from his chair, at the end of the table, was growing this magnificent flowering pink dogwood tree, its branches spreading throughout my whole kitchen.

She woke with a start, a sheen of tears on her cheeks. "Anything other than a dogwood would have had zero impact on me," she says. "But I *love* dogwood trees more than anything; I believe they are the most beautiful tree in the world."

Alma decided to stay, with the certainty granted by her dream that whatever her husband was on the outside, he contained, unknown even to himself, some magnificent efflorescence of soul. For years, she didn't tell him her dream; it was a keepsake for her, a talisman for them both. Often when she looked at him, she could see only the magical tree. Then slowly, almost miraculously, her husband began to open up. The marriage, on the cusp of final winter, put forth tentative new buds. "The dream lets me accept things the way they are. Now, whatever is happening inside me, I hear Pink Dogwood say, 'Get a grip on it, don't get upset or rattled. It's been too long to give it up now.' Besides, this man needs someone to take care of him—no one else is dumb enough to do it!"

Her Healing Dream had revealed a deep, impossible truth that lay beneath the veil of apparency. Marriage *is* both a life and a death—a death of the small self, down to dry bone and ephemeral feather (the Greek word *tholos* means both "bridal chamber" and "grave"). All relationships are betrayals—of private hopes and longings that can never be satisfied through another; of fantasies of perfection, total security, and eternal harmony. Parts of us must fall by the wayside; branches must be pruned, so that the tree may live. Sacrifice—literally, "to make sacred"—becomes an act of affirmation, allowing some mysterious blessing to enter a place made empty.

Alma's dreams, her reverence for them, awed me. Conventional wisdom, pop psychology, the consensus of her friends, all gave her every reason and right to break free. With their three children all grown, why not simply divorce? In a society where marriage is a contract that comes up periodically for renewal, where people seek warranties on happiness, it seems crazy to settle for less than one is entitled to—most of all in love.

Was Alma just beaten down? Or had she found in her Healing Dream that mustard seed of faith that moves mountains?

Her dream had presented an idea so strong as to blow all others before it as chaff before a gale. It spoke on behalf of the third presence that may arise out of two, that presence which shows how much greater a relationship is than the sum of its parts. It revealed that the taciturn, oppressive man to whom Alma had devoted her life contained a fragrant, flowering spirit. Even if only she could perceive it, if only her vision could nurture and sustain it—and slowly, encourage it to bloom—that would be, for her, love's crowning glory.

The Dream Society

Now I know that it is not out of our single souls we dream. We dream
anonymously, communally, if each after his fashion. The great soul of
which we are all a part may dream through us, in our manner of dreaming,
its own secret dreams. . . .

> —*Thomas Mann,* The Magic Mountain

ealing Dreams not only are well informed about our intimate relationships but are shrewd social observers. They are remarkably
attuned to the clamor of community, the nuances of the body
politic, even the fate of the earth. They chafe at boundaries. They wriggle
free of our solitary nets, and head into open water, seeking a greater con-
clave of souls. This idea may disturb us a little. It has been standing policy
in psychology to treat dreams as private creations that speak to the dreamer
alone. Dreams, after all, can be transgressive, championing the rude, lewd,
and wholly unacceptable. What if they were enacted on the social stage?
When Julius Caesar dreamed he was sleeping with his mother, his royal
soothsayer told him it meant he would soon possess the mother city,
Rome. Caesar duly marched southward to take the capital. Would he and
the world have been better off if, instead of setting out on the road to

conquest, he had brought his dream to a therapist to work through his Oedipus complex?

In dreamwork, we are counseled, wisely, to "keep the lid on the pot"; to always "withdraw the projections" back from the outer world to the inner one. "The purpose of dreams," one Jungian told me, "is to undermine group identification, oppose collective solutions, and spur individuation." But Healing Dreams crave a give-and-take. They confront us with our own unmet social potential, calling upon us each to know ourselves as part of the whole. Has psychology been too eager to bottle up the dream in the consulting room, forbidding it a collective life?

Clan Dreaming

In dreams, writes the psychoanalyst Erich Fromm, "we are concerned exclusively with ourselves . . . in which 'I am' is the only system to which thoughts and feelings refer."[1] Yet the privatization of the dream remains a peculiarly Western practice. Dreams in many cultures—the Plains Indians,[2] for example—are key components in social problem solving, with vital public and even political implications. My Cree Indian friend Sylvia, known in her community as a dreamer and a healer, finds the notion that her dreams might come for her alone puzzling. She doesn't see their characters as simply aspects of herself wrapped in symbolic clothing. For her, a dream is often a social occurrence, to be shared with her own extended kinship network and sometimes with the entire tribe.

I have heard many instances in the course of my research of what might be called "clan dreaming." A cable TV executive named Linda asserts, "I rarely dream about myself. Mostly about other people." Linda had grown up in Georgia with a rich heritage of American Indian and African ancestors. Her ninety-seven-year-old aunt is still known as a healer. Her grandmother, a well-known local root doctor, taught her the " 'guess what I'm thinking game'—she'd hide things in the room or behind her back, ask me what the object was, what was its color, and I'd have to somehow 'see' it." It is a game I have heard described by African *sangomas* as part of the intuitive training of gifted individuals. Linda has had the family gift since she was a small child, when she first began dreaming "little previews of things that would happen."

"It's as if I'm fully conscious and watching a movie," says Linda. "As if I'm in a darkened theater, seeing the scenes lit up in front of me, feeling the emotions of the people on the screen."

When Linda was in her twenties, she dreamed that her distant cousin Delores was being rushed down a hospital corridor on a gurney. *I am even "told" the name—Arlington Hospital. Then I am sitting in a waiting room, in the middle of a semicircle consisting of Delores's mother, my mother, and my three sisters and her three sisters—the whole clan! I can see Delores with a bloody sheet pulled over her, and feel she has died a violent death.*

"When I came out of that dream," Linda recalls, "I could hardly catch my breath. Such fear! As soon as I woke up, I ran downstairs and told my mom." By coincidence, Delores's mother was visiting that morning, but she wasn't impressed: "This could be a dream about yourself," she told Linda. "About anyone."

"You don't understand," Linda insisted to her. "*These* kinds of dreams don't make mistakes—they're *real.*"

Two weeks later, a grief-stricken Linda attended Delores's funeral. Soon after the dream, Delores' ex-boyfriend had broken into her house and shot her, then himself. As it turned out, Delores had just started dating someone else—a man who worked at Arlington Hospital. She had told none of her kin that her ex-boyfriend had been calling and threatening to kill her. The family was devastated. "Since then," says Linda, "whenever I get a 'message' about someone, I try to find a way to pass it on."

As much as she dares, Linda has brought her "social dreaming" into her work life. "There was a woman in my office at a public TV station, snappish, crabby, no friends on the job. One night, I dreamed about a man I knew immediately was her dad, though she'd certainly never spoken of him. It was a lovely dream, with a festive air—neighbors coming over, eating, everyone having a great time. He gave each person a dark brown chocolate baguette."

She could find no personal associations to the dream images. "The next day, I got up my nerve, and said, 'Virginia, I think I had a dream about your dad.' I described this short man with a small moustache, in a little derby, who was so generous. She got teary eyed. It turns out her dad's been dead for fifteen years, but I'd gotten his appearance and personality to a T. Every Friday, she told me, he'd go to the neighborhood baker and buy a huge box of chocolate buns and hand them out to all the neighborhood kids." Their office relationship became more harmonious. With the memory of her father's generous interest in people restored to her, the woman herself took on some of his sociability. Linda had, in effect, had a dream *for* her; by sharing it with her, she helped to heal the strained atmosphere of the workplace.

Dream Helper

Dream-sharing customs vary from culture to culture. The Zuni people of New Mexico have a tradition of making public their "bad" dreams, while "good" dreams are sometimes withheld even from close relatives. Among the Quiché of Guatemala, all dreams, even small fragments, are shared immediately with family and tribe.[3] An Australian aborigine told me, "We have a saying, 'Share it out before the next sunrise.' We tell our dreams to the group, because different people have different gifts and might help understand it." It reminded me of the informal dream groups that have sprung up in Western societies over the past several decades—until he added an intriguing comment: "We often meet each other while we're sleeping."

There are a number of cultures where members are said to deliberately dream about each other. The shamans of Siberia's Yakut tribe conduct an evening ceremony using the shoulder blade of a deer, then ask participants to pay close attention to their dreams. The next morning, dreams are recited and interpreted for guidance—not only for the dreamer himself but for the other members of the group. There have been even more exotic accounts of dream sharing throughout history. After Islamic soldiers conquered the island of Rhodes from the Knights of St. John in 1522, a monastery was built in which collective dream techniques were practiced.

Writes one scholar: "Master and disciples purified themselves bodily, mentally, and spiritually together; they got into an enormous bed together, a bed that contained the whole congregation. They recited the same secret formula together and had the same dreams."[4] Rabbi Zalman Schachter-Shalomi speaks of a Jewish ritual called a "dream assembly." A group of people says a prayer together at a certain time of night, "when the Shekhinah [divine wisdom] removes her veil." They close their eyes when the evening prayer reaches the words "Guard our going out and our coming in." Then, he says, "Those who joined in prayer together will be joined together in a dream."[5]

On several occasions, I have dreamed about friends in meaningful ways, and they about me. Sometimes they are relatives, but more often they are people I have been drawn to by what Goethe called *Wahlverwandtschaft* ("elective affinity"). It is a term roughly equivalent to the novelist Kurt Vonnegut's inspired neologism from *Cat's Cradle,* the *karass,* a group bound by mutual sensibilities, affection, and fate. If you want to know who's in yours, watch who you dream about.

I once decided to organize a series of informal experiments to see what would happen if I invited my karass into my dream space. At the time, I stood at a difficult crossroads. I asked friends and family to incubate a dream that might help me find my way. A number of them devised informal rituals—lighting candles and incense and meditating before bed, putting a slip of paper with my name on it under their pillows, or just visualizing my face as they went to sleep.

Several reported having vivid dreams that, upon examination, had as a common thread images of cups and glasses. One dreamed that white wine was being poured into my eyes through the hollow stems of two wine glasses "for medicinal purposes." (A month later, I was prescribed my first pair of glasses, after a test involving eyedrops.) Another saw "a counter laid out with paper cups with pills in them, administered by a nurse in a white uniform." Another friend, Sally, had a vivid, elaborate dream:

I am in a very large old mansion with many rooms. We are sitting around a ceremonial table on which plastic party cups filled with water and peach-colored flow-

ers have been laid out, two hundred glasses at least. We see the water quivering, as if from an earthquake. Then a great wind blows, and a hand comes in, pointing, and we hear a huge voice, like the voice of God: 'Ask and you shall receive!' The flowers begin to blossom. I see flames growing out of the petals.

I was fascinated. The day before, a psychologist friend (who was also a nurse) had encouraged me to do an active imagination exercise regarding my predicament—at the time, bad health, money trouble, an existential loneliness I couldn't shake. The image had arisen in my mind of a prisoner in a bare stone cell, desperate for water. The setting became so vivid that my mouth grew parched. I could barely swallow, managing only to croak out, *Water. Please.* My friend asked me to close my eyes and stick out my tongue, whereupon she began to drip water into my mouth. It felt like blessed rain in a desert. Driven by an ever greater thirst, I demanded more, and she brought me plastic party cups brimming with water, which I gulped down greedily, one after the other. I felt I was in a sacred ritual, drinking the medicinal waters of life.

Somehow this scene had been amplified in Sally's dream, a dream that seemed sanctified not only by the elements—earth, water, fire, wind—but by the hand of God Himself. I found her dream's emphatic "Ask and ye shall receive" affecting. It is hard for me to reach out when I am in need. Sally's dream helped me find the courage and humility to send a letter to sixty friends revealing my situation and asking for assistance. I discovered to my surprise that helping hands had been waiting all along—hands that would, in months to come, lift me willingly over hurdle after hurdle.

Several other friends had dreamed of healing rituals that night. Rick, who told me he rarely remembered his dreams, had one strong enough to wake him in the middle of the night:

Howard Badhand, a Lakota shaman, is standing behind me and putting a necklace around my neck. The necklace consists of four red cotton prayer ties, which are usually filled with tobacco and sewn up. These are unusual ones in that they are oblong and very large—they cover my throat, almost like a choker. As Howard is tying the necklace around the back of my neck he says, "Pray any-

body," which I take to mean, "Pray to anybody." My heart was beating thump-de-thump, and my chest felt opened.

I assumed Rick's dream had to do with my own illness, which was in my throat, and felt grateful to receive his vision of a Native American blessing. But it turned out to have an unforeseen meaning: a week later, in a routine checkup, Rick was diagnosed with a recurrence of lung cancer. Shortly thereafter, he was invited to Boulder for a ceremony conducted by none other than Howard Badhand. Rick asked me to come along. Late one night, in a pitch-black room sweetened by burning sage, we found ourselves praying together for healing—our own, each other's, everybody's—in a moving *yuwipi* ceremony, which featured large, oblong, red cotton prayer ties. Rick sang out his prayers hoarsely—the cancer had moved into his throat, its "choker" impinging on his vocal cords. It marked the beginning of our companionship on a journey that took him well past his medical prognosis. His dream's message became his watch-word: he "prayed anybody" from Hawaian *kahunas* to top oncologists, and became a regular participant in Lakota sun dance ceremonies.

Rick's experience was something I was to see duplicated in other "dream helper" ceremonies: my request that people dream on my behalf produced Healing Dreams for them. It has the logic of a spiritual folktale: if you want to heal yourself, resolve to heal another. The dreams had drawn a magic chalk circle that summoned powerful forces into all our lives.

Dreams in Community

One society that reportedly had extensive dream-sharing regimens was the Temiar Senoi, a jungle tribe of ten thousand living in the Cameron Highlands of Malaysia. Researcher Kilton Stewart reported in 1954 that if, for example, a child dreamed he had been attacked by a friend, his father would advise him to tell the friend about it. The friend would be advised by *his* father to give the dreamer a present and to go out of his way to be kind to him, in case he had offended him. "Thus," said Stewart, "the aggression building up around the image of the friend in the dreamer's mind became the basis of a friendly exchange." Later in the day, dreams would be discussed by the entire community, and the messages and insights they contained would become part of the tribe's rituals and their behavior in waking life.

Whether Stewart's Rousseauian portrait can be taken at face value or was, as many anthropologists claim, just romantic confabulation, remains an open question.[6] Anthropologist Robert Knox Dentan, who made two trips to Malaysia in 1963 and 1974, could find few traces of the world Stewart compellingly described. One of Dentan's informants summed it up best, perhaps, when he poignantly told him, "We used to have true dreams—but no more."

Yet this dispute scarcely matters. Decades of research have revealed that many tribal cultures give dreams a central role in their collective lives. Anthropologist Barbara Tedlock reports that dreams are of such integral importance to Mexico's Maya that one out of four tribal members are initiated as "day keepers," their term for dream interpreters. And the tales of the Temiar Senoi, whether apocryphal or historical, have been an inspiration to those seeking to bring dreams into Western social discourse.

One such person is the Unitarian minister Jeremy Taylor, who began running dream groups while performing alternative civilian service during the Vietnam War. He was assigned to do community organizing in Emeryville, California, an "all-black, working- and under-class" city. Tensions between blacks and whites in the group ran high, and meetings often degenerated into polarized name-calling sessions.

One day Taylor suggested that they stop talking about waking life and instead start sharing their dreams. Many confessed they were having "nasty, racist dreams . . . of being attacked and menaced by sinister, hostile and dangerous people of other races."[7] Taylor feared that discussing them would pour gasoline on the fire. Instead a more open form of dialogue began to develop. It became clear to everyone, writes Taylor, that "these ugly, scary, dark, powerful, sexy, violent, irresponsible, dangerous dream figures were vitally alive parts of their own authentic being."[8]

Cynicism started to evaporate. "Authentic personal likes and dislikes began to replace ritual 'politeness,' and blundering patronizing comments, and repressed fear. The energy that had previously been squandered in maintaining the repression and projection suddenly came welling up . . . as spontaneous surges of vitality and well-being . . . creative possibility and enthusiasm." The group dreamwork contributed to a style of interracial, grassroots political organizing that eventually helped elect the first black public officials in what had once been called "the most corrupt community in California."

In a world where "community" too often means "people like us," dreamers are sometimes dismayed to find themself face to face with, even in thrall to, denizens of society that they in waking life try to avoid. In dreams, I've consorted with sleazy pimps and thieving hoodlums; aging bikers and liquored-up Indians; a "con-man guardian"; "a short, fat Sherpa woman"; a "villainous, common Italian guy"; a skinny junkie girl; humpbacked, senile old Jewish grandmothers; an acne-scarred Mexican teenage hooker. Yet some of the figures I encountered had unexpected qualities, or even did me great boons. The con man in my dream got me out of the army by bribing an officer with a stolen emerald; the Sherpa woman was my guide through a treacherous mountain pass; the bikers were ardent hedonists and loyal friends; and it was the teenage hooker who gave me a highly informative lecture about the interplay between the thymus gland and the lymph system!

But it is hard to avoid the fact—indeed, it is a little mortifying—that these images are near-cartoonish stereotypes of race, class, and gender. Even in those of us who pride ourselves on an acute social conscience, prejudices against the "other" have deep psychic roots. Certainly, I could find unacknowledged aspects of myself in these broad-stroke dream-characters: in every uneasy distancing from another person, it is usually ourselves we are rejecting, those wounded parts that certain our greatest wealth of soul. But their very closeness, at once intimate and intimidating, makes them stark reminders of what is ignored, repressed, and denied—not just in the psyche, but in society at large. Dreams are the great levelers.

Such images—each one a vivid, personal encounter—undermine the social rituals of status and position, the ego's preposterous contention that some of us are "above" or "below" others, and that we can sever our own fate from that of our neighbors. The dream world has no gated communities. A pastor who runs church dream groups is amazed how unerringly dreams present what she calls "the alternative wisdom of Jesus, which insists that we honor the least among us, and love the unlovable."[9] Though we may be only too glad to see the dream's upside-down society dissipate in the morning sun, it tells us that all whom we meet, if seen with the inner eye, are potential companions, teachers, and loved ones.

Dream Politics

Dream-sharing can be an unlikely source of social conciliation. During the 1970s, a pitched political and economic battle erupted between real estate developers and houseboat dwellers in the picturesque bohemia of Sausalito, California. In response, a resident named John van Damm started a mimeographed broadsheet subtitled *A Waterfront Community Dream Journal*. He began publishing its pastiche of dreams, poems, and drawings when the paranoia of the water folk had been ratcheted up to breaking point by constant harassment from developers, sheriff's deputies, construction workers, and gun-toting guards.

In the midst of it all, van Damm printed a dream of a prominent houseboater in which *she had slept with one of the most hated developers.* Here, in blunt fashion, a Healing Dream stated a constitutional article of the dreamworld: At our core, we all touch; our differences are only skin-deep.

"The community was outraged—at us for printing the dream, and at the woman for even *having* it," van Damm recalled. "But the image couldn't be ignored. It said, very graphically, that the developers were people, too—that we shouldn't demonize them but find our common humanity. The point almost couldn't have been raised in any other way." The woman's outrageous dream image became a catalyst that helped reframe the dialogue. The dynamics of the simmering social warfare shifted, and a peaceful resolution was eventually found. Van Damm wondered if he hadn't stumbled on a new form of "dream politics."

Of course, it is scarcely new. The Iroquois, for example, brought the dream into the social sphere to an almost unheard-of degree. They believed dreams represented the wishes of the soul, the divine force they called Ondinnonk, and required outward expression if the individual—and society at large—were to remain healthy.

The Iroquois had medicine men whose specialized function was recognizably psychoanalytic: "certain persons, more enlightened than the common . . . [who] see the natural and hidden desires that it [the soul] has . . . though he who may have had the dreams had completely forgotten them." They even used free-association techniques, urging patients to "declare . . . whatever first occurs to them" in order to uncover their "inborn desires, often unknown to themselves, upon which the happiness of individuals depends."[10]

A spirited instance of the dream in Iroquois social discourse was the midwinter "dream-guessing rite," a sacred game in which groups of men and women would run through the village, bursting into dwellings and upending furnishings while posing riddles about dreams that contained a "soul wish." In what was known as the Feast of Fools, or Ononharoia ("turning the brain upside down"), celebrants would not leave until the wish—whether for food, a beautiful ornament, or a sexual liaison—had been guessed. The desire had to be either enacted through ritual or bought off with an appropriate gift.[11] Here was a ceremony whereby the dream literally invaded social space, insisting on being heard and acknowledged. The "hidden and forbidden" elements of the individual psyche were unequivocally expressed. The dream became public and animate—an autonomous actor rather than a mere commentator.

What kind of society resulted? Though we must rely principally on the writings of seventeenth-century Jesuit missionaries for an answer, these accounts characterized the Iroquois as "modest in dress, often rather shy in heterosexual contacts, and although premarital affairs were freely permitted to the young people and divorce and remarriage were easy for adults, chastity and marital fidelity were publicly recognized ideals." Despite our notions of what havoc the dream unloosed might wreak upon society, the dream-honoring Iroquois of centuries past developed a set of mores that is strikingly contemporary.

Sometimes, however, notes the anthropologist Anthony Wallace, "the fulfillment of dream wishes took priority over other proprieties." This fidelity could sometimes lead to darker enactments. Wallace notes the 1642 case of a Huron man who dreamed he had been taken captive and burned alive, a torture widely used by various tribes. In order to avert this ill fortune, the council decreed that fires be lit in the cabin where captives were traditionally held, the dreamer tormented with fire, and a dog killed in the ritual manner of a captive. There are reports of a man's finger being amputated with a seashell because he dreamed he had been captured and all his fingers cut off. These apotropaic ceremonies, as they are known in anthropology, are not uncommon in disparate cultures that give great credence to their dreams.

But no society could function were there not implicit limits placed on dream enactments; the psyche, as Freud well noted, contains more sexuality and aggression than can be expressed without catastrophic social results. Among the Iroquois, the drama of enacting a horrible dream would usually halt at the last moment. Thus, a man whose dream-wish was to kill a French soldier was satisfied to receive his coat. Certainly, instances were reported where a dream promoted positive social change. One story is told of an Iroquois woman, unhappily married into a tribe far from home, who wandered into the woods one night and saw the moon come to her as a beautiful lady. In her dreamlike vision, the lady declared that each tribe was to give the woman gifts—tobacco from the Tobacco Nation, for example, and robes of black squirrel fur from the Neutrals. As word of her vision spread, gifts were exchanged and intertribal feasts held in many villages. The missionary who reported it noted a positive outcome: "This poor unhappy creature found herself much better after the feast than before." Here a dream vision brought healing to both an individual and an entire society.[12]

To gain a modern perspective I spoke to Orren Lyons, leader of the Onandaga, a tribe of the Iroquois, about the social power of dreaming. He confirmed that the Iroquois still use dreams in collective decision-making. "The day the chief is presented and raised, for example, the question is put to the public at large whether anyone had a 'dream of significance' the night before.

"Usually we don't see our dreams as personal," he added, "though sometimes they are—you need to be able to tell if a dream's because you had too much pizza last night, or if it's a special message for everyone."

"How do you tell?" I asked him.

"We just *know*. We've got ten thousand years of knowing. It's no big deal— just a normal part of our lives."

The incorporation of dreams into social life is common to many cultures. Bob Randal, my Australian aboriginal friend, tells me, "Dreams give us direction, so we share them, especially if it's prophecy-type dreaming. But in that case, the elders will discuss it, examine whether the person is someone who's shown proof of his accuracy. Say this person had a true dream the last four times, maybe they'll listen to him the fifth time."

Clearly, however, some cultures have descended into chaos when the unconscious was given too much social credence. I had the good fortune to once spend an afternoon with Sir Laurens van der Post, Jung's friend and biographer, shortly before he died. In the sweep of our conversation, I mentioned the the late-nineteenth-century Paiute Ghost Dance, where the dream of a prophet named Wovoka had galvanized Plains Indians tribes into a last attempt to restore their vanishing world. If this dance were performed, the vision promised, the buffalo would return, fallen warriors would spring from the earth, and society would enter a new golden age. Though Wovoka's dream had emphasized peace, the Sioux interpreted it as a call to resistance. The movement triggered a brief war that proved to be their last hurrah. "They ran into the soldiers' guns believing their ghost shirts would stop the bullets," I told van der Post. "Isn't this what we fear? That dreams don't tell the truth, and we follow them at our peril?"

Van der Post, whose writings make clear his own passionate belief in dreams, replied by summing up his core belief: "A dream is never false. Every detail is there for a reason, and has a meaning." He offered an example that he was familiar with from his many years in South Africa. A young girl of the Amacoza people dreamed that her tribe needed to sacrifice all their material possessions—"to eat up all their cattle, which was the greater part of their wealth. The dream said that on the day they consumed their last worldly goods, their ancestors would come out of the sea and drive out the white man."

The tribe, he recounted, took the girl's dream literally. As they began to slaughter their cattle, the area's governor, Sir George Gray (who was later to make a study of Maori dreams and mythology), tried desperately to persuade them to consider other interpretations. "They wouldn't listen. The girl told them, 'It's another trick of the white man to keep you in their power.' All Gray could do was ready all the supplies he could to move up to the frontier and await the inevitable famine. The Amacoza kept faith with the dream, and hundreds of thousands died as a result. They didn't see the dream's symbolism."

What, I asked him as the afternoon shadows lengthened, did he think the symbolism was?

"That they mustn't be preoccupied with the material world and its values but rather turn back to the spiritual values of their ancestors. You've got to see imagery both literally *and* symbolically. Only then will the dream never betray you."

The Dream on the Social Stage

And Pharoah had a dream; he was standing by the Nile, and there, coming up from the Nile, were seven cows, sleek and fat, and they began to feed among the rushes. And seven other cows, ugly and lean, came from the Nile after them; and these went over and stood beside the other cows on the bank of the Nile. The ugly and lean cows ate the seven sleek and fat cows. Then Pharaoh awoke.

According to the account from Genesis, Pharaoh declared a national emergency after his nightmare, rounding up every forelock-tugging sage in the land to divine its meaning. We look wonderingly at his panic. It was just a dream—of six-thousand-year vintage, but not unlike our own, with its mishmash of the familiar and the topsy-turvy. But there must have been something inexpressible about *this* dream, something that so trembled with portent that Pharaoh was willing to beg a jailed Jewish seer named Joseph for help. Heeding his Hebrew prisoner's famous interpretation—seven years of good harvests, seven years of bad—he began a massive public works program, erecting the granaries that saved his people from famine and his kingdom from extinction.

We tend to view such accounts as quaint biblical footnotes. The days when a single person's dream could set a national agenda are long past. But consider, for example, the famous Healing Dream of Mohandas Gandhi. During a period of horrifying civil unrest in India, with daily reports of torching, looting, and rioting, Gandhi had spoken at public meetings to beg for restraint. Shouted down by the agitated crowds, unable even to get his letters published in newspapers, he felt helpless to advance his goal of nonviolent struggle. He retreated to a friend's summer home to fast and pray for a solution. After a week, he awakened one morning with a startling dream.

In his dream, all of the warring religious factions in India—Hindus, Muslims, Parsis, Jains, Buddhists, and Sikhs—had forsaken their own holy festivals in order to gather together in prayer and public procession (*hartal*) on a single day. A psychologist might have categorized Gandhi's dream as mere wish fulfillment, a compensatory response to hopes dashed by waking realities. But Gandhi took it as instruction, demanding that Nehru and the Congress party follow the dream's directives and "call upon all the religious sects in India to practice *hartal* at once."

His own party greeted the idea with some derision. Gandhi, undaunted, sat down to write a series of remarkable personal letters to religious leaders across India, recounting his dream and inviting them all to gather beneath its nonsectarian banner. Surprisingly, nearly every religious leader he notified accepted, organizing their followers to gather in the streets for massive worship ceremonies. Not only was violence reduced, but the various Indian factions opposing colonialism—previously disorganized and feuding—now found a common voice. The movement paralyzed the colonial administration with its first successful general strike. The government was forced to rescind a series of hated acts and restore to Indians the rights of British citizenry, including freedom of assembly, press, and local elections.[13] Gandhi's dream helped free an entire country.

Nor is it so long ago that Martin Luther King Jr.'s extraordinary phrase "I have a dream" mobilized a nation's conscience (although his biographers have debated whether he was referring to a literal prophetic dream or merely using a rhetorical device). A dream, once loosed, becomes a living presence with unpredictable effects upon the destinies of all whom it touches. Marion Stamps, a community activist in Chicago's infamous Cabrini Green housing projects, was one person inspired by King's vision. She had dedicated her life to building social equity for families in that crumbling monument to failed urban policy, which had become a no-man's land terrorized by armed warfare between rival drug gangs.

Before going to bed one night in January of 1992, she prayed fervently for guidance, and a dream shattered her sleep: *The Lord tells me He wants me to plan a four-day feast.* Her dream spelled out an elaborate plan. She was "told" to put out a flier inviting the gangs to a "unity feast." On the first night, a Friday, each of the gang leaders was to bring fifteen of his top people. In her dream, she had seen it unspooling like a movie, each delegation sweeping into the room in their gang colors—the Disciples in blue, the Cobras in green and gray, the Stones in their red and white, the gold-and-black Vice Lords. She saw herself making welcoming remarks as the representatives, each at their separate tables, listened intently: "I'm calling you all out—it's Nation Time!" On the second night, said the remarkably specific dream, all the community leaders would meet to decide on a program of change. On the third day, the decision of the group would be announced at a Sunday church service replete with choirs and worship ceremonies. The following day would be a community-wide gala celebration.

Marion woke up stunned, and wrote down her vision word for word.

The next day, she regaled her minister, her sister, and her friends with her amazing experience. Though some encouraged her, others told her not to take chances, and her dream languished unfulfilled. Three months later, on Easter, she was playing solitaire and felt she'd entered "a different state. I lay down. I wasn't really asleep, I was sort of nodding off. And all these words came to me."

She groped for a pen, and the words flowed onto the page. It was as an open letter to all residents, spelling out all the details of her great dream. She made up flyers, then walked up and down every block, handing them out to anyone she met. Her whirlwind of activity led to an appearance on a popular local radio show. Gang members from what she calls the "tribes" of the Near North Side began phoning her, and miraculously she was able to bring about a temporary peace. Freed for a time from fear and division, people organized a march on city hall to demand new solutions to the unchecked violence and chronic unemployment in the community. By that summer and fall, there were new youth recreational programs, revitalized social services, regular family nights, and "rap sessions."

Marion says she learned to pay attention to her "subconsciousness" in the early days of the Movement: "If the spirit says boycott, you boycott. If the spirit says go to jail, you go to jail. Because the spirit is a collective energy of everybody. . . . You feel all these forces pouring into you, saying you've got to do what the spirit says to do."

Ultimately, she succeeded in putting together a version of the four-day event. A Friday-night group of mostly women held a get-together. "We danced and we sang and we talked and we reminisced, and did a lot of soul sharing." The next day's fund-raiser was an abject failure, and the Sunday event, when the different "nations" were supposed to announce a long-awaited peace, was called off when the Cobras dropped out. But that Monday, she remembered fondly, "We had this great big old block party. We had about three thousand people. Everybody, the children, the elders, everybody came—it was beautiful."

Within weeks of the party, a young boy was gunned down in a gang-related shoot-out, another innocent bystander in the senseless turf war. The tragedy brought the gangs to the table for another shaky truce. Marion realized that her dream might never literally come to pass, but it had revealed "some kind of groundwork, a blueprint; it was an outline in terms of what God had laid out for me to do."[14]

She did not live to see her dream fulfilled. She died a few years ago, at the age of fifty. Today, Cabrini Green is being razed to make room for a real estate development that will displace the nascent community she fought so hard for. But she remains an example of how a Healing Dream may circulate, issuing from the dreamworld to the individual, from the individual to society, and from society back to the individual, gathering momentum as it goes.

What Happens to a Dream Denied?

But what if a dream is confined within the individual psyche, never to escape? In a book entitled *The Third Reich of Dreams,* the German journalist Charlotte Beradt catalogued the dream lives of three hundred of her fellow citizens during the rise of Nazism. She found that while her informants felt constrained to go along with the devastating rending of the Weimar social fabric, their dreams were telling the dark parallel story.

Beradt heard the first dream that alarmed her in 1933, three days after Hitler seized power. Her acquaintance Herr S., an industrialist, dreamed that propaganda minister Joseph Goebbels visited his factory and had all workers line up in two rows facing each other. Herr S., who employed many Social Democrats who had opposed Hitler's rise, was forced to stand before them all and raise his arm in the Nazi salute. Goebbels watched him impassively as it "took me half an hour to get my arm up, inch by inch." Finally when he did manage, "Goebbels said coldly, 'I don't want your salute' and turned on his heel out the door. There I stood in my own factory, arm raised, pilloried right in the midst of my own people. I was only able to keep from collapsing by staring at his clubfoot as he limped out. And so I stood until I woke up. "

The dream, says Beradt, "swept him off his self-made foundations, destroyed his sense of identity and left him disoriented." It recurred again and again, each time with humiliating new details—in one, Herr S. found himself struggling to lift his arm until his backbone literally broke. Such nightmares, she began to suspect, were becoming common, yet remained each dreamer's private hell. The atmosphere was becoming so poisoned, the ground so treacherous, that people were afraid to tell each other their dreams.

Until she was compelled to leave the country in 1939, Beradt continued to compile her dream history. She quietly asked the people she normally came in contact with to tell her their dreams—dressmakers, neighbors, an aunt, the mailman— without revealing her purpose. She had to write her notes in code, camouflaging them as family anecdotes (Hitler, Goering, and Goebbels became "Uncle Hans, Uncle Gustav, and Uncle Gerhard") and hiding them in the bindings of books scattered throughout her large private library.

Beradt's work sheds light on the power of truth that Healing Dreams wield, and how, to society's tragic loss, that power can be reduced to a voice crying in the wilderness. It is worth citing, for example, the case of a forty-five-year-old eye doctor who dreamed in 1934:

> *Storm Troopers were putting up barbed wire at all hospital windows. I had sworn I wouldn't stand for having them bring their barbed wire into my ward. But I did put up with it after all. I stood by like a caricature of a doctor while they took out the window panes and turned a ward into a concentration camp—but I lost my job anyway. I was called back, however, to treat Hitler because I was the only man in the world who could. I was ashamed of myself for feeling proud, and so I began to cry.*

Writes Beradt: "The doctor awoke in the middle of the night, spent and exhausted as people often are when they have been crying in their sleep." He remembered one of his assistants had appeared for work at the clinic that day wearing a Storm Trooper's uniform, and though he'd felt indignant, he didn't protest.[15] The dream is a stark reminder of how ordinary citizens became complicit in the Nazi monstrosities. The man resolves inwardly to protest, but intimidated, he stands by passively. He becomes a "caricature," as does anyone who cannot find a way to bring forth what is within, and whose behavior is at odds with personal truth. Dreams hold us accountable: his dream tells him he is personally responsible for keeping Hitler alive.

The Nazis' future victims, too, were dreaming. Very early in the Reich, when some Jews still believed there could be an accommodation, a young girl who feared her Semitic-looking nose would brand her as Jewish had a dream that eerily suggested the totalism of the Shoah, the Holocaust. Her dream, which occurred before race laws were in full force, contains awful premonitions of the crematoria to come:

> *I went to the Bureau of Verification of Aryan Descent [which did not exist under this name, and she had nothing to do with any such office] and presented a certificate attesting to my grandmother's descent, which I had obtained after months of running around. The official looked just like a marble statue and was sitting behind a low stone wall. He reached over the wall, took my paper, and tore it to bits, and threw the pieces into an oven that was built into the wall. And he remarked, "Think you're still pure Aryan now?"*

Another woman's dream, years before the Final Solution, was also hauntingly prophetic: *All at once I found myself lying at the bottom of a pile of corpses with no idea how I got there—at least I had a good hiding place. Pure bliss under my pile of bodies, clutching my papers in their folder.*

These dreams remarkably prefigured many of the horrors that were not yet manifest—the subversion of medicine into torture and human experimentation; the elimination of the unfit and racially "impure"; the contempt for civil procedure; the breakdown of individual psychological autonomy, allowing evil to run rampant. The uniqueness of these dreams, Beradt noted, is that they were not produced by conflicts in private life or personal psychological wounds but in response to a public realm of lies and imminent violence. Before the totalitarian ruthlessness of the Nazis was fully revealed—when, as she wrote, "the regime was still treading lightly"—many already knew the facts in their dreams.[16]

It struck Beradt that the dreams tended to be unusually straightforward:

"These dreams adopt forms and guises which are no more complicated than the ones used in caricature or political satire, and the masks they assume are just as transparent as those worn at carnivals." Beradt, in fact, used terms we often hear when people describe a Healing Dream: "particularly intensive, and unerratic . . . composed in a generally coherent, anecdotal, and even dramatic fashion, making them easy to remember . . . When retold any number were prefaced by the words, 'I shall never forget this.'"[17]

She was amazed that even seemingly unexceptional people were envisioning the "true apparitions of a new order."[18] "On the basis of widespread experience," Beradt concluded, "one can safely assume that a great number of people were plagued by very similar dreams during the Third Reich."

Beradt's observations raise an intriguing question: Could countervailing forces arising from the psyche have mitigated fascism before it attained its final, distilled virulence? If pre-Nazi Germany had been honeycombed with grassroots dream groups—if people had shared their nightmares, spoken them aloud—would this have acted, in some small way, as an inoculation against totalitarianism, allowing people to draw courage from each others' inner visions?

Or what if people had simply *believed* their own dreams? We often think of Nazi Germany as a cautionary tale of the unconscious run rampant, when the civilized ego-structure of a nation is overcome by its unleashed id, and the blind directives of Eros and Thanatos gather the collective force of an avalanche. But might it be more accurate to say its citizens had become deaf to their own unconscious, blind to their own nightmares and mute to the psyche's expression?

There is one well-documented nightmare that helped a man dare to throw himself before the onrushing juggernaut. Franz Jaegerstetter was an Austrian who, before World War II broke out, publicly refused Nazi conscription, one of the only such cases for which we have a detailed dossier. During his trial, he testified that his actions were inspired by a powerful dream: *I am in a valley, seeing a great train gathering speed as it comes down a mountain, watching in amazement as hundreds and then thousands and finally millions of people jump on. I am debating doing this myself when a booming voice proclaims, "This train is going to Hell!"* He knew, come what may, he could never get aboard this terrible conveyance carrying such a great part of humanity into the abyss. In 1938, with all the barbarous pomp of Prussian militarism, Jaegerstetter was convicted of treason and publicly beheaded.

But a dream, once shared, does not die. It becomes a living seed, putting down roots in the world. I was told this story by Daniel Ellsberg, the man who blew the whistle on the so-called Pentagon Papers during the Vietnam War, so incensing President Nixon that White House "plumbers" were dispatched to burglarize his office. Ellsberg was put on trial for violating national security and narrowly evaded a long prison sentence. He went on to become a passionate antinuclear protester, focusing his outrage on weapons of mass destruction. "When I sat on the tracks to block the freight train into the Rocky Flats nuclear weapons plant, where they were machining enough plutonium bomb triggers for a hundred, a thousand Auschwitzes, I thought of Jaegerstetter's dream. I took comfort that I was doing what was right, and that I could endure the consequences."

Clinicians not infrequently report that patients have terrible nightmares about nuclear annihilation. Psychologist and author Gayle Delaney writes about a client who, after deciding to reduce her analysis to once weekly after becoming pregnant, dreamed:

> *A nuclear holocaust has occurred. I am in a room; I look out and see a mushroom cloud with multiple colors. I think, "Oh shit, someone finally did it." I decide I would rather die immediately than linger on with radiation sickness, yet I am attempting to survive. Then, due to the catastrophe, civilized restraint is gone in the world: I encounter people fighting, engaged in lethal combat—there were no more normal controls.*

Delaney concludes, "The patient's associations dealt mostly with her frightened feelings about reducing her visits to me to one time per week. We attributed this apocalyptic dream to a rather mundane and nonviolent concern: her fear of the possible symptomatic consequences of reducing the analytic frequency." It is true that even the most titanic-seeming dream may, on one level, address one's ground-level concerns. Still, is this dream really so different from those catalogued by Charlotte Beradt? Perhaps the patient's psyche is trying to call attention to the silent specter of nuclear holocaust in an era when, despite the cold war's end, the nuclear "club" is still gaining new members and thousands of missiles remain on alert.

Poet Michael Ortiz collected many dreams of nuclear apocalypse in his book *Dreaming the End of the World*. He sees them as an emergent modern mythos—initiations into a collective psychological death and rebirth to banish the possibility of self-destruction. In the following examples, ordinary people confront the awesome potential of the world's arsenals:

- *The place where we lived had been nuked and I, with my family, was trying to escape. We were walking and carrying some things, but not much, and there were hundreds of other people walking, too. . . . The banks of the motorway were too high to see over, and there was no traffic, no cars. The shock came and the real horror hit home as we went to where the bridge went over the road and met hundreds of people walking in the opposite direction. There was no place to go, no refuge. It affects us all.*
- *There was a layer of red dust covering everything. If you breathed it would kill you. . . . We walked twenty miles away where there wouldn't be so much radioactive dust. I carried my brother. We could see the mushroom cloud while we were walking. We'd eat grass on the way. The mushroom cloud was very scary. We were just trying to survive. Sometimes the air was black and we couldn't see.*[19] [This one from a nine-year-old girl.]

It might seem strange that I would classify these nightmares as Healing Dreams but they are precisely that—as much as the dreams of those who glimpsed the impending horrors of Nazism. Our dreams may entice toward wholeness or scare us into it. But first we must be willing to face them. As nuclear technologies spread like dandelion seeds, the urgency to eliminate war and its roots in society—and in our hearts—is more pressing than ever. Our dreams force us to grapple inwardly with some of the more horrible aspects of our world, goading us to find a means to transform them.

One wonders sometimes if we should not follow the example of the

Roman emperor Augustus, who issued a proclamation that anyone who had a dream about the fate of the republic was duty bound to announce it in the marketplace. Writes Dr. Montague Ullman: "As long as nothing of importance [from the dream] is allowed to find its way back into the society, the individual is left to his own devices and has no choice but to absorb its mysteries within his own personal consciousness or unconscious. No room is left for any challenge to the social order."

The bomb, our dreams tell us, is outside of us and within us. When I page through my old notebooks, I am struck by how often my dreams in the period before my illness were about nuclear holocaust. *There is an atomic bomb in the garage about to go off,* warns one entry. *World War III breaks out and all major cities blow themselves up,* reads another. *I'm in Mexico—are we far enough from the fallout?* A decade later, the government released a study suggesting that up to seventy thousand cases of thyroid cancer—including, perhaps, my own—were caused by the radioactive iodine in fallout-contaminated milk drunk nationwide by children during the fifties atomic testing era.[20] Body and soul, our dreams tell us, we are bound to the fate of this world, as it is bound to us.

The German philosopher Georg Hegel once remarked that if the dreams of a certain historical period were collected and analyzed, they would form "an accurate notion of the spirit which prevailed at the time." What sort of prevailing spirit appears in dreams of contemporary Americans and others around the world, and what might this mean for our future? Ortiz reports that as common as dreams of apocalypse are, he has seen few dealing with ecological catastrophe, despite the hole in the ozone layer, the accelerating extinction of species, global warming, and the decimation of the rain forests. He proposes that even dreams may be subject to a form of "psychic conservatism," adding, "It may be a number of years before the psyche can fully and sharply imagine—and therefore respond to—ecological catastrophe."

But individuals are receiving a call, some through visions of environmental devastation, some through elegiac visions of the beauty of the endangered earth and its wondrous living beings. My Cree friend Sylvia tells me that though her dreams are usually only for her own tribe, for the past few years her dreams have begun instructing her: "It is time for all cultures to share information about the continuation of humankind." A number of her people, she says, are getting the same story in their dreams, a message "to be prepared to unite in hardship. Long ago, our elders dreamed there would be climate changes, the food chain would be damaged, there would be less abundance. My dreams show me this is coming, a time that will be hard, like the Dirty Thirties in Canada." She says her dreams have been very graphic, showing smaller harvests, "even the grass not as green." Others in her clan have had similar visions. Her sister one night heard a booming voice, startling her awake in the middle of the night, giving information about climate changes to come. "Her husband heard it too," Sylvia says, adding drily, "and he's Russian!"

Her dreams make her feel, she says, "an urgency to remember the knowledge I learned as a child and share it with my people. My dreams are of me digging up roots, showing where to find them. How to plant what I need, whether in marshy ground, prairie, woodlands."

A friend told me an unforgettable, haunting dream she had fifteen years ago, which she is only now coming to understand: *I'm on the shore and see dozens, then hundreds of dying, beached whales. Suddenly out of their blowholes spurts a geyser of brine mixed with blood. I am horrified.* Years later, similar incidents, along with other signs and portents of the slow agonies of the natural world, began to occur. We are all too used to ignoring the "deep news" from the psyche until it is ratified by the daily paper and the six o'clock report. Many dreams today speak of what the Hopi call *koyaanisqatsi*—life without sacredness, leached of soul, riven by disharmony. Many indigenous people say the trees and animals and rocks and streams are "telling" them our situation has become dire, that Mother Earth is groaning. Can we create a society that draws water from the well of dreams and has the courage to drink deeply of it together—before the time for dreaming is past?

The Invisible
Community

The recognition that the psyche is self-moving, that it is something
genuine which is not yourself, is exceedingly difficult to see and to admit.
For it means that the consciousness which you call yourself is at an end.
You discover you are not master in your own house, you are not living
alone in your own room, there are spooks about that play havoc with
your realities, and that is the end of your monarchy.

—*Carl Jung*

If dreams reflect society as a whole, they also are a society unto themselves, inhabited by a teeming populace. Most of the time, these are familiar figures of our lives—friends and enemies, parents and spouses,
children and neighbors. Sometimes, however, a flood of astonishing living
images pours into our dreams from a source that seems beyond the personal psyche. Such beings (for it is hard to think of them as anything else)
are the wellsprings of folklore and myth. In the ancient past, their visits inspired religions—Muhammad's dream of an "angel in human form," dis-
playing on a silken cloth the holy Koran; Mormon patriarch Joseph
Smith's vision of a golden being; the Buddhist Tilopa's tutelage by blue
Vajradhara; the biblical Jacob's wrestling match with an angel.

Such stories often read to the modern eye like moldering dispatches
from some long-ago age of miracles. We feel bewildered by accounts from

other times and places claiming that deities, demons, angels, ancestors, and celestial messengers once made routine house calls. Tales that the healing god Asklepius appeared for the drowsing seekers in the Greek dream temples strike us as ancient-world versions of Elvis sightings. Where are these gods now? Why do they not make themselves known to us? Today our dreams (at least the ones we tell each other) overbrim with what Freud called *Tagesreste*—the "day residue" of our jobs and relationships, the rustlings of quotidian angst. Trite phrases like "listen to your better angels" or "the devil got into me" are a far cry from the titanic experiences catalogued in the world's holy writs.

But the truth is that more people still have encounters with compelling dream figures than feel comfortable admitting it. I have interviewed a surprising number who attest—often with reluctance, after assurances that their sanity will not be questioned—that the door between the worlds stands as open as ever. I have heard descriptions of "coaches," "guides," "archangels," and other beings variegated in appearance and attributes. A typical comment is that such dream beings seem "autonomous, acting on their own; not like anyone I'd ever met, or could make up." Some people describe their experiences as blissful, others as hectoring. Other times, these dreams inspire the dictionary definition of *awe*—"fear mingled with reverence"—as in those Annunciation paintings where Mary has her arm thrown across her face in a vain attempt to deny the bright angel.

Such incursions are still accepted in traditional cultures, where the denizens of the dreamworld have not yet been banished. Joseph Shabalala, the South African minister who founded the famed choral group Lady-Smith Black Mambazo, matter-of-factly claimed that his songs and arrangements were sung to him by children he would see in dreams "floating between the stage and the sky. They teach me exactly this sound." The thirteenth Dalai Lama, talking in a recent TV broadcast about the difference between "important dreams" and ordinary ones, casually mentioned receiving in his sleep fresh teachings from the fifth Dalai Lama, a historical figure known for his ecumenical skills.

That such encounters were known among North American Indian tribes is evidenced by the Blackfoot tribe's *spomitai* ("people above"); the

Cheyenne's *maiyun* ("mysterious beings") and the Ojibwa's *pawakan* ("dream spirits"). Nor have the spirits ceased to appear, at least to those who are receptive. When Sylvia was a six-year-old girl on the Cree Indian reserve in Alberta, Canada, she had a searing dream that singled her out as one who could see what others could not. In her dream, she saw an uncle die in a car crash—heard the sickening crunch of metal, the brittle rain of glass on pavement, the man's dying groans. A few days later, the tragedy came to pass. Terrified that she had somehow caused it, she waited for days before plucking up the courage to tell her beloved grandfather. He responded in the way her tribe's elders have for centuries when a child is discovered with such a gift. The time had come, he gently told her, to teach her the way of the dream.

She remembers her grandfather, who was also the tribal chief, sitting her on his lap during council meetings, asking her to report her dreams to the circle of elders. After a few years, a teacher began to appear in her dreams, a spirit "grandfather" (*mushum*). Sylvia says he seems like an ordinary person, "except I've been seeing him all my life, and he's never aged a day." She describes him as being between thirty and forty years old, dressed in cotton jeans and a sandy brownish shirt "the color of fall leaves," wearing a cap with a brim that doesn't conceal his gentle, compelling eyes.

At first, she says, she was too awed to know how to respond. But as she got older, she learned to ask him questions. "He's very calm. He explains things in a way I won't forget, and he never rushes." The being has shown her ways to lessen the negative impact of events that would happen in the future, and has helped her with family problems. He always talks in an archaic Cree dialect. "Either he doesn't know English, or he refuses to speak it!" Sylvia, living in a culture in which such experiences are normative, does not feel she created her "grandfather" through an act of imagination, or that he symbolizes a grandfatherly aspect of herself, or a "wise old man archetype." He simply *is,* just as much, in his own way, as she herself is. "He once told me," she says, "'We came to help you, and you to help us.'"

Her simple statement neatly encapsulates the mutual need for concourse that connects the dreamer and the invisible community. "It's like I have two jobs," she says, "one during the day and one at night. There's so much they want me to learn. Sometimes I have to ask them to leave me alone for a while."

She laughs, but her pixie-ish face looks momentarily careworn. Sylvia works as a play therapist for children suffering the ravages of reservation life—fetal alcohol syndrome, abuse, and families losing hope. Her dreams sometimes show her ceremonies to be performed by her tribe for restoration and healing. She feels she must not only transcribe the dreams as accurately as she can, but see that the visions become reality. "It's a big responsibility to receive them," she says. Once she was shown a special drum ritual whose name she whispers but asks me not to repeat. ("My elders would be mad at me—these are secrets.") Her dream teachers once showed her how to construct a special lodge, down to the position of the offering fire and where the specific sacred foods were to be placed on the altars. When she described it in a council, one very old man rocked back on his heels. *"Who taught you that?"* he demanded, astonished. He had recognized it as an obscure historic rite not performed in her area for two hundred years. The preparation to bring such a dream to life requires time, expense, and emotional investment. "Spiritual is not a category, it's every moment of life," Sylvia says. "It's what you do seven days a week, three hundred sixty-five days a year, waking or sleeping. The spirit world helps me, and I help them in return."

Hearing Voices

Sylvia's compact with the spirit world is an ancient one, deeply embedded in tribal tradition. For a modern Western person suddenly enveloped in such dreams, the task of understanding—of making relationship—may be more difficult. What seems culturally exotic or anachronistic becomes burningly relevant. One wonders, faced with a dream-being, the same things as if any stranger had come through the door: *Who are you? Where are you from? What do you want?* Such encounters elicit emotions ranging from amazement, fear, delight, and even indignation.

My own most vivid brush with the invisible community took place during a ferociously condensed period of a few months. At an agonized choice point in my medical journey, I had abruptly felt haunted and hovered over by, for want of a better word, presences. In one visitation, *I am shown a glistening green field with an aquamarine stream meandering through it, the scene as lucid as a Tibetan scroll painting. I see an ancient glass bottle hovering in midair, its pure water being spilled out by an invisible hand, until half is emptied on the ground. The air feels heavy with menace. "This," thunders a voice, "is the doing of Hecate!"*

I had first identified the bottle with my thyroid gland, a vessel containing very waters of life. Half of it was slated to be removed in surgery, a prospect that made me queasy. But who was Hecate? I vaguely recalled her as a witch in a Shakespeare play. When I looked her up in *Bullfinch's Mythology,* I discovered she was a Roman deity, a mistress of magic and sender of nightmares "mighty to shatter every stubborn thing." I was only later to discover that Hecate was also associated with dream interpretation itself. Known as *phosphoros*—a substance that shines in darkness—she embodied, suggests analyst James Hillman, the principle that what is born in the dark must also be seen in the dark: we must submit to a dream's mystery, that is, before we can solve it. To approach dreams according to the way of this goddess is to first "abandon attempts to find their dayworld use."[1]

Though in waking reality we map the route of our own destinies, Hecate, who was the guardian of unmarked crossroads, proclaims that we cannot detour around her. If we wish to change our fate, we must acknowledge her dream-doings in our viscera. At my own fateful crossroads, not knowing where to turn, I heard in more than one dream a voice making oracular pronouncements, usually in one or two sentences I could remember word for word. It was not a version of my own voice, nor the voice of anyone I've known. It was often very loud, like a shout in a great hall, or a proclamation echoing like thunder down a valley. It was as genderless as the voice chip on an answering machine. Part of me wanted to stopper my ears; part of me desperately wanted to keep listening.

I was to discover in later research that this voice is not uncommon in Healing Dreams. Sylvia calls it an "intercom voice," describing it as if coming from a loudspeaker: "That voice doesn't mince words. It tells it like it is. It hits a sore spot sometimes, like if I'm procrastinating, or need to change an unhealthy behavior." She describes the voice as "booming," as does Dr. Brugh Joy, who refers to "the booming voice [in my dream] that led me out of medicine." A Navajo man once told an anthropologist how his people identified a bona fide dream spirit: "When our ears ring, he is telling us what to do, for he has been out and traveling, and is trying to give us a message."

Anthropologists have commented on the "imperative mood" and "didactic speech" of the presences described by Native American visionaries. The beings use an "authoritative structure of communication," often a "direct address in the form of commands or instructions" that are "exceedingly brief and condensed." Jung, who observed that "archetypes speak the language of high rhetoric, even of bombast,"[2] believed the occurrence of a voice in the dream most often represented "some truth or condition that is beyond all doubt." St. Teresa of Avila, however, who spoke in detail about the "locutions" bestowed on her ("The words are perfectly formed, but are not heard with the physical ear. . . . I have to listen whether I like it or not") cautioned that some voices come from "good spirits," some from "evil ones," and some are "caused by the intellect itself, or by the spirit talking to itself."[3]

The latter is an astute psychological comment: such voices could be speaking for one's disowned perception. It is true that we tend to deny our awareness, often missing the subliminal cues trickling in from the peripheries of consciousness. But such explanations are inadequate to an experience invariably described in terms of a powerful sense of "otherness," where one is "taken" elsewhere, "shown" or "told" things by a mysterious guiding presence. Exclaimed the Persian sage Rumi: "Everyone understands this voice when it comes. It speaks with the same authority to Turk and Kurd, Persian Arab, Ethiopian, one language!"

A thirty-four-year-old accountant named Wanda was offered a lucrative new position in another state just as she discovered her New York company was about to be liquidated. She meditated one night before bed, promising to faithfully follow any guidance she might receive, and had an unusually vivid dream: *I am in an open country setting. I am struck by the vibrancy and richness of the green of the grass. In the Voice that I distinctly know as that of my guide, I am invited to accompany it on a tour.*

In the dream, she walked through the building of her new prospective job, feeling the seduction of its power and prestige. Then she was shown her childhood home and her parents, and told by the Voice that it would be a significant betrayal if she took the job. The Voice said, in a typical proverblike utterance, "It is as important to know when to leave as when to stay."

Sitting on the page, the words sound like a bromide. But it is the peculiar quality of such dream voices to give even the most banal-sounding sentiment the weight of revelation. Wanda woke up deeply impressed; turning the phrase over in her mind. Pondering its implications, she felt she had been given her answer. She decided "with trembling heart" to turn down the job, not knowing what might follow. A few months later, on a car trip down the eastern seaboard, she stumbled upon a North Carolina town whose vibrant greenery strongly reminded her of her dream landscape. Though she had "never in my god-awfulest moments" imagined living in the South, she sensed this was to be her new home. (This was confirmed in another dream by her "guide Voice," which stated simply: "This is where you are to be.") She has lived there happily, in a new life and new profession, for over a decade. About the Voice, she says, "It has never ever lied. It communicates on an entirely different level. There is no time or space dimension in it, yet it is intensely personal. This Voice does not say, 'You must obey.' It just shows me."[4]

Sometimes an authoritative voice presenting spiritual instruction in a dream sounds like the very voice of "God," such is its aura of ultimate authority and illimitable wisdom. A man told me how, when he was a college student uncertain what direction to take, he was addressed by a dream voice: *I hear the word HELP! It's the loudest word I've ever heard, but uttered in a strange monotone, like a radio. I think I must be dying. I wake bolt upright, heart pounding.* "After I thought about it," he says, "I decided the voice was both the earth and God calling out, saying 'Help Me.' It is a strange idea, to think that God might need human help, but this was my clear impression." (The notion that Creation depends on us is a paradoxical insight of many mystics, as expressed by the poet Rilke: "All becoming has needed me / My looking ripens things.") The man finished college and then entered the ministry, feeling he'd received a draft notice from a place at once far above him and right beneath his feet.

His experience is not dissimilar to that of a young Catholic named Anthony, who at age twelve heard a voice from the sky saying, "You must become a priest." Anthony was bewildered—having attended a strict Catholic school, he had no real interest in the priesthood and felt a terrible conflict over this inner calling. But there was a crucial difference: his story is a case study in *The Interpretation of Schizophrenia*. Having chosen a career as a mathematician, Anthony had begun in adulthood exhibiting "schizoid tendencies" and obsessive disorders. The root of his problems, his therapist determined, was a lingering psychic wound from a hypercritical, domineering mother, whose voice he had internalized.

Freud once commented that the superego is largely auditory. Perhaps this accounts for the voices heard by, say, paranoid psychotics, which are often those of some parental, castigating deity. Psychologist Julian Jaynes characterizes the range of voices heard by schizophrenics: "They converse, threaten, curse, criticize, consult, often in short sentences. They admonish, console, mock, command, or sometimes simply announce everything that's happening."

Psychiatrists use the term "command hallucinations" to refer to experiences in which patients are ordered by God, Jesus, the devil, demons, aliens, or the like to perform certain deeds—anything from saving the world to committing mayhem. Aside from the issue of clinical pathology, a certain healthy skepticism is justified when it comes to visions. Even the mystic St. John of the Cross recognized the need for discrimination and analysis, dispensing sound psychological advice in theological terms: "The devil causes many to believe in vain visions and false prophecies, and strives to make them presume that God and the saints are speaking with them; and they often trust their own fancy."

Every spiritual tradition speaks of various classes of, as it were, God's authorized representatives. In the Jewish tradition, for example, the angel

Gabriel acted as an appointed intermediary "to bring man to God and God to man." Writes one commentator: "The dream is a manifestation of God in search of humanity and of our human need to recognize our own innate divine powers."[5] Jung placed such dream figures under his definition of archetypes, which he saw as emissaries from some deeper source of wisdom. Though they could be regarded symbolically, the archetypes also seemed to have "their own initiative." They could, he wrote, "interfere in a given situation with their own impulses and their own thought formations. . . . They come and go very much as they please, and often they obstruct or modify our conscious intentions in an embarrassing way." It is similar to the way Tibetan Buddhists conceive of the deities of their iconography, from the fierce *mahakalas* to the playful *dakinis*—as self-existing life energies, agents provocateurs of greater awareness, personifications of that aspect of consciousness that will peck diligently at the eggshell of ego until a truer selfhood hatches out.

I once asked spiritual teacher Chögyam Trungpa Rinpoche if he understood the Tibetan pantheon to be literally real. "Not exactly," he said, and I felt a swell of relief at Buddhism's cool rationalism, its wakeful regard for the particulars of *this* world. But then he smiled again, grating his molars together, loudly, the way the Khampas of his native province do when they want you to know they mean business. His grin turned tigerish. "That's why they can get in anywhere. Come right in your window—or through the walls!"

Having imaginal characters that one seemingly has not created tearing around one's psychic dwelling place is a vertiginous experience. One is confronted by something that is at once both "inside" and utterly "beyond." The Western mind finds such experiences deeply disturbing. When the poet Robert Duncan was given hallucinogenic mescaline in 1952 in an experiment conducted by Stanford University, he had a vivid vision of what he called "the World Tree," huge and jeweled like a mosaic. As awed as he was by its majesty, he burst into tears when he realized he was "seeing something I hadn't made, I hadn't drawn, and that somebody else hadn't made." What perturbed him was that his creative process didn't seem to be the sole source of this magnificence. It not only flew in the face

182 · *Healing Dreams*

of his "refusal to have any mystical experience," his credo of the concrete and immediate—it flouted his insistence that, like a Muslim rug that takes a lifetime to knot, his life would be "made out of thousands of threads that I myself have tied, thread by thread."

Such experiences threaten our psychic autonomy, our well-settled habitation of our own minds and bodies. That Western civilization, particularly under the guidance of the Church, turned away from such things is reflected in the dictionary's rendering of the word *daemon:* the first definition is "an inspiring or inner spirit"; the second, "a demon; a devil." Though daemons were viewed in the ancient world as guides, guardians, and sources of inspiration existing midway between the divine and the human, Christian doctrine is full of warnings like St. Paul's: "Ye cannot drink out of the cup of daemons and the cup of the Lord."

In the view of such thinkers, the psyche must be, like a monotheistic God, only singular. But this is at odds with the plurality of our makeup. The daemons/demons of our dreams put a face on our full human potential for good or ill. We feel their presence when we are consumed by a powerful urge, on fire to manifest an idea, or driven by a talent that craves embodiment. We acknowledge them in our language when we speak of the "green-eyed demon" of jealousy, call a great racer a "speed demon" or a superb mathematician a "demon with numbers." We crave their inspiration; we fear their possession. We don't wish to be "taken over," yet who does not long to be seized by a great passion or a transcendent thought?

In dreams, we experience our inner universe as a tumult of beings of varying purpose and appearance demanding true engagement. We can glimpse, in the Roman Apuleius's description of the daemon, what we stand to lose by denying them outright: "our guardian; our watcher at home, our own proper regulator, a searcher into our inmost fibres, our constant observer, our inseparable witness, a reprover of our evil actions, an approver of our good ones . . . our forewarner in uncertainty, our monitor in matters of doubt, our defender in danger, and our assistant in need."[6]

The poet Yeats wrote of his own visionary encounters with "the Daimon, who would ever set us to the hardest work among those not impossible," adding, "I am persuaded that the Daimon delivers *and* deceives us."[7] Discussing the archetypes, Jung advised that such images be carefully interrogated. He suggested a middle path, whereby we "expose ourselves" to the archetypes "without identifying with them, and without running away, for flight from the unconscious would defeat the purpose of the whole proceeding. We must hold our ground."[8]

We usually react to our predicaments in dreams as we might in waking life. I most often experience my dream-self as a responsible, reasonable, even aggrieved party. It is the *others,* whether dazzling or menacing, sublime or ridiculous, who seem to make all the trouble. But the dream ego—the part that feels like "me" in the dream—is the point of view that's already known. It is precisely the "outsiders" of the invisible community who contain an unknown portion of being. They bear the unassimilated parts of our personality of which we are most needful, yet which the ego often deems least worthy—or secretly feels least worthy *of.* They splay out before us our unlived lives; immerse us in unfamiliar feelings and disturbing new perspectives, desires and terrors and wisdom barred to a narrower selfhood. We may ignore them if they seem too humble, flee from them if they seem too awful (or too majestic), distance ourselves from them until we hear only faint echoes of their voices on the breeze. Yet they remain, awaiting only the ripening of our appetite (and fortitude) for discovery.

In our encounters with the invisible community, hermeneutics—the science of interpretation named for Hermes, quicksilver messenger of the gods—becomes paramount. But Hermes (also known as Mercurius, the "mercurial" essence of change) symbolizes the slipperiness of meaning itself. In the Middle Ages, he was seen sometimes as "a ministering or helpful spirit, a comrade and assistant," other times as an "elusive, deceptive, teasing goblin." Contradictions do not magically disappear in the realm of the archetypes. Imaginal beings can be inscrutable, even two-faced, in their dealings. They are not mere symbolic stand-ins but vital mysteries. We do not always welcome, or even recognize, these instigators of growth, these torchbearers from parts unknown. Perhaps an unease at their shapeshifting ambiguity was behind the ancients' obsession with intricately codifying the invisible realm. The third-century Greek philosopher Iamblichus catalogued "distinctions among imaginal persons in terms of their beauty, their motion, their luminosity and energy." He maintained, for example, that the heroic *phasmata* were "subject to motion and chance and show magnificence; that angels do not speak; and that daimons give rise to dread, but their operations are not as rapid as they appear to be."

Many cultures had almost hairsplitting hierarchies of such figures. The gods of Olympus were said to dispatch specific intermediaries for certain purposes. Telesphoros brought true dreams. In the *Iliad,* Oneiros, a more general dream god, was sent by Zeus to stand at Agamemnon's head and tell him to go to war; yet it is Hermes who visits Preon to warn him he is sleeping among enemies. To the Hopis, the water spirit Palulukon appears specifically to condemn the dreamer for sexual misconduct or aggression. Among the Maricopa, the eagle tells the dreamer he will become a great singer.

Religious training has always included spiritual exercises—the rapt contemplation of statues and paintings, the repeated visualizing of deities in every detail—to ready the initiate for a direct encounter with a higher wisdom, and provide the ineffable with suitable raiment. Thus, the "dream-teacher" experience could be interpreted according to which recognizable form they chose to manifest. Our civilization has impoverished us of these ancient symbols and practices without providing substitutes.[9]

How can we know when, or how, or even whether to pay heed to the numinous inhabitants of our dreams? I can recall being carefully quizzed by a Tibetan *tulku,* or incarnate lama, when years later I described my own strange experiences to him. What time of the night did I have these dreams? he wanted to know. (Tibetans consider the hours leading up to dawn as the domain of prophetic dreaming.) Did I see the figures or just hear them? After ten minutes of questioning, the lama gazed at me with equanimity. "Sometimes," he said, "you might consider doing what they tell you."

Dream Icons

Though members of other cultures grow up with their gods, we grow up with pop stars and politicians, magnified through television as effectively as the gods were evoked in rituals and epic recitations around a fire. I have been surprised to note that Healing Dreams often press these modern icons into service, imbuing them with the qualities the ancients found in their deities. In a charming book entitled *I Dream of Madonna,* the author collected dreams in which the chameleonlike diva appears as a cross between Aphrodite and the blessed Virgin Mary, an angel of female empowerment, comfort, and a sort of divine mischief.

One thirty-nine-year-old woman dreamed of ascending to the third floor of a house owned by a group of feminists. It had a skylight through which she could observe the starry panoply of the evening. She gazed up in wonder and expectancy, and

> *in one sudden, miraculous moment, Madonna appeared in and across the wide expanse of night sky. She was a projection, an apparition, a Madonna in the flesh and performance all at the same time. She was visible to everyone looking at the sky at that time. The effect on me was total. I realized in a great surge of revelation that this was what we were working toward all this time, that this was the dimension I had missed.*

Another middle-aged woman dreamed she was helping a friend prepare a TV special about Madonna. As they talked about the goddess, she realized her friend was dressed in a gold-flecked gown with a blue cowl and had turned into the Virgin of Guadalupe. In her dream, she shook and became tongue-tied. The Virgin offered her a drink of "mother's milk" in a plastic medicine cup. Yet another woman dreamed of Madonna in a floor-length blue velvet robe. Madonna took her to a bathroom lit with votive candles, bathing her tenderly as her song "Like a Prayer" played on the dream's "soundtrack." A halo of golden light appeared behind Madonna's head as she *poured water from her hands down my forehead. . . . After finishing this ritual, she wrapped me in a warm fluffy towel and led me back to my bed. That glow round her head was still there, and as I looked up at it she bent to kiss me and then disappeared. I felt like I had been baptized by love and sex, that Madonna had somehow cleansed me of past experiences with a violent ex-lover. In the dream I experienced great relief from letting go of these painful memories, and I cried with joy from Madonna's gift.*

Here, truly "like a Virgin," Madonna dispenses blessings, protection, mystical sacraments, spiritual cleansing, healing. The persona of an often vapid pop star becomes a container for primal spiritual forces. We might imagine that a number of the demigods of other cultures were once living, charismatic "stars" apotheosized into supernatural status when they began appearing in people's Healing Dreams.

The Church has declared the singer Madonna sacrilegious. But it has also been made uneasy by a rash of Marian visions that in recent years have cropped up around the world, drawing adherents to what might be called unauthorized Virgin Mary sightings. Direct personal communication with the divine bypasses churches entirely (perhaps one reason St. Paul attributed to daemons the sin of disobedience). If in waking life we submit ourselves to many authorities—the needs of family; the judgments of society; the requirements of employers, loan officers, tax accountants, and traffic cops; the catechisms of church or temple—the invisible community cares little for conventional hierarchies. The dreamer is faced with an inner authority independent of the outer world. Official scripture may pale beside an original, signed epistle delivered straight into one's hands, its ink still drying. Some such experiences may be, by any standards, purely self-delusional. Others are those instances when the "mask of God" becomes translucent; when we glimpse behind the façade a terrible glory, an unbearable solicitude, an inimical reflection, or a surpassing sweetness. In such moments, perhaps we are being taught something nonnegotiable, in words straight from the lips of insatiable Truth.

Of Answering Angels

Jewish mystical life from the sixteenth to the eighteenth centuries was inhabited by supernatural guides called *maggid* (literally, "one who relates," a term used for itinerant preachers). Also known as "answering angels," such beings were said to appear in dreams in response to waking queries, bearing helpful, divinely mediated replies.

According to Hayim Vital, a disciple and chronicler of the great sixteenth-century cabalist Isaac Luria, the quality of one's own *maggid* depended on one's level of spiritual achievement. "Sometimes the *maggidim* are true, and some there are such as tell lies." In fact, he asserts, the angels' very creation springs from the deeds of the person to whom they appear, "therefore their nature will be in accordance with these actions." (Scholar Harold Bloom comments that an angel "whose capacity for deceit depends upon the relative virtue of his human creator is a remarkable image for the equivocal nature of dreams.")[10]

A Sufi sheikh once told me there are three spiritual levels of dreaming: "At a higher level of consciousness, you're at a holy place, or with a great teacher or an angel of light. These are direct revelations that require no interpretation. You're actually there. At the intermediate level, it is like hearing a wonderful teaching story, a beautiful sermon translated into a few movie images that convey an hour's worth of talking. Then at a basic level, there's the work on your personality, childhood issues, sexual things for which you don't need a sheikh—you can ask your therapist!" He, too, claimed that the type of dream experience one had depended on one's spiritual attainment.

I cannot strictly hold with this meritocratic view: the "gods" speak loudly to sinners and saints alike (though the difference may lie in the capacity to understand and willingness to follow). Among the Kagwahiv people, shamans, who were powerful dreamers, were described as *ipaji,* or possessed of power. But it was also said that "anyone who dreams has a little *ipaji.*"[11] "Perfectly ordinary people can have utterly extraordinary dreams; exceptional people can have pedestrian ones. It's been my observation that most dream-beings tend to be anti-inflationary, more like the homespun "angel second class" depicted in the movie *It's a Wonderful Life* than the heavenly creatures with archangel wingspans seen in Renaissance paintings.

Karl, a soft-spoken midwesterner in his forties, has had a lifelong relationship with such instructive dream figures. Raised in a fundamentalist family where even mentioning dreams was taboo, in an Iowa town of six hundred souls where dreams were condemned from the pulpit as the devil's lure for the virtuous, Karl learned early to keep his experiences to himself. "I didn't dare even *read* anything about dreams. It was like a revelation to me when I grew up and found books that said this stuff happened to other people."

Throughout childhood, Karl told me, he lived "a parallel existence," protecting this "treasured" side of his life, speaking of it to no one. His dreams, he says, were "the more real part." A deliberative talker, he chews over each word as if tasting it for the first time. "I learned about the things I wasn't getting in my waking life—like lessons in what you might call emotional intelligence." From as early as he can remember, he had encountered a particular guide in his dreams, a thirtyish woman with long dark hair, gentle and good-humored. "I've been in love with her all my life. Although I'm physically attracted to her, the love I feel for her is much more than sexual. In fact, I've never had a sexual dream involving her. She taught me how to deal with my emotions, especially my anger, my tendency to lash out. She would never scold me—she would reward me with her presence whenever I had done something well."

The woman disappeared in his own early thirties, telling him there was nothing more she could do to help him. It was a farewell, and Karl was devastated. Later, she reappeared, but the relationship had changed: "Now we're more on an equal footing, though we both miss the way things once were." In recent years, a girl has been added to the relationship who seems to be the woman's daughter, "a very exuberant, unrestrained teenager; I seem to be her mentor."

Karl's dreamworld is less an exotic realm than a neighborhood populated by long-term friends, acquaintances, and even rivals: he occasionally dreams about "someone who seems to be a sort of nature god, powerfully built, with dark bronze skin, green plantlike hair, and piercing eyes. He has a deep distrust of people in general, and of me in particular. He seems to be the father of the dark-haired woman. He told me he'd be watching me, and that if I made a mistake, I'd regret it." Karl shakes his head. "He is a challenge."

Such a dream seems to fairly beg for Freudian interpretation. Karl describes his mother as cold and distant. His childhood longing to be cuddled by her went unrequited. We might paint a scenario that, lacking the motherly nurturance he craved, Karl's psyche conjured up a dream woman as an oasis in an emotional desert. In a Freudian interpretation, the muscular nature god might be a child's-eye view of a threatening father, a symbol of unresolved Oedipal conflicts stirred up by his desire for his mother's embrace. But Karl, who functions at a healthy level in his waking life, does not see his odd companions as ambulatory symbols. They are who they are, he insists, with personalities as subtly different as real people.

He finds their presence in his life mysterious and edifying, though he is often at a loss to understand the purpose of their comings and goings. Once, he says, "I had a dream in which I barged into a meeting in what looked like a corporate board room, and there were *all* my recurring dream people! I got upset—it was like they were secretly strategizing behind my back. I told them that in the future, I'd appreciate it if they'd cut out the mumbo-jumbo and tell me straight out what was on their minds, instead of using all these symbols! I remember a white-haired man—this gruff, stocky guy in his late fifties who always teases me and pokes fun at my shortcomings—laughing his head off over this."

Like the Greek gods, such figures sometimes seem to take a certain delight in befuddling mortals, posing riddles, seducing us into trying to catch the wind or lasso the moon. A friend told me about a dream that underscored the autonomous lifeways of such dream folk:

I'm in some sort of clinic. I ask the woman behind the counter, "If this is a dream, can I touch you?" She says, "Yes." I reach out and shake her hand. To my amazement, her hand is warm and solid and feels just like the outer world.

> *Then I turn to a nurse walking down the hallway, and she gives a glance to the woman behind the counter, sort of like, "Oh, she figured it out." I get a tremendous feeling that this is their life, walking around in dreams, just like we have jobs out here. The nurse says something like, "Now that you know this is a dream, you know that we have a lot of information on you."*

It is an attitude that anyone who has encountered such figures would recognize—a wry, even sardonic amusement at our attempts to reduce them to mere representations, any more than we ourselves would submit to being viewed as game pieces in another's mind game.

Joining the Invisible Community

In our society, concourse with the invisible realm and the "information" it offers is generally viewed with some disfavor. Descriptions of individuals who talk regularly with dream spirits are found mostly in anthropological reports of tribal societies—and are thought to properly belong there. But I have met through my research a surprising number of dreamers whose life history would be instantly recognizable to any indigenous elder. These are people who, in a sense, live within the invisible community, counting its members as part of their own circle. Though in another culture they might be overtly identified as shamans, they work in all vocations, from businessmen to environmentalists, artists to scientists. They seem to cluster in what are known as the helping professions—not surprisingly, for in indigenous societies, most shamans are also healers.

If there could be a typical cross-cultural profile for those who have such experiences, it would be roughly this: A child has precocious visionary experiences (Sylvia says she remembers leaving her body and "flying with the birds" when she was still in her cradle); hears voices and sees invisible companions; suffers a bout with life-threatening illness; finds a mentor who provides reassurance and instruction (the biblical seer Samuel, born in a time of skepticism about prophecy, was encouraged by the elder, Eli); receives spiritual pedagogy in dreams, including an unfolding exposition of a life mission (the dream teacher may even begin appearing as a daylight apparition); finally embarks, sometimes with no little inner resistance, on a life of compassionate service.

Our culture does not generally acknowledge much distinction between this type of giftedness and mental illness. Indeed, in some people, the syndrome may be symptomatic of (or lead to) delusions of grandeur, "possession," or a general inability to distinguish between fantasy and reality. But even when the shoals of childhood are successfully navigated, and an odd talent reconciled with the business of ordinary life, such a calling often portends a life of some hardship and austerity. Such people are, in a sense, always on call, exquisitely sensitized to subtle influences, whether from the other world or this one, and faced with the difficulty of finding sympathetic companions.

I first met Laura Lawrence when she got up to speak—hesitantly at first, but then with mesmerizing conviction—at a medical seminar. A psychiatrist with graying blond hair and calm, slate blue eyes, she convincingly recounted a personal healing she attributed to a vivid dream. Years later, a scrap of paper with her phone number surfaced from a pile of notes, leading to a series of extraordinary conversations that detailed the life history of a modern shaman.

As far back as she can remember, Laura's dreams have been filled with unseen presences she often refers to as "the We" because of their characteristic first-person plural style of address. She can think of no other term for this "intelligence beyond mine," which she says "taught me the rules of empathy" as early as kindergarten. "My mother tells me that I might be upset if a kid was mean to me, but if he was cruel to other kids, I was inconsolable. I felt their pain more than my own." Her acute sensitivity caused her emotional turmoil: "I remember thinking about suicide when I was five, only I didn't know how." Then one afternoon, lying on her back gazing at the sky, she had a transcendent experience. "I was no longer my body. There was just this sense of the vastness of universe. I felt I was completely connected with everything around me, yet at the same time, just a little speck in this enormous creation." (Hers is as good a description as I've heard of what scholars of mysticism term the *mysterium tremendum,* absorption in the grandeur of the cosmos.)

In keeping with the life story of many shamans, Laura suffered a serious illness: "They thought I had leukemia when I was a teenager," but she claims her blood-test markers mysteriously normalized after several powerful meditation experiences. (Though misdiagnosis remains the most likely explanation, her story is uncannily similar to one Sylvia told me. She, too, was once diagnosed with leukemia. Then she had a vivid dream that she was in a coffin, but "I didn't want to be there, so I just climbed out of it and continued to 'walk my day.'" A month later, her doctors discovered that her blood counts had returned to normal, attributing it to a misdiagnosis.) Laura's own cycle of suffering and healing, she says, solidified her connection with "the We," giving her a sense of being "part of something much bigger. The pain was happening for a reason that would unfold one day, though I didn't know when."

It helped lead to her career as a doctor of the mind, though she is hard-pressed to find normative descriptions of her dreamlife in psychiatric texts. She describes a special category of dream in which she seems to inhabit other characters. "I'll experience firsthand the different viewpoints of these 'dream people;' I'll feel their personalities, even have their memories—as if I *am* them."

She cites a repetitive dream that unfolded in growing detail over a period of months, in which her central identity was a twelve-year-old Cambodian girl in a small, poor village. "I am living a wonderful life," she recalls with a small smile. "My family is close, we have relatives in the neighboring village." In the dream, she returns from a visit to her aunts and uncles to find her town burned to the ground, her family murdered. "It's pure devastation. I feel such an intensity of feeling, such horror, that I want to die of grief."

She sees village children emerging from the forest where they had hidden during the massacre, all younger than she, crying and terrified, begging her to help. She feels an unfamiliar sensation arise from deep within her twelve-year-old selfhood, an iron resolve to get them all to safety. As the dream unfolds, she and her small retinue are captured by enemy soldiers and forced on a death march. Twice, late at night, they try to escape, and twice they are caught and threatened with instant execution. But they make a third attempt, fleeing into the woods, shaking with fear as the soldiers' boots clomp through the grass by their hiding place.

Finally, the frightened young band straggles toward an isolated farmhouse. At first the farmer wants to turn them over to the soldiers, but the wife argues, and finally, with much misgiving, he yields to her. The farmwife contacts a charity group that has been spiriting refugee Cambodian children out of the war zone. They are taken to a European city and finally to America and safety.

Laura had this vivid dream over and over again. She would wake up to hear "the We" audibly telling her, "We will send you this until you pay attention." Then it stopped. She had no idea what to make of it. It had seemed so real, but she could extract little personal meaning from it and laid it aside.

Six months later, a Cambodian engineer was referred to her practice. A mother with several young children, she had developed carpal tunnel syndrome and could no longer function at her job. She had begun to feel suicidal. When Laura asked her to recount her life history, the psychiatrist was stunned to hear the very story she had been dreaming, reproduced in every detail.

Typically, Laura does not recount this as an amazing anecdote of the occult, but in terms of how it assisted her in diagnosis and treatment. "It was helpful to have, in a sense, experienced her life from the inside, to be so aware of her personality, her strength, her survivor's guilt. I got her to open up to the horrible grief at seeing her home and family destroyed, which had added so much sadness to her current situation. Her remorse had deep roots."

Laura let nothing slip of the foreknowledge that had magnified her empathy a thousandfold. But inevitably, a moment came when the woman stopped in midsentence, stared at her hard, and said, her voice trembling, "I know you know all about this. How *can* you?" Only then did Laura tell her about her dream, right down to specific people she'd seen thrown to the ground, bayoneted or kicked to death when they could no longer keep up with the parade to a killing field. The woman listened, her hand clamped on her mouth, eyes welling with tears. When Laura told of a man who had been murdered in a particularly agonizing way to dissuade anyone else from considering escape, the two women wept together at what was, in effect, a shared memory of a season in hell. Laura had been "told," at the end of her dream, that the young woman had decided to become an engineer to honor her slain father. Here was the key to unlock the deep despair she felt at being unable to function in her chosen profession.

On another occasion, Laura had a series of dreams in which she was living the life of a stunning girl in her twenties: "She had a super body, in great shape, very attractive, if maybe a little cheap." The young woman had bleached-blond hair and painstakingly applied maquillage. She wore seductive short skirts, had a boyfriend who was a heavy cocaine user, and was sexually promiscuous. Laura, a classically trained psychiatrist, might under other circumstances have interpreted her dream in psychological terms: here was a dream creation of her own suppressed libido, or a personification—albeit caricatured as a kind of "inner slut"—of a sexy, outrageous flair she needed to integrate into her personality.

But she had instantly recognized in her dream production the directorial signature of "the We." One day, a middle-aged secretary suffering from severe depression was referred to her. "She was very plain-looking, no makeup, limp brown hair, overweight. She had been involved with an emotionally abusive man on and off. When I asked her about her past, she refused to talk about it. A few sessions into treatment, I suddenly realized *this* was the woman from my dreams."

Laura could hardly trust the association—the dream figure couldn't have been more different from the wan, demoralized creature before her. After she had seen the woman for several months without being able to pry out a word about her past, Laura asked a single, pointed question about sex. Then the floodgates opened. Out tumbled a lurid tale of a Ferrari-driving, sex-partner-swapping coke dealer she had fallen in love with in her early twenties, and a reference to a traumatic wild party. The woman then fell silent, clearly mortified. 'I've never told anyone about this," she said, her voice thick with emotion. She started and halted, then sat in silence. Finally, Laura told her she'd had a dream she thought was about her. 'What was I wearing?' the woman asked, testing her.

When Laura described the outfit she had seen, indeed, had worn in her own dreams—"an outrageous, bright red bustier, cut so low cut it barely covers my nipples; tight black leather miniskirt; black stockings with a seam up the back; and four-inch heels"—the woman gazed at her, shocked, then said in small, subdued voice, "God gave you that dream so you could understand me." The woman poured out the sordid story of the orgiastic affair that began her descent into a life of empty, self-hating debauchery. It came out in a single, cathartic rush that proved to be the turning point of her therapy. Later the woman told her, wonderingly, "All these months, you'd known, but you didn't judge me, because *you* were there, too."

Unlike many new-age visionaries, eager to market themselves in pricey workshops, Laura has shunned the limelight, preferring to be left alone to do her healing work with those patients who cross her path. She finds herself periodically subject to roaring influxes of information in her dreams, which she describes as a "disembodied exchange of knowledge." She struggles to describe the quality of this experience, which feels like "a flow of compressed data coming in so rapidly I can't begin to interpret it, but afterwards, I just know more." She laughs self-consciously. "I know it sounds grandiose."

Laura, who says some of her patients refer to her as "the witch doctor," is still trying to come to terms with her gifts, still on a learning curve with her mysterious tutors. "The We," she says, "always indicated this was to be a hands-on lab course. Definitely *not* an academic survey." Though Laura's "data transmission" is unusual, hers is the typical Healing Dream pedagogy that instructs through powerful subjective experience. Such dreams often push us beyond ourselves, insisting we must inhabit foreign skins, see with strange eyes, feel with others' senses.

Some dream teaching has the character of what Hindus call *darshan* ("holy presence")—Buddhists call it *abhiseka* (literally, "a sprinkling") or "pointing-out instruction"—in which an actual state of consciousness is said to be transmitted from guru to student. Some dreams have a similar quality of initiation. I spoke to an award-winning photographer named Gary, whose ethereal images are often inspired by dream symbolism. But the dreams that have been most important to him, that remained with him indelibly years later, were those which made him feel—in his heart, in his gut—a potential for authentic being. He unhesitatingly called one to mind:

> *I am in a windswept desert, arguing with God, who wants me to do something more than I feel capable of. There is an old man over my right shoulder, walking behind me, whom I can't see. He interrupts my diatribe and I hear his voice: "You don't understand—God wants you to do what you really want to do!" Then a dust devil arises and whirls me around. I look up, and am awed to see the moon and stars and sky wheeling around me.*

Gary says his dream didn't so much change his ideas about life but subtly influenced the way life *felt:* "It left me with the distinct impression that wholeness really is possible." It is as if he had been spun for a moment on some central cosmic axis, like the biblical Joseph, who dreamed the very moon and stars had bowed to him. The dream's offering was the unique sensation of being centered and complete. I was deeply moved by the poignancy in his tone. Arguing with "what God wants" is what we all too commonly do—to embody what is most heartfelt can often be more difficult than halfheartedness. Like many of us, Gary often feels himself to be made up of contesting selves, inner contradictions pulling one against the other. The dream has given him an enduring sneak preview of a state of integrity. The special feeling is a homing device, guiding him toward life situations that radiate the same special sense of wholeness. Gary had a subsequent visit from another dream teacher:

> *I am on a golf course in a snowstorm. About twenty feet away, I see an Indian in full regalia—feathered headdress, a breastplate of bones, buckskin leggings. He doesn't seem to notice I'm there. He very deliberately puts a white tee in the snowy ground, and places the white ball on it. I watch as he takes a few practice swings, then in one graceful motion he arcs back his club—which also has feathers*

attached to it, like some ritual implement—and whacks the ball. It instantly dis-
appears into the snowstorm, though his gaze seems to follow its invisible trajec-
tory. Then he finally looks at me, his eyes peaceful and full of authority, and says
with a small smile, "Hole in One! " I am about to start angrily arguing with
him for being so sure of himself—I hate that attitude—when I wake up.

Gary professed not to understand his dream, only its strange admixture of agitation (his) and peace (the Indian's). I suggested he look at the pun: perhaps the dream was saying, "Whole in Oneself. Holy in One." He laughed aloud, clapping his hands: "That's it!"

Though we profess to crave it, we resist our fullest capacity for being. We look for it outside ourselves, but it remains invisible. Gary's dream is a droll iteration of the *mysterium tremendum,* where figure becomes ground in some primal purity of white on white, and our painful dichotomies merge into grace. The scenario is akin to a Zen archery demonstration: the target is beside the point. The point is to *lose* the point, to be immersed in a moment with no past, present, or future—a moment that emerges from nothing, disappears into nowhere. Through the beauty and dignity of his actions, the "golfing master" reveals that there is no goal, no bull's-eye, no eighteenth hole—only the journey.

A teacher, as anyone who studies with a wise guru or mentor finds, can't wave a magic wand (or a nine iron) to make us whole. But he or she can demonstrate that the thing is possible. Dream teachers, too, give us the experience of a state of being not normally accessible. Someone has played a clear, unquavering note for us; whenever we hear it in the chord and discord of this world, we resonate, and draw nearer its source.

The Teachings of the Just

Sometimes this note is sounded so early in life, with such clarity, that everything that follows is shaped by it. Myron Eshowsky is a short, powerfully built man whose streetwise persona is belied by a slight speech impediment, the product of partial deafness. A psychologist and social worker under contract in the state prison system, he is also a dreamer who, like Dr. Laura Lawrence, tells what amounts to a classic shamanic autobiography transposed into midwestern America.

Myron remembers feeling changed by an early, near-fatal bout of childhood pneumonia, after which, he claims, "I could sometimes tell my parents what would be in the next day's papers." By the age of five, he says, he was subject to visionary experiences—the psychologist in him knows others might call them fugue states—in which he would seem to enter a place deep inside the earth. "I would go to this city made out of gold, streets, buildings, everything," he says matter-of-factly, "with people walking around from thousands of years ago."

"I spent my early life in the spirit world," he says, "and my adulthood learning to be in ordinary life." Myron considers himself to be "self-raised"—his parents, discomfited by his strangeness, emotionally withdrew. His family life, he says tersely, "could feel pretty poisonous." Fortunately, he found a deliverer—his Russian Jewish great-aunt Soshie, a folk healer and "plant doctor" who revealed that she was descended from a long line of dreamers. She would hold his hand and demand that he confide his dreams. He described the mystifying ones of the "ancient men in old rabbinical robes with long beards and dark, Semitic features" who called themselves the Just Ones. "They were as real as real could be," he remembers. "They'd touch my hand and I'd feel it." When he described his visions, she nodded. "She'd tell me she knew about the places I went and the people I saw, but a lot of folks didn't, so I had to be careful who I talked to about it." It was Aunt Soshie who would light the candles in order to, as she put it, "vision through fire," chanting Yiddish and Hebrew prayers and promising to dream on Myron's behalf for wisdom.

Her dreams told her, she said, that he had been chosen. She told him the old wise men were ancestors who were watching over him, and who would gradually teach him the way of "taking others' suffering into your own soul in order to heal it." His aunt taught him to repeat special words he didn't understand, murmuring them like mantras. Soon the Just Ones would appear even when he was awake, emerging, he says, as if out of a "wall of mist."

To the modern ear, this is a disturbing picture: the "crazy old aunt" from the old country, imposing superstitions from the shtetl on an impressionable child with an already tenuous grasp on reality. But from another viewpoint, Myron was being apprenticed—trained, as shamans have always been, to cross between the visible and invisible worlds. This sort of tutelage is common in tribal societies—children gifted in dreaming are routinely guided by special elders to make contact with ancestral spirits. In Myron's dreams and visions, his teachers would sometimes explain the tangled intricacies of his family dynamics. He was once "told" that two of his aunts had been diagnosed psychotic, information he was able to confirm later. Depending on our perspective, we might see Myron as the incipient victim of hereditary disease who grew up in an intolerable family pressure cooker, or the recipient of an ancestral gift his unlucky aunts had not had the strength and guidance to creatively develop.

Not that Myron's path was smoothed before him. He grew up in 1950s Indianapolis, on the edge of a simmering black ghetto, in a section of town populated with "people from the Kentucky hills, Bible thumpers." In a neighborhood where the New Testament was part of the elementary school curriculum, his was the only Jewish family, and he grew up isolated, picked on as "a killer of Jesus." A respite from playground persecution only came when he was seven, and a Japanese American family with two sons had moved in. The two new boys quickly became the next scapegoats. One day, when the local bullies picked up rocks and began to chase them, Myron found his own hand tightening around a stone. He dropped it in horror, fleeing to the special spot in the woods where he did his dreaming.

"The Just Ones showed up," he recalls, "and I asked why those two kids were hated."

"What do you see in the eyes of those two boys?" the Just Ones asked.

"Wild, open-eyed fear," he responded.

"And in the eyes of the people that chase them?"

"The same wild-eyed fear look," young Myron said, wonderingly.

After years spent trying to put his strange experiences into context, Myron, today an accredited psychotherapist, formally identifies himself as a kind of urban shaman—although, he says, "Really, I just want to be an ordinary guy, drink beer, watch Green Bay Packers games."

But the Just Ones won't let him. One day, he says, he had a "strong dream," the special kind he calls a "spiritual visitation." A Just One appeared and "started showing me all these drive-by shootings in different cities by different gangs. Then he said, 'We want you to take it to the street. Bring healing.' He was emphatic." Myron says his first reaction to the dream was to protest. He knew nothing about gangs, had no idea how to even make contact with one. But at one o'clock the next afternoon, he got an unexpected call: a grass-roots organization he had never heard of wanted him to talk to a group of gang kids as part of an experimental class on spiritual development. Assured that only a handful of gang members were likely to show up, and that the staff would forward most of the questions, he assented.

When Myron arrived, the class had swelled to forty-five formidable-looking African-American kids decked out in gang regalia, rowdily demanding to hear "the shaman man." But as he told his story, they grew quiet. "When I started talking about how people would be called to be a healer in indigenous cultures, and about the invisible world, they stopped giving me shit." Long after the class was supposed to end, he spent hours talking with one kid at a time. "Each of them," he recalls, "was basically telling me ghost stories. People they had known who had gotten shot, family members, older brothers, friends who'd been killed, coming to them in a dream or walking through the room in broad daylight."

Within weeks, Myron received another invitation. At a two-day campsite with forty kids sleeping in tents, he found himself having to mediate peace among members of three Southeast Asian gangs—Vietnamese, Laotian, and Cambodian Hmong—whose ethnic differences put them at one another's throats. Most, ranging in age from twelve to seventeen, already had arrest records for everything from drug dealing to armed robbery to murder. Eshowsky induced the wary kids to improvise a "ceremonial ritual theater, to dance the conflict and get past the verbal stuff" as he pounded hypnotically on his drums, hoping that "the healing spirit would come to them." By the end of the two days, there was an unlikely peace that held for three years without a shooting.

The night before he had gone, Myron had dreamed about "the biggest, toughest sixteen-year-old imaginable, who the dream told me would be my key to the whole situation. Underneath, he was a healer, and I was to tell him that." He recognized him the minute he saw him—swaggering and full of bluster, he dwarfed the other kids, alternately menacing and coldly aloof. But after Myron won his trust, he confessed that he had been having "ghost dreams" about his ancestors since he was a little boy.

Myron told him this meant he'd been chosen. "I said he had to study with a Hmong shaman, with someone who gets it." By the end of the second day, the boy had been transformed into a mediator, using his burly authority to compel even the most stubborn holdouts to participate. Watching him, Myron felt a lump in his throat. It was as if, at last, he had been able pass on Aunt Soshie's gift of initiation.

Myron reports that his aunt, now long dead, still shows up in his dreams. A few years ago, she appeared to tell him that his girlfriend, Karen, was his destined spouse. He argued inwardly, until Karen called the next day to tell him of a strange dream she'd had. An old woman had appeared, and told her in a Russian accent, "Myron is your husband." Myron invited Karen over to see a home movie. "It had my great-aunt in it, but I didn't tell her. The minute Aunt Soshie appeared on the screen, she yelled, 'That's the one from my dream! Who *is* she?'" Myron and Karen are married today, a fact he credits to a timely ancestral intervention.

Teachings from the Dead

With Myron's account, we have crossed into the zone of the uncanny, a region that must be demarcated in any honest mapping of the landscape of Healing Dreams. But perhaps we should not be taken aback. Accounts of ancestors who guide the living from beyond the grave go back as far as recorded history. Most societies have believed that departed loved ones may return in dreams to teach, to warn, to help navigate life's treacherous passages.

I first met the novelist Amy Tan on a bandstand on a San Francisco pier, where I was playing guitar with her "lit-rock" group, the Rock Bottom

Remainders. Amy is a pillar of this ragtag collection of bookish rock 'n' roll wannabes. We were performing for public radio, so listeners missed seeing the author of *The Joy Luck Club* tricked out for her signature show-stopper, the kitsch classic "These Boots Are Made for Walking," in thigh-high black boots, a studded choker collar, and a cat-o'-nine-tails.

Later, over good greasy burgers at a local dive, Amy—as prolific a dreamer as she is a writer—told me that she has as many as twenty dreams a night. Some are invariably flying dreams—a skill she says she learned from her murdered friend Pete. Shortly after his death, still grieving his loss in the middle of the trial of his assailant, Pete appeared in a dream, offering to take her to "this place where I live now." They arrived in an idyllic setting where every creature, from elephants to camels to people, had the ability to fly. He directed Amy to a booth where she could rent a pair of cheap wings ("since you're not dead") for a quarter. She was having a splendid time swooping through the air until she was struck with the absurdity of flying with her cut-rate wings, and immediately began to plummet to the ground. Terrified as the ground rushed toward her, she remembered her wings had been working fine a minute before, and felt herself once again wafting aloft. This cycle of soaring flight, loss of faith, and precipitous fall repeated again and again, with all the emotions of flight's elation and the sickening plunge toward death, until something clicked. "I finally figured out the point: it wasn't the wings that were letting me fly, it was my own self-confidence."

Pete's dream teachings continued every night through the grueling nine months of the murder trial. In one dream, Amy was being chased by something so horrible she was afraid to look back. The harder she ran, the more her feet seemed mired. Pete urged her to turn around to face her pursuer. Though petrified that it would catch up and kill her, she finally wheeled around and saw that it was a character half-remembered from childhood: "Old Mr. Chou, the mythical guardian of dreams, who lets you in a door and gives you your dreams for the evening—a mythical being who's supposed to be benevolent, but suddenly becomes evil." Old Mr. Chou was so surprised to see her looking at him that he vanished. She realized in that instant that it was her own fear that gave power to her phantoms. Facing them, she could break the spell. Pete had enabled her to have an experience of fearlessness that began to subtly percolate through her waking life.

At the end of the trial, Pete informed her it was time for him to go. Amy was angry. She remembers yelling, "Who are you to decide? You have no right! This is *my* dream!" Pete was adamant; he described a new friend he would arrange for her to meet in the future. "I did meet the person he talked about," Amy says, "a fiction writer, and we became good friends. She was one of the first people to encourage me to write novels."[12]

Her account has many characteristics of other "teachings from the dead" I have heard: the dreamer visits the departed in his new "place" and has a glimpse of his changed existence; there is casual conversation, consolation, instruction, or advice bearing on the dreamer's present circumstances. It is as if the deceased wanted to use his postmortem vantage point to help the dreamer. The teaching is a mixture of wisdom gained since passing away, and resolving the relationship on necessarily new terms.

A few months after meeting Amy, I came across another case involving a court trial and a visitation from the dead. A woman whom I'll call Shirley was married to a commercial pilot who loved to fly his own much-fussed-over private plane in his spare time. One day, skirting Hayden Pass near Colorado's San Luis Valley, Ken's plane had gone down. The crash investigators found, says Shirley, "he had experienced aerodynamic flutter— which is to say, a wing fell off. He took a nosedive and was killed."

Shirley was grief-stricken, although she says she'd had a premonition something was going to happen months before the accident. They'd been married for thirty years, she explained, but suddenly she and Ken had been making out like two kids. A week before he'd died, he'd sat out on their patio singing "Beautiful, Beautiful Brown Eyes," the song he'd sung when he courted her. She sensed an entire cycle of their life together was about to end. When she and some friends saw the TV news flash that a light airplane had crashed, "We never said a word to each other. We knew."

At the urging of her lawyer, Shirley had brought suit against the plane's manufacturer. Ken, an expert pilot who'd flown missions in the Korean War, had taken loving care of the airplane—why had it fallen apart? But as the years of long-drawn-out legal maneuvering ground on, she found herself succumbing to the stress. She'd have bouts of hives that lasted for six months, her throat swelling until it restricted her breath. When the first court date drew near, she found herself uncertain whether to go on. In the midst of her confusion, she had a stunning dream of Ken. "I saw him so clearly," she tells me. "The only way I know how to say it is: he looked *new*. His body, his skin. No wrinkles. Just sitting in a rocking chair. He said, 'I bet you're surprised to see me.'" Then Ken rose smoothly from his chair and ambled down a hallway lined with tilted pictures. "I've come back to straighten these up," he told her. She followed and found herself in a room with brownish wooden chairs for seating an audience, and a white easel in front. Then she awoke.

Feeling Ken wanted her to "straighten up the picture" of his death, she made the decision to proceed to trial. The stress symptoms disappeared a few days after her dream. Months later, as the trial got under way, she recognized the courtroom as the room she'd dreamed about, complete with the lawyers' whiteboard. She found the trial itself "fearsome," she says, but Ken regularly appeared to encourage her. In one of these dream visitations, she found him sitting at a table with a pencil and paper, "like he was trying to figure out what had happened." He drew a diagram of a mechanical part, turned the paper around, and pushed it across the polished surface for her to examine. A few days later, her lawyer, explaining what investigators thought had gone wrong, told her the "trimtab actuator" had broken, and drew a picture of the defective part.

"It was exactly what I'd seen in my dream!" Shirley exclaims. This precise part, she tells me, turned out to be the crucial piece of evidence of the aircraft company's negligence—and perhaps chicanery. "After my dream, that same part was found missing from the wreckage held in storage. Some representatives of the company had been allowed into the warehouse to examine the plane, and they'd gotten the mechanic to take the part out. Then it disappeared."

In an example of the law of unintended consequences, the company's various stratagems backfired, and the jury awarded Shirley a hefty settlement. I spoke with her shortly after the trial's resolution. She told me, with a mixture of fretfulness and serenity, that Ken seemed to be "getting ready to leave." He had begun acting, she says, as if he had other things to do. In a final dream, *Ken and I are in my backyard, happily playing music like in old days. But we begin to run out of songs and I notice a whole new group next door, playing new songs. One has an upright bass, and wants me to join them. Ken doesn't seem to mind.* "Maybe," she wonders, "it means the music of us continues, but a different kind, and with different people."

The Healing Ancestors

It is not only those who have been close to us who appear in dreams when we are needful of help. In most traditional cultures, the invisible community that surrounds us includes a lineage of ancestors stretching back for generations.

Claude Makabella, a cheerful, round-faced man from a clan in northern Mozambique, told me a story of a healing visit from a vanished world as we sat in a lush backyard on the outskirts of Johannesburg. Dressed in a patterned purple-and-white shirt depicting an ancestral spirit (*mndago*), his short-cropped hair just beginning to gray, Claude recalled how, as a young man working as a clerk in a medical clinic, he had been diagnosed with double pneumonia. He was given antibiotic cocktails, but they'd proved useless. His condition grew critical. Suddenly, he saw in his room an astonishing sight. "First, there was a great strong wind. Then a short man in short trousers, with a long beard came into my hospital room! I couldn't move. I was half-awake, half-asleep. It was as if I was in the bush, in the veldt. I could see trees, grass. Then I saw people digging my grave!"

"You were dreaming this," I suggested to him.

"No, my eyes were open. These people were real! That is the mystery. Then I was back at home. I saw an old man with an old stick with a carved head on it, the stick of a nobleman. I woke up, and I could breathe. I was healed." When he described the figure later to his mother, she recognized him instantly: "She told me, that is your great-grandfather from my father's people."

Several times when I've been in crisis, my late grandmother has appeared to me, a Jewish *zaida* offering the earthy counsel I found slightly foolish when she was alive, but which in my dreams resonates with wisdom. In many cultures, the ancestors mingle with the living. But for us, the people of the past seem merely quaint. We think of them indulgently, not quite taking them seriously—until they show up on the doorstep of a dream. Then they are no longer sepia-toned daguerreotypes, posed stiffly in their starched Sunday best, but are vibrantly alive. (I once dreamed of my grandmother perched on the wing of a biplane, a young, vivacious woman with her head thrown back, laughing.)

A woman told me she dreamed: *I am cooking a meal for my husband and children, but there is a spice that is missing from the dish. I go looking for it in a "communal area" where many people gather. Then I see my late father, who I'd sometimes been estranged from, sitting in a chair, tipped back, just beaming at me. He looks so good, I tell him, "I've missed you so much," and he says, "I've missed you, too." We hold each other and hug, and I feel utterly loved.*

"It was like he was really there," she says. "Like I was a child, knowing the smell of him, feeling his scruffy five-o'clock shadow." She realized the "spice of life" she was seeking was this unbreakable, still vital bond. Perhaps our ancestors are our missing ingredient.

Moving forward, we brush the trail behind us; reinvent ourselves, as if from scratch. I rarely think about my familial past or ethnic identity. I am, I tell myself, a universalist, an itinerant just passing through. But once I dreamed: *I learn that our family name is the Polish word for "grail"; I feel a thrill of purpose: I am no longer just me, but the descendant of a noble lineage, charged with upholding some great cause.* In another dream, *a strange man, some distant relation, is entrusting me with an eighteenth-century ledger containing hand-drawn maps of our "ancestral estates." I leaf through the pages, gazing at panoramas reminiscent of a Gainsborough painting—green landscapes lush with meadows, hills, streams, and stands of forest. My heart beats in amazement. "We own this?" I ask the man, who smiles in assent. "This is ours?"*

I can still summon up the feeling—a breathless rush of security, an unfamiliar sense of being *landed*. My clan is by and large unpropertied, dispersed, any farflung kin lost in Auschwitz and Treblinka when Polish Jewry was burned to stubble. But in my dreams I have a patrimony, a personal heritage spanning centuries; I know a place beyond Diaspora, and am part of a people beyond the grasp of mundane time.

Agatha, a chic urbanite, dreamed that the strong, ruddy women of her family's rural past had invaded her house. Her parents had rarely spoken of them when she was growing up. Her people had long since drifted to the city, fleeing the backwardness of an existence based on the soil. But here were these sturdy and buxom women in her basement (which in her dream was called a "roots cellar"), talking and laughing as they put by winter stores and strung up clotheslines. Their ease and naturalness set her wondering what her family had lost in its rush toward modernity. Her heritage now seemed like a rhizome, a forgotten store of inward nourishment.

"Don't look back," we tell ourselves, even as the voices of the invisible community whisper about where we come from, reminding us that as hard as we try to be somebody, we already *are;* and as diligently as we strive to acquire, we already *have*. To acknowledge the ancestors is to look backward—perhaps, in a positive sense, to *be* backward. People speak of the lost sensibility conveyed in their dreams—of sociability and simplicity; the conferral of a blessing they didn't know they ached for. Some even recount dreams of the farthest ancestors, those who slept by firepits at the crack of human dawn—ancient ones insistent on kinship, imploring us to remember our stewardship of the Garden.

In our era, the past is vanishing like smoke. The ancestors and gods and spirits who speak through dreams were once welcomed into the circle of community—were among its essential members. But who now will listen to them? The cultures that honored them are dying, their very languages becoming extinct. The thread of received wisdom that has sustained us is stretched thin to breaking. Shorn of memory, we no longer recognize as part of life's fabric those who have come before us. The voices of the myriad beings, visible and invisible, who surround us grow faint, though they are still talking in our sleep.

The Inca kept track of history by a system of knots on a cord, all time existing on the same thread. Our dreams, too, are a continuum, revealing, if we care to look, that we do not exist alone, but in a skein of relationship with all that has been, all that is, and all that shall be.

Binding the
Wound of Time

Have you also learned that secret from the river, that there is no such
thing as time? . . . The river is everywhere at the same time, at the source
and at the mouth.

—*Herman Hesse,* Siddhartha

e think we know Time. What we've done in the past stays
done—you can't unfry an egg. The present is palpably now.
The future's down the road, and not ours to see: *que será, será.*
But the picture of Time given by Healing Dreams is wildly different. It is
fairly certain that if you watch your dreams closely, you will find occasional instances of outright prediction. These are usually odd bits of
trivia—you dream about a friend you haven't seen in ten years, and she
calls the next day; or an image from a dream shows up in a movie you see
a week later (you're sure it wasn't in the previews).

Most often the dream portrays some happenstance that will stand out
from normal routine. Karl tells me that when he was ten, he dreamed: *I go
to my school superintendent's house to collect the weekly fee for my paper route. As
I walk up to the porch, I notice that the windows are completely black, and I hear*

a woman crying. "I didn't think much of it," he says, "other than that the dream somehow felt strange." He did in fact have a paper route that included the superintendent's home. A few weeks later, as he went to collect his money, he was shocked to see "the house was exactly like my dream—the black-curtained windows, a woman's piercing cries. I knocked, and someone I didn't recognize opened the door and asked me to come back another time. When I got home, I found out the superintendent had died of a heart attack that morning." Karl has had similar dreams throughout his life but finds their purpose, if they have any, opaque. Although they often have a recognizably eerie feeling, he can't be sure they will be predictive until the events they foretell actually happen. "I've never been able to figure out what it is I'm supposed to *do* with them, if anything," he says. "I guess they're there to show me there's more to life than meets the waking eye."

More, indeed: if such dreams are real, they batter down our usual ideas of time in a hailstorm of paradox. They force us to revise our most hallowed axioms about causality itself. It is generally assumed that if cause A (an event) produces effect B (a memory), then A *must* have preceded B in time. But in such cases, B precedes A—the law of cause and effect is mocked by what amounts to "backward causation."

I have always regarded so-called precognitive dreams with an almost urgent fascination. How amazing it would be to peer around time's corner, to know in advance the outcome of some crucial choice. But the first instances in my life, too, were trivial. In my early twenties, I worked as a chef in a ski lodge at the foot of Wyoming's magisterial Grand Tetons. One night, I had an exceptionally vivid dream: *I am in a helicopter, soaring and swooping between high mountain peaks.* Early the next morning, I pulled into the parking lot and saw, for the first time before or since, a helicopter sitting there, its blades glinting like dragonfly wings in the rising sun. I knew in an instant that the dream was mine for the asking. Seeing the pilot standing nearby, I sauntered over and, like a ten-year-old tugging at the sleeve of a Ferris wheel operator, asked for a ride.

The pilot looked me over, shrugged, and said, "Hop in. I've got some gas to burn." The blades shuddered, then spun, and we hummed into glorious flight. The exhilaration of diving and climbing among glittering peaks was as I had dreamed. We didn't exchange a word. No fee was ever discussed. I never found out who he was, or even what he was doing there. When I shook his hand good-bye, we smiled over our stolen moment aloft, then he and his mechanical marvel beat their way back into the sky.

Afterward, I puzzled over the implications of this odd non sequitur. Had it been a completely free choice to go over to him, thus triggering the enactment of the dream? Or did I only *think* I had chosen, while both the opportunity *and* my decision were somehow foreordained?

After a few more such incidents, I found myself faced with an ancient bugaboo—the notion of a nonnegotiable and inadvertent Destiny. In an era of limitless options, the very idea sounds archaic. But these early encounters subtly altered my sense of orientation in Time. I no longer felt anchored in the safe harbor of the present, but adrift on a horizonless sea, my temporal compass spinning.

I will dispense here with the age-old debate over whether or not precognitive dreaming is "real." I hold with Greek writers like Macrobius and Artemidorus of Daldis, who included in their classification of dreams such categories as *oraculum* ("direct prophecy") and *visio* ("prevision of a future event") because they had empirically observed them. Their ideas were reasonably opposed by Cicero, who wrote in *De Divinatione:* "From the visions of drunkards and madmen, one might doubtless deduce innumerable consequences by conjecture which might seem to presage future events. For what person who aims at a mark all day will not hit it? We sleep every night, and there are few on which we do not dream; can we wonder then that what we dream sometimes comes to pass?"

There is certainly a place for scientific skepticism, which holds that all foreknowledge is folklore, its supposed instances mere confabulation, fraud, coincidence, self-fulfilling prophecy, or faulty memory. I can only second Charles Richet, a Nobel Prize–winning nineteenth-century scientist who, when mocked for attempting a methodological study of clairvoyance, replied: "I didn't say it was possible. I only said it was *true.*" If, as quantum physics tells us, time is an illusion, it should not surprise us that Healing Dreams could contain images whose "payoff" might not occur

until days, weeks, months, or even years later. But this raises a troubling issue: There may be aspects of our dreams we cannot possibly understand
until some future event reveals their meaning! In fact, it is often the very
element in a dream that, indigestible as a pebble, steadfastly resists all interpretation, and later manifests in waking reality.

I've discovered that people have their own ways of distinguishing such
dreams when they occur. One woman described the unusual "bright colors," then added: "It's like a TV with the sound turned off. People are talking and nothing comes out of their mouths, like a silent movie." Another
told me her "strong dreams" about the future are always "very storylike.
They have a beginning, middle, and end, don't ramble, tend to be short
and to the point." In the same spirit, a Jewish cabalistic source reads,
"When a dreamer sees his dream very clearly, as if he were actually awake,
with the result that when he awakens he recalls every detail without the
slightest omission, this is to be taken as a sign the dream will be quickly fulfilled."[1]

Modern researchers intrepid enough to take the phenomenon seriously
have made similar observations. Professor Robert van de Castle, who performed a study of hundreds of precognitive dream reports, has concluded
that in 90 percent of the cases, the imagery "would be most accurately described as realistic" rather than symbolic. The vast majority pertained to
events within a twenty-four-hour period after the dream. They tended to
impress themselves upon the dreamer by being more vivid and colorful
than ordinary dreams. Details would refuse to fade away, no matter how
hard the dreamer tried to put them from his mind. Such dreams often repeated themselves on consecutive nights, even several times in a single
night. Most seemed to be nightmares warning of personal danger and,
sometimes, collective disaster. He notes that twice as many women as men
have such dreams.

But description is not explanation. A precognitive dream is precisely the
sort of inconvenient datum that demands new models of reality—including the strange notion that information may be bombarding us from the
future. If so, there is an equally paradoxical corollary: If we are today receiving information from the future, then our present—which is our *past's*

future—may be sending its particulars "backward," toward what has already happened!. But even the concept of "to and from" when applied to this enlarged view of time is a case of the blind men and the elephant—of drawing conclusions on the basis of the trunk or the tail. The Healing Dream, perhaps, provides a glimpse of the entire beast. As always, dreams insist upon the integration of all parts into a whole, even when those parts appear too contradictory to belong to any animal but a chimera.

Exploring the Time Paradox

J. W. Dunne, an early aeronautical engineer who devoted the second half of his life to the study of precognition, wrote in his 1938 book *An Experiment with Time:* "If prevision be a fact, it is a fact which destroys absolutely the entire basis of all our past opinions of the universe."[2] Dunne spent years observing his dreams with a meticulous ardor, discovering a surprising number that presaged events to come. Keeping careful records, he developed a complex theory called "serialism," in which the present, called "A," was only part of a constellation of other A's existing in the past and future. Writing down his own dreams, collecting those of friends, combing each one for portents, he was surprised at how often the other A's bled through. Much of the content was inconsequential. He dreamed, for example, of a farmer herding three cows using a stick held in an odd position, then saw the identical sight the next day. Similarly, an unusually painted lifeboat he'd dreamed of showed up the next morning on a beach.

Dunne concluded that though the phenomenon "bristled with peculiarities," dream precognition was not confined to "an abnormal few"; for it was not merely some individuals' "supernormal faculties"[3] that produced this odd temporal warping, but rather the nature of time itself.

Dunne took careful note of recurrent patterns. Most events, he observed, transpired within "a two-day limit." He even speculated that the experience of déjà vu could be the result of having *actually* seen something before—but in a dream. He noted that unusual life events were more likely to be precognitively detected by dreamers. If a person were living a monotonous life, in which each day's events resembled the next, the phenomenon was less likely to occur.

I have noted down my own list of such dreams' bristling peculiarities. I have been struck, for example, by how often precognitive dreams are almost myopically literal, showing the dreamer only the exact visual perspective they will have when the future event occurs. Steven, a well-known family therapist, was a junior high school outcast, longing to be accepted by a group of cool kids who treated him with pure disdain. One night, he had a vivid dream that *the tough leader of this crowd is riding his bike on the hill known as Austin Bluffs and sails straight off into the abyss.* Steven woke up sobbing. A therapist might have gently counseled that his dream stemmed from suppressed aggression at the humiliations inflicted by the bully. When Steven saw the boy the next day at school, he told him about his dream and promptly burst into tears, cementing his "uncool" reputation with the kids he'd yearned to impress. A few days later, up at the bluffs, Steven saw the bully crest the hill on his bicycle and, just as in his dream, hurtle into empty space. Horror-struck, his heart pounding, Steven raced to the precipice expecting to see his broken body far below, only to find that the boy had tumbled into a shallow unseen ditch right at the cliff's edge. The dream had presented an accurate picture, but one precisely cropped to Steven's future vantage point. (Perhaps, too, it did reflect an element of hostility. The ditch was filled with poison ivy, and the bully spent a week in itching agony—though Steven's tears show Healing Dreams' power to create empathy even for a nemesis.)

Others have remarked upon such dreams' odd perceptual limitations—the ability to peer into the future but unable, in Steven's case, to see over a mound of dirt. A London psychologist told me a vivid recurring nightmare she'd had since adolescence: *I am in a hotel room. My father has been killed in a plane crash. A dwarf is in front of me, weeping and begging me to forgive him.* Decades later, while staying in a hotel abroad, she received an awful phone call. Her father had been killed in a helicopter accident in Africa. A few days later, there was a knock on the door. Answering it, she was startled to see a man she took for a dwarf, tearfully imploring her forgiveness.

Then she realized that the man, who turned out to be the surviving copi-
lot, was *down on his knees.*

The British playwright and man of letters J. B. Priestley, who collected
many hundreds of such accounts (and who once wrote a popular play
based on Dunne's serialism) cites the case of a man who had "a very vivid
dream" containing an absurd image—an Indian canoe sailing through the
air across his landlocked city's town-hall square. Nine years later, the man
was standing in the town hall after his father's unexpected appointment as
lord mayor, and glancing out the window was stunned to see "a fully
painted Indian war canoe," floating by as if in midair. Running to the window, he looked down to discover that the canoe was a theater prop
perched atop a moving cart full of equipment. Another woman wrote
Priestley that she had dreamed that an orange tiger with large fangs had
jumped on her and brought its face within inches of her own. Oddly, she
wasn't frightened. The next day, browsing in a toy store, her daughter had
crept up on her and thrust into her face a large hand puppet with movable
jaws that had all the features and coloration of her dream tiger.

Several parapsychologists have speculated that for our hunter-gatherer
ancestors, who had to contend with surprise attacks from real saber-
toothed tigers, precognitive dreaming may have been an adaptive trait. Being able to anticipate an assault from an animal or an enemy, or to intuit
the location of water or game or shelter, were life-or-death matters in an
unpredictable environment. If so, perhaps there was an evolutionary advantage conferred on those who could foresee a situation in the exact way
it would unfold, gaining a critical margin of readiness.

I have noticed that this cognitive function becomes more active when
one is in unknown and possibly risky surroundings, such as traveling in a
foreign country. Exploring India years ago, wandering at random with my
passport, return ticket, and remaining hundred dollars strapped to my leg,
I was invited by a Sikh filmmaker to drive to Kashmir to vacation in a
houseboat on a lake. It sounded like a wonderful adventure—he'd proposed that we continue on to Ladakh to see a renowned "oracle" and from
there try to sneak across the border into Tibet. I began making plans. But

the night before we were to depart, I had a clear, disturbing dream: *I see a swimming pool elevated on pillars. In it, dark, swarthy men are "committing fratricide" with curved knives. The pointless butchery turns the water red with blood.*

The dream changed my mind about going. My friend later wrote to say that the trip had been a disaster. Bloody riots had broken out between Muslim separatists and Hindus in Kashmir directly on his route. (Swords and daggers had been common weapons.) Hours before he had arrived, a European had been pulled from a car and stabbed to death, and the U.S. State Department had issued a travel advisory. One thing after another had gone wrong on the journey, and he'd finally been forced to turn back. (In subsequent years, the fraternal violence was to escalate to the point that senseless civilian massacres in Kashmir have claimed tens of thousands of lives.)

I am reminded, too, of the story of a sculptor friend who was invited to Moscow to collaborate with a group of local artists. Shortly after his arrival, he had "a very elaborate dream," the most striking feature of which was: *I'm in a market, and I run into a girl with bright green clothes carrying two water buckets.* Two days later, the Russians he was traveling with were called away, and he was left in the uncomfortable position of a stranger who didn't speak the language in a city that must be warily navigated. His dream, however, had left him feeling confident that all would be well. Standing mutely on Arbat Street, he suddenly saw "this girl walking up in a tight green outfit, carrying two brand-new pails! It turned out she knew the two artists I was with, and best of all, was an exchange student who spoke Russian and English. She became my guide for the rest of the trip."

Memories of the Future

One of the observations that most intrigued J. W. Dunne was what he came to call "integration"—a precognitive dream's tendency to blend together images of both past and future. He describes once reading about a lion-hunting expedition, then dreaming that night: *I am watching from the window of a country house as a lion that has escaped a zoo hunts down and kills a goat in a cornfield.* The next day, picking up another book at random, he happened to open to a passage in which a leopard escapes from a menagerie, shows up near a country house, and kills a goat. It was as if his dream had taken a "day residue" from the past ("lion hunt") and seamlessly woven in elements from a future perception ("zoo," "country house," "goat"). Dunne speculated that this meant that a dream's "associational network . . . stretched backwards *and* forwards in time."[4]

A psychoanalyst might speculate that Dunne, forgetting he had read the book, had chosen it from the shelf because he subconsciously knew it contained some elements of the previous night's dream. If so, it would have been a roundabout use of one of the key tools of psychoanalysis, association, in which the dreamer is encouraged to link new elements to those in his dream in hopes they will lead him to long-buried incidents of emotional trauma. The unshakable assumption is that dreams and their associations concern the patient's past, and analysis will reveal how that past is affecting his present, freeing him to shape a new future. To propose that the future *also* affects the present rattles the foundations of the house that Freud built. It is no wonder that Freud, in a posthumously published essay, felt moved to categorically state that "the creation of a dream after the event . . . alone makes [so-called] prophetic dreams possible."

But future dreams imply that some dreams are created *before* the event. We are inconveniently faced with both a remembrance of things past and a remembrance of things *future* (a kind of *pre*membering). If that is so, who can say that our psychological equilibrium is not affected by memories of both past and future, much as Dunne's lion dream was a blending of these two opposing "streams" of time? It leads to a worldview not unlike that of the White Queen in *Alice in Wonderland,* who screams in pain *before* she is accidentally pricked by a thorn, and huffs: "It is a poor sort of memory that works only *backwards!*"

Intriguingly, the Tibetan term for precognitive dreams translates as "memories of the future," which firmly links the phenomenon to the memory function. This may be less nonsensical than it sounds. If one eliminates the factor of temporal ordering, memory and precognition have certain similarities. Both are perceptions of noncurrent events. Both are subjectively distorted versions of an objective experience. They are perceptions separated by an interval of time from the experience they represent (or *pre*present); in both, an event occurring at another time causes the formation of a mental trace. We might even speculate that the experience of déjà vu is the stirring of one of these "memories of the future," forgotten until the event actually occurs. (One woman told me bluntly: "*Whenever* I experience déjà vu, it's because I've dreamed it before.")[5]

Dr. Jule Eisenbud, a classically trained psychoanalyst, found himself beleaguered by instances of future dreaming in his own practice. He concluded that the future events revealed in such dreams could be treated in the same way as the day residues of the immediate past that show up in normal dreams—that is, as clues to personal issues needful of attention. He insisted that such seemingly magical occurrences should not be exempt from the nitty-gritty of psychological work. Why, he asked, would a given patient dream of a *particular* occurrence if it did not have acute psychological significance for him? What clues to his underlying emotional conflicts might be found by analyzing his dream's subtle distortion of the future event? The psychiatrist Merloo suggested that even being prone to having such dreams is a strong clue to the personality: "Premonitions and precognitions as we experience them in the therapeutic relationship are related to . . . a special danger-mindedness, and a special pull toward mastering the future through predetermined imaginings and schemes."[6]

Healing Dreams, however exotic, are intent upon the growth of the soul, presenting us with psychological challenges of the highest order. Indeed, it sometimes seems as if precognitive elements are as much attention-getting devices for difficult emotional issues as outright prophecies. A theological version of this idea can be found in the sixteenth-century writings of Benedict Pererius. Speaking of those dreams that "prefigure" and "foreshadow" events, he stated: "God sometimes intends that dreams be hidden and incomprehensible for a while so that their truth may be the more firmly recognized and acknowledged through the consequence itself and the succession of events."[7]

Healing Fate

It is common in folklore (and, it would seem, in fact) that dreams call attention to impending catastrophe. An Australian aborigine told me, "When you have a warning dream, you wake up with your heart beating as if you've been running. This can tell us someone in the family will die." But even if we can recognize a dream as a warning about the future, what then? The Jewish Zohar says, "When one's dreams foretell evil, he is thereby intended to try to nullify this evil before it comes to pass." But how? What do we *do* with a future dream?

The anthropologist Anthony Wallace gives the account of a Seneca tribesman who had a warning dream that "a certain young woman was alone in a canoe, in the middle of a stream, without a paddle. The dreamer invited the young lady to a 'dream-guessing' ceremony at his home. Various people gathered and tried to guess what the dream was. Finally the dream was guessed. A miniature canoe with a paddle was thereupon presented to the girl. This ceremony was expected to forestall the dream disaster from happening in real life."[8] Such "apotropaic rites," are frequently observed in tribal societies. Michael Harner, who underwent initiations with Amazonian shamans and has tried to adapt their practices for Western audiences, recommends: "If you have a big dream that you are injured in an automobile accident, that is a warning for you from the guardian spirit that such an accident will occur. You may not be able to prevent it, but you can enact it symbolically by yourself or with a friend in a very minor way, and may thereby prevent its serious occurrence."[9]

Of course, it is hard to evaluate the "efficacy" of such an act due to another time paradox: if we try to avert or deflect an event seen in a dream, and the event never comes to pass, how are we to know if it would *ever* have happened? If it does not, did our tactic of avoidance "work," or was our dream just groundless fantasy in the first place?

A case that sheds fascinating light on this conundrum can be found in H. F. Saltmarsh's compendium *Foreknowledge*. A London housewife designated as "Mrs. C." dreamed *she is being followed by a monkey, an animal that fills her with loathing.* When she awoke, she told her husband, who suggested she take the children for an after-breakfast walk to shake off the nightmare's lingering cobwebs. As they were strolling down the street, she encountered, to her horror, "the very monkey" depicted in her dream, which weirdly began to follow her. The act of trying to escape the dream had, as if in a folktale, caused its fulfillment.

We like to imagine that we are masters of our own fate. It is no accident that the word *will* is both a future conjugation and an expression of inner resolve. We intend to *will* our future into being, to shape it on our own terms. We toss the grappling hook of our intention forward in time, hoping it catches on an outcropping so that, testing the tautness of the rope, we might pull ourselves up toward our goal. But what if it is only a fishing hook, our climbing rope an angler's line—and though we think we pull ourselves up, we are instead being reeled in by our Fate?

I once asked my Cree friend Sylvia if she thought a future event seen in a dream could be changed. She's never been able to do it, she tells me. For one thing, the "grandfathers" often grant her only ambiguous "clues." (Sometimes, she says, "they'll laugh at me.") Even in the case of clear dreams that later come true, "They just give me time to prepare. They give me the strength to deal with what is about to happen, because I already have some familiarity with it. It's like a replay—you know what to watch for."

She has often dreamed of deaths in her extended clan, including that of her late father, who she says is now one of her guiding spirits. One night he came to her in a dream and told her that her mother-in-law would soon die. The woman had a heart attack a few days later. "The doctors had told us she'd recover. But I said no, and urged my husband to spend time with his mom before she was gone. He did, and she died unexpectedly just days later. So the dream gave him a little extra time to clear things up."

For many tribes, premonitions have more to do with what *could* happen than what *must* happen. The Lacandon Maya of Mexico say that "dreams are a 'kind of lie,' foretelling the future 'but not as a face value.' " Medieval Christian theologians spoke of the "future contingencies" revealed by God in dreams.[10] From this standpoint, dreams are not inescapable fate but more like extrapolations from a current balance of forces, where a change in one variable can yield a different result. If we choose to learn by paying heed to a dream, could that not alter the equation and produce a new answer?

Shannon, a twenty-seven-year-old single mother, told me: "One morning my six-year-old had a nightmare that he'd been hit by a van. It really bothered him. All that morning, I'd catch him staring off into space. I'd ask, 'What's wrong?' and he'd say, 'Mom, my dream was *so* scary!'

"That afternoon, we went to the store. Normally he's tugging on my arm like kids his age do, pulling ahead when you're going *aagh!* trying to keep them near you. But this day he was walking behind, holding my hand and looking around kind of fearfully.

"Just as we were about to step off the curb into the parking lot, a big van zoomed right past us at top speed. It was very sudden. If my son had been two steps ahead as usual, he would have been hit. He looked up at me, his face white as a sheet, and said, 'Mom, that was *just like my dream!*' " Shannon is convinced her son's hesitancy may have saved his life.

Louisa Rhine, the wife of famed ESP researcher Joseph Banks Rhine, examined four hundred dreams of future events that the dreamer, armed with such foreknowledge, might conceivably have been able to avert. She found that in only one-third of the cases were such efforts even made. Rhine added that in dreams that followed a definite sequence, it was sometimes possible to recognize the pattern in waking life soon enough to avoid catastrophe. She relates the case of a woman who dreamed that her coachman fell from his driver's seat one snowy Christmas Eve and cracked his skull. Months later, on Christmas Eve, while clip-clopping down a street in her carriage, she suddenly recognized the landmarks from her dream. When her coachman pulled up in front of her home, instead of waiting for him to open the door as usual, she jumped out just in time to see him tumbling headfirst from his perch toward the cobblestones. But she was there to break his fall, and presumably save his life.

Many spiritual teachings say our possibilities become circumscribed when our lives are shaped by habitual actions, patterns, and mental attitudes. Healing Dreams often bid us to decisively break those habits, to pay minute attention to what we normally overlook. The grip of the accustomed is a firm one, and the task of change always wrenching, but it may be better than some invisibly looming alternative. As the poet William Blake once pointedly wrote: "If you go on so, the result is so."

One reason we "go on so" is that we rarely bother to interpret our dreams. It is an omission akin to leaving a letter containing a vital message unopened on the breakfast table. Even when we do open it, we too often read it through a filter of preconception that edits out key words. In dreams as in waking, we hear what we want to hear. Sometimes we refuse to believe even a favorable dream premonition if it doesn't fit the ongoing pattern of our lives. In the *Odyssey*, Penelope is convinced that her husband Odysseus has died on his voyages, yet has a dream that seems to portend his triumphal return. The dream leaves little doubt as to its veracity: she even sees the image of an eagle, which says "with mortal voice," "Here is no dream, but something real as day, something about to happen." The next day, she confides her dream to a visitor, adding she is sure it is "too good to be true."[11] Ironically, the stranger to whom she is speaking is none other than Odysseus himself, returned to her in disguise.

Though dreams, too, often come in disguise, sometimes we conceal them from ourselves. Thelma, a *sangoma* priestess I met in a shantytown on the outskirts of Johannesburg, told me: "I once prayed for money. I did worry a little that if I got too rich, I might ignore my healing practice, but I just needed more room for my students. That night, I dreamed that my grandfather was telling me I needed a better house. He gave me a number like a phone number, six digits, which I realized could be a number for the Pick Six lottery. I had sixty rand, but I thought the ticket cost more, so I didn't do it. Then the next day, I saw the winning number was exactly the one in my dream. I cried for a week—it paid out a million rand!"

It is a common theme in myths: the hero is granted a vision by the gods but fails to carry out instructions. Such myths suggest that we human beings are always left to exercise our free will, proceeding fallibly on such knowledge as we can glean, to forge our destiny. To rely overmuch on dreams for anything more than a special sort of truthtelling—often a paradoxical one, at that—can put us in the position of the sorcerer's apprentice, expecting the otherworld to do our work for us. The Aguaruna Indians of Peru, who use dreams in daily decision making, believe previsions are only "emergent possibilities, events that are developing." To them, a future dream is not an immutable destiny, but an invitation to a creative response.

The Jewish Zohar, too, counsels that dreams can only indicate a direction: "When one dreams of good, he is meant to strive after its fulfillment." We might argue that a dream heeded is only a self-fulfilling prophecy. But what of those instances in which we seem to set out in no particular direction yet arrive mysteriously at our dream's doorstep? I have been astonished how dreams have shown me the very street signs of some life crossroad I will reach only years later, after much spiritual mileage. Looking back through my well-thumbed dream notebooks, I have sometimes found a current situation described down to its particulars. It is as if, ascending a fog-shrouded mountain, low on supplies, we were to stumble across a miraculous sight—a crate containing the very provisions we need, along with a set of maps left by someone who had already reached the summit. Marvelous coincidence! But then we see, with a chill, the name stenciled on the side of the box—it is our own. We have been in some mysterious way following in our own footsteps.

When I was first dating Carolyn, I tried to incubate a dream about what our future together might hold. That night, I dreamed:

I am invited to go in as partners on a house in a community that's becoming very pricey. On the front part of the property facing the narrow unpaved street is a small shack. In back is a good-sized house shaped like an upended boat. (I think of the purported ship's beams photographed on the top of Mount Ararat, claimed to be the remnants of Noah's Ark.) The house, which I'm told was built in the thirties, sits on a ridge facing over the city, with a panoramic view of the plains beyond. But the ceilings seem too low. And I'll have to sign a mortgage for millions of dollars. It's no bargain, but there is no way to avoid paying "mansion prices" on this now mansion-filled street. I think I will have to just make the commitment and figure out how to pay for it later. I realize if I demolished the shack, the property would be worth more.

I did my best to puzzle it out. At the time, I was renting a small, somewhat rundown house, though not strictly speaking a shack. Perhaps our relationship was symbolized by this big house that we could "go in on" together. (The Noah's Ark reference implied a refuge from life's floodwaters, as well as pairing off two-by-two.) I worried about the image of the low ceiling, which spoke to my fear that the potential for spiritual growth in the relationship might be limited: would there, I wondered arrogantly, be enough intellectual headroom? The "high cost" might mean I was getting in over *my* head. Making a commitment would demolish the shack of my solitary life (and my "small self?"), but this might increase the relationship's true "worth." The original meaning of *mansion,* the dictionary says, was "a staying, abiding, an abode, a sojourn" (from *manere,* to remain). It was very much in the spirit of Carolyn's and my relationship—we had agreed to remain with each other for a time, without knowing more. Whenever we found ourselves in limbo, I would think back on this clear dream, aching for a clue.

Six years later, we found ourselves at a crucial juncture. Still not living together, I faced suddenly having to move out of my "shack." Carolyn had to move, too, and had unexpectedly come into enough money for a down payment when a house her mother owned burned down and they'd gotten an insurance settlement. Still uncertain about moving in together, I began to help her look for something to purchase. I discovered, after years of paying little attention to the housing market, that there had been a real estate gold rush in Boulder. Prices had doubled, then tripled. "Housing Costs Drive Out Middle Class" screamed the headline in that week's local paper. It didn't look promising.

One day Carolyn called to tell me she had came across a house she loved. When we drove up to it, I was amazed to see that it matched, with some precision, the one I'd dreamed of years before. It was on a ridge with a panoramic view of the city, on what was once a low-rent dirt road adjoining the city's greenbelt. Parcels on this now well-paved block had so soared in value that million-dollar mansions had been erected where matchboxes had once stood. (There was a reminder of the neighborhood's humble origins directly across the street—a small, tumbledown shack.)

The house, though relatively small, was barely affordable. Carolyn told me, discouraged, its ceilings were much too low, made more so by the large exposed beams that made it feel like the hold of an old sailing vessel (an effect enhanced by weathered wood paneling that resembled the seaworm-eaten siding of some long-sunken ship). Jutting from the back of the house was a very large wooden deck, on which the previous resident had bolted an old ship-captain's bell.

I had never told Carolyn my dream—I'd been leery about plunging into the relationship issues it raised. Now, as I related it, I wondered aloud about the dream's reference to the thirties—the house had clearly been built much later. There was a silence. "Didn't you notice?" she asked. "The street address is thirty-thirty. Third Street. The *thirties.*"

She equivocated about putting in an offer and was devastated when another party swooped in with a contract. But I told her not to despair—my dream had left me certain the house was hers, and I advised her not to commit her money elsewhere. A few weeks later, on the afternoon the other party was to close the deal, they suddenly got cold feet; the realtor called Carolyn back and offered it to her on the spot. She didn't hesitate.

Could I have somehow confabulated all these connections? The philosopher C. D. Broad once compiled a list of alternative explanations for supposedly precognitive incidents:

1. A person has already subconsciously inferred a future event from existing data or trends.
2. A person initiates, without being quite aware of it, a course of action likely to fulfill an unconscious goal reflected in his dreams.
3. The supposedly precognitive dream sets up a conscious desire the person acts upon so as to bring it to pass.
4. Someone else somewhere has consciously decided to do something, and the apparent "prediction" of their subsequent actions is a feat of telepathy, not precognition.
5. The laws of chance sometimes do produce extraordinary coincidences.

226 • *Healing Dreams*

But here, very nearly, was a case of none of the above. Carolyn hadn't previously considered buying a house at all until a wild series of unforeseen events came to pass, all of which had to take place within a certain time window for the dream's fruition: her mother's house had unexpectedly burned down; Carolyn had spent a year completing the paperwork and insurance, dickering to get the money that she would later decide could be used for a down payment; the land under the charred husk of her mother's house had been sold only scant weeks before, providing needed additional cash; a realtor friend I hadn't spoken to for years had called me and told me about the Third Street house, which had just gone on the market; I was debating moving in with Carolyn, as I had been in the dream, only because my landlord had suddenly decided after seven years to terminate my lease.

I felt oddly prepared for this critical juncture—I had contemplated the "low-ceilinged" house image for years, anticipating a moment of reckoning in our relationship. The dream had not shown an outcome, just a choice point; in the end, we decided not to move in together. At the same time, the dream had affected the unfolding of events. Because of it, I had counseled Carolyn to sit tight and wait rather than give up and buy a different house, and so influenced the outcome.

The fact remains, I could not fully interpret my dream without knowledge—indeed, experience—of future events on which it seems to have been hinged. What an outrageous state of affairs: the dream had handed me a jigsaw puzzle with crucial pieces missing from the box! Perhaps this is why traditional cultures often preserve a "true" dream even if its meaning in the present is unclear. The Old Testament prophet Habakkuk, for example, claimed that the Lord had instructed him to "write the vision; make it plain on tablets. . . . For there is still a vision for the appointed time. If it seems to tarry, wait for it; it will surely come." (Habakkuk 2:2–4). The Hopi long preserved a prophecy, handed down orally and via stone pictographs generations before the white man came, foretelling tall "buildings of crystal" on the eastern shore, men's voices carried over "spider webs," "sticky black ribbons" crisscrossing the landscape, and "houses in the sky."

The great Plains Indian warrior Plenty Coups (1848–1932) dreamed when he was not yet ten that he was summoned by "a voice at midnight." He saw a buffalo bull transform into a "Man-person" wearing a buffalo robe, and followed him into a hole in the ground. Plenty Coups's description is filled with the visual and tactile immediacy characteristic of the Healing Dream: "I could see countless buffalo, see their sharp horns . . . smell their bodies and hear them snorting. . . . Their eyes, without number, were like little fires in the darkness. . . . The burrs that are always in their hair would scratch my skin. I felt their warm bodies against my own."

He was frightened, but came to no harm. His journey seemed to go on all night and the next day. But then, the buffalo without number that had blackened the plains "were gone, *all!*" In their place, he saw "strange animals from another world" that were not buffaloes, but had spotted hides, and "lay down, not as a buffalo does, but differently." These began to eat the tall grass. He could not understand it. Only the coming years revealed that he'd had a prophetic vision of the decimation of the great buffalo herds and the coming of the white man's cattle to the rangelands.

In Plenty Coups's dream, he emerged from the hole to see an old man sitting in an unfamiliar place. This turned out to be the very spot he was living at the time of the ethnographer's interview. "This very house, just as it is, these trees which comfort us today, and a very old man sitting in the shade, alone. I felt pity for him because he was so old and feeble. . . . 'This old man is yourself, Plenty Coups,' the Man-person told me." Plenty Coups, who became a farmer and conciliator, had witnessed his people's destiny and his own personal future in a single childhood vision.

Big Dreamers

It is not surprising, perhaps, that a man destined to be a great chief would be vouchsafed a dream of his people's fate. The Sufis believe the dreamer's status in waking life determines whether a future dream concerns world-shaking events or personal matters: "On the eve of great battle," a sheikh once told me, "if a corporal dreams of success, it means he'll survive. But if a general dreams of success, it means military victory." Other cultures have similar ideas. The Mohave Indians believe that there are two classes of future dreaming—"omen dreams," which do not necessarily show what will happen but what *could* happen, and the rarer "power dreams" shamans have, which are believed to be prophetic. But are the prophet and the priest (or for that matter the CEO or the Speaker of the House) somehow designated dreamers of big dreams?

Franklin, a seventy-one-year-old Methodist pastor, once told me in laconic midwestern cadences a story of what he calls his "strange dreaming." Some years ago, he dreamed that a friend and church worker named John Chapman murdered someone. "I saw him standing there, gun in hand, and someone came out of this hotel-like building, and bang!" He hadn't seen the person who'd been shot, but when he awoke, he reasoned it must have been his friend's wife, as he was under the impression they hadn't been getting along. "The dream was so strong, my body was shaking! I went to work at eight that morning convinced he'd killed her, but lo and behold, he came into the staff meeting and everything was fine."

But the dream continued to trouble him. "It was like the very core of my being had been shaken up; it was mentally and physically the most powerful dream I've ever had. After three days, it began to evaporate a little. But on the fourth day, watching television, I saw the scene from my dream! Same hotel-like place, and the same story of someone coming out, a man waiting for him with a pistol who shoots and kills him." The "hotel" in the news broadcast was New York's Dakota apartment building; the man with the gun was Mark *Chapman,* and his victim ex-Beatle *John* Lennon.

As a pastor, Franklin is perhaps a shaman of sorts, albeit a gently bewildered one. As a man responsible for his flock, it is perhaps not surprising he'd dream about a member of his congregation. Yet he had seemingly dreamed of an event that made the world stop in its tracks for a few sorrowful days to mourn the falling of one more man of peace. Robert, not even a Beatles fan, remains "utterly flabbergasted—it's puzzling why I of all people would have seen this before it happened."

A friend of mine named Anna also had a dream of a shocking public tragedy. In April of 1999, she dreamed *I'm in a high school cafeteria, hiding under a table from two men with shotguns. I see their feet, the barrels of their guns, and the bottoms of their long black trenchcoats. I'm scared to breathe.* She had been so stunned she'd written the scene into a screenplay she was working on. A week later, two heavily armed students in long black overcoats walked into the cafeteria of Columbine High School in Littleton, Colorado. They opened fire as their classmates and teachers cowered under the tables. The boys had been part of a clique known around the school as the Trenchcoat Mafia.

The more I thought about it, the less baffling it seemed that Anna might have "tuned in" this awful event. She lived in nearby Boulder and had a high-school-aged daughter, whose safety she always worried about. More significantly, her most vivid childhood memory—of her family's unsuccessful attempt to escape from Hungary after the 1956 Soviet invasion—had clear analogies to her dream's violence. Her group had sneaked up near the border and wound up spending the night in a field. But the soldiers found out. Anna recalls: "We were hiding in a haystack. I could hear people around us being captured and shot by this faceless enemy. I didn't dare peer out. I could hear them yelling 'Stop!' and then *bang-bang.* I was seven or eight. It was the most petrifying experience of my life."

It is almost as if some principle of resonance were at work connecting past and future—joining the fearful young Anna, who concealed herself from her would-be killers, to the terrorized children who would soon crouch beneath tables as gunfire rang out around them, hoping to escape the notice of their friends' murderers. Somehow she was pre-tuned to the wavelength of an event yet to come.

Other times, however, the connecting principle is harder to understand. Pamela is a nurse from Iowa in her early forties. The simplicity of her life is reflected in her hobbies, which she lists as "baking, gardening, reading, sewing, and working with animals." Hers is not the profile of a leader, a mystic, or a seer—she calls herself "a completely ordinary person"—but in the early eighties, after her mother's death, she suddenly began having psychic dreams and visions. She was alarmed. She'd been taught by both her church and her parents that "only God could do this stuff, psychics were witches and the next thing to devils, and I would go to hell." She found herself struggling to reconcile her strict Roman Catholic beliefs with her growing interest in new-age metaphysics.

Then she started to have a repetitive dream. She saw *this really little girl, maybe two years old, in a very dark hole, wedged in so tight she couldn't move. She had a cut over her eye, she was scared and crying, and I would call out to her to try to comfort her. I remember her tiny hands trying to raise up to grab mine.*

Each night, the dream unfolded with more detail. "In the next phase," she recalls, *I'm seeing how she'd stumbled into an old abandoned well, kind of like in old westerns where the cowboy walks on a rotting board and falls through. I also saw that she was in Texas.* Night by night, the cast of characters grew.

> *Some nights I'd see firemen working to get her out, feeling their frustration. I saw her mom, and could feel her intense maternal instinct and her bone-tiredness. I saw this one reporter pushing her so he could get the first scoop—I was so angry at him!*
>
> *Each night, the curtain would open a little more. I would run through the whole story like a movie—the little girl falling in the well, getting stuck, crying, not being able to be rescued, people gathering, then finally a rope going down and her being pulled out. I'd go to bed praying and wake up praying for those people in my dream, whoever they were. It was a little exhausting.*

A month later, what became known as the "Baby Jessica" story broke. A Texas toddler had fallen into an old well and became wedged in its narrow aperture. Her ordeal became a worldwide cliffhanger as firemen struggled against time to tunnel in and rescue the scared child before she succumbed to exposure. For Pamela, it was a revelation. "I learned you don't have to be some Buddha or a spiritual leader to have incredible intuitive insights—everybody has these abilities." Still, it remained perplexing. "I always thought when you had premonitions, they were given so that you could help, so you could prevent something bad. But the only help I could give this little girl was my prayers."

She continues to dream about "disasters of all kinds, some famous, some private, but always about a person in distress. Sometimes I think they're reminders for me to think of the big picture in the midst of life's petty stuff." Pamela still asks herself the inevitable question many do who have such dreams: "Why me? How could it be there was no separation between me in Iowa and that little girl and her folks in Texas? It made me realize that we are all so deeply connected. Well, isn't that what they teach us in Sunday school?" What began as a challenge to her faith has rooted it more deeply in the ground of compassion.

History Past and Future

> Innumerable mirrors of the future transmit their
> images to the eons of the past. —*Myoē*

Pamela's lingering question is a penetrating one. Why, indeed? Do events on the world stage cause, in *Star Wars*–speak, a disturbance in the Force— a sympathetic resonance that sets hundreds, thousands, even millions of minds vibrating like tuning forks as a titanic chord is about to sound?

One spring night in 1902, encamped with his infantry company in South Africa, far from any newspaper or mail, J. W. Dunne dreamed he was

> *standing on high ground—the upper slopes of some spur of a hill or mountain. . . . Here and there in this were little fissures, and from these jets of vapour were spouting upward. In my dream I recognized the place as an island of which I had dreamed before—an island which was in imminent peril from a volcano. I gasped: "It's the island. Good Lord, the whole thing is going to blow up!" . . . Forthwith I was seized with a frantic desire to save the four thousand (I knew the number) unsuspecting inhabitants. Obviously there was only one way of doing this, and that was to take them off in ships. There followed a most distressing nightmare, in which I was at a neighbouring island, trying to get the incredulous French authorities to dispatch vessels of every and any description.*[12]

Some days later, when his company received their next mail pouch, it contained a newspaper with the headline: "Volcano Disaster in Martinique: Town Swept Away in Avalanche of Flame, Probable Loss of Over 40,000 Lives, British Steamer Burnt." (Dunne wrote that as he was reading the newspaper in haste, he mistakenly saw the figure 4,000 instead of 40,000—another example of the peculiar "literalism" of such dreams. His dream was partly about the real event and partly about reading the shocking news.) As in Pamela's dream, his vision was accompanied by feelings of sympathy, a desperate desire to help, though the catastrophe could not be prevented.

Is it possible that certain events are immutable? Dunne's volcano is Nature at her most merciless. The terrible event *must* happen, and we can only watch, helpless, like the Plains Indian prophets whose visions foresaw the onrush of American Manifest Destiny, but in the end could do nothing to stop it. J. B. Priestley, analyzing his collection of hundreds of precognitive dreams, estimated that just under half of dreams that came true concerned death and tragedy, while the other half were predictions of trivial, seemingly insignificant events. Both types, on opposite ends of the spectrum, seemed to possess a certain inevitability. He suggested that it is in the large space between these two extremes, where most of life is enacted, that we can exercise the greatest free will.

Is there a "soft future" and a "hard future," one written in sand, the other carved in stone? Perhaps it is to these latter the Zohar speaks: "Nothing takes place in the world but what has previously been made known, either by means of a dream or by means of a proclamation, for it has been affirmed that before any event comes to pass in the world, it is first announced in heaven, whence it is proclaimed to the world."[13]

Maybe it is the sheer number of witnessing minds and the force of collective emotion—in cases such as the *Titanic* disaster (where some nineteen precognitive dreams were documented, some by passengers who heeded their premonitions not to embark)—that determine the strength of the "signal" from the future. Do we have a future dream about a world event not because we are seeing something about to happen but because the future, where it has *already* happened, is sending its collective gasp of amazement back to us, like radio waves propagating outward from a supernova?

Physicist Fred Alan Wolf suggests that every conscious observation sends one "probability wave" toward the future and another toward the past, so that our past, present, and future minds are all significantly associated.[14] More than associated, he says, but bound: "Information can flow from past to present and from future to present. Thus it implies the existence of both the past and the future 'simultaneously' with our time."[15]

I thought of this notion of temporal simultaneity while reading about a museum that exhibited a giant hologram of a woman blowing a bubble. As visitors walked along, a sequence would unfold: the woman would bring the bubble blower to her mouth; a soap bubble would form; and then the bubble would pop. The observer could view these events as linear and causal—as past, present, and future—but the time sequence is an illusion. The entire activity is already present within the hologram. The woman is ever raising the toy to her lips, blowing her evanescent bubble, seeing its soft explosion—all at the same time.[16] It suggests what quantum physicist and former Einstein colleague David Bohm called a "nonlocality," where all points in space-time are in touch with all other points.

Bohm once theorized that as the present unfolds and becomes part of the past, the past still continues to exist: "The past is active in the present." An illustration of this principle can perhaps be found in the case of Stefan Ossowiecki, a Russian-born clairvoyant, who was studied at the University of Warsaw because of his apparent ability to derive, from often featureless ancient artifacts, extraordinarily accurate knowledge of their geographic and historical origins. Ossowiecki maintained that when he held the objects, he could see scenes from the past unfolding before him like a three-dimensional movie, just as if they were happening now. His eyes would move back and forth as if responding to actual physical presences. He would see not only landscapes and buildings but individual lives being lived out, which he said he could fast-forward through or pause to examine as he wished.[17]

Tom Brown, Jr., a well-known modern wilderness "tracker," describes the occasion when an Apache shaman he called Grandfather taught him about what he referred to as "the veil." Alongside this apparent world, the shaman said, is another one, which can be penetrated through a radical emptying out of our preconceptions and a suspending of analytic thought. Explaining that the veil "knows no time," Grandfather insisted that ancient events could be experienced in the present by one who knew the technique. After years of apprenticeship, Brown claims to have had this experience one day, when he "saw" a band of Indians from centuries before making their way through the pine barrens. He saw one of them drop a stone berry-masher along the trail. He later went back to the area and located the artifact, which he found buried beneath a pine tree root. It turned out to be made of a river rock typically found hundreds of miles distant, along the Delaware River.[18]

Knower of the Three Times

Sometimes it seems only indigenous cultures remember how to navigate this backward-and-forward world of time. Anthropologist Geoffrey Gorer writes, in his 1935 book *Africa Dances:* "Their idea of time is extremely peculiar. The present, the past, and the future are inextricably mingled. . . . Most dream experiences are believed as implicitly as physical ones. . . . It is my belief that natives, without the inhibitions which our view of time and a causal universe impose upon us, regularly dream the future as much as the past, and as vividly, with the result that the ideas 'present,' 'past' and 'future' have no meaning to them as they have to us."[19]

It suggests a notion of time radically different from everyday experience, similar, if anything, to the Australian aboriginal Dreamtime, in which ancestral time back to Creation is considered part of the present. Much has been written on this enigmatic concept. One book defines Dreamtime as "the creative activity of a primordial being leaving lore and landscape in its wake." But Bob Randal, a member of Australia's Pitjantjatjara tribe, told me, "Dreamtime's the white people's word. They may think they understand it, but they don't." The aboriginal word *tjukurrpa,* he explained, implies the totality of past, present, and future. "It's not just some way-back 'creation time.' It's now, *and* the past, *and* the future—all of it!" he said, making an inclusive, circular motion. (A similar idea, perhaps, is implied in the honorific applied to a great Tibetan lama—"Knower of the Three Times.")

In the geometric fantasy-cum-spiritual parable, *Flatland,* we are asked us to imagine an inhabitant of a two-dimensional universe. When a sphere first touches his planar world, he sees a point that becomes a widening circle as the sphere passes through, then dwindles in diameter back to a point and vanishes. No one can convince the Flatlanders that the weird and mystical series of events they've witnessed are evidence of a single, unified entity called a three-dimensional object.

Perhaps we three-dimensional beings have a similarly shortsighted relationship to a fourth dimension, commonly conceived of as time. Healing Dreams may be a glimpse of a greater "nonlocal" reality passing through our usual plane of existence—some fourth-dimensional hypersphere where past, present, and future are all at once (just as the dimensions of length, breadth, and height are present "all at once" in a solid object). Nor are a mere four dimensions adequate: physicists like A. S. Eddington, John Wheeler, and Richard Feynman have suggested that there are not one but *two* separate time dimensions, one of the past-to-present-to-future variety ("directed" time) and the other, at a quantum level, an omni-directional time that travels both backward and forward. The latest mathematical investigations of what physicists call hyperspace have led to the conclusion that we live in a universe made up of at least *ten* or more dimensions.

Fred Alan Wolf, with whom I once shared a long car ride through the forests of rural British Columbia, believes that post-quantum physics argues for a peculiar mutability of time itself. "If the future communicates with the present," he said, his excitement bordering on agitation, "then the present must be communicating with the past, which would mean that time is just not fixed." As we talked, I drifted back to a conversation I once had with an American Jewish man ordained as a leader in the eight-hundred-year-old Halveti-Jerrahi order of Sufism. "In our tradition," he told me, "fate is not immutable. But if you don't do the right thing with a dream—or, worse, do the wrong thing—your fate gets locked in. If you continue as a slave of past habits, the dream will come true. But a sheikh can, by interpreting a dream, actually change the thrust of its outcome."

As Sufis are apt to do, he launched into a teaching story:

"A man who had recently become a dervish had a powerful dream that a big, frightening black snake had emerged from his belly. He lived outside the city and didn't have time to journey to see his teacher, so he sent his servant to bring the dream to him, ask him to interpret it, and bring back the answer. But as the servant walked to town, a friend fell in beside him, pestering him until he told the man's dream. The friend laughed: 'It means his guts will come out of his stomach and he'll die.'

"The servant reached the teacher and began to relate his master's dream. 'Stop!' said the sheikh. 'It has *already* been interpreted. Now go back and see what has happened.' And when he got back, his discovered his master had suddenly died."

In Sufi doctrine, he continued, the interpreter of a dream has the power to "change or even deter its meaning. The act of interpretation itself is a creative event." He added, "You can't unread the letter once it's read. Maybe in its unread state, it has more possibilities."

Something was tugging annoyingly at a corner of my mind. I realized why this idea sounded so familiar: It was the paradox of Schrödinger's cat, a brainteaser used to illustrate the nature of quantum reality. Schrödinger's famous thought-experiment posits that a cat has been confined in a sealed box with a device that has a fifty-fifty chance of emitting a poison gas and killing it. The cat exists in both potential states—alive *and* dead—until the box is opened and the cat's condition is "read" by an observer. The metaphor means that a quantum wave, which is indeterminate, "collapses" into a determinate, verifiable state out of a cloud of probabilities only when it is measured. This is the so-called "observer effect" in quantum mechanics, where the act of observation itself causes a potentiality to become an actuality. When it comes to dreams, *interpretation* may be the act of measurement that "collapses the wave function," bringing forth meaning out of a cloud of myriad (and sometimes conflicting) possibilities. If an uninterpreted dream, says the Talmud, is like an unopened letter, could it also be like an unopened Schrödinger's cat box?

Schrödinger was passionately interested in the nature of time, once stating that Einstein's theory of relativity meant nothing less than "the dethronement of time as a rigid tyrant.") Einstein in 1928 bluntly disagreed: "We cannot send wire messages into the past." Einstein adamantly opposed the notion of precognition, that particles (let alone thought) could whiz back and forth along the world-lines of curved space-time. His modern heirs, however, argue that this is precisely the implication of his theories, as well as the measurable outcome of later experiments. (Physicist John Wheeler's "delayed choice" measurements, for instance, imply that a choice made in the present determines what the past *had to have been*.)[20]

We can be forgiven for feeling a painful stretching sensation as the mind tries valiantly to wrap itself around such paradoxes. The best analogy from quantum physics, writes Wolf, is that "the river of time has two counter-streaming currents. Information coming from the future as well as from the past influences the present." He bids us imagine that this river of time is filled with bottles containing messages, some floating upstream from the great ocean of information in the past, others flowing downstream from the mountain of information in the future. We reach into the river to pluck one out—the equivalent of looking into the box containing Schrödinger's cat. But rather, in that moment of reaching for it, "a past bottle and a future bottle coalesce into one bottle." Only then does a message appear in the bottle explaining the situation at the present moment—a message that takes into account past and future probabilities.[21] In this theory, our present moment is not separate from the past and the future—it is a confluence of them. (Dunne anticipated this model when he conjectured: "Was it possible . . . that dreams—dreams in general, all dreams, everybody's dreams—were composed of images of past experience and images of future experience blended together in approximately equal proportions?"[22])

Some of Wolf's interpretations of quantum theory seem to provide a weird logic for the apotropaic warding-off rituals of tribal societies (like that of the Seneca man who tried to keep his dream of a woman stranded in a canoe from coming true by making a miniature replica). Wolf suggests that quantum waves moving from the present *toward* the future meet and clash with waves coming *from* the future. If the waves "match" and produce a combined wave of a certain strength, then "a real future is created from our present point of view, and a real memory of sequences is created in the future." Is it possible a ceremony—or even a dream itself—

sends a wave toward the future so complementary in pattern as to mitigate the one roaring toward the present? (In the dream realm, a symbol is real—perhaps it has the same "wave form" as the actual event.) Wolf postulates that our present is "broadcast" to many possible futures, while many potential futures are broadcasting back in time to us.[23] Which ones link up to create reality depends on factors he calls, somewhat mysteriously, "resonance" and even "meaning."

Healing Time

What *is* the meaning of these strange phenomena? The idea that the present is joined in living relationship to the future and the past—that time is a circle, not a line—is characteristic of traditional cultures, where ancient Creation time and the prophetic future are woven together in art, in ceremony, and even in perception. To experience time as the dream reveals that it shakes loose a pillar of ego-centered living; for it is the ego that is time-squeezed, haunted by the might-have-beens of an irretrievable past; by a present that sifts away like sand, ungraspable; by a future of nerve-wracking uncertainty. The Tibetan ritual of the Kalachakra ("the Wheel of Time") speaks of two kinds of time, one "black," the other "white." Black time is represented as clockwise, the time of the everyday, hemmed with regrets for the past, hopes and fears for the future, anxiety and scheming in the present. But "white time" moves counterclockwise, unwinding the constricted logic of ego; here, the three times are fused into a moment. The wound made by the arrow of time is salved and healed.

The notion of "healing time" may rightfully strike us as odd. Time just *is*—as immutable and onrushing as the tide. But the Healing Dream suggests that the modern condition is not only soulsick but timesick. An acquaintance of mine, an award-winning, overscheduled L.A. screenwriter with multiple projects on the boil, confided she has been having the same repetitive dream since she was twelve: *I am rushing around, by car and airplane, to get to appointments I can never make on time. Then a voice announces: "This is the Farthest Place from Anywhere. It takes four and half hours to get here, but only fifteen minutes to get back."* She laughs at the ironic goad: "In my dream, everything is about time; but none of the time makes sense." Her dream tries to cure her not only of her tendency to speed madly through life, with never enough hours in the day, but also of our supposedly sensible notions of time itself.

In our culture, we are pleased to view ourselves as commuters along the time line on the sleek monorail of the present, leaving behind an encumbering past, free of a preordained future. This is how we have been socialized to experience time. But the phenomenologist C. J. Ducasse has argued that, in view of quantum physics, past, present, and future must be considered only psychological states with no real meaning in physical terms. My dream experiences have often led me to feel I am living partway in a future that is already taking form, one foot in a past that is still alive and even in some strange way malleable. Sometimes this sensation is deeply disturbing; other times, I've found it oddly comforting. I feel less separated from my past, present, and future selves; they are with me, and I with them, curiously joined at the hip.

My future dreams have come to seem less like inescapable fate than trajectories that reach their end point only in the absence of a course correction. I think often of the question posed by Scrooge to the Spirit of Christmas Future: *Why show me this if I cannot change?* Each moment is a fulcrum of choice; every act, every thought is consequential to the future, and perhaps even to the past. Beholding the seed, I cannot but feel I stand in the rustling shade of the tree it will become—and the one from which it has fallen. Perhaps such a worldview, of all three times "present" at once, explains traditional peoples' sense of kinship with generations departed, as well as their obligation to the "seventh generation" to come.

For the Time Being

The Hopi language does not designate past, present, and future tenses but rather two temporal forms—the "already manifest" and the "not yet manifest" (or "coming into being"). The already manifest is our commonsense objective world. But the coming into being, they say, belongs to the subjective realm. Both the remote past and the future are denoted by subjective word forms. This may be one culture's iteration of the plausible notion that only the present truly exists, while the past is reimagined and the future conjectured. But it seems to contain the nuance that we have a hand in all three times, are full creative participants. The Hopi verb for the not yet manifest is *tunyata*—"to think, to wish, to cause."

"Our minds are time machines," proclaims physicist Wolf, "able to sense the flow of possibility waves from both the past and the future." But is that mind that senses time's waves yet held tightly within its grasp? Or in Healing Dreams, do we become observers *outside* time, just as museumgoers observing the hologram of the bubble blower can see past, present, and future in a single long glance?

The intrepid J. W. Dunne suggested that by "disengaging from the trammels of self-conscious existence," one becomes "an observer at infinity." The Healing Dream may have a vantage point in what he referred to as "Absolute Time." Jung, too, wrote about "an existence outside time which runs parallel with existence inside time. Yes, we ourselves may simultaneously exist in both worlds, and occasionally we do have intimations of a twofold existence. But what is outside time is, according to our understanding, outside change. It possesses relative eternity."[24]

The Healing Dream immerses us in the palpable reality that we are more than we think we are, allows us to escape, for a moment, being boundaried creatures in a boundless universe. Perhaps the gateway of dreaming leads to what mystics call the Timeless. Or perhaps we are experiencing, first-hand, the quantum physicists' version of things—waves upon an ocean, giving the appearance of objects moving through space in time, but in reality just undulations in a spacetime continuum.

But when it comes to the Eternal, science, at last, fails us. We are in territory to which only poets lay claim. T. S. Eliot, in "Four Quartets," presents us with both a conundrum and a promise:

> And we shall not cease from exploration.
> Time present and time past

Are both perhaps present in time future,
And time future contained in time past. . . .
What might have been and what has been
Point to one end, which is always present. . . .

And the end of all our exploring
Will be to arrive where we started
And know the place for the first time.

Chapter 9

The Otherworld

Joining Heaven and Earth

We have placed in you a substance,
a seeking, a yearning, and
we are watching over it and won't let it be lost,
but will bring it to its destined place.

—Rumi

What happens if you gaze into Eternity, and Eternity gazes back?

Several years ago, national newspapers seized on the story of the young CEO of a multimillion-dollar Internet company who resigned his position after a vivid dream of "a remarkable being clothed in brilliant white light." The man said the Christ-like apparition held a glowing blue sphere, and entrusted him with key insights about humanity's place in the cosmos. One of his former colleagues, who had previously regarded him as an entrepreneurial genius, was quoted calling him "a crackpot." But the man's vision had a real-world outcome, inspiring him to invest millions in the start-up of an "e-commerce" company whose aim was to produce revenues for environmentally friendly causes.

His story is a vivid reminder of the power of otherworldly visions, even in a distinctly worldly age. Dreams of divinities and heavenly realms have instigated religions, fueled the imaginings of poets and madmen, emboldened saints and suicide bombers. Dreamers have told me of visits to fantastic places where they beheld, unforgettably, an eternal order that both underlies and transcends our day-to-day reality. The encounters caused them to question many of their previous assumptions, even to reorient their lives and work along the lines of their spiritual vision. Whatever we may think of such accounts, we must take seriously the power and mystery of a dream that leave an indelible brand upon the soul. But it is hard to know what to do with these travelers' tales and their news of a far country.

I might be more likely to discount such dispatches had I not once had my own strange dream concerning a dear friend. Nancy Wilson Ross was the sort of mentor every young seeker on the path should have the good fortune to meet. She had studied with Carl Jung at Kusnacht. She had been an adventuress in Asia; a war correspondent (she'd stood at arm's length from Hitler when he shuttered the Bauhaus); the author of a bestselling novel (the now obscure *The Left Hand Is the Dreamer*); and finally a kind of unofficial abbess of a Zen center in San Francisco. Solicitous and shrewd, she made everyone she took under wing feel surfeited with gifts and talents. She would divine your uniqueness, then hold you mercilessly accountable for it. She was living proof that one could lead a spiritual life while keeping one's feet firmly rooted in terra firma.

I'd met her when she was in her mid-seventies, still glowing with the vitality of a woman half her age. I'd visit her in her loaned house on a grand estate, staying up late talking and laughing, quaffing tumblers of what she called "the Mellon elixer," a privately distilled whiskey with which the famous philanthropic family kept her generously stocked.

Nancy was an unfailing correspondent, seeming to know exactly when to call or write with a timely observation, a morsel of encouragement, or the name of a contact she was convinced you had to know. "I was born," she would say assuredly, "with the caul over my eyes"—a sign in Irish folk culture of a clairvoyant child. As my professional life ate up too much of my private one, we'd lost touch; her last letter had sat in silent reproach for six months on a corner of my desk. But one night during this hiatus in our friendship I was struck by a vivid dream:

> *Nancy is going to be inducted by a Gathering of the Immortals, and I am to be her escort. But I've started out late. By the time we arrive at our destination—a magnificent Grecian amphitheater of brilliant white marble—there are no seats left on the concentric stone benches. Instead, we have to stand in the aisle as a white-robed Speaker unscrolls a document made of human skin and recites a glowing encomium to Nancy.*

The dream had unsettled and awed me. I had thought of phoning her right away, then hesitated. I owed her a letter, not some quick call about a cornball fantasy. But the vision refused to dissipate. Worried, I called her house and left a message. A mutual friend got back to me the next day: Nancy had been taken to the hospital the very night of my dream suffering from a myocardial infarction. She had lingered several days near death, then had rallied and was making a full recovery.

When I told Nancy my dream during her convalescence, she just laughed: "You were born with the caul, too, my boy. Better get used to it." She was soon back on her feet, brushing infinity aside to return to life's perishable wonders. But I brooded over my dream. What *was* that place, anyway? It was so "heavenly"—the afterlife as an Olympian toga party. At least the dream maker had spared me wings and gilded slippers. Imagery of heaven—typically a kind of Pearly Gated community reminiscent of ancient Athens—is well dispersed in Western culture. But it's not a dream scene I've experienced before or since. I've heard the same sort of thing from unlikely sources, such as my Cree friend Sylvia, who told me she once dreamed: *I'm in a huge, very ornate building made of marble where some kind of teachings are going on. Everything is circular, the halls, the floors—even a circular stairway.* "Being a nature person," she says, "I could never figure out why it wasn't outside." Another woman, who'd grown up so deep in the West Virginia hill country her family didn't have books, get a newspaper, go to movies, or own a TV set until she was seventeen, remembered a childhood dream of being in "another dimension and time. I saw the biggest marble plaza, with large marble columns, and men and women with white robes tied with rope sashes and long flowing hair. I'd never seen people like that. There were incredible flowers whose brilliant colors I haven't seen to this day. I knew I was in a real place, in the presence of God's folk."

The author Aldous Huxley, imaginer of brave new worlds, wrestled with the thread of consistency running through such otherworldly reports. He notes in his book *Heaven and Hell* that Socrates described an "other earth," complete with mountains and rivers and buildings, whose common stones surpassed the most precious jewels in purity, brilliance, and intensity of hue. Huxley wondered at the similarity with experiences on mind-altering compounds such as mescaline or lysergic acid, visions of

vast and complicated buildings, in the midst of landscapes which change continuously, passing from richness to more intensely colored richness, from grandeur to deepening grandeur. Heroic figures, of the kind that Blake called "The Seraphim," may make their appearance, alone or in multitudes. . . . Almost never does the visionary see anything that reminds him of his own past. He is not remembering scenes, persons or objects, and he is not inventing them; he is looking on at a new creation.[1]

Huxley would have been interested to learn that the images of dream sleep are now thought to be activated by compounds in the body, the beta-carbolines, also found in psychedelic botanicals.[2] He concluded that, whatever their source, all visionary experiences are of the "same species," their "preternatural aesthetic" deriving from "the stuff of the mind's antipodes." He continued to puzzle over their universality: "Why this should be so," he wrote, "we have no idea. It is a brute fact of experience which, whether we like it or not, we have to accept—just as we have to accept the fact of kangaroos."[3]

If a numinous aesthetic is a staple of the mystical dream, the images it illumines vary from dreamer to dreamer. The futurist and visionary David Spangler once described for me a Healing Dream featuring a Supreme Being of more pagan character:

I'm looking at a house I lived in as a child. A large but not fat woman comes out, almost as tall as the house itself, wearing a voluminous dress. I go up the walkway to the front door, then realize her dress is the walkway, the lawn, every-thing—the whole landscape is coming from her dress, which I now see is a mass of brilliant plant life. She herself is made of fleshlike vegetation. I approach her with trepidation, realizing that at any moment I could be absorbed by her, and that I'm walking this earth at her suffrage. The closer I get, the greater the possibility I will be engulfed. Terror wells up. Yet I say to her, I'm here, I'm willing to be absorbed. Like, Lord, here am I. She smiles, as if to say, No, not this time.

A psychoanalyst might have a field day with the image of a gigantic, en-gulfing matron associated with a boy's childhood home. But the dream, Spangler says, was a spiritual turning point, a direct encounter with the Great Goddess of all living things. "I'd passed some initiation. I surren-dered to utter powerlessness. I stopped putting out that energy we all ex-pend shielding ourselves from the world. I realized to approach the sacred is to risk everything. In my dream, I'd taken an irreversible step."

Such dreams of an embracing eternal order augment or transcend our usual religious categories. It is as if the dreamer has gone straight to the Source. Yet such experiences may sometimes place them on a collision course with theological dogma. Roger, a therapist, told me of a dream that became a touchstone for all his beliefs. In it, he was given a guided tour of Creation by the "Power of the Universe":

This Power takes me through realms of life where colors are richer, smells more wonderful, tactile feeling so much more intense. I wake up for a minute, see that our reality is actually concurrent with this one, then I say silently, Let's go back, and am instantly returned to this ecstatic experience. The Power of the Universe then shows me a map, which I see has a quadrant that "God" rules, a little con-tained world. This, the Power implies, isn't the real Immensity. Finally, feeling as full as I could be, I decide to return to this life.

Roger says the sense of a larger "concurrent reality" has lingered for twenty years. "It's right next to me, even as I'm just getting in and out of the car to go shopping. I'm *still* living out the questions that dream provoked—not just philosophically but what it means here in the sensuous world." The dream communicated the same understanding given to religious mystics throughout history: the Divine is a vastness beyond all conception, yet its resplendent glory is right under our nose.

I heard a different sort of divine encounter from actress Martha del Grande. After years of living at a plateau of success, Martha had taken up residence in her own private hell. In her early thirties, her husband had left and moved to California. She had bought a decrepit rooming house in Toronto she planned to fix up but soon found herself impossibly deep in hock, taking care of two small kids and an infirm father-in-law. She poured what money remained into the crumbling structure, watching it run out through every leak in the plumbing and hole in the floorboards.

"Pretty soon," Martha says in her self-mocking way, "I was cracking! One evening, my father-in-law was taking a bath, reached up, and tore off the soapdish holder. I just went nuts, crying and carrying on. I scooped up my little daughter, ran to church, and told the priest I wanted to make open confession. He listened, then said essentially, 'You're about to flip out. I'm gonna pray for you, but you need to get into therapy.'" That night, Martha had a powerful dream:

My body is all covered in big running sores, my hair is dirty and matted in dreadlocks, I'm wearing sooty clothes, smoking cigarettes, and cursing a blue streak: Goddamn sonofabitch! Then I hear a laugh, and see a light. A face appears, then a body like an angel. And I say, Motherf---er! You love me, don't you?

And he says, I love every cell in your body.

Then I say, Who the hell are you—Jesus?

And he says, Yes, I am. I brought you up to heaven to show you how much I love you. Then, as if he has an X ray that shines clear through me, he shows me all my sins, which flash onto a big neon sign like a scoreboard.

You know all of them? I ask.

Yes, but I love you anyway, he says. Love you like nothing on earth.

I say, Well, if I'm in heaven, I want to see everyone else who's here!

There's just you and me, he says. The way it works here is, I look at you,
and you look at me.
But I'm not ready for that! I tell him.
He agrees. That's why, he says, I'm sending you back.

Then Martha awoke, filled with an "ecstatic love like you can't conceive." Although she began seeing a therapist, the memory of that love was
to help her weather crisis after crisis. "I can't remember exactly what it felt
like, because we can't contain that intensity of feeling here on earth. But I
know it's the only thing that's real, the only thing that really exists in the
universe. And that knowledge keeps me going."

Many Heavens

Neither Roger nor Martha feels entirely comfortable hanging their hats in
the cloakroom of organized religion. Out of the almost infinite variety of
spiritual experiences reported around the world, some of them resulting in
sustained religious enterprises, who is to say which is intrinsically "true"?
The founder of Japan's Sukyo Mahikari religion dreamed of an old,
white-haired man standing on a white cloud washing clothes in a golden
tub, which he interpreted as "Su-God" (the Lord God) telling him to undertake a cleansing mission. The eighteenth-century Islamic reform leader
Sheikh Ahmad dreamed in his youth that he was taken to Paradise, where
he saw "figures and colors which dazzle the intelligence," and was received
by the Twelve Imams. A Salish Indian friend's husband had a massive heart
attack while on a hunting trip near Pendleton, Oregon. He had dreamed,
she told me, that "he was walking to a place on the other side, a shadow of
this world with trees, water, animals, people; you know, the 'Happy Hunting Ground.' He said it was beautiful," she said, adding for my benefit,
"like what *Indians* would think is beautiful."

What are we to make of dreams' varying models of a sacred realm beyond the apprehensible? Are we surrounded by multiple otherworlds, each

with its own assigned broadcast frequency, awaiting only the tuning of our dream receivers? Dreamers sense that they have encountered something eternally preexisting—beings and worlds fed not just by our own imaginings, but by that which is behind all imaginings. These experiences seem so self-contained, so self-proclaiming, they find it hard to question that they have been *somewhere*—only where?

The Sufis say there exists a dimension created out of the subtle matter of thought itself, the *alam almithal*, sometimes called "the country of the hidden Imam." (A twelfth-century Persian mystic named Sohrawardi said it might best be referred to as Na-Koja-Abad, "the Land of Nowhere.") It is conceived of in some Muslim traditions as a plane of existence born from the collective imagination of many people over time.[4] Islamic scholar Henry Corbin coined the term "imaginal" (as distinct from imaginary) to denote an experientially authentic, yet nonphysical realm that appears fully realized on its own terms:

> [It is] an intermediate world, the world of Idea-Images, of archetypal figures, of subtle substances, of "immaterial matter." This world is as real and objective, as consistent and subsistent as the intelligible and sensible worlds; it is an intermediate universe "where the spiritual takes body and body becomes spiritual." . . . It is the scene on which visionary events and symbolic histories appear in their true reality. The organ of this universe is the active Imagination.[5]

Corbin is careful to specify that even the most vivid otherworld dreams are also symbolic, though the impact of the raw experience can overwhelm even the most spiritually sophisticated traveler. Once, just before dawn, the tenth-century Tibetan Buddhist sage Gampopa had a prodigious dream: he saw himself *wearing silken robes adorned with holy images, in ornaments of pearl and silver, drinking golden nectar from a skullcup, beholding a bodhisattva on a lotus seat in a field of flowers, framed by a brilliant, multicolored aura.*

The dream, the text comments, "bore no relationship at all to his previous habitual thinking." Gampopa awoke so confused he forgot to put on his robe and ran naked to his guru, Milarepa, to plead for an explanation.

Milarepa at first informed him he had been merely "caught" by his dreams: "Dreams are unreal and deceptive, as was taught/By Buddha Himself/To collect, supply and study them/Will bring little profit." Having sounded the proper cautionary note, however, Milarepa asserted in a different vein: "And yet, your dreams were marvelous/Wondrous omens foretelling things to come!" He went on to explain the symbolic meaning of each adornment: "The white hat on your head indicates that your View will go beyond the 'high' and 'low.' . . . The magnificent Vajra skull you dreamt of holding shows that you will illustrate the truth of Voidness. . . . The Bodhisattva in the Lotus Posture signifies that you, the young Bodhisattva, will abide not in Nirvana but with great compassion will transform your body into many forms to help the mother-like sentient beings."[6]

Otherworldly visions are often a potent mix of what feels like actual experience compounded with symbolism that matches the dreamer's preconceptions. Dream researcher Fariba Bogzaran studied a group of lucid dreamers to compare their conscious understanding of "the Divine" with their experience of it in dreams. Approximately one third of her subjects subscribed to the existence of a personal God, while the other two-thirds believed in an "all-compassing Energy" or other impersonal forces. Tabulating their dreams, Bogzaran found, not surprisingly, that the majority of those who held with a personal God encountered a divine personage, while those who saw divinity as impersonal had experiences matching their beliefs. For example, one believer in a personal God dreamed:

> *I am floating and see the back of a throne. A chair arm, solid and massive, is cut into a marble block. I creep around the side and see a person's arm on the marble chair arm. The hand is old, but firm and strong, like a carpenter's. The sleeve is white and full. The fingers are curved downward over the edge of the arm—relaxed but full of life. I can't see higher than the elbow from my position, but I know it is God without any doubt.*[7]

By contrast, a person in Bogzaran's study who believed in a more impersonal divine force reported the following dream: *Before me appears a moving picture with numerous interwoven cycles—like the workings of a clock. It is also like patterns of pulsating light and shadow. No complete cycle can be seen.* Each image conveys in differing terms something rarely experienced in waking life—the sense of Something so vast that its workings dwarf human comprehension, allowing only a partial vision of its infinitude.

The geography and demography of the otherworld is so diverse that it often leads people outside the bounds of their faith for answers. Bernadette, a former anatomy instructor reared in a strict, churchgoing home, might have remained a self-described "dyed-in-the-wool Catholic" were it not for a Healing Dream that made her believe there were things that "either the Church wasn't telling me on purpose or the priests didn't know any more about than I do."

Before the Vatican II reforms, when the Church still used its power of Imprimatur to decree which books were best suited to the faithful, Bernadette felt a "burning desire to know about other belief systems, what great minds had thought in other cultures, what *their* experience of God was like." But leaving "Holy Mother Church" remained a daunting prospect: "I was afraid to be an outcast," Bernadette says. "To be all alone, maybe never finding my way to God or to heaven." In the midst of her anguished reflections, she had an extraordinary dream:

It is a jungle scene. I see a person frantically hacking a path through the vegetation. Then I seem to recede back until I can see the entire earth. From this aerial viewpoint, I perceive that this person is trying to get to the Land of Light, which in the dream is located at the North Pole. But I see with happy surprise there are many paths leading to this Land. Some appear as footpaths and have scattered travelers, others have ruts made by wagon trains, some are very broad, tree-lined avenues, some are even superhighways, but they all end up at the same place. I also notice that many of the travelers are not getting to their destination. They pause to embellish the path, or create edifices alongside the path which they then stop to worship.

The dream occurred twenty-five years ago, she says, but "if it were last night, it couldn't be more vivid. I was comforted. The vision told me it was not wrong or evil or sinful to try another path. I was finally free to leave the only way I'd ever known." Secure in the knowledge that religious institutions were at best way stations, at worst roadblocks, and never final destinations, Bernadette went on to study a variety of spiritual paths, eventually being ordained as an interfaith minister.

A patient of Jung's once described an otherworldly dream he'd had of a gigantic construction site where people of all races and creeds were erecting a complex of buildings that reached to the sky. Jung promptly informed him that they were building "the new religion," one which would supersede the sectarian approaches to God that had dominated human history. He had been to this place himself, he explained to his startled patient, adding that this great work would not be completed for another five hundred years.

In every religion, there are those who seek to shatter the shell of iconography and dogma to penetrate to some kernel of universal truth. The Sufis seek *fana,* a dissolution of outward religious and cultural identity, so that *baqa,* the new man, might arise. The Trappist iconoclast Thomas Merton, distinguishing between sentimentalized mysticism and genuine "transcendence," noted that St. John of the Cross was "hostile to visions, ecstasies, and all forms of 'special experience.'" Merton suggested that the Christian vision of God and the enlightenment of Zen had in common a "psychic limitlessness,"[8] citing with favor the Zen admonition against substituting images of the divine for actual illumination: "If you meet the Buddha, kill him!" Even in the tantric traditions of Tibet, the elaborate pantheons are understood to be emanations of *dharmadhatu,* the formless, all-pervading Ultimate, devoid of preconception.

It is a view similar to that of the anonymous fourteenth-century Christian author of *The Cloud of Unknowing,* who was skeptical about seekers who put too much stock in visions:

> In their mental fantasies they penetrate to the planets, and make a hole in the firmament, and look through! They make a God to their liking, and

give him rich clothes, and set him on a throne, and it is all much odder than any painting! They make angels have human shapes, and plant them about, each one with a different musical instrument. . . . The work of our spirit does not go up or down, sideways, forward, or backward, like some physical thing.[9]

Here we are being urged not merely to see but also to see *through*. Behind the myriad guises of the divine in Healing Dreams is a Source that begs our notice in the things of *this* world. The Teton Sioux leader Lone Man said a "Thunder Being" taught him in a dream: "This earth is under the protection of something which at times becomes visible to the eye. One would think that this would be at the center of the earth, but its representations appear everywhere, in large and small forms."

The Dark Night

St. John of the Cross viewed heavenly visions as time spent in "swaddling clothes" at God's "gentle breast" before attaining spiritual maturity. "When they believe that the sun of divine favor is shining most brightly upon them," he writes with a certain irony, "God turns all this light of theirs into darkness." It is not God's punishment, he explained, but a loving pedagogy, an immolation in God's "dark fire" to "strip the soul" of its vanities. Only after many such "dark nights" is the soul sufficiently emptied out to be filled with divine light.

Katharine had never read St. John, had never heard him describe the spiritual pilgrim's time spent bereft in the wilderness. She called her dark night of the soul simply "the Vacuum," or the Black Year. There seemed no escape from deepest depression—the kind of despair in which darkness wraps itself around the heart and squeezes the life from each dawn.

She loosened its coils slightly walking through a park near her home, marching ten or fifteen miles a day, one foot in front of the other, like a soldier in a defeated army too stubborn to surrender. Striding past other strollers symbolized and redeemed ever so slightly her sense of being an interloper in the world of the daylight folk whose lives somehow functioned. One day as she wound around the path, feeling more than usual a suicidal emptiness, she passed "a little old man with a cane." He said a few innocuous words as she brushed by, "something funny about how tense I looked, how strained my posture was." After she passed him, she recalls, "These odd feelings of total freedom rushed through me, kind of a physical euphoria. It was weird. I looked back, but he wasn't there."

She doesn't know if the strange encounter was somehow the cause, but that night, she had a "most amazing" dream:

> *I am in a vacuum, floating and whirling around. I feel as if everything is being sucked out of me, and I'm utterly terrified. Then my point of view pans back, like a camera in a movie to give a larger picture, and all around me is the image of two hands. Big hands, like the hands of God. As if the vacuum were contained and even protective, encapsulated by a divine Something.*

The vivid dream "just snapped me into a brand-new perspective." It seemed to effect a near-instantaneous cure. She felt the dark weight lifting the very next day as thoughts of the future came flooding back. The Black Year, it now seemed to her, had had a secret, higher purpose all along. "I somehow *had* to have everything taken from me, *had* to feel completely alone, to receive spiritual deepening." The sun continued to burn off the fog. Within a week, she had volunteered to work in a nearby women's shelter, using her near-forgotten degree in psychology to counsel cancer patients. "I knew I had some healing force inside me that everyone has. I was using the gift of the Black Year to help people empower themselves in their own darkness. Before that dream, all I could think about was dead trees, winter coming. Then, suddenly—I know this sounds a little ridiculous—it was spring."

Other dreamers described similar "dark nights" culminating in otherworldly Healing Dreams. Chuck, who for thirty years had been a successful computer scientist, suddenly came down with chronic fatigue syndrome. Life became a dead zone lit in vaporous gray, its people, places, and things reduced to sketches in charcoal. One night, at his breaking point, he dreamed *I'm in a room in a house trying to pry a dead body out of the wall and put it into this box. I guess the box is a coffin, but it's also a rectangular piece of fine furniture with an enticing finished top, in the middle of which, I'm surprised to see, is a keyhole.* He realized with horror that the coffin was meant for him. But later, in an active imagination exercise, he looked through the keyhole and was shocked to see it was flooded with brilliant white light.

Still sick and depressed, Chuck was startled by another vivid dream:

> *I'm in San Francisco. Water is coming up through big cracks in the streets and the sidewalks with such force it is breaking the pavement. It is somewhat frightening. I climb a hill toward this big cathedral in the middle of town. Inside it, an incredible party is going on—a real celebration. It's a charismatic kind of service, very high energy, people literally swinging from the chandeliers, long tables set up and lots of feasting going on. It was great fun, even though I didn't know a soul there.*

In this dream, the waters of healing literally break through the old personality structures with a power so undeniable it intimidates him. Forces from deep within the psyche are welling up. He can no longer remain stuck where he is. High on a hill, overlooking the disintegrating city of the self, he discovers at its center a truly holy church—a place of uplifting merriment, whose rafters ring with joy and whose tables groan with soul food. It is religion become spirit. When he told me his dream, he grinned from ear to ear to remember this "really great time I had."

Shortly thereafter, Chuck found himself attending a psychology workshop, somewhat skeptically going along with an exercise in which people paired off and repetitively asked each other, "What do you want?"—a tool, the leader said, for bringing out unconscious goals, desires and drives. "After you go through all the surface stuff you *think* you want, you do get down to some pretty basic feelings. The dream seemed to have primed me for this in some way," Chuck says, "because the answer that fell out of my mouth was, 'Doing exactly what I'm doing right now.' Then I was overwhelmed with the same sense of joy I'd felt in the big cathedral. The room seemed to evaporate. There was a visual sense of an endless array of windows, a light that went from carmine to golden to a brilliant white. All sense of self, of space and time, was gone. I felt as if my soul was coming into existence, a sense of the real me. I seemed to hear a voice say inwardly, 'All is well with the world.' It only lasted a few seconds, but it left me dazed, barely functioning for days."

Chuck's dream led him to a dramatic change in vocation. He now felt a strong impulse to "work with the dying." As his symptoms of chronic fatigue subsided, he began to volunteer at the hospital as a nurses' aide, then was invited into the hospital chaplaincy. He protested that he didn't have the training or experience, but under the chaplain's gentle pressure, he gave in, following the man around as an intern. Chuck now runs a group at a local hospital for people who have had near-death experiences. He has, in a sense, made his own church within the Church, with the authority of one who has journeyed from death to life, from crumbling gray pavements to, for one unexpected moment, a shining City on a Hill.

Going to the Mountain

Although he had written a scholarly book on the Bible, Reynolds Price had always described his spirituality as "unchurchly," though "strong currents of impersonal force have pressed against my thoughts since infancy." Poet, essayist, novelist, and playwright, an honoree of the American Academy of Arts and Letters, he was at the pinnacle of his career when suddenly he plummeted down into the abyss. Medical tests uncovered a ten-inch tumor in his spinal cord, a dire malignancy of the central nervous system. The operation to remove it, though initially successful, led to his gradual paralysis.

Throughout his decline, his nights were tormented by "long credible nightmares . . . far more shapely and terrifying than any I could remember." In one, he found himself in a Caribbean hotel staffed by "real vampires who'd learned to tolerate the tropical sun. At first they were affable, charming me with perfect service, but actually waiting till they'd lowered my caution and could drain me dry." Bad dream followed bad dream, murderously unrelenting.

Then one night, when he was about to enter a five-week course of ionizing radiation, he had "the single strangest experience of my life." He'd seemed to waken at dawn, he wrote, but "not propped in my brass bed or even contained in my familiar house." Instead, he was lying fully dressed in modern street clothes on a slope by the Sea of Galilee in the time of Jesus. He could make out a dozen men in rough cloaks slumbering on the misty ground by the shore. *I am really here,* he marveled: he could see in remarkable detail the men's simple tunics, feel the night chill lifting as dawn turned the land tan and rose, smell the smoke of breakfast fires wafting from stone huts in the fishing villages of Capernaum and Bethesda just to the north.

Then one of the sleepers awoke, and he saw it was Jesus, "like the lean Jesus of Flemish paintings—tall with dark hair, unblemished skin and a self-possession both natural and imposing," dressed in a "twisted white cloth round his loins." He and Jesus waded together into the cool water twenty feet from shore. Jesus scooped handfuls of water over Price's head, letting it splash onto the purplish surgical wound on his back, then spoke once—"Your sins are forgiven"—and turned to go back to shore.

"I came on behind him, thinking in standard greedy fashion, *It's not my sins I'm worried about.* So to Jesus' receding back, I had the gall to say, 'Am I also cured?'

"He turned to face me, no sign of a smile, and finally said two words— 'That, too.'" Then, Price wrote, "with no palpable seam in the texture of time or place, I was home again in my wide bed."

He was astonished at this "concrete visual and tactile reality unlike any sleeping or waking dream I've known or heard of." It betrayed none of the surreal logic or the jerked-about plot of an actual dream. Nothing had resembled it "in five decades of a life rich in fantasy and longing."

Though he had cause to be dubious about it during the years of anguish that followed (one convincing nightmare portrayed his vision as "manufactured with fiendish cunning from Nazi propaganda, and somehow planted in me by Joseph Goebbels, Hitler's master liar"), the dream remained a consoling companion. He could summon at will the feeling of the "curative hand" that had bathed him.[10] Though he was never to have a restoration of his physical health, Price continued to feel surges of well-being flowing from his experience, and meditated with constancy on the mystery of forgiveness.

Coming Down: The Dream Embodied

Such Healing Dreams fall into a pattern common to shamans and mystics of all places and times. Some dire and dark defeat—through illness, perhaps, or loss and depression—is catalyst for a visionary experience. Only when the biblical Job is reduced to a sick, lonely pauper lamenting on an ash heap does God reveal to him the vastness of the cosmos. It is a well-known spiritual trajectory, where a descent is the necessary prelude to transformation, and infirmity the hard bedrock of a new wholeness.

San Francisco psychiatrist Louis Vuksinick knows this journey first-hand. A mild-mannered, sandy-haired man in his late fifties, partial to blue Oxford shirts and regimental ties, he seems an unlikely candidate to be carried away by mysticism's wild torrents. But like Reynolds Price, he was engulfed by a strange dream in the midst of a terrible physical trial. Hospitalized for six months when a near-fatal accident crushed his legs and pelvis, Vuksinick dreamed one night: *I am led to an opening in the ground. The passage downward is covered with dismembered body parts. At the deepest level underground, I enter a labyrinth and am taken to a chamber where a huge monster with blazing red eyes holds its captives, many of them children.*

It is the sort of Underworld dream that can be found in many accounts of spiritual initiation. But he and the Freudian analyst with whom he was training at the time were unprepared. "I never believed a dream could change your life or cause spiritual growth," Louis says. "The analyst's job was to rationally dissect it, to find the underlying conflicts and emotional traumas. I didn't know what to do with this." Then another titanic dream burst upon him, repeating for three consecutive nights:

I am looking up at the huge mountain which dominated the front view from my childhood home. A bright mystical light is glowing about three-quarters of the way up the center of the mountain. It marks the confluence of two great rivers, the Snake and the Siskiyou. Behind the confluence is a cave with a treasure. The scene then becomes a photograph with the date 1932 boldly displayed.

His psychoanalyst proposed that the mountain symbolized his father who had been a coal miner, while the cave was clearly a metaphor for his mother. "Even the mystical lights, he told me, were parental symbols—the whole thing was nothing but disguised family issues! At the time, I accepted it." But on the fourth night, Vuksinick dreamed that Jung himself appeared and handed him a book on dreams. The next day, thumbing through the index of a Jungian text, Vuksinick found that, rather than as a reflection of Oedipal conflict, Jung interpreted a confluence of rivers as a symbol of the powerful fluxes that lead to psychological integration.

When his analyst accused him of using Jung's ideas as "resistance," Vuksinick decided to leave. He began to experiment with somatic relaxation exercises, which unexpectedly produced an alarming series of physical symptoms. His body would suddenly go into convulsive paroxysms, becoming hot and painful. He would be awakened by "loud popping sounds" in his head. "Particles and brightly colored lights" danced before his eyes, while high-pitched buzzing sounds rattled his eardrums and sharp, incapacitating pains shot along nerve pathways. Over time, the sensations led to states of bliss, but his euphoria was often followed by depression. He feared he was losing his grip on sanity.

His experience, unbeknownst to him, could be found described nearly word for word in the autobiography of Gopi Krishna. A former clerk in India's Public Works Department who became a celebrated visionary, Krishna had taken up his own study of yoga, faithfully performing its psychophysical exercises in his spare time. But like Vuksinick, he was disconcerted by a sudden eruption of bizarre physical symptoms: "roaring sounds and weirdly moving lights," heat like "the ruddy blast from a furnace . . . scorching and blistering the organs." He, too, experienced violent shocks along his nerves, and a flooding brightness, at first "a thin stream of radiant essence," then "an effulgent, cascading shower of brilliant vital energy into my brain," which created a spiritual awakening.

Vuksinick had never been exposed to, or even interested in, Eastern philosophy or religion. But his dreams, it appeared, had other designs. One dream presented him with the florid image of a black female Buddha statue *sitting upon a golden pedestal whose legs are snakes. Suddenly an electric charge animates the statue and snakes. The black Goddess transforms into a winged being. A transparent curtain is pulled aside and a lovely woman disrobes. Two men approach her in preparation for ritual intercourse.* He woke with "electrical energy coursing throughout my entire body." Later he was to learn about the goddess Kundalini, represented as a snake coiled at the base of the spine, who transmutes sexual energy into spiritual transcendence. His Healing Dreams, he began to believe, were leading him toward yoga's ancient mystical goal, a union of spirit and flesh. He concluded this was the hidden meaning of his first dream of the *Snake* River and mystical light. (He later discovered that the first lecture on kundalini in the West had been given at the Jung Institute in 1932—the very date he had seen emblazoned on his dream mountain.)

The confluence of physical and spiritual forces initiated by his Healing Dreams caused a peculiar transformation of his psychiatric practice, sometimes enabling him to physically sense the source of his patients' distress. In one case, he began to feel a severe pain in his left foot whenever he saw a certain patient. One day he asked the man if anything had ever happened to his own left foot, and a long-concealed secret spilled forth: As a depressed teenager, the man had once been on the verge of commiting suicide with a pistol. At the very last moment, he had taken the gun from his head and shot his foot instead. After this revelation, the therapy took a successful turn. Vuksinick's empathic physical sensations have acted as a sort of bodily Morse code: pain in the genitals, he says, alerts him that a patient has suffered childhood sexual abuse; abdominal cramps relate to "severe power issues." On one occasion, after a catalytic session that proved a breakthrough for one patient, he experienced an attack of pain so severe he went to the emergency ward, though no physical basis could be found. "That such a deep illness (psychological) of the patient could be taken into the analyst's body and then released," his diary entry reads, "struck me as what a shaman attempts to do when he takes in another's sickness in order to heal it."

Cracking Upward: Spiritual Emergence

Vuksinick, flung from the orderly orbit of classical psychoanalysis by near-hallucinatory, psychologically overwhelming Healing Dreams, often feared he was going mad. The area of psychology that addresses such inner upheavals, sometimes referred to as "spiritual emergence," is a recent, still spottily accepted addition to the practice of mental health care. Psychologist James Hillman, who had met Gopi Krishna and carefully studied his case, points out how closely the yogi's symptomology resembled a psychotic episode. Many spiritual traditions, too, have recognized how razor-thin the line is between delusion and illumination. "To our loss in the West," writes Hillman, "we are so lacking in an adequate context that we indeed go to pieces at the eruption of the unconscious, thus justifying the psychiatric view."

When the famous psychologist Robert Johnson was studying with Jung in Zurich in 1948, he had a singular, overwhelming dream (which, interestingly, also featured Eastern religious motifs and imposing snakes). Jung told the young man emphatically, "You have been claimed for an inner life. You must focus on containing these energies, or they will destroy you."[11] Johnson has chosen to spend long sojourns in India, feeling at home in a place where such experiences are better understood.

But many people in the West are left to grope their own way through this type of Healing Dream, without help or even comprehension. I spoke to several people whose alarming otherworldly dreams, seen through a psychiatric lens, might well have led to a pathological diagnosis. Susannah's journey began with what she calls an "initiation dream" of a coffinlike object. As she drew closer to it, she *saw a steamer trunk, revolving in the black of space, which I am "told" belongs to Hitler.* The object hung silently in the Stygian dark, supremely ominous, filling her with terror.

The bleak dream was a prelude to a horrendous descent. She married an Iranian man after a whirlwind courtship, only to find he was prone to ungovernable rages—once going out into the sheep pen of their small farm in the middle of the night to bloodily slaughter all the animals. A self-described "relaxed Muslim," he would later inform her—in a chilling echo of her dream—that he had responded enthusiastically to the old Nazi propaganda films the Iranian government had distributed to schools during his youth.

Trauma piled upon trauma. After becoming pregnant, Susannah dreamed: *I am visiting friends and discover a room where a woman is hanging from the rafters. For the first time in my life, I smell death.* The moribund odor of the dream haunted her days. She was soon to learn, to her horror, that her baby had died inside her. Not long after, she was stricken with cervical cancer. Finally, unable to bear her husband's mistreatment, she divorced him.

For many years afterward, she says, she was tormented by what she calls "underworld dreams." In one, she fell down through the floor and in the basement and encountered a "family of the dead," watching in horror as a skeleton mother nursed a skeleton baby. Similar imagery has been noted in the bizarre dreams that characterize the onset of schizophrenia (such as these related by P. Carrington: "a man sweeping up a girl's bones and throwing them into a sanitation truck . . . the dreamer lying down in a coffin from which her parents had just risen . . . people turning into skeletons").[12] Skeletal images are also characteristic of shamanic initiatory visions—in many indigenous cultures, the ceremonial costumes of tribal shamans are decorated with skeletons and skulls.

Gradually, Susannah's dreams took off in strange new directions. She encountered the "goddess of the underworld" and was bitten by a snake, feeling herself grow dizzy and finally succumb to its poison. But in a subsequent dream, the goddess wrapped the snake around her arm so that it might bite her between thumb and forefinger—a technique, Susannah later learned, purportedly used by the ancient priestesses of Isis to induce altered states. These were followed by dreams in which she seemingly was being initiated by all the world's spiritual traditions. She was never a religious person ("the word God made me cringe"), but suddenly her dreams were filled with the sacred rites of "all different orders—Judaic, Christian, Native American, Tibetan, even an African tribe with painful female circumcision"—which now admitted her into the fold.

Susannah struggled to maintain her balance: "I just kept trying to see it all on a metaphoric level, to get some sense it was normal; that this had been part of the human psyche throughout the ages." Her dreams oscillated between light and darkness, ascent and descent, shaking her apart until she feared madness. She had nightmares about the fate of the earth, about toxic waste sites and "the environment decaying from lack of care." For weeks, she dreamed of incidents in World War II as if she were experiencing them through the eyes of their participants. She would find herself on a train going to a concentration camp. She witnessed a horrible surgical experiment being performed on a little girl by a Nazi doctor; then in another dream, *she* was the doctor. (As we have seen, the Healing Dream often places the dreamer inside other lives, other bodies, causing a sometimes painful widening of the sympathies.)

These horrors, in turn, gave way to "raptures": She would dream of *walking through a shining gate and seeing a grass-covered hill at dawn;* or of *being drawn into the sky in a million pieces;* or *expanding to the size of the earth, covering it and raining my love down upon it.* Sometimes she would wake up vibrating with joy, "ecstatic, like God was running up my spine." She would emerge from such dreams feeling "not yet willing to shrink back into my ordinary personality, as if the inner and outer realms were still meshed."

Today Susannah often feels herself living "in two worlds at once." She has vivid flash memories of her dreams when she is awake. Her boundaries feel permeable: "I can feel the energy of a place or a person when I first come near them, like stepping into an ontological field that affects me physically."

But in the clear depths of her ice-blue eyes are flickers of soul trouble. Intelligent and empathetic, there is an aura about her of what psychologists call "inappropriate affect." Her facial expressions don't always match her words; her body language seems at one moment too guarded, the next too sprawling. The wariness of one who is wounded—and fears to be wounded again—appears to struggle with her ideal of all-embracing love. When she describes her expansion to the earth and stars, I do not question her joy, but wonder how much it is tinged with what Merton called the "elasticity of ego," which nuances even the most glorious-feeling spiritual ascent with a subtle inflation.

Studies using the MMPI (Minnesota Multiphasic Psychological Inventory) have also correlated "dream bizarreness" with schizoid and paranoid states. But Susannah's rich and complex experience cannot be simply pathologized. I rather get the feeling of someone whose dreams are re-shaping her, as a hammer shapes heated metal on an anvil, annealing with heat and blows and shards of light a new form. The Healing Dream often finds entry in brokenness.

As others described their own mystical dreams, a pattern began to emerge. First would come a dream of personal or even global destruction, heralding a period of dark depression and disintegration; then, later, dreams that seemed to throw open the gates to growth and shining re-newal. It is a pattern remarkably similar to that noted by Dr. John Perry. In the 1960s, Perry founded a now-defunct clinic for young people suffering acute schizophrenic breaks. "If the person's journey into the unconscious psyche is given the empathy and understanding it deserves," wrote Perry in his book, *The Far Side of Madness,* "his experience feels like the 'altered state of consciousness' that it is, and not like craziness. Then, too, the psy-che can get on with its work without having to combat an uncompre-hending environment."[13] Though this approach may sound naive in light of today's knowledge of the biochemistry of mental illness, Perry claimed that, treated sympathetically, some patients' dreams and visions lead them through transformative crises more typical of a spiritual initiation, begin-ning with images of death and leading finally to a personal rebirth—even a "mystical apotheosis."

Growing Wings to Heaven

This archetypal connection between death and heavenly ascent was perhaps the deeper meaning of Freud's only published childhood dream—a dream so vivid that he recalled it throughout his life: "I saw my beloved mother, with a peculiarly peaceful, sleeping expression on her features, being carried into the room by two (or three) people with birds' beaks and laid upon the bed." Such mythic figures, from the bird-headed shamans of the Lascaux cave paintings to the ibis-headed gods of Egyptian tombs, link the image of flying with the journey to the land of the dead (though Freud declared in adulthood that it represented his forbidden incestuous desires and castration anxiety[14]).

Many traditions say that we commute to the invisible realm in an immaterial body capable of flight. The image of "getting your wings" to go to heaven is in keeping with this common motif. We have all had flying dreams in which we buzz the treetops, but the flights some dreamers have described to me—seeing, as if they were spacewalking astronauts, the whole earth spread out below them—seem another order of magnitude. Psychiatrist Louis Vuksinick dreamed: *I'm on a flying mattress. Light globules are racing from every direction toward a central point. When they collide there is a huge explosion of light and sound—ecstasy. Looking down, I see the whole of South America. Each country is illuminated from deep within with bright, neonlike light, and each has a distinctive color.*

My Cree friend Sylvia describes "flying into the universe" in her dreams, "seeing the round earth below, glowing bluish green, so different from the pictures, like the difference between black-and-white and color." Diegueno Indian shamans believe that if they dream of putting their hands around the whole earth, "this signifies all-embracing knowledge, the highest degree of wisdom that a dream can symbolize."[15] St. Jerome told about dreams of "flying over lands, and sailing through the air, and crossing over mountains and seas."[16]

One of the most famous accounts of spirit flight was that of the Oglala Sioux medicine man Black Elk. At the age of nine, he contracted a mysterious disease that left his body swollen and comatose for twelve days. As he hovered near death, he dreamed that he flew on the wings of two spirit warriors in the form of geese, coming face to face with the ancestral Grandfathers of the six directions, who told him he would become a defender of his people.

At the time of his dream, the Sioux could still hope to retain their land and their patrimony. Later, as the last vestiges of the Indian way of life were being eradicated, and his people—defeated, despairing, hungry— were consigned to reservations, Black Elk, then twenty-seven years old, had another series of remarkable visions in which he flew to an otherworld located at the center of an unknown mountain range. It was, he says,

> a beautiful land where many, many people were camping in a great circle. They were happy and had plenty. Everywhere there were drying racks full of meat. The air was clear and beautiful with a living light that was everywhere. All around the circle, feeding on the green, green grass, were fat and happy horses. . . . I floated over the tepees and began to come down feet first at the center of the hoop, where I could see a beautiful tree all green and full of flowers.[17]

Two men wearing "holy shirts" painted with symbols told him they would give him something to bring back with him to help his people. Then he fell back into his body. The next day, he painted "ghost shirts" in the sacred manner he had seen in his dream. "I thought if this world would do as the vision teaches, the tree could bloom here, too." Then, during a ceremony, he had another vision of the "beautiful land that was all clear and green in living light." This time, twelve men came toward him and, telling him he would meet "Our Father, the two-legged chief," brought him to the holy tree. Standing against it was a long-haired man whose body was painted red, but who "was not a Wasichu [white man] and he was not an Indian." He was, Black Elk says, "a very fine-looking man," but he could not "make him out."

As Black Elk watched, the man's body dissolved into "all colors of light" until he was surrounded by pure effulgence. "He spoke like singing: 'My life is such that all earthly beings and growing things belong to me. Your father, the Great Spirit, has said this. You, too, must say this.' Then this being "went out like a light in a wind." Finally, Black Elk saw twelve women who commanded him, "Their way of life shall you take back to earth." When he emerged from his vision, he taught the songs he had heard to his people.

His vision helped spark the rebellious spread of ritual dancing that was soon under way on all the reservations, from Pine Ridge and No Water's Camp on Clay Creek, to Sitting Bull's camp on the Grand River. But that winter, the Wounded Knee massacre ended his nation's dream of revival. Five hundred U.S. Cavalry soldiers butchered mostly unarmed men, women, and children. Black Elk charged at the soldiers repeatedly with his sacred bow ("which was not made to shoot with"), wearing a shirt on which he had painted all the elements of his visions—the flaming rainbow, the spotted eagle, the sacred tree.

When years later he told his vision to his biographer, he described himself as "a pitiful old man who has done nothing, for the nation's hoop is broken and scattered. There is no center any longer and the sacred tree is dead." Black Elk felt anguished that he had failed to fulfill the mandate of the upper world: "It is hard to follow one great vision in this world of darkness and of many shadows. Among these shadows, men get lost."[18]

Down to Earth

Their way of life shall you take back to earth. The Healing Dream is ever demanding that we bring the two worlds closer. Through all our human trying and failing, the shining otherworld remains, enjoining us to complete the mystical circuit.

Indeed, the geography of the otherworld, of the lands of *alam-amithal,* is almost always circular, tracing the geometry of wholeness itself. Black Elk's round "hoop" and "great circle" are kin to depictions in brilliantly colored Tibetan *thangka*s of the kingdom of Shambhala, resplendent at the center of rings of mountain ranges. Shambhala, in Tibetan legend, was a land whose inhabitants became enlightened. Like Brigadoon or Avalon, it exists eternally in a sort of parallel universe, continuing to appear to those with special faculties and purity of spirit. My own teacher, Chögyam Trungpa Rinpoche, spoke of Shambhala both as an inspirational myth—a symbol for how we might live together in the here-and-now—and as an otherworldly place whose buildings, people, and landscape he saw in great detail in his own visions.[19]

A number of Tibetan lamas have offered personal accounts of their visits to this mysterious realm. When he was a teenager, Khamtrul Rinpoche went on a meditation retreat to a holy place in Minyak, in eastern Tibet. He had been told by his guru to recite 400,000 prayers to the saint Padmasambhava, but "being young and lazy," he recited only half. Still, meditating in a sacred cave, he had "an amazing dream."

He saw the most beautiful girl he could imagine who "behaved so seductively toward me that all the atoms in my body began to dance." She offered to guide him to the kingdom of Shambhala. Looking closely at her, he saw that she had extra eyes, one between her brows and two on each foot and hand; she was actually the goddess White Tara. She predicted that he would not remain a monk but would instead marry a woman named Dolma (which later came to pass).

Khamtrul Rinpoche sailed through the air with the goddess, flashing northward over snowy mountain ranges and deserts until he came to a "great circle of mountains that looked like a gigantic open lotus with thirty-two petals." The houses there were "splendid golden-roofed palaces decorated with brilliant jewels and lovely rainbows." All its people dwelt in peace and harmony ("there was no sense of you and I, no competition or discord"), all were free from sickness, and all were wealthy—whatever a person desired would spontaneously appear. Khamtrul was also told that here were "counter-agents" composed of "powerful, exalted wisdom" that could defeat the destructive weapons of our world.

Khamtrul was presented to the king, who "shone with such radiance that I was unable to look directly at him. He dissolved first into light, then into a lama, who gave me a number of empowerments. After that, everything disappeared like a rainbow except the girl and myself. We began to express our love for each other." Then he suddenly found himself back in his cave, and it was dawn. "I don't know if dreams are true or real," he writes, "but this dream was very vivid indeed."[20]

There can be little doubt that such experiences are the basis for our religious doctrines of paradise. It might be surmised that many great spiritual leaders have visited these "places," which are less towering holy metropolises than well-organized, thriving, compassionate societies that, their emissaries always insist, could be emulated by us. Heaven on earth, dreamers throughout history have been told, is ours to gain, and ours to lose.

The life of the visionary may become given over to the task of trying to transliterate, as it were, the beauty he or she has witnessed into life on solid ground. This may not be so simple. Some, as the exhilaration fades, feel a corresponding letdown. This world seems only a dim, tarnished version of the golden one, a trap for the spirit, built of matter's all-fettering density. Our real bodies seem ponderous next to the ethereal ones we are issued in our dreams. (Perhaps this is the basis for those nightmares where we are trying to run but are stuck in slow-motion, captive to our weighted flesh.)

Roger, for example, told me a once soul-shaking dream: *I'm given an entrance exam I know I can easily pass. Then I am taken to meet God. Through His eyes, I see the town I grew up in, but without sentimentality, knowing all its beauty and ugliness, its wealth and poverty. I realize that without dualities and opposites the physical world wouldn't exist. God is looking at all creation with love, and there is no lack.*

Here is a deeper version of divinity, with both dark and light included in the holy order of things. But Roger remembers feeling deeply depressed for a period following the dream, a "dysphoria" not uncommon after a sublime inner experience: "I went from absolute clarity and love, to falling out of grace back into this world. It radicalized my whole consciousness—I knew, and still do, that our usual model of reality is not the reality we truly live in." Roger eventually regained his sense of inspiration; the holiness of everyday life became, for him, an article of faith.

But it can be difficult to reconcile the sullying impurities of the here-

and-now with the numinosity of the otherworld. That this world falls so far short of paradise becomes an unshakable knowledge with which the visionary is now burdened. There is good reason spiritual teachers so often emphasize being "grounded" in ordinary life and humble practice, reconciling the upward mobility of the spirit with the earthward rootings of the body and soul.

Jacob's Ladder

"And he dreamed and, behold, a ladder was set up on the earth, and the top of it reached to heaven; and, behold, the angels of God ascended and descended on it." Perhaps the most interesting aspect of Jacob's Healing Dream is its vibrant sense of busy, shuttling two-way traffic between down here and up there. The ancient Taoists expressed the same thought in terms honoring nature's sacred order: heaven waters earth; water vapor rises from earth to make clouds; sky rains down: earth potentiates heaven, and heaven, earth. (Black Elk's spirit-women gestured toward the "beautiful world," with its "sky all blue and full of yellow light above the greening earth," telling him, "Your nation's life shall be such.") What is gained in the divine world, as its denizens tell the visiting dreamer, must be brought back within the scope of personal and collective life—family, work, and relationships; business, politics, and communal caring. All religious traditions recognize a dynamic interplay between this world and the other one, and the benefit of striving to make our lives a bit more "on earth as it is in heaven."

In Tibetan visualizations, one imagines this world is *already* a sacred realm, and the people we meet every day gods and goddesses (though all too often, asleep to their own true nature). Every morning the Dalai Lama gets up at four to perform his ritual prayers. He sits with three tiers of flat ornamental baskets in his lap—a sacred layer cake, symbolizing the entire universe—then pours handful after handful of silver rings, shells, and semiprecious stones in a cascading waterfall, a shimmering mandala of offering, visualizing that he possesses everything, and is giving it all away.

"Taking care of our blue planet," he murmurs, "is nothing special, nothing sacred, nothing holy. It is simply taking care of our own house."

At a recent museum exhibit, eight of his monks delicately tapped metal funnels primed with colored grains of sand, guiding the thin streams that flowed out a little more than a grain at a time, painstakingly creating a mandala of the kingdom of Shambhala. It emerged over weeks at a patient, elephantine pace. By the time the labor of love and spirit was completed, 722 deities jostled in a nine-foot-square representation of a sacred palace at the center of a wondrous realm. Such a mandala is considered an ideal world where "every building is a divine palace, every sound a prayer, and every being a god." It is a heaven, to be sure, but not a never-never land; rather, a here-and-now land, if we would but make it so.

Healing the Shadow

Some evil dreams appear as good—
Only an expert sees they presage ill;
But only a master of the art
Can recognize good dreams
When they take on ominous forms.

—Milarepa

Yet if there are heavens, there must be hells. If it is true that Healing Dreams open us to a greater vision of reality, that vision must inevitably include the dark as well as the light, the Below as well as the Above. A revelation would be incomplete that shows us only what we wish to see, and omits what we wish we did not. Jung used the term "shadow"[1] for those hidden parts of ourselves that do not fit our conscious ideals—our shameful wants and embarrassing lacks; our venom and our vanity. The shadow appears in our dreams in the guise of the characters and predicaments we most fear and despise. We know we've had a close encounter with our shadow when we find ourselves describing it in telltale vocabulary—*outrageous, horrifying, idiotic, cheap, disgusting.*

Yet shadow dreams, in their refusal to kowtow to the idealized self, offer a deeper knowing of ourselves and world we live in. They dig up buried truths and lay them at our feet like reeking, dirt-clotted bones. It is to our tragic loss that we strive, upon awakening, to sweep these "gifts" under the rug. The shadow images in our dreams, Jung suggested, represent our undeveloped potentialities—those parts of the personality which are still "becoming;" inner places where "we are unfinished; we are growing and changing." These aspects of the psyche take on a negative cast only because they have been so thoroughly disowned.

Shadow dreams force us to face not only our own unresolved contradictions but the truly pressing human questions: What *do* we do with our hatred, greed, lust, and avarice? With the commotion in our bifurcated hearts? ("The good I would do," wrote St. Paul, "I do not; the evil I would not, I do.") The shadow comes to us in our dreams like some dark fallen angel, demanding that we wrestle it for an answer. Such dreams are rarely cool and cerebral but are hot, visceral, nightmarish. We are murdered, or are ourselves murderers; we are chased by rank beasts and fanged monsters, accosted by harridans and thieves; we discover half-human creatures living pale and scabrous in our own basement. We don't want to *interpret* them— we want to forget we ever saw them.

People who consider themselves spiritual often equate the good with what is beautiful and harmonious, forgetting that there is such a thing as an ugly truth. An image the ego finds most bitter may be the best medicine for the soul. A friend of mine named Maureen, a spiritual seeker for some forty years, was deeply involved with an esoteric group. "I was trying tremendously hard to follow all the tenets," she told me, "which said that I was an unawakened person, just a collection of jumbled parts that might someday, if I did everything right, become enlightened." After a few years on this path, Maureen's quest for illumination culminated in a powerful dream. One of her teachers appeared in the form of "a majestic clock, so enormous it stretched all the way up into the heavens." But when she asked to see herself in the dream, to her disgust, "I was shown a steaming turd! This did *not* help my sense of worthiness."

She was repulsed and discouraged. It was only months later that she had a sudden insight that yielded a deeper, more affirmative meaning: "I realized the dream was saying my teacher was entirely mechanical, while I had within me the beginnings of organic life." What had first seemed a dark verdict passed upon her now liberated her to leave the group and find her own path. She had discovered in herself the fertile humus—what the old alchemists called the *prima materia,* the raw material—that is the very basis of all real growth yet is the despised thing thrown out on the compost heap.

Her story is reminiscent of a Sufi teaching tale of Ibn al-Imad: "One day I was carrying something disgusting in my hands. My companions imagined I was carrying it with the intention of mortifying my soul, because in their eyes I was much too lofty to stoop to carrying such a thing. I replied that it was simply that I saw that God did not disdain to create such a thing. How then was I to disdain to carry it?"

But most of us disdain to carry that part of ourselves we deem most unworthy. Instead, we deny it, project it upon others, pretend it doesn't exist—anything so as not to feel its coiling presence in our soul. It is as if a bloated corpse had bobbed to the surface of the river of consciousness, and we scramble to marshal our alibis—*I wasn't even there; I had nothing to do with it*—despite the fact that now its head, hair still wet, lies upon our sweat-dampened pillow.

It falls to our dreams to bear witness. In contrast to the sometimes sentimental tone of heavenly apparitions, shadow dreams are tough-minded, hardboiled—more Raymond Chandler than Kahlil Gibran. One of their most unnerving qualities is a most acrid sort of sarcasm. How is it that a Healing Dream, which we presume is a veritable gift from God, could so cruelly jeer at us, be so taunting, harassing, and shaming? Perhaps the dream scoffs because it sees right through us, piercing our defenses and our well-fabricated rationales. It calls to mind the saying of Jesus: "What man thinks important, God holds in contempt."[2] Its sardonic wit is a peerless attention-getting device, for the tender skin of our self-regard is easily bruised. Most people can recall a mortal insult or scathing put-down long after other details of a conversation have faded. The shadow makes corrosive use of our ego's pitch-perfect memory for slights; it is the town crier of Dreamland, shouting out the embarrassing news.

Given its ever-challenging appearance, it is no wonder we are literally scared of our own shadow. We may try to flee, but this rejected other remains at our very heels. Our shadow figures—be they demons, grotesques, low-lifes, wild animals, kidnappers, or killers—are carriers of qualities we need to acknowledge. We apprehend them as destroyers, but they may be deliverers, redressing the imbalance between the ego and the raw powers of life. Without them, we would be doomed to superficiality, to that spiritual consumerism that buys into only what looks flattering in the mirror. Writes the analyst Marie-Louise von Franz: "We need a shadow. The shadow keeps us down to earth, reminds us of our incompleteness, and provides us with complementary traits. We would be very poor indeed if we were only what we imagined ourselves to be."[3]

The emotionally fraught dynamic between self-image and shadow springs to life in the classic *Dr. Jekyll and Mr. Hyde,*[4] a story that author Robert Louis Stevenson claimed came to him in a rip-roaring nightmare. His dream tale still glowers at us from some dark cul-de-sac of the soul: Dr. Jekyll, a brilliant medical man determined to nobly serve the world, invents an elixir to liberate the human race from its evil side. But something goes wrong. Quaffing it late one evening, he is transformed into his evil twin, the terrible Mr. Hyde. At first, Jekyll is surprised to find his nighttime outings as Hyde strangely exhilarating—the ugly little man has an impulsivity and brute force he lacks, the carnal appetites he dared not fulfill. But as Hyde assumes more and more of his personhood, he is stricken to find that his former self begins to recede.

Hyde is described in terms that immediately suggest we are in the presence of the shadow. He is a mail-order catalogue of undesirable traits— one minute full of "black, sneering coolness," the next consumed by fear, lust, or rage. He is "pale and dwarfish," for he has been chained up in the basement of consciousness and denied a chance for healthy growth. The other characters can barely describe the "hitherto unknown disgust, loathing and fear" that they feel in his presence. The shadow inspires the nameless dread of a truth too long entombed. (As Freud once observed, the sense of the uncanny stems from the return of the repressed.)

One of Dr. Jekyll's colleagues vows to investigate the horrid little man, punning "If he be Mr. Hyde, I shall be Mr. Seek." He surmises, with un-intended irony, that the creature "must have black secrets . . . compared to which poor Jekyll's worst would be like sunshine." Yet, as a diary discovered after Dr. Jekyll's death makes clear, it is precisely because the good doctor's sun—the shining face he turns to the world—is so bright that the shadow he casts is black. The most poignant secrets the diary reveals are those of a tormented psyche. Born to a large fortune, gifted, honorable, and beloved, he is yet miserable and despairing, submerged in an existence that is "nine-tenths . . . effort, virtue, and control." Pinched and cramped, in thrall to "the dryness of a life of study," he nonetheless holds a disdainful attitude toward his unfulfilled desires. Living in a state of "profound duplicity," he leaps at the chance to literally separate his good self from his bad self: "If each could be housed in separate identities, life would be relieved of all that was unbearable." The desire to be rid of our worst foibles is one few of us have not felt; and Jekyll's strategy, to judge from the multiplicity of our characters, is one we all know.

But when Jekyll drinks down the "blood-red liquor" of his potion, he is in for a rude surprise. Rather than finding his "evil" side safely compartmentalized, he is overwhelmed by sensations of "something indescribably new and, from its very novelty, incredibly sweet. I felt younger, lighter, happier in body; within I was conscious of a heady recklessness . . . an unknown but not an innocent freedom of the soul. . . . When I looked upon that ugly idol in the glass I was conscious of no repugnance, rather a leap of welcome. This, too, was myself. It seemed natural and human."

Here Stevenson brilliantly evokes the energies that are locked in the shadow just as liquid water is locked in a block of ice. The shadow is indeed "natural and human." Mr. Hyde possesses life force, energy, sensuality, unfettered exuberance. But this shadow self is also coarse and dangerous, as the unassimilated parts of the self usually appear. Our repressed traits, which have lagged behind the rest of the personality on its journey of development, are often raw and raucously destructive. The shadow is the reversed mirror image, the nemesis, of the persona. Hyde sets out to stomp on Jekyll's confining pieties and suffocating sentiments, even annotating the good doctor's favorite holy books with "startling blasphemies" and, tellingly, trashing his father's portrait. His is a howl of rage from a soul that can bear self-denial no longer.

Hyde finally turns murderous. The only solution, Jekyll determines, is suicide. He cannot live with his contradictions—the good self must triumph. It is a tragic ending. But the real tragedy is Jekyll's terrible psychological naivete—his belief he can become purely "good" by suppressing his "bad"side, and then, when he can no longer deny it, finding no choice but to give over to it without restraint. (The story illustrates a common fear of the shadow: offer it your hand, and it will rip off your arm.) Dr. Jekyll fails, miserably, at the task of integration required of anyone who would be whole—to learn to live in creative tension with both the dark and the light (and to forthrightly question which is which).

Fortunately, the laboratory of the human psyche is better equipped than poor Jekyll's basement. A more fruitful experiment might have been for the physician to heal himself by absorbing some quality of his hidden Hyde—to loosen the grip of duty and social nicety; to acknowledge his sexuality and his anger; to abandon the quest for moral purity and admit to human fallibility. If we cannot "eat" some of our shadow, it will eat us. Ignored, it becomes a leech, and finally a monster, gorging on our life's blood. It is a story we know well from the tabloids—the minister who inveighs against greed from the pulpit, then is caught fleecing his flock; the senator who sponsors bills to legislate others' morality, then is exposed in a tawdry tryst. Denied, the shadow becomes ever more deformed, growing in power, projected irrationally upon others, while its host becomes anemic, a pale reflection of full human potential.

We usually allow ourselves only the most narrow range of options for dealing with our shadow material. We may try to hide it from those around us; diminish it through mockery; deny to ourselves that it even exists; determine, futilely, to battle it to the death; try to outrun it by speeding through life, hoping it will never catch up (though it remains firmly attached to our feet). Ironically, all it may take to come to terms with the shadow is an unprejudiced gaze. We may see, to our surprise, it is not the pure evil we thought it was. The closer we look, the more its seams show and, through them, glimpses of something quite human, merely costumed as a devil.

I can recall once having a terrible dream: *I am trying to kill a black, writhing "devil-crab" by stepping on it. If I don't, it will turn into a whole human being. But its shell is impervious.* The creature, which my dream also called a "bug," *seeks more ways of growing. Blood is best—it finds a tube of it in the fridge.* I had awoken with a sense of sinister horror—surely, I thought, this was an image of cancer taking over the body. But bringing it to my dream group, my black monochrome picture revealed other colorations. Under their gentle prodding, I admitted that *I* often felt trapped in my own defensive shell, not knowing how to get out. ("Crabs *outgrow* their shells" one advised. "They molt.") My life as a writer had been feeling constricted and lonely, a Victorian-era scrivener in his garret. (In my dream diary, I had even misspelled *writhing* as *writing*—I was afflicted with a "writing bug.") "You say this thing wants to turn into a whole human being," said another. "Well, isn't that what *you* want?" Someone else chimed in: "And isn't it true that 'blood *is* best'? Would you rather be bloodless?" A member of the group who'd been poring over a dictionary while we talked suddenly laughed: "Did you know," he asked, "that the archaic meaning of "writhe" is "to misinterpret"? It was revelatory to look at the dream from a fresh vantage point—one in which my "devil" might be, as was Jekyll's Hyde, a neglected aspect of my own "stepped-on" desire for more being. Perhaps I needed to offer my misinterpreted shadow a little of my life's blood (here sitting unused, on a shelf in the fridge, like a leftover).

In the Tibetan *chöd* ritual, the practitioner conjures up the most terrible demons he can imagine and symbolically offers them his body—limbs, head, and bloody heart—to free himself from dualistic illusions of good and bad, self and other. We may not wish to go that far. But there is always something we can offer our unappeased demons—if not a hand, perhaps just the tip of a pinky—to see what happens. The psychologist Robert Johnson advises a brief ritual enactment, since the unconscious can scarcely distinguish between real acts and symbolic ones—drawing, dancing, sculpting, or writing a story to acknowledge the shadow; burning something or burying it. He calls this technique "shadow upkeep." He describes how, when he complained of chronic exhaustion before his lectures, a friend gave him some odd advice: He should go into a private room just before his talk, wad up a dampened towel, and hurl it with all his might at the floor, letting out a shout. Even this small act of deference to his shadow, Johnson said, worked a minor miracle: "When I walked out to the lecture platform, there was fire in my eyes. I had energy and stamina and voice. I did a courteous, well-structured lecture. The shadow backed me, but did not overwhelm me."[5]

When the shadow approaches us, we usually respond with dismay. We treat it as a derelict demanding a handout, a murderer chasing us down the street, a thief in our house—it wants something from us, maybe even our life. In fact, it is *we* who need to take something from *it;* it is because we need it that it comes to us, in ruthless compassion, to be reclaimed. When we feed our demons a little food, we may find that something very peculiar happens—they stop trying to devour us. They may be satiated when we simply acknowledge their existence—and thus, implicitly, our own, for we are nourishing our own soul.

The Murderers of Sleep

I once asked a sweet Tibetan lama what his favorite movie was.

"What kind of movie?" asked the young lama, who spoke good colloquial English. "Old, new? French, American?"

"New," I answered. "American."

"*Natural Born Killers,*" he said promptly, reveling in my surprise. "I *loved* that movie! It reminded me that passion, aggression, and ignorance are in me, too. In another life, under other circumstances, maybe *I* would be this murderer." Here was a man in touch with his own shadow traits and, not coincidentally, one of the most cheerful and compassionate people I've ever met.

For most of us, however, it is natural to see our shadow as our enemy, for it seems intent on our bloody demise. Dr. Jacob Zieghelboim, a prominent oncologist, had long promised to tell me about a shattering dream that had followed his own diagnosis of cancer. But whenever I asked him, he demurred: it wasn't a good time; it was too personal; he was still working it through. Years after his recovery, he shared an account of a nightmare that, he wrote to me, "announced a transformative force of such magnitude I cannot help but feel it was healing." I include it here, abridged only slightly from his unpublished memoir, as important testimony to our shadow's relentless pursuit:

> *I walk out of my house and step into my car, which is parked in my open garage. As I am about to drive away, a blond, blue-eyed, athletic man opens the passenger door and sits by me. I am startled. I have never seen this man before. Something about him frightens me.*
>
> *We drive to a consulate or embassy where I am supposed to retrieve important documents. As I wait in one of the offices, the man pulls a machine gun from underneath his jacket and takes the employees hostage, demanding money from the office vault. I am petrified. I don't know what to do. I fear being perceived as an accomplice, and that my reputation will be ruined forever. While these thoughts race through my mind, the man begins wantonly shooting, and I see people falling dead or seriously injured. Chaos reigns, and I run for my life to get away from the murderer.*

Like Dr. Jekyll, Dr. Zieghelboim is placed in thrall to a murderous nemesis—here, as blond and blue-eyed as Zieghelboim is dark-haired and brown-eyed—who inspires fear and loathing. Maybe, the doctor reasons, he can keep up appearances, retrieve his credentialed identity, but his Hyde-like double forces his complicity in wild adventures that end in murder.

His dream, as he relates it, becomes a series of escapes and captures involving his shadow figure. He gets away and buys a one-way ticket to a foreign land, but while he finds relief making small talk with an old high school friend in a restaurant, the murderer reappears and silently joins them at the table.

> *I know by his looks that he is saying to me something like, "Did you really think you could get rid of me, little boy? You must be kidding!" I am oppressed by his presence, and overwhelmed with fear.*
>
> *The three of us are now in my kitchen, listening to the television news. The anchorman describes a massacre that took place that morning, and gives a detailed*

description of the murderers. Benny, my friend, realizes that the description of the
assailants fits me and the man. He stands in front of the TV dumbfounded, and
I know my well-kept secret is out, and nobody will ever believe I had nothing to
do with the atrocities.

I pull a gun from somewhere and aim it at the real murderer. He looks at me
with disdain and says: "You will never dare to shoot me. You will chicken out."

"I won't," I reply, and proceed to pull the trigger.

To Zieghelboim's dismay, there is no bullet in the chamber. The murderer laughs mockingly. Indignant, the doctor aims a second time and pulls the trigger:

I hear a very powerful explosion that fills the room with smoke. When the smoke
dissipates, I see that the bullet has shattered the man's head, and that he lies mo-
tionless on the floor. In the background, I hear the sounds of police sirens ap-
proaching my home. I feel greatly relieved. I know that I shall have to pay for my
acts, and that I will surely go to jail. I also know that it will be for a short time,
and then I shall be free.

Years later, Zieghelboim remains "awestruck" at his dream. Being victimized by the coldblooded felon, he says, symbolized how he felt after discovering his cancer—exposed, frightened, vulnerable to destructive forces that seemed "evil, wreaking havoc on my reputation and on the social and professional image I had built for myself over many years." The diagnosis, he says, meant he could no longer pretend all was well or that he was "an honest, law-abiding citizen of unblemished reputation." The doctor, the lawful enforcer of health, was suddenly thrown in with the criminal element of cancer (ironically, of the specific type he specialized in treating).

Although Zieghelboim did successfully treat his disease—at one level, his dream symbolized his medical triumph over his would-be murderer—the telltale mark of the shadow is too prominent to ignore. As usual, the mortal enemy (and companion) mocks, threatens, and cajoles; no matter how the dreamer tries to shake him, he stays stuck to him like glue, implicating him in his ruinous business. In the dream, the good doctor doth protest too much, swearing to whoever will listen that he and the murderer have nothing in common, that he is an innocent bystander. But in fact they are fellow travelers and co-conspirators. When he shatters the murderer's head with a bullet, he becomes a murderer himself.

The dream made him realize, he says, that his soul was a balance of creative and destructive forces. It freed him from "the inner conflict between my innocent side, 'Mr. Everything's All Right,' and this aggressive social outcast." Zieghelboim realized over time that his cancer/murderer helped to "liberate me from my gross misunderstanding of the world of God, our creator and our destroyer, the totality of everything. When God hears some of us—clergymen, doctors, whatever—invoke in His name a world without loss, disease, or death, He knows us to be false prophets."

His dream, he says, was the catalyst of a new psychological and spiritual maturity: "I could never return to the childlike perception that dominated my first thirty-seven years. It thrust me out of innocence into the turmoil of adulthood's hard beauty."

It also marked a radical life change. In his dream, he realized his actions would be judged harshly by society, that "the ruling order would not tolerate my bypassing its regulations and taking the law into my own hands." Later, as he began to tansgress the rules and routines of his outer world, questioning the dogmas of his profession, acting out in his personal life in ways that shook his marriage to its foundations, the distance widened between him and his friends, colleagues, and family. He did become, for a while, an outlaw of sorts, a man on the run from accepted norms. As his dream had symbolized, he wound up buying a "one-way ticket." He enrolled in radical psychological training, sought spiritual teachers, and eventually traveled as far as the Himalayas on his quest. His dire escapade with the shadow, he says, "liberated me from the oppression of conventional responsibilities, societal and professional obligations, and my own conditioned responses." It was some time before he returned, full circle, to a medical practice, but one infused with an acceptance, even an appreciation, of the denied, unconscious forces that may contain the seeds of healing. Today he uses innovative techniques that combine leading-edge oncology with a mind-body approach once viewed by his colleagues as an outlaw area of medicine.

Through the Looking Glass

The realm of the shadow is a turned-around world where right is left and wrong is right. Shadow dreams are, like good conjurers, masters of misdirection. They tell it like it is by telling it like it isn't. Indeed, such dreams seem to have a hidden agenda—that we forsake for a time our staunch categories of good and bad as blinders obscuring our view of the Whole.

The rules of this mirror world are so difficult to sort out that spiritual teachers often discourage their students from putting much stock in dreams at all, lest they misinterpret them and go astray. The Tibetan saint Milarepa once counseled a disciple that "a devoted yogi should never cling to dreams because, by doing so, you will eventually expose yourself to the influence of devils." But on the same occasion, he instructed three disciples to remember their dreams that very evening. Two of them had wonderful dreams filled with spiritual beauty. But his chief student, Gampopa, told him the next morning "in remorseful tears" that he'd had "a very bad dream."

"We do not know whether it was good or bad," Milarepa replied equably. "Do not come to a conclusion about it too hastily. Now tell us about it."

"I slaughtered many people of different races and stopped their breath," Gampopa reported, trembling. "Oh, I must be a sinful person with bad Karma!" He was shocked when Milarepa was instead elated. The dream revealed to him, he said, that Gampopa would liberate many sentient beings from the prison of Samsara by slaying their self-centered delusions.[6]

If almost everything turns out to be the opposite of what it seems in this Möbius-strip universe, it is not necessarily the dream's fault. The ego, with its often superficial values, can be easily deceived by appearances. In the fairy tale, Beauty can't see the Beast's pure spirit beneath his awful exterior. The Beast has been the Prince all along; it is Beauty who has failed to notice, stuck in her partial point of view. In daily life, we may gravitate toward those who flatter us with a kind lie, while our adversary is the only one willing to tell us the awful truth. It is precisely this spiritual myopia that Healing Dreams seek to cure.

In our dreams, our shadow people appear to be creatures of lack or malevolence. But if we have the courage to look deeper, they may offer us indispensable gifts. Zuni Indian rituals feature dancers in the hideous inside-out costumes of the mudhead clowns. Mythology says these beings were created when a brother and sister god committed incest and produced ten deformed sons, each with contradictory traits and sacred gifts for mankind. The one named Small Mouth gabbled constantly, but bore an offering of delicious sweet corn. Water Drinker was always thirsty, yet it was he who offered the water gourd. Great Warrior Priest was a coward who brought humanity blue corn. Black Bat was afraid of the dark, but was far-seeing in daylight. Old Youth was the group's selfish yet clairvoyant advisor.[7] To receive the gifts offered by our own shadow people requires a willingness to embrace paradox.

It also requires an ability to look unflinchingly into what seems loathsome. President Lyndon Johnson once dreamed that he was the aging Woodrow Wilson. He was horrified—Wilson's shriveled, wheelchair-bound body symbolized to him impotence, weakness, defeat. But we might well wonder: if Johnson had looked more closely at the shadow figure that filled him with such revulsion, might he have found the personal and political qualities to avert the calamities of his presidency? All Johnson could see in the image of Wilson was enfeeblement. But Wilson was a visionary peacemaker, the founder of the League of Nations, the opposite of the horse-trading wheeler-dealer from the Lone Star state. It was Johnson's fear of appearing "weak" that helped plunge the country ever deeper into the quagmire of Vietnam, crippling his domestic agenda and finally rendering him politically impotent. Perhaps his fate was an example of the psychological proverb that the shadow denied is projected outward as destiny.

Whereas Johnson's shadow side was that of a crippled idealist, the shadow figures of a middle-aged woman named Claudia were imperious Nazis. She encountered them in a dream so powerful it led her, previously a rather unreflective person, to begin a course of psychotherapy at the age of fifty-four:

> *I am confronted with two enormous Nazi figures, one male, one female. They look like characters from an old comedy program, camp commandant "Colonel Klink" and a fat, motherly Gestapo lady. They order me to complete a list of tasks before they come back from their errands. I'm terrified, because they'll kill me if I don't finish.*
>
> *As I sit there paralyzed in fear, a young woman comes over to help me. She seems filled with love and a sense of playfulness. We sit down to go over a list of orders which, when we actually look at it, turns out to be titled, "Twenty Things I Love to Do," and is to be carried out as a scavenger hunt! She goes right to item three, which is a colorful graphic object shaped like a heart and a couple of breasts, and says, "Here's where we're going to start."*

The frightening Nazi figures in Claudia's dream—"they were huge, ten feet tall"—are not as menacing as they first appear. They are even faintly comical, despite their life-and-death authority over the dreamer. The dream introduces a redemptive female character who has penetrated the security perimeter of the dictatorial complex. She represents a force capable of liberating the imprisoned self through eros, nurturance, and the powers of the heart. It turns out that the Nazis, ironically, are ordering Claudia to *play:* sometimes our shadow has to imprison us, even threaten us with execution, to spur us toward the smallest manifestation of vitality.

She woke up "stunned," realizing how her life had been permeated by a sense of intimidation since childhood (on one level, the Nazi couple represents her parents), and how much she felt hostage to her need to please others. "The wisdom of that simple dream knocked me over the head," she says. It laid out a new agenda, a treasure hunt that would help her— even force her—to make a priority of what she truly loved, and to do it from the heart. "At that time, I'd been compulsive about always making lists, trying to do things in a masculinized, rationalistic way, but it wasn't working. The breast/heart symbol the girl pointed to embarrassed me, it was so crude and direct. The whole dream was saying, Live your life differently. Do it, or die." She started therapy shortly thereafter, then left her job "to give myself a year to go to the opposite side, to trust myself to be spontaneous and outrageous—to go crazy in my house, stay up all night, sleep all day, not finish reading books, not work." At the end of this somewhat chaotic year, she completed her training to become a therapist.

Claudia's dream illustrates that the shadow almost always has some characteristic—a hidden birthmark, as it were—that suggests it is not irredeemably evil. But we can easily miss this when a dream is challenging us to learn under enemy fire. Good, too, may be ruthless; life is fierce when we refuse to grasp its gift with both hands; truth turns ugly when it is derided. Shadow dreams goad us toward understanding using confrontation and crisis, daring us to see through their malevolent masks even as they seem to threaten our very sense of existence.

Shadow Teachers

Since transformation often demands the downfall of our self-image, it is not surprising that our shadow teachers are sometimes ugly, old, poor, and decrepit. Such figures are dispossessed of all the ego holds dear. They are the antithesis of our idealized selfhood. At the same time, they embody that wisdom which transcends surface appearances.

A friend once sent me a powerful nightmare about an ancient crone that utterly terrified her. In her dream, Chloë is struggling through hip-deep snowdrifts and howling winds to get to school, where she has an appointment with "a big male authority figure." She battles her way through the blizzard to an old-fashioned schoolhouse that looms "black and blue in the moonlight, like some gothic set." But there is no refuge inside the ominous building, which turns out to be "full of snow and hung with big icicles." She tries dutifully to climb a huge staircase, but then, exhausted, lies down in fetal position.

I'm just curled up there, moaning, "I can't do this. I can't go on." Then, glancing up, I see a dark figure coming down the stairs from above me, almost hidden in shadow. It is a very old, bent, female "crone," like a witch, and she is wearing a long, pointed false nose, tied around her face with a string. She begins to weave back and forth, as if blind, searching out the air in front of her with a furled umbrella. She seems to be trying to "hone in" on me. I struggle to scream or move or catch hold of the umbrella, but I'm paralyzed with fear. I know that when the umbrella is pointing straight at me, I will die.

She woke up "sitting upright in bed, screaming at the top of my lungs, shaking, tears streaming down my face, and—the worst part!—I could *still see* that figure. It melted from sight in a second or two." The terror stayed with her for days.

Chloë had been going through a great personal crisis. A late-returning doctoral student in a field she loved, she had been admitted into one of the country's top departments, staffed by the best authorities in her subject. But after years of heavy course loads, low-paid teaching assignments, and mounting debt, the whole exercise had begun to seem fruitless. The academic pressure was unrelenting. The job market for Ph.D.s in her field was cinched tight. Her health was becoming precarious. She had entered premature menopause—perhaps, she suspected, from the sheer, molar-grinding stress.

The dream tableau formed a picture of what school had become for her—a sunless world where all life is frozen. The very place she'd once viewed as a refuge is as frigid as the world outside. In the dream, she has borne all that she is able. Her refusal to go on is childlike, regressive, but a refusal nonetheless. She expects to be upbraided by the man in charge, but instead a powerful female symbol, a mythic hag, makes a dramatic entrance, coming straight for her. The unwanted attention of shadow figures is typically up close and personal—here, even radar-guided! The blind hag can maneuver in the shadow world, because she is its denizen.

Yet this terrifying figure contains some clues that its nature is not as evil as might appear. The crone wears a disguise so obvious even the strings of her false nose show: she is at once a real witch and someone wearing a Halloween costume, which, judging by its flimsiness, might be easily removed. Instead of a blind person's cane, she wields an umbrella—more like Mary Poppins, that emissary of magic and possibility, than grim Hecate.

The language of the dream leaves little doubt as to her function: the word *umbrella* derives from the Latin *umbra,* meaning "shade" or "shadow." Instead of "home in," the dreamer has written "hone in." To hone is to sharpen, to make a blade keen by rubbing it against a hard surface, an apt metaphor for the shadow function. (One thinks of the martial arts slogan, "My enemy is a whetstone against which I hone my spirit.") The old woman "searches out the air," as if avid for the very oxygen of life. A "witch" is an ancient emblem of supernatural female power. She "weaves back and forth," the pun suggesting a bringing together of diverse threads upon a loom. Perhaps it is Chloë's fate itself that is being woven: grown dull with travail, she is being sharpened for a new destiny by her mysterious adversary—one who "points straight," and may be an inner guide to salvation.

Chloë told me she was literally too frightened to investigate this figure any further. (Our shadow images are so frightening, writes one analyst, "because the ego is so strong . . . they must be frightening in order to make their values known."[8]) Six months later, I dreamed that Chloë's apartment was empty and boarded up, as if condemned for demolition. As is my habit after a vivid dream, I called her and discovered she had taken the difficult, decisive step of quitting school. She was in the process of moving to New York to resume a vocation as a poet. She sounded happier than she had in years. Clearly, her dream had decreed an end to life as she knew it; she had to surrender, or risk suffering a terrible collapse.

But typical of the shadow, the dire warning also contained the seeds of a new life. The crone is a symbol of hard-won knowledge. Being blind, she cannot be deceived by appearances. Being ugly, she is past caring what others think of her. She is a harbinger of the second half of life, the time when many people attain a purity of calling, a memento mori not to waste precious time looking back.

Chloë's encounter with this archetypal figure reminded me of a Buddhist story that highlights the dual nature of the shadow as both tormenter and catalyst for spiritual change. The biography of the Tibetan sage

Naropa also begins on a campus, India's great Nalanda University, where he held the position of chief pandit.[9] One day he was sitting beneath a tree poring over a book of spiritual knowledge, when suddenly, we are told, "a terrifying shadow" fell across the page.

He looked up and saw before him a repulsive specter: a hag with thirty-seven ugly features: lame, humpbacked, eyes "red and deep-hollowed," a nose "twisted and inflamed," a face webbed by wrinkles with a "yellow beard streaked with white." This nightmarish interloper demanded to know if Naropa understood the words or the sense of the text he was reading. When he answered, "The words," she smiled, but when he added, "*and* the sense," she wept and gnashed her teeth, calling the scholar, in essence, a phony. With a fierce cry, she clapped her hands and disappeared.

Naropa was thunderstruck. But he suppressed his disgust to ponder the details of the vision's appearance. He realized the crone's thirty-seven deformities represented not only the "thirty-seven marks" of the misery of Samsara but also the "thirty-seven kinds of creative potentiality." (Here, again, we see the archetypal function of the shadow—to show us not only our limitations but our hidden possibilities and to suggest that they are mysteriously linked.)

The vision changed Naropa's life. He decided to leave the university to search for a guru. But instead of finding enlightenment, he stumbled upon a series of horrific scenes that challenged all his sacred precepts. In the course of one day, he was asked to kill a deer with an arrow; to cook a fish alive; and to help a man who had impaled his own father on a stake. Every time, after he had righteously refused to act, the secret symbolism of the forbidden scene was revealed. The brutal hunter, he was told, was actually the slayer of ego-centered duality—"the fleeing deer of this and that/On the mountain of the body believing in an 'I'"; the wriggling fish he was asked to cook was "the fish of habit-forming thoughts"; and the stake was being driven through the heart of the "parent" of delusion.

Finally, on the verge of suicide, Naropa met the fierce guru Tilopa ("a dark man with protruding, bloodshot eyes") who explained that the nightmarish figures and events were only instructional guises of the teacher: "We have never been apart, but were like a body and its shadow," he tells him, adding that his horrifying forms were shaped by Naropa's own "de-filements . . . so you did not recognize me."

Those who teach us spiritual lessons, in dreams as in life, are hard to recognize in the daunting appearance of the shadow. I spoke with an artist whose interest in spirituality had been casual and desultory until he had a puzzling dream:

> *I am climbing up a mountain in a spiral pattern. The path is very narrow, and I have to cling to the rock wall for all I'm worth. I come around the bend and there is a yogi with matted hair, dressed in a loincloth, dirty, smelly, almost growing out of the rock. And I'm going to have inch past, practically on top of him. I reach a point where we are nose-tip to nose-tip. Just then his closed eyes fly open. I'm terrified he's going to kiss me full on the lips. I wonder if I would rather jump off the cliff!*

His dream is a telling metaphor for the steeper segments of the spiritual path, often represented by a spiral because such ascents are never direct, but circumambulatory—and narrow, forcing us to tread one step at a time. We do often feel we would rather die than embrace our own shadow, even if it bears the gift of wisdom. This dream-teacher's eyes are wide open, for he has attained wakefulness. He is "like a rock," and cannot be swayed by the superficial. His gaze and his presence—even his embrace—can no longer be avoided. Once we are on a path, the only direction is onward. Such confrontations with what one psychologist calls "the intolerable image" can snap the ego like a twig. Yet the requirement to confront one's scariest demons—often transferred onto the teacher in what psychoanalysis calls "negative cathexis"—seems a necessary step for anyone seeking genuine sanity, and not merely "cheap and easy grace."

An encounter with the shadow leads us toward both higher wisdom and deeper compassion. One of the first obstacles Naropa encountered on his journey was a leper woman without hands and feet, whom he arrogantly ordered out of his way. When she pleaded she could not move, he "closed his nose in disgust" and jumped over her, even though, the text sarcastically notes, "he was full of compassion." The leper woman then rose into the air in a rainbow halo and scolded him for not seeing that she, too, belonged to "the Ultimate." Chastened, he vowed to humbly open his heart to anyone he met, but soon, on a narrow road, he found "a stinking bitch crawling with vermin." He again held his nose and jumped over the suffering animal, only to see it, too, rise in a dazzling rainbow, chiding him: "All living beings by nature are one's parents."[10] Being kind to others is easy when they are lovable, but shadow figures are often beyond the pale of what we feel we can bear. Healing Dreams tell us in no uncertain terms: you, too, *are* that—the scorned, the sick, the mad, the inimical.

From one perspective, not only our own spiritual imbalance but also the ills of the outer world spring from a refusal to embrace the shadow. As Freud pithily noted, "The ego thrusts forth upon the external world whatever within itself gives rise to pain." From discordant families to uncharitable deeds, from our rejection of others to a simple failure to care, from sectarianism to outright warfare, the principle seems to obtain. By embracing the shadow-other, we may begin to heal not only our divided hearts but our sundered world as well.

The Touch of Evil

Still, the invitation to touch and be touched by the shadow, even in a dream, often seems too horrible to contemplate. It does not feel "life-affirming"—quite the contrary. Dreams of spiritual initiation so often contain images of blood and death because this is how the task of integrating the shadow feels—it is nothing less than a dismemberment, albeit of an outgrown aspect of the self.[11]

Phyllis, a successful female corporate executive, had only a passing interest in mysticism until she had a startling Healing Dream:

> *I am in a subterranean chamber, like a catacomb, lying on an operating table. A huge black being stands over me. He's a bird-man, wearing a cape with many symbols, performing surgery on me while I'm fully awake. He makes a cut in my navel, pulls out something that looks like a grid, and shows it to me. Then he*

touches me and there's no pain. I look down and see the scar where he made the incision.

"It seemed so real," she told me, "that when I woke up, I looked down at my stomach to make sure there was no actual scar! I realized later that my whole life to that point had been organized on a grid, placing every-thing—job, relationships, thoughts, feelings—in neat labeled boxes. I had accepted society's tendency to value only the rational." In her dream, it was as if this viewpoint was, in solemn sacrifice, being excised from her flesh. Her therapist was alarmed that her underworld dream might be a literal warning of a health crisis or personal danger. But Phyllis was convinced it was "an initiation from the subterranean parts of my psyche. I didn't know what it meant, but it felt sacred." The bird-man, a classic intermediary be-tween the worlds, performs a sort of cesarean; she must be cut open to give birth to new awareness. She marks the dream as the beginning of a profound change of mind that caused her to eventually leave the corporate world. She now works as a psychologist in Washington, D.C., enjoying suc-cess with a clientele of corporate, government, and military leaders seek-ing access to their inner lives. She has herself become that half-avian figure who brings together the above and the below in the name of healing.

The encounter with the shadow is often bloodsoaked because it involves the dismantling of an overcherished ego ideal. The outward persona, often represented by the body itself, must be torn asunder so that the forces within can emerge. The approach counseled in esoteric traditions is always the same—a difficult, painful surrender to the process of death and recon-stitution. In the Arabic *Book of Ostanes,* it is said that a spiritual aspirant will eventually be confronted by the tormenting shadow-being symbolically known as the Prince of Andalusia. At that time, the seeker has "no weapon against him save resignation, no charger but knowledge, no buckler but un-derstanding." If he is able to wield these three weapons, which in effect open him to his own shadow, the prince will die, then will come to life again and give the seeker great powers.[12] (Chen Man-Ching, the modern progenitor of the martial art of tai chi chuan, dreamed one night that his arms had been amputated. But after his dream, he could not be beaten in combat, seeming to execute his "pushes" without even touching his opponent.[13]) One psychologist proposes a watchword when meeting the shadow: "Nothing can destroy you; nothing intends your destruction, though these are the very words it utters. What is intended is your ends, not your end: finally, your enlightenment and placement in the cosmos."[14]

Sympathy for the Devil

It is difficult to picture enlightenment, however, when facing the fearsome dark. There is a deity known in Tibetan mythology as a *mahakala*, usually depicted as a pitch-black, fanged, burning-eyed demon trampling on naked human corpses, ornamented with garlands of severed heads. He looks in every particular like our imagination of a devil. (Indeed, horrified early Christian missionaries believed his image in religious paintings to be a representation of Satan himself.) Yet he is considered a protector of the holy dharma who "drinks the hot blood of ego." The corpses he treads underfoot symbolize his ultimate conquest of the small self.

This *mahakala* principle appears in our dreams as the shadow, which speaks, sometimes with bloodcurdling ferocity, for those truths masked by ego's tendency to grow cozy with self-deception. Theologian John Sanford points out that although the devil is called the Father of Lies in the New Testament, in fact "the shadow never lies; it's the ego that lies about its real motives."

Still, sometimes we have shadow dreams so black and toxic we seem to have met the devil himself. There is a palpable aura of "something wicked this way comes," as distinctive as the smell of sulfur or the taste of ashes. But the character the dream identifies as the devil is often paradoxical— at once a terrifying presence and a speaker of truth—as in this striking dream told to me by writer Katharine Ramsland:

I am entrusted with caretaking a farm. My main task is to watch over one cow that has a tendency to act out. I look out the window and see it chasing other cows and biting them. I'm about to try to get it under control when I see a strange man walking toward the house. I open the door, and see over his shoulder a short, fat, black, potbellied bull covered with fur, standing upright, looking at me with human eyes, one hoof raised in greeting. The man says to me, "The devil approves of you." Oddly, his statement doesn't frighten me. Instead I feel liberated. The man comes into the house and shuts the door behind him. He seems worried, and says I should spend more time talking to a preacher. But I tell him, "I always know everything the preacher will say, and it never applies to me." The dream ends with me wondering if the devil approved of my behavior, or of the essential me. That is, have I been damned before I even get to do anything wrong? I have a vaguely sensual feeling, somewhere between freedom and uneasiness.

What are we to make of such a figure? The medieval Church, perhaps even the modern one, would say Katharine's soul was imperiled by the Prince of Darkness, and that she should indeed "talk to the preacher." But the figure in some ways has more in common with a pagan deity than with the source of all evil. It was Zeus, after all, who took the form of a bull to visit humankind—particularly women—and impregnate them with divine seed. Katharine was surprised that the devil was "smiling and waving, very relaxed and confident. I felt embraced, as if I were a part of him by my very nature." The experience disturbed and thrilled her. She sent copies of her dream to friends, soliciting their opinions of this strange encounter. Should she be afraid for her soul?

But the more she examined the dream, the more it seemed an enticement to throw off some inner shackles. She had always disapproved of her own "wild and devilish parts," but here she was receiving official sanction, as it were, to "act out," to kick up her heels like the cow she was supposed to control. It gave her permission to explore her "bad-girl side," erotic, transgressive, desirous. Indeed, the devil is often a representative of the sensate—and the sensual. When we give in to our high spirits—once the divine function of the half-goat Roman god of wine and song, Pan, on whom the Church's image of the horned devil was based—we say, with a secretly pleased smile, "The devil made me do it." The shadow speaks on behalf of the body and will not allow it to be cast aside in the name of piety or a dry, vitiated "goodness."

The dream, Katharine says, "emboldened me to be who I am. It changed the way I pursue my friendships, how I extend myself to people. Now I'm less likely to compromise my integrity just to have a guy in my life." It also was the beginning of the end of her marriage. "My ex-husband was raised in a fundamentalist home, so I had cut the wild part of me away, pretending it didn't exist. But now there was nowhere to run; the devil knew me, no matter where I went. And somehow that was okay." Her newfound ability to embrace the contradictions in her own nature has affected the psychotherapy practice she has kept up in addition to her writing career. "I've become a kind of 'dark-side therapist,'" she says. "People confess things to me they've never told anyone, because they can sense that I won't judge them."

Our dreams seem to advance a theology that allows a more subtle interplay between dark and light, akin to that which inspired the builders of Notre Dame to place demonic-looking gargoyles, scowling and gaping, on the very eaves of the house of God. Jung notes that some early Church fathers believed that "God rules the world with a right and a left hand, the right being Christ, the left being Satan."[15] Scholar Harold Bloom points out that Satan, in the Bible, is not a proper name but describes a functionary, "'*the* Satan,' which is a court title, akin to our 'prosecuting attorney.'... He is an authorized adversary."[16] The shadow advocates the whole truth and nothing but; in the court of dreams, there is no option of pleading the Fifth. It may well be that there is "objective evil" in the world, but is not the greatest part caused by our denial, on the witness stand, of our own personal demons?

Giving the Devil His Due

In the controversial film version of Nikos Kazantzakis's *The Last Temptation of Christ,* Jesus of Nazareth's mother asks her child about his visions: "Are you sure it's God? Are you sure it's not the devil? If it's the devil, the devil can be cast out."

"But what if it's God?" replies the Son. "You can't cast out God."

It is a question posed by the Healing Dream to anyone who wishes to get beneath the surface of things. Those who choose to face their shadow dreams sometimes find themselves facing almost theological quandaries. What is evil? Is it outside, implacable, irredeemable? Or inside, mutable, a wounded part of ourselves that we have never dared touch? Can the devil, as it were, be redeemed? The Healing Dream is always pushing us, enticing us, and even frightening us into a more inclusive embrace of life—one that can only be experienced beyond the grasp of duality. The Sufi sage Rabi was once seen running, carrying fire in one hand and water in the other. When she was asked the meaning of her action, she replied: "I am going to light a fire in Paradise and pour water on Hell, so that both veils disappear."[17] To be sure, we often find it hard to understand what the shadow dream is trying to show us. We refuse, over and over, the relationship it proposes between the profane and the sacred, refuse to fully confront the difficult question posed by the Taoist sage Lao Tzu: "Between good and evil, how great is the distance?"

The Taoists, who extolled the virtues of "the low, the dark and small," devised the yin-and-yang symbol to illustrate how the universe was constantly regenerated by the action of opposites. In its design, black and white exist in dynamic relationship, interpenetrating each other. Similarly, the path of the shadow may require adopting opposing points of view until some superior synthesis arises. This requires unusual courage and discipline. Both/and is a far more challenging proposition than either/or. Writes Robert Johnson: "To stay loyal to paradox is to earn the right to unity."

The sage Abu Sa'id al-Kharraz offered perhaps the most elegant summation. When asked, "Through what have you known God?" he promptly replied, "Through the fact that He brings opposites together." Healing Dreams challenge boundaries between shadow and ego, self and other, "good" and "evil"—even sometimes, we may find, between dreams and reality itself.

Chapter   11

The House of Dreams

Healing the Rift Between the Worlds

I do not know how to distinguish between our waking life and a dream.
Are we not always living the life that we imagine we are?
                                                    —*Henry David Thoreau*

They tease me now, telling me it was only a dream. But does it matter
whether it was a dream or reality, if the dream made known to me
the truth?
                                                    —*Fyodor Dostoyevsky*

There came a time in my life—several months, perhaps, though it felt
interminable—when dreams and reality drew closer than I could
ever have imagined. The images, moods, and imperatives of the
psyche pushed brusquely into waking life. Ordinary events glowed with
occult significance. The literal became symbolic, the symbolic literal: I felt
like the proverbial man who sees a stick in the road at dusk, mistakes it for
a snake, and, persuaded by his own mental projections, keels over from a
heart attack. I no longer knew if I was haunted by my own phantasms or
glimpsing another sort of reality altogether. It seemed as if I had, as in
faerie legends, eaten the food of the invisible world, and was now in its
thrall.

I talk to my Cree friend Sylvia about this whenever I have the chance.
Given how little such issues are discussed in mainstream Western culture,

it's been a comfort. "Indians don't make a big distinction between what's real and what's a dream," she said to me once over a cup of coffee. "It's *all* real." Her "grandfathers" appear not only in her dreams, she confided, but when she is awake. "One just shows up, in daylight. I can see through him. Like a shadow with color."

"Translucent," I suggested.

She nodded, then was suddenly caught by how absurd our conversation might sound, a taxonomy of angels on a pinhead: "Someone once told me I was a borderline personality," she pronounced gravely, then erupted into peals of merriment.

I laughed, too, a little uncertainly. My own less dramatic experiences had sometimes scared me witless. "See, the real and the not-real have some things in common," she said, sliding my napkin toward her and drawing a circle on it. "Say this is the waking world." She superimposed another circle intersecting the first. "And this is dreaming." Then she shaded the shared area at their juncture with a crosshatching of lines. "Just like this space is in both circles at the same time, our elders say we can exist in different dimensions at once.

"It's hard to translate," she added with a small frown. She pondered for a moment. "It's like this"—and she interlaced her fingers, gazing down at them placidly. "Reality and the dream just . . . overlap."

I was fascinated by this cross-cultural glimpse beyond our rigid dualisms of waking and dreaming. Our linguistic forms allow for only two cases— the subjective ("in here") or the objective ("out there"). But this was something in between. The diagram on Sylvia's napkin was familiar from the so-called Venn diagrams taught in geometry class, where the shaded area, belonging to both domains and to neither, is labeled rather poetically as a "null set." In the medieval world, this same figure was known as a mandorla and is found at various Christian sacred sites.

The more I've looked, the more I've noted how many societies have recognized a realm of awareness between waking and dreaming—not only recognized it but cultivated it, as in this tenth-century Hindu tantric text: "In order to acquire continuity of consciousness, unaffected by lapses into unconscious states, you must hold yourself at the junction of all the states, which constitutes the links between sleeping, dreaming, and waking: the half-sleep or Fourth State."[1]

There are few modern Western references to this "fourth state" of awareness; those we have tend to be linked to the theory and practice of art. The eighteenth-century German Romantic poet Novalis declared: "*To dream and altogether not to dream:* This synthesis is the operation of the genius by which both activities are mutually reinforced." French poet André Breton called for "the future resolution of these two states, so contradictory in appearance—dream and reality—into a kind of absolute reality, or surreality."[2] While Breton might be a little disappointed to see his coinage reduced today to describing aesthetic weirdness rather than the revolutionary mode of perception he proclaimed, we sometimes use "surreal" to describe those life moments so hard to believe that it feels like we're dreaming and awake at the same time. When reality seems to behave with the plasticity of imagination, one cannot escape the sense that one is straddling the worlds.

While we lack terminology for this fourth-state experience, other cultures not only name it but seek it out. The Zulu refer to the House of Dreams (Indlu Yemaphupha), a period in a shaman's initiation when the dreamworld stakes an insistent claim on the waking one, and the two seem increasingly commingled. The American writer James Hall, in the midst of his training as a Zulu *sangoma,* describes having the following experience sitting by a river:

> For me, waking and dreaming had merged. I looked at the rock closely. The microscopic was suddenly enlarged, and I watched granules of stone being chipped away by the powerful, ceaseless, erosive force. The noise was tremendous, nightmarish. . . . What followed were repeated visions that superimposed themselves on the sun's reflection sparkling over the rushing water. They were visions of flood waters raging up that narrow valley, a tidal wave between the sheer stone cliffs, engulfing and killing me [though] I knew that I was still on that rock. I was not so much terrified as puzzled and

unnerved . . . hearing snatches of music and singing that weren't really there, and glimpsing visions that disappeared as soon as I became aware that a figure moving against the tree was not physically present.[3]

It is a piercing vision of the world, at once minutely observed, yet densely overlaid by images that lend meaning and mystery. In my efforts to fathom this, I have had the sensation of trying to recover a lost way of seeing, drawing on personal experiences, as well as accounts by mystics, scientists, anthropologists, poets, and hinting testimony from members of traditional cultures. Even those gifted with a sort of "second sight" seem at a loss for words, as if trying to describe Totality through the tunnel vision of the human condition.

The sixty-six-year-old Australian Pitjantjatjara shaman Kurunpa Malpa (Bob Randal) was sent off to a boarding school when he was seven, one of some 45,000 aboriginal children displaced by the government's attempt to eradicate their culture. When he returned, he threw himself into study with elders who still followed the ancient traditions. He describes how young men would be initiated into a special form of seeing through fasting and sleep deprivation. "The elders sing and tell stories, get you into a state," he says, "and then you find you're in both places, the dreamworld and this one—first fifty-fifty, then maybe eighty-twenty.

"I did this in Arumland. Staying up late, around the fire, a man said he would show me the spirits. He said to look at the trees, not straight but just off to the right. Then I saw them, the spirit people! They looked just like real people, happy people." Although it sounds more like fantasies produced by fatigue and low glucose levels—when the brain's bleary pattern-making might reveal a face in the eye-headlights and mouth-grille of a car—Kurunpa insists, "The song brought them out. You go to 'beauty-rock' sites, look for them, and they will tell you things."

The thread of this hidden world, he says, gradually becomes woven into the ordinary fabric of life. He describes "day dreams" that happen "just to the side" of normal perception, many times during the day. "These are very soft," he adds, "like a butterfly that sits for a moment on your finger. But if you can listen, your life completely changes. Even if you ignore them, they still keep coming. The love is always around you. It doesn't give up." He sighs and smiles sweetly, wondering if I'm understanding: "Another life is *right beside us*," he says, tapping my arm for emphasis. "If you look, it will show itself. At any time, we are walking on three or four other footpaths—if only we could see."

Of course, most of us assume that we *already* see, despite the insistence of both mystics and cognitive scientists to the contrary. Though we may feel we are awake to our surroundings, our perceptual apparatus functions, in philosopher Henri Bergson's words, as a "reducing valve" of consciousness, subliminally filtering our experience, automatically weeding out what seems extraneous. There are times, however, when these mental gears disengage, and a world bursts forth, pulsing with new significance. The poet William Blake wrote, "If the doors of perception were cleansed, man would see everything as it is, infinite." To the ordinary person, he remarked, the sun looks like a burning golden coin; but to him, the sun was a Heavenly Host chorusing *Holy, Holy, Holy*. Blake termed this seeing that merges inner and outer realities "double vision."

We are given to believe that this is the private preserve of mystics. But as Jamake Highwater, the part-Blackfoot, part-Cherokee author of *The Primal Mind,* observes, "There is absolutely nothing 'mystical' in the notion that everything that happens to us, everything we think, everything we envision, imagine, conceive, perceive, dream, and intuit is a real and vital part of our lives."[4] Highwater was once told by an Indian shaman:

> You must learn to look at the world twice. First you must bring your eyes together in front so you can see each droplet of rain on the grass, so you can see the smoke rising from an anthill in the sunshine. *Nothing* should escape your notice. But you must learn to look again, with your eyes at the very edge of what is visible. Now you must see dimly if you wish to see things that are dim—visions, mist, and cloud-people. You must learn to look twice at the world if you wish to see all that there is to see.[5]

"Seeing doubly" is not an unfocused, inattentive state, but requires a different *kind* of focus, a different *means* of attention, though Western philosophers have for the most part ignored or even opposed it: "[We] can never bind and join our dreams . . . to the rest of our lives," Descartes pronounced, echoing the Greek philosopher Heraclitus, who posited an iron distinction between an objective reality (waking, consensual) and a subjective one (dreaming, private). Yet this neat boundary line was opposed by Socrates in the Dialogues, who wrote that it could never be said with certainty "whether we are asleep and our thoughts are a dream, or whether we are awake and talking with each other in a waking condition." Another philosopher caught by the notion of some rough equivalence between waking and dreaming was Friedrich Nietzsche, who in *The Dawn of Day* subversively argued that both are only variations on a theme:

> Real life has not the freedom of interpretation possessed by dream life; it is less poetic and less unrestrained—but is it necessary for me to show that our instincts, when we are awake, likewise merely interpret our nervous irritations? . . . that there is no really essential difference between waking and dreaming? . . . that all our so-called consciousness is more or less fantastic commentary on an unknown text, one which is perhaps unknowable but yet felt?[6]

Nietzsche's remarks deftly anticipated the work of modern cognitive psychologists, who tell us that consciousness, waking or sleeping, is produced by similar neurological mechanisms (the so-called continuity hypothesis). I believe that I am awake because I feel my fingers hitting the keys as I type these words, feel the pressure of my chair and the soughing of my breath, hear the stirring of birds and the distant rush of traffic outside my window. But immersed in a vivid dream, do we not also feel, hear, see, and otherwise experience apparent events? The brain is a sort of virtual-reality generator, providing us with a convincing sensorium, whether the input is from the outer world or the inner one.

We insist waking perceptions are more real. But how objective are they? By the time we become aware of it, the world "out there" has already been mediated. We don't see objects directly but as retinal images turned upside down by the eye's lens, so already a representation—a symbol—of the original. Our sense-perceptions are altered by memories, emotions, and preconceptions (telling me, for example, that the orange-yellow cylinder on the tabletop is my favorite Ticonderoga pencil, not a carrot stick). The physicist Ilya Prigogine writes: "Whatever we call reality, it is revealed to us only through an active construction in which we participate." Does this not also describe the dreamworld?

Add to our picture of "objective" waking life a variety of dreamlike states experienced throughout the day—lapses in attention, daydreams, hypnotic absorption in music or TV, perceptions colored by anger, or desire, or the buzz of subconscious gossip. Recent studies of the physiology of dreaming have even challenged the common notion that we dream only during the REM (rapid eye movement) phase of the sleep cycle. Dreams have also been correlated with the orchestrated functioning of various parts of the brain when no REM is occurring.[7] The implication is that we could be experiencing dreamlike states during times other than sleep. It may be, as philosopher Ludwig Wittgenstein wrote presciently, "Like the endlessly permeable consciousness of wakefulness, dreaming may have no set or fixed nature." How often do dreams and waking overlap? And how do we know?

Lucid Dreaming

One type of awareness that blurs the distinction between waking and dreaming is the state that researchers call lucidity. Usually, when we are engaged in the action of a dream, we credulously believe that its people, objects, and events are real: our heart pounds when we're pursued by a dream tiger; we feel sexually aroused by our dream lover. But people occasionally report "waking up" within their dreams and regaining the power of conscious action. In this lucid state, the dream is abruptly exposed as a fiction, a magical stage set where we are free to step outside our assigned role, even to deliberately change the plot and characters. One is in the dreamworld, but not *of* it.

Dutch psychiatrist Frederik Willems van Eeden first coined the term at a 1913 meeting of the Society for Psychical Research, where he summarized his conclusions based on three hundred of his own experiences. He described, for example, waking in his dream and performing an experiment within the dreamworld: he took a "fine claret-glass" and struck it with his fist as hard as he could, but it remained intact. Yet when he glanced back at it, the glass was broken. "It broke all right," wrote van Eeden, "but a little too late, like an actor who misses his cue. . . . This gave me a very curious impression of being in a fake-world, cleverly imitated, but with small failures. I took the broken glass and threw it out of the window, in order to observe whether I could hear the tinkling. I heard the noise, all right, and I even saw two dogs run away from it quite naturally. I thought what a good imitation this comedy-world was."[8]

There is debate in the dream community over the value of lucidity, with some taking the viewpoint that it is merely a case of the ego trying to usurp the unconscious and impose its control-freak agenda upon the dreamworld. (A similar contention was put forth by the medieval sage Almoli, who maintained that "true dreams are the result not of one's choice, but of the will of God," and those who impose their own will—whom he labeled "sorcerers"—have unreliable dreams, because "the contents are self-determined."[9])

One lucid dreamer told me how he had become adept at manipulating his dreamworld, conjuring up at will rooms full of beautiful, compliant women. But once, when he was amusing himself by "flying over Detroit, knocking over the hats off men," one of his made-up people *reached up and grabbed his foot,* unnerving him so much he awoke. Another time, as he was trying to make all the bell towers in a dream-town chime at once, a brass band came unexpectedly marching down Main Street, drowning them out.

Finally, one lucid dream forced him to wonder if the dreamworld might not have purposes beyond his own. He asked one of his dream people, a portly banker with a gold watch fob, "What do you represent?" and was stunned to hear a voice boom out of the sky: "The Unexpressed Characteristics!"

"Of what?" he asked, and the voice thundered back, "Of the Happy

Giver!" The man remembered that he'd once heard the expression "The Lord must be a happy giver" at a church fund-raiser. He began to wonder: "That Voice-That-Knows—well, *who* knows? Jehovah? Buddha? My inner self? A spirit guide? I'm no longer so sure my dream characters are just mental Play-Doh."

Apart from playful experiments, lucid dreamers say the experience of "awakening within their dreams" enables them to successfully confront situations that would normally terrify them. By consciously facing down a pursuing monster, for example, they conquer inner fears. They rehearse positive outcomes that can be transposed to real-life predicaments. Some go even further, claiming they have gained a new spiritual perspective on the nature of waking life, similar to that expressed by the Russian philosopher P. D. Ouspensky: "When a man begins to be aware, in a dream, that he is asleep and that what he sees is a dream, he awakes. In the same way a soul, when it begins to realize that all visible life is but a dream, approaches awakening."[10]

Twenty-five hundred years ago, Sakyamuni Buddha declared that the world of apparent phenomena was insubstantial, by using a series of similies: What we take to be real, he said, is like an optical illusion; a flickering butter lamp; a cloud armada; the reflection of the moon in water; a city composed of sounds; a soap bubble; a shooting star; a rainbow; and of course, a dream. Many compare lucid dreaming to Tibetan Buddhist "dream yoga," which prescribes that we regard the dreamworld and the waking world alike as mind-stuff. As in lucid dreaming, the practitioner develops an ability to become aware within the dream state, then learns to dispel its illusions. (If one dreams one is threatened by fire, counsels a typical instruction, one should say, "What fear is there of fire in a dream?" and then transform the fire into water.[11]) As it happens, however, dream yoga presents a view several degrees stranger—a hundred eighty, to be exact—than the Western paradigm of the lucid dream.

"You should view *waking* experience as if it is a dream," explains Dzigar Kongtrul Rinpoche, a married Tibetan lama in his thirties, as we sit on the porch of his retreat cabin high above Colorado's San Luis Valley. "This means seeing that appearances have no inherent existence, any more than a tree seen in a dream is a real tree. When you perceive even 'real' things as not solidified, you don't feel such attachment or aversion to them, so you're less trapped in Samsara." He restlessly crossed one leather boot over the other as his brother, a robed monk, sat perched on the railing, intermittently eavesdropping. I got the feeling that Dzigar had endured his share of questions about the fabled exotica of Tibetan dream practices.

When it comes to the interpretation of dreams, he borders on dismissive. Certainly, there may be reasons to do so (though Dzigar claims this is "not of such interest to the Eastern mind"); but this pursuit is for those who are "confident in their realization that dreams are nothing." Dreams, Buddhists believe, are part of the same spectrum of dualistic delusion as waking life. "Just don't make such a big deal about dreams," he asserts. "*Especially* the amazing ones. Most people have enough trouble taking their waking life seriously!" His smile has an ironic tilt. I've heard this rhetorical maneuver from various lamas for years: *Yes, we have special dream practices. No, working with dreams is not very important, even a distraction.* They're tired of Westerners grabbing the dessert tray without first ordering a meal—especially when tray, meal, table, and even the diner himself are viewed as equally "devoid of essence."

Dzigar won't say much about his own dreams beyond that he "has a lot of déjà vu." He admits, with a small sigh, that "there are signs of accomplishment in dreams of how far you've come in your spiritual journey," but he looks diffidently away when I ask what they are.

His brother breaks the silence. "There are four types of accomplishment dreams," he offers helpfully. "One, 'capture.' That means recalling the dream within the dream. The second is 'manipulate,' increasing your power to act voluntarily while dreaming. The third is 'pacify,' which means to calm whatever is a hindrance. And then there is 'manifest,' doing whatever you want to do—transform yourself into a bird or a fly, travel to different worlds and times."

Dzigar glances at him sharply. He's said enough.

My own teacher, Chögyam Trungpa, though similarly tight-lipped on the subject, was fond of quoting a "slogan" of the Indian sage Atisha: "Regard all dharmas [i.e., the "ten thousand things" of this world] as dreams." In his translation, Trungpa suggests how, rather than being obscure or occult, such a view is psychologically liberating: "The slogan means to regard whatever occurs as a phantom. . . . You can see that your hate for your enemy, your love for your friends, and your attitudes toward money, food, and wealth are all part of discursive thoughts. Regarding dharmas as dreams means that although you might think that things are very solid, the way you perceive them is soft and dreamlike."[12]

The other day, I had a reminder of the tenacious solidity of our waking projections. Late for the post office and desperate to get off an Express Mail parcel, I saw a strapping young man in a sport-utility vehicle pull into the handicapped parking spot right next to the door. I felt annoyed that he would misuse this privilege while I jockeyed with other last-minute arrivals for a space three rows back. He became the focus of my irritation. I bounced mental daggers off his rearview mirror. Then, as I was running up to the door, I saw him sidling in front of me—painstakingly, using a walker, his withered lower limbs in stark contrast to the built-up torso I'd glimpsed through his car window. I waited to hold the door for him, and he thanked me warmly, making me more abashed at what had been, in effect, a waking hallucination—a pinch of perception, mixed well with frazzled assumptions. Such incidents of mental projection happen to us daily—many spiritual doctrines would say on a moment-to-moment basis. We name and label things before we really know what we're seeing. I would have saved myself considerable aggravation had I remembered to "regard all dharmas as dreams."

Still, how far do we dare to take this? We tend to think of someone who "lives in a dreamworld" as the type who'd go shopping and forget he'd left the dog locked in the car with the windows rolled up during a record heat wave. The Dalai Lama has joked, when asked about dream yoga, "There are a lot of people who mix up their sleep with meditation, but not quite intentionally." There is a difference, he suggests, between recognizing the illusory nature of reality and stumbling around in a daze. Yet I have been told by several lamas that dream yoga begins with recognizing the dreamlike qualities of daily life—a practice known as *trekchö*. Here the practitioner is urged, upon waking up from a dream that just moments before seemed so real, to contemplate the similar insubstantiality of the daytime experiences to come.

Whether "waking" within a dream (lucid dreaming) or "dreaming" when awake (*trekchö*), dream life and waking life are placed on more equal footing, the better to transcend both. A lama once told me, chortling, a story by the great teacher Mipham, concerning a heated argument between Dream and Waking:

One day Waking was heard to remark snidely, "You, dear Dream, are a lie."

"You, friend Waking," responded Dream, "are equally deceptive."

"You are more so!" exclaimed Waking, mightily offended. "I dream that I am eating a stupendous banquet, yet I wake up with an empty stomach."

"It is no different with you," replied Dream languorously. "You go to sleep in your bedroom, but when you dream of being caught outside in a rainstorm, you can feel yourself get soaking wet!"

They were about to come to blows when a judge intervened in the debate, wisely ruling that each party had merit. "It cannot be that if a dream is true, waking is false, or vice versa," he pronounced. "All problems in the world come from mistakenly seeing these two as opposite, when they are really on the same side."

The lama and I drove back to the suburban house where he was staying, whereupon he challenged me to a video race-car game belonging to his host's son. We sat on the carpet, shoulder to shoulder, as our cars careened around the track. I tried to steer my digital driver around a series of bizarre obstacles, swerving to avoid jouncing, neon green bombs hurled at me by the competition—a red-robed lama twiddling a joystick with a small, easy-going smile.

"Recognize no differences between appearances in dreams and those in waking experience," he murmured, as my race car flipped end over end and burst into flames. "Then, even if you dream that a tiger has your head in his mouth, you're still happy." But I found it hard not to be anxious even amid the whimsical carnage of a cartoon demolition derby. Adrenaline sang in my nerves. I wanted to avoid being blown to bits. I longed to roar unobstructed into the straightaway. The game was becoming, in video-game lingo, a highly immersive environment, a too-perfect example of how readily we buy into phantasms. The lama deftly avoided the swirl of slippery blue goo I splattered before his onrushing vehicle. As I smacked into a bright orange barrier, he whizzed past the victory flag and then, with the aplomb of a champion, graciously took his winner's lap.

The Bee and I

The lama later explained that in dreams, the "mental body" is "open and flexible," and so has more possibilities than in normal daytime existence. By erasing rigid distinctions between waking and dreaming life, he told me, "you can learn to not only transform your dream but change your reality."

An incident sprang to mind that gave me an inkling of what he meant. I was sitting in a friend's yard one day enjoying the sun when a bee landed on my bare chest. I have spent years trying to overcome my innate revulsion to insects. (I sometimes use a Buddhist practice that counsels imagining that after limitless lifetimes, even the lowliest bug must have once been your parent.) Summoning up with some effort an attitude of benign curiosity, I soon became entranced by the rainbow sheen of its wings, the odd waggling movements of its golden thorax, the incessant dipping motion of its antennae and tapping of its legs. It became a dream bee, an apparitional creature that I had never really seen before. I forgot my city-boy fear it might jab me with its stinger. The bee and I were sharing a surreal interlude. When my friend came back outside, she let out a small shriek—it was a big bee—but I begged her silence with a glance. She crept up and we both watched an amazing sight—using its back legs, the bee neatly scraped off its load of pollen onto my chest in a tidy yellow pile and calmly whirred away. Had I seen the bee as a dangerous insect, I would have swiped at it, either killing it, driving it off with an angry buzz, or annoying it enough to deliver a nasty sting. Instead I had changed my "waking dream" of the bee, and in some spiritual variant of the Heisenberg principle, the perception had altered my experiment's outcome.

We suffer, says Buddhism, because we grasp at or flee from our own projections, taking them for real. But Buddhist teachers contend that self and other have no more intrinsic existence than a dream: more often than not, we are directing our desire and repulsion at our own phantoms. Dream yoga is practiced not as a mental parlor trick, but in order to wake from our too-solid delusions, which in turn unblocks the flow of compassion (or "resonating concern") for our fellow beings.

Waking Up to Dreaming

When we think of enlightenment, of spiritually "waking up" (the word *Buddha* comes from the root *budh,* meaning "awake"), we imagine it as an otherworldly, unattainable mystical state. But all spiritual paths worth their salt insist that we can live in the worlds of the transcendent and the here-and-now simultaneously.

The whole idea of a "waking dream" may seem like an invitation to delusional living—we'd be bumping into walls as we tried to walk through them, jumping out windows thinking we could fly—but the practices are heuristic. Regard the world *as if* it were a dream, and see what happens. We invest the world with our imagination in any case, interweaving it unwittingly with everything we perceive. We might as well play consciously with this dimension of our experience. If we were to visualize everyone we meet as a *bodhisattva* (for what scripture does not tell us that the most miserable beggar could be a disguised angel?) or imagine that every creature we encounter was, in another life, our father or mother, would it not evoke an attitude of respect and tenderness? If we imagine the world differently, such teachings say, the world will return the favor. Pick any person in your life, invest them with a new fantasy, and watch how over time, even instantly, their behavior and very appearance seem to change. To be sure, the response we get stems from subliminal cues (a benign look creates a different effect than a hostile glare), but perhaps our perceptions themselves are reality-generating fields. Perhaps our vaunted selfhood is process and flux, subject to subtle emanations. Perhaps, when we allow our imaginal world and this world to interpenetrate, we engage in a sort of co-creation.

In the Koran, the story is told of the first day the queen of Sheba entered King Solomon's palace. The queen, mistaking its crystal flooring for a pool of water, picked up her robe so as not to wet its hem. Solomon used the occasion, writes Henry Corbin, to point out that "every object, perceived at every instant, is a 'new creation' . . . The crystal floor is imagined as water. . . . But precisely because it is 'imagined,' the Image, once recognized as such, betokens something that is not illusory, but real and meaningful: for indeed, to recognize it for what it is is 'to wake up,' and to invest it with one's marvelous power."[13]

This creative power, nowhere greater than in dreams, is what charges the world with meaning. "The only reason God placed sleep in the animate world," the Sufi mystic Ibn 'Arabi (1165–1240) wrote, "was so that everyone might witness the Presence of Imagination." Bringing this imaginative presence into our lives, notes Corbin, enables us "to raise sensory data to a higher level, to transmute the outward envelope into its truth,"[14] apprehending the world in its fullest glory. Similar insights abound in virtually every spiritual tradition. The story is told that the Brahman Narendra, before he became the great sage Swami Vivekananda, sat one day in the temple garden proclaiming to a friend how "silly" it was to believe that everything was God. Why, if this were so, he exclaimed disdainfully, "This jug is God. This cup is God. Whatever we see is God. And we too are God!" His guru, Sri Ramakrishna, came out of his room at that moment and blessed him with a touch that instantly awakened insight: "Spellbound, [Narendra] immediately perceived that everything in the world was indeed God. A new universe opened around him. Returning home in a dazed state, he found there, too, that the food, the plate, the eater himself, the people around him, were all God. When he walked in the street, he saw the cabs, the horses, the streams of people, the buildings were Brahman. He could hardly go about his day's business."[15]

According to a contemporary's account, "when the intensity of the experience abated a little, he saw the world as a dream. Walking in the public square, he would strike his head against the iron railings to know whether they were real."[16] Narendra's experience—reminiscent of the Zulu concept of the House of Dreams—illustrates a remark made by a British theologian: Since we already exist within God, we do not so much seek Him as "explore into Him."[17]

In the House of Dreams, even small experiments can be life enhancing. For example, I don't have a dishwasher, and so I have to do my dishes by hand. I often see this as drudgery, a time-wasting nuisance, and let them pile up. But sometimes I remind myself to see the job in another way. Some of my dishes, gifts from a friend, are a luminous, handpainted burnt orange. In another era they would have been someone's treasured possession; now they're items anyone discerning can pick up in a megastore. But if I treat them as precious, remembering to appreciate their texture, colors, and shapes, I find my resentment dissolving. I sometimes even imagine that as I'm washing them, I'm cleansing my world and my mind of impurities, and they seem to glow in silent signification. Mostly I see them as irritating dirty dishes. But in either case, I am washing my *dream* of the dishes: in one dream, they are annoying. In another, they are an opportunity to "transmute the outward envelope into its truth." There is a hopeful Zen story about a monk who was not regarded as intellectually gifted enough for the holy teachings. He was given a job sweeping the temple. But his teacher instructed him to imagine as he swept, "I am sweeping away my anger. I am sweeping away my attachment. I am sweeping away my ignorance." Thus, it is said, the monk became enlightened.

Synchronicity

The place where the invisible world and the visible one conjoin is situated at the furthest edge of our understanding. There are some rooms in the House of Dreams that we can only peer into through the keyhole. Jung regarded the phenomenon he called synchronicity as one peek into the mystery of how reality itself is constructed.

We have all experienced some form of synchronicity in our lives—

those times a book falls open to a page containing the very thought we'd just been engrossed in. Or the other way around: sometimes, the world falls open. A friend of mine was once sitting in his cabin reading *The Dream of the Grasshopper* by Laurens van der Post, a book about synchronicity. He had just gotten to a passage about an African folktale in which a woman is summoned to a tree by a dream; as she sits beneath it, the tree crashes to the ground and kills her.

"At that moment," my friend said, "lightning struck a hundred-year-old tree right outside my window, and it came crashing down." At the time, my friend was battling cancer. He took this not as an omen of death, but as a reflection of his titanic struggle. He told me he often experienced dreamlike waking states that he referred to as "the field of healing. Anything and everything happens to you when you're in it."

Jung defined *synchronicity* as "an acausal connecting principle" through which internal states—dreams, fantasies, or feelings—seem to be tangibly linked with events in the material world. Such occurrences can feel jarringly surreal. According to Marie-Louise von Franz, "Synchronistic events constitute moments in which a 'cosmic' or 'greater' meaning becomes gradually conscious in an individual; generally it is a shaking experience."[18] Jung, during the period he was storm-tossed by his own confrontation with the unconscious, had a "big dream" about a being with the wings of a kingfisher, sailing across a sky that was also the blue water of the sea. "Since I did not understand this dream-image," he wrote, "I painted it in order to impress it upon my memory. During the days when I was occupied with the painting, I found in my garden, by the lake shore, a dead kingfisher! I was thunderstruck, for kingfishers are quite rare in the vicinity of Zurich and I have never since found a dead one. The body was recently dead—at the most, two or three days—and showed no external injuries."[19]

Here a synchronistic event acts as an amplification—almost a confirmation from heaven—with respect to a dream. The figure of the man with kingfisher wings, whom he called Philomen, was the dream personage Jung credited with teaching him the "objective nature" of the psyche. It was as if the creature had broken the dream's version of TV's fourth wall, showing that the hard-and-fast boundary between the imaginal life and our life in this world could act like a semi-permeable membrane.

Here Lie Dragons

Others would label this viewpoint pure solipsism and superstition: what a paralyzing way to live, if every random coincidence were an omen—as if the world revolved around us, pointing out things for our edification. Even Jung, who began his study of synchronicity believing that "meaning" was the signal characteristic of such events, later decided that they implied a hidden principle more likely to be explained by science than psychology.[20] Collaborating with physicists like Einstein colleague Wolfgang Pauli, he began to wonder if such occurrences didn't suggest something about the very composition of the universe. He remarked that it often seemed to him that "matter is only a thin skin round an enormous cosmos of psychical reality," or even, "psyche and matter are two different aspects of the same thing."

His colleague C. A. Meier proposed the idea of a third aspect, a *tertium,* an unknown factor beyond mind and matter that synchronistically produces effects in both realms. Canadian dream researcher Jayne Gackenbach sent me the reminiscences of a Cree woman named Erin that exemplify this paradigm.

Erin recalled that her mother's legs once became so badly swollen with infection that the doctors wanted to amputate. But Erin's *kokum* (grandmother), a well-known healer, took her mother home from the hospital vowing, "You're not going to cut off my child's legs." Erin remembers quietly watching the healing ceremony with her three brothers. Suddenly they were amazed to see "spiders coming from inside my mother's legs!" Gackenbach pointed out it was no doubt their susceptibility to suggestion—it was her *kokum* after all, a persuasive authority figure, who had first pointed out the "spiders." But Gackenbach later wondered if her explanation wasn't "my white academic arrogance." After all, she reflected, the technique had worked—Erin's mother is walking today, and is a healer herself. Gackenbach, who specialized in lucid dream research for several decades before becoming deeply involved with the Cree community, carries her speculation a step further: "If I'd been at that healing and chirped up with my Western understanding, I might have disrupted some shared alternate reality crucial to the healing. Though I may feel the need to ascertain objective 'reality,' I've learned that for them, the whole issue's relatively nonexistent."

Many native peoples claim that the dream is an active force, walking in this world, leaving visible footprints. Is it possible that beyond our standard map of reality, in a region still labeled "Here Lie Dragons," lies a great terra incognita? I have no way to evaluate—or corroborate—the "truth" of the downright apparitional. My Cree friend Sylvia has told me about two dream symbols that have been with her since childhood. One, a white wolf, appears when a dream is meant for all the Indian people in Canada. When a white bear comes, she knows it pertains to her or her relatives. The bear arrives at night, she says, in her bedroom, when "there's something I need to see." She climbs on its back and flies to distant locations.

"You mean, you *dream* about a white bear," I interject.

"No, he's really there."

"How do you know? Do you wake up and still see him?"

She gives me a look. "I turn on the *light*," she says, as if explaining something patently obvious, "and I still see him. He's there, like a real bear. I can reach down and stroke him and feel his fur."

One struggles to understand, to affix labels. Perhaps it is an instance of hypnagogia, the unique state between waking and sleeping well documented by dream researchers. Images seen in this state tend to be exceptionally sharp, detailed, and lifelike. (As one subject stated of an imagined face: "I could see the grain of the skin.") They tend to be vividly colored, luminous, and solid-looking, "like a movie in 3-D." They often induce "feelings of heightened reality." Even subjects who realize that such fantastic sights are internally generated, and who know their eyes to be shut, report that the visions appear to be "projected five or six feet in front of them, impinging upon 'real' space."[21] In this form of consciousness, as one writer describes it, "Metaphors are experienced as actualities."

A friend of mine, a university English instructor, once breathlessly called me a few days after she had taken her beloved nineteen-year-old cat to the vet to be put to sleep. Now, she told me, her voice a combination of delight and distress, "He's been showing up in my room in broad daylight when I'm wide awake. Today he rubbed up against my leg, and I actually *felt* his hair." It was so similar to Sylvia's descriptions, I didn't know quite what to say, though the rational explanation would be a hallucination triggered by grief.

A South African *sangoma* named Claude told me a similar tale of the House of Dreams: "In 1946, I went to the river where the women used to wash the clothes. I saw some women drying shawls by the river, but when I got nearer, they were not there. Disappear! They were the water people, who live underneath the river." After that, he dreamed of them for many nights. He says that each dream, in a time dilation common to other-worldly visits, was "as if I was learning for six months. They taught me about different type of herbs, and gave me medicines to drink."

(His story is starkly similar to one a young Pawnee boy named Small told a historian in 1850. The boy had fallen asleep while hunting along Nebraska's South Platte River and had been taken to an underwater animal "lodge." He awoke sitting by a fireplace surrounded by an assortment of creatures, with a big snake guarding the door. For four nights, each animal in turn taught him its powers.[22] He insisted his experience was real.)

As reality blends into dream and back again, the Western mind grasps at, but fails to find a conceptual handhold. Either something actually happens, or it does not; there is no room for anything in between. Yet many indigenous cultures accept that one can dwell almost amphibiously in two realities. Anthropologist William Merrill, writing about the Mexican Raramuri, has observed that for them, "Dreams are real events. On numerous occasions, people would describe to me quite incredible personal experiences, but fail to mention that the events had taken place in dreams until I asked. This does not mean that they do not distinguish between their waking and dreaming lives, but that they attribute comparable reality to both." The reality ascribed to dreams extends to waking experiences that would normally be classed as hallucinations. Merrill gives the example of a woman named Rosario who "saw" a Catholic priest and nun playing in the sand near a hot spring. She ran to get her husband and children to witness this strange sight, but when they returned, the clergy were gone. The family concluded they must have been "water people" who had slipped back to their home in the stream.

I have a story of my own, an anecdote I keep stored in "the gray bin" where I toss those things that are neither black nor white. One night, just out of college, I had been playing music into the wee hours with a group in a nearby town. Seeing that I was tired and concerned about the icy roads, a new acquaintance invited me to stay overnight in a house his girl-friend had recently inherited. The spare room was still unfurnished, but the carpet was plush, and nestling in a few blankets, I quickly started drift-ing off to sleep. I was startled to suddenly hear a woman's operatic soprano, trilling effortlessly up and down four or five octaves. One minute it was al-most deafening—her voice seemed right inside my ear—then as distant as the wind in the treetops. It was shockingly distinct, with an almost clichéd, echoing "ghostliness" that made it seem less frightening than faintly ludi-crous. I had the image of a Brünnhilde-like figure in an armored breastplate and horned helmet, an operatic caricature straight out of a Marx Brothers movie. The incongruous thought came to mind that I was hearing some-one singing German lieder. The voice quickly dissipated, swallowed by a hiss resembling radio static. Uneasy but too tired to stay awake, I sank into a deep sleep.

The next morning at breakfast, I mentioned, slightly embarrassed, my dream of a bedside musical recital.

"That was Auntie Jewel," my new friend promptly responded.

"Auntie *who?*"

"She was a German opera singer around the turn of the century. This was her house." I was dumbfounded. "We've heard her, too," he reassured me, adding, "You were sleeping in her old practice room. "

I do not offer this as evidence for the survival of the human personality after death. But I remain at a loss for a rational explanation—no mention had been made of the home's previous owner, and I barely knew my hosts. From that moment on, I was more sympathetic to the belief system of the shaman, who insists we are surrounded by invisible influences we do not make up in our heads.

Living in the House of Dreams

Sylvia, Claude, Rosario, my friend who saw her dead cat, the diva-haunted couple, and I could be deemed to have suffered a transient perceptual disorder. But this species of experience is found among all peoples on every continent in every historical era. Only the degree to which it is acknowledged, suppressed, interpreted, or medically treated varies from society to society.

Consider the story of Frances H. I first met Fran, a lively sixty-something with short-cropped gray hair and owlishly large glasses, at a conference, where she'd held a small room spellbound with her tale of recovery from a severe head injury. She'd never spoken about her ordeal in public, and her initial tentativeness made the narrative all the more poignant. Dressed in a bright blue peasant blouse and heavy turquoise jewelry, using her politically incorrect cigarette like a laser pointer, Fran, with her deep, gravelly voice, was soon narrating her to-hell-and-back story with the panache of a performance artist.

Fran had been a successful accounting executive, a woman who had broken through the glass ceiling in what was then a man's game. But one sunny day, stopped at a light in rush-hour traffic, the world as she knew it ended. "I remember seeing a large van to my right, edging onto the crosswalk," she recalls. "I noticed a car barreling up behind me in my rearview mirror. The last thing I remember thinking is, 'I hope this guy sees the red light.'"

The horrendous crash left her with what is known as a "closed head trauma injury," which typically causes severe brain damage. "I had to re-learn the difference between 'hot' and 'not hot,' because I'd burn myself like a baby. It was chaos to perform a simple task like brushing my teeth, because I would start and not stop. I'd find a half dozen wet toothbrushes and empty toothpaste tubes in the ashcan. I couldn't remember if I'd really done something or not."

She doesn't remember most of the three years after her accident. Her math abilities were gone. Through sheer grit and a quotient of grace, her verbal abilities slowly returned. "My spoken vocabulary is now beyond my fifth-grade reading skills," she remarks drily. She's had seizures from a flash camera, from high-tech car alarms, and from high-frequency sounds emitted from traffic poles that guide the deaf at busy corners. But she has come a long way from the shattered, useless days that once stretched featurelessly before her. She attributes her progress to a series of curious encounters with the invisible world.

One afternoon, living in what felt like perpetual twilight, she had the sudden sensation someone was in the house with her. She looked up and saw "a pantomime, being enacted right in front of me. Like a badly focused slide, I saw young men seated at classroom desks. One stood and held up a piece of paper. As my focus cleared, I saw it was a crossword puzzle." Not knowing what else to do, Fran dutifully opened her morning paper to the crossword page. One of the young men nodded. "Then I saw his crossword puzzle page fill in with letters. I got a pencil and copied what I saw." It was the beginning, she says, of relearning to read and write.

Another day, she says, she "saw" an entire team of baseball players. "They were all in their proper positions in this baseball diamond that suddenly appeared in my living room, but they were all missing an arm or a leg. Each had a cane they used with great skill." Fran, who had abandoned hope of learning to use a cane when she was in the hospital, imitated the ballplayers' motions, learning bit by bit to maneuver. "Now I'm very clever with my cane," she says with a grim smile. "I can put it right in your instep if you hurt my feelings."

Fran had once been been a special education teacher for retarded adults. The slow, patient teaching methods of her apparitions were not foreign to her. "When the same group of guys showed up and said, 'Typewriter,' I got the old clickety-clack from the closet." She began, under their tutelage, to learn to type again, discovering in the process that she could write powerful, evocative poetry.

Not all her encounters were benign. Early in her treatment, Fran had been given Prozac, a common enough prescription. But in her case, it seemed to trigger "terrifying hallucinations which would go on forever." One day, lying in bed at home, exhausted, "the neighborhood noises seemed to stop and I got very scared. A figure came through the inside wall of the house and materialized in front of me—a handsome man, dressed in black, with a black leather portfolio. He opened it, pulled out a contract, and gestured to me to sign it. Then I realized he was a death salesman—a death collector. I screamed, and actually called 911. As the neighbors were almost breaking the door down to see what was happening to me, he wafted out the window."

Fran's psychiatrist considered committing her to an institution. Eventually, she refused to take her medications, reasoning that unlike her drug-induced nightmares, her previous hallucinations had done her no harm—and perhaps had even done her some good.

Slowly, her dreams began to change. "All night long, I'd see figures accompanied by music so all-encompassing it was as if all the universe were held together by this sound." Or she was given a necklace made of "gold and jewels on strands of light energy, an object of incredible beauty. When I would tell people about these dreams, all I could say was, There's real, and there's *real,* and then there's *realer than real.*" After each of the big dreams, Fran's doctors were surprised to observe breakthroughs in her course of recovery, which she calls "my major adaptive shifts."

Today, says Fran, "I have 'paraphenomena' in the daytime, nightmares when I'm asleep, hallucinations and encounters with spooks in broad daylight." But she's proud she's learned to live with her frequent dream visions as well as her petit mal seizures. Once, on a bus, she noticed an elderly man sitting next to her. "I've seen you before," he told her in a kind, creaky voice, "but I always thought I'd frighten you away." When she looked again, he was gone. Fran, who had long stopped caring what others thought, strode up to the bus driver and demanded he tell her if he had seen the man. "He's on my bus every so often," the driver allowed cautiously. "He always speaks to a particular person, always sits in the same seat." He looked at Fran appraisingly, then, deciding it was all right to elaborate, muttered, "I've seen him get on, but never off. He's *my* ghost. Other drivers have their own ghosts," and opened the door with a pneumatic hiss.

"How do I live with these experiences without going crazy?" she asks me with a flash of indignation. "In the medical context, all this is pathological. I hadn't taken Spook Etiquette 101! I was clueless about how to explain it, let alone live with it."[23]

Fran now regularly attends dream groups—"my salvation," she says—but also has found a toehold in the medical system. She runs dream groups for head trauma survivors referred by doctors, rehab therapists, and workmen's comp. She once persuaded a few brain injury support-group leaders to hand out a questionnaire to elicit their patients' experiences. Says Fran wryly, "Many of the patients asked, 'Why doesn't anyone want to know what I see and hear at night in my dreams and hallucinations? They only ask for the time and date. They never ask me what the voices *say*.'"

The Underwater Lodge

The medieval mystic and physician Paracelsus cautioned against confusing the true imagination (*imaginatio vera*) that sees into the hidden nature of things with pure fantasy (which he called the "madman's cornerstone"). Despite the relatively happy ending to Fran's story, there are psychological pitfalls in the House of Dreams. Notes the Reverend Jeremy Taylor, who has done dreamwork in residential facilities with schizophrenic and autistic teens: "Dream narratives of whacked-out kids are the same as normal kids. The difference is their ability to wake up from the dream and ask, What was *that* about? For the schizophrenic kids, the dream doesn't end; they don't distinguish between 'primary process' and consensual reality."

M. L. von Franz concurs: "You only have to go into a lunatic asylum to see the victims of the dream world. Someone is living in a dream that he is Napoleon. Another, when you begin to talk to him, tells you confidentially that he is really Jesus Christ, but nobody seems to understand him. They have been swallowed by the dream world. . . . The dream world is beneficent and healing only if we have a dialogue with it, but at the same time remain in actual life."[24]

John Schultheiss is a climber who, after suffering a severe fall, found himself in an altered state of consciousness that he credits with saving his life. It included a vision of a man who seemed to help him stagger back to civilization, then vanish. He spent a year investigating the phenomenon he dubbed "stress-based initiation," paying particular attention to the mysterious "phantom companions" who have been reported by everyone from Himalayan climbers to desert explorers. In his book *Bone Games,* he cites the case of Lindbergh's "cockpit angels," whom the exhausted pilot saw guiding his solo flight across the Atlantic; and of Captain Joshua Slocum, who, after sailing solo circumnavigation at the turn of the century, claimed his ship was kept on course by "Christopher Columbus's navigator" as he lay struck down by a fever during rough weather in the mid-Atlantic.

But Schultheiss also catalogues hallucinations that were not only valueless but also life-threatening. He quotes from a report on the survivors of a Dutch liner torpedoed in the South Atlantic. They spent eighty-three days together on a life raft before being picked up by rescuers. A young Italian-American named Izzy experienced a series of compelling visions:

> Izzy thought he was "going a mile a minute" on a motorboat captained by a silent Charon-like figure; then he was in the middle of a fleet, near "a big hole, where guys were going down for a cigarette"; then the torpedoed ship was resurrected from the deep, with men swimming over to it, the ship's cook serving them ham and eggs; a lunchroom, with coffee, hamburgers, doughnuts, pie. These scenes occurred over and over that first night, and again and again Izzy tried to swim away from the raft to reach the illusory food, drink, warmth, safety; if his friends hadn't restrained him, he would have swum away into the darkness and drowned.

A filmmaker friend of mine named Marty told me of a similar experience. He'd been riding a rubber raft alongside a father-and-son kayaking team, shooting a segment for the PBS children's series *Zoom*. Suddenly the stream turned into raging whitewater. He and his cameraman hit a tree jutting from a small island, barely managing to grab hold of a branch as their raft sailed into oblivion. They hauled themselves onto the island to await help.

The day was clear and sunny but freezing cold, and while the producers on shore called for a helicopter rescue, Marty warded off hypothermia by exploring the terrain. At the far end of the island, by a spit of land that protruded into calm water, "I saw the answer for us. There was a little wooden raft like Huck Finn's, with a pole! I didn't know what it was doing there, sitting in this golden light. I almost got on it, then thought I'd better go back to tell the others." When he got back to other side of the island, he looked behind him and was startled to realize there was no raft, no calm water. Had he climbed aboard the imaginary craft—"which to me was as utterly real as you are sitting there"—he would have been swept downstream. These stories reveal the negative, perilous aspect of the "underwater lodge"—it is also the realm of the Sirens, luring the unwary toward a submergence, possibly forever, in the depths of the unconscious.

Freud wrote emphatically: "*Psychical* reality is a particular form of existence, not to be confused with *material* reality."[25] Children especially have trouble distinguishing between the inner and outer worlds. One vivid dreamer told me how as a child she jumped off a rock and broke her ankle because, having convincingly experienced flying in her dreams, she was certain she could do it in real life. Another told me how he performed a similar childhood experiment—but out a second-story window, occasioning a few months in traction!

Perhaps out of caution, our culture trains us early to ignore the imaginal, making it subject to belittlement, mistrust, and neglect. Children are not permitted to live in both worlds but are pressured early to renounce their fantasies. "Having an active imagination" becomes the patronizing "just imagining things." Psychologist Mary Watkins, an impassioned defender of the imaginal realm, describes this crucial turning point in her book, *Waking Dreams:* "We discarded the stuffed dogs, the fairy kingdoms, train empires, aspirations for stardom, and for early death. We turned in the secret notions that we could fly (if only given a chance), or be a tree, a Robin Hood, or a dog. The imagination is laughable. It is a lot of silliness and fairy dust and pale pastel colors which caught us like cobwebs in our eyes, blurring what is really before us—our practical, having-come-to-terms-with-reality life."[26]

Most of us are discouraged early from treating imagination as remotely real. A bombardment of media surfeits us with the prepackaged, ghostly icons of consumer culture. Imagination becomes "image." We live increasingly within what one writer has called "technology-mediated half-realities." Though we seek it more ardently than ever, the magic of the world withdraws from us—most especially the world of nature. Where once we were nourished by its sphere of sensibility, now we settle for its scenery (or, poorer substitution, the TV "nature shows," which have become commensurately popular). Humanity risks becoming the lonely sovereign of a world from which the psyche has been banished. Wrote Jung of our present plight: "No river contains a spirit, no tree is the principal of life in man, no snake contains the embodiment of wisdom, no mountain cave is the home of a demon. No voices now speak to man from stones, plants or animals; nor does he speak to them believing they can hear. His contact with nature has gone, and with it has gone the profound emotional energy that this symbolic connection supplied."[27]

Perhaps it is this keening sense of loss that accounts for our continuing fascination with those indigenous peoples who have not entirely lost contact. The anthropologist Lee Irwin maintains that within some Plains Indians societies, there are still traces of a life where "the shaman's world is the world in which all human beings live, a world seen and enhanced through dreams and visionary experiences, in which the boundaries between waking and sleeping have retained their transparency. The shift from waking to dreaming is continuously broken down into subtler states and gradations until the metaphor of 'life-as-dream' takes on an increasingly vivid signification."[28]

This view of reality, Ernst Cassirer wrote, is not merely theoretical, practical, or technological, but "sympathetic. . . . [Traditional peoples] by no means lack the ability to grasp the empirical differences of things. But in [their] conception of nature and life, all these differences are obliterated by a stronger feeling—the deep conviction of a fundamental and indelible *solidarity* of life."[29] As a Navajo chant expresses it: "The fir tree, the gathering waters, the dew drop, the pollen, I become part of it."[30] Thus is the world and one's place within it transformed.

There is a Tibetan story in which the sage Marpa the Translator went to seek instruction from a yogi on a sacred island. Marpa had spent years gathering gold dust to offer in exchange for his teachings. But when he gave the precious sack to the yogi, the man turned it upside down and, leaving Marpa dumbstruck with horror, let the shimmering motes of gold scatter to the wind. "What need have I of your gold?" the yogi demanded, laughing fiercely. "All the world is gold to me!" He stamped his foot, and Marpa saw that the dirt, the plants, the air itself were alive with scintillas of beauty. Healing Dreams show us that this world is golden. The "imaginative faculty" transmutes reality, revealing a dimension that stands behind and beyond apparent forms. (André Malraux, speaking of the Chinese pictograph for "flower," wrote: "What the symbol is to the flower, the flower itself is to something else.") The Japanese Zen sage Myoē, a St. Francis–like character who recorded hundreds of vivid dreams in diaries he kept over forty years, seemed to his contemporaries to live in a waking dream. He once wrote a letter to an island he loved, apologizing for having been too busy to visit it and care for it, then ordered his monks to hand-deliver the message! Acknowledging that people might look askance at sending a letter—especially one so filled with sentiment—to an "inanimate" island, he wrote that he often had such impulses, but "in order to accommodate the irrational ways of the world, I kept my thoughts to myself."

The Hidden World Speaks

But what if Myoē's island were to send a letter back? Everything in the world is alive, say native peoples, and each thing and creature has its own secret purpose for existing. In the reversal of the base and the exalted so common in dreams, the lowly dung beetle of Egyptian cosmology rolls the ball of the sun across the sky. Today, in an era when species are being extinguished at an unprecedented rate, we are belatedly discovering the inexorability of this dream logic, for even the humblest creature is vital to some process once deemed beneath our notice. Nothing within the great dream of life is without meaning—or without a voice, should it choose to speak, and we deign to listen.

It is said that when our connection to this great dream is most broken, when we have become deaf to its cries and whispers, the invisible world may manifest itself, demanding parity. On May 5, 1996, on the Navajo reservation near Window Rock, Arizona, during one of the worst droughts in tribal memory, a mother and daughter living in a hogan in remote Dinnebito Wash were visited by two holy ones. The story, as I have pieced it together from friends on and near the reservation, is an extraordinary contemporary claim of outright visitation—of a Healing Dream made visible.

Irene Yazzie, ninety-six years old, blind and unable to talk after suffering a devastating stroke, and her daughter Sarah Begay, known as "a good soul who made little things for the elderly," lived on an isolated patch of land on the disputed boundary of Hopi territory. Then, one day in May, Irene, long silent, suddenly spoke: "They are coming today."

"Who's coming?" her daughter Sarah asked, but then, getting no answer, went back to her sewing machine. Twice more, her mother made her cryptic announcement. A few hours later, a sudden wind arose that made the hogan shake. A noise like a whirling bullroarer seemed to surround the house. Sarah stepped outside, the wind-swirled grit forcing her head down, and saw two beings, one blue and one white, who gave off a brilliant light. All around them sacred cornmeal was falling like rain. When she asked who they were, they proclaimed: *We have always been here. We have been to six mountains and there are no offerings. We are angry because you have turned from your traditions, no longer pray or do ceremonies, no longer take care of the old ones.* She was told to tell the Navajo people to return to the ancient ways. Then they vanished.

Sarah staggered back inside and fell into her mother's arms. Then she jumped into her pickup and sped off to find the nearest hand trembler (diviner) to explain the incident. The hand trembler told her the "holy people" were, as one of my informants put it, "pretty pissed, and there would be hell to pay. It was like a prediction of the end of the world, but the people had a chance of maybe forestalling it if they prayed and performed the old rituals."

When it was discovered that the holy beings had left footprints outlined in blue and yellow corn, thousands made their way to the pilgrimage site, drawn by the good reputation of the two women in the community: "These women weren't thought of as crackpots who would make up a story," my friend tells me. A holiday for a day of prayer was declared, with Navajo president Albert Hale giving each tribal employee four hours off, with pay, for religious observances. The Navajo came by car, tour bus, pickup, and motorcycle, along rutted and rocky dirt roads, to observe the footprints, which, despite attempts to shelter them for posterity, soon were washed away. The reservation community—only five percent of which, by some reckonings, still follows the traditional ways—is still trying to come to terms with the occurrence. People have predictably divided into skeptics (who think it was a ploy to claim contested land), agnostics, and believers (who, though Sarah's description of the beings was sketchy, are convinced she saw the legendary Twin Gods, Monster Slayer and Born for Water).[31]

Just as a Healing Dream may come to us in crisis to restore balance to the psyche, might such phantasms from the otherworld appear when society is afflicted with what the Hopi call *koyaanisqatsi,* life out of harmony? Many would no doubt chalk up this vision of the Holy Ones to a transient folie à deux of two isolated, otherwise sane back-country women. But what is the rational explanation for the extensively witnessed apparitions that occurred in 1916, the fourth year of Europe's Great War, in an obscure peasant hamlet a hundred miles north of Lisbon? It began with three children out tending sheep who claimed they saw a beautiful young man, who called himself an "Angel of Peace," appear out of a snow-white cloud. On May 13, 1917, a "beautiful lady" who said she came "from heaven" manifested to the same children, calling for peace in a time of global bloodshed and asking them to return on the thirteenth day of each month. They described her as being "composed of the aura," translucent or transparent.

As word spread, the new Portuguese government—an anticlerical republic ruled by a motley revolutionary alliance that had executed thousands of clergy as enemies of the state—was unable to discourage the crowds. On October 13, 1917, between seventy thousand and ninety thousand people gathered outside Fatima in a torrential downpour. Some of the most skeptical, antiecclesiastical officials reported the final display in the same terms as more reverential members of the crowd: the clouds had suddenly parted, and what observers took to be the sun, "like a great silver disk," began to rotate as if it were a gigantic pinwheel, brilliant beams of color radiating from its rim. It had seemed to sweep down from the sky in a zigzag motion, and when it ascended, the muddy ground had been dried to baked clay, and the clothes of the assembled were dry.[32]

We will never know with any certainty what happened on that day. A religious visitation from on high? A UFO sighting? A remarkable collective delusion? Here we are in a zone unknown, of folktales about Brigadoons and Avalons, of lands that emerge from mists and vanish back into them. Whatever cultural trappings we apply to the strange visitations at Dinnebito Wash, Fatima, and other such places throughout history, it would seem that the otherworld occasionally does break full-blown into this one. Something, some peculiar alteration of the psyche—or of reality itself—can turn this waking everyday world into a dreamscape.

Telos

Our task is to stamp this provisional, perishing earth into ourselves so
deeply, so painfully and passionately, that its being may rise again,
"invisibly," in us. We are the bees of the invisible.
—*Rainer Maria Rilke,* Letters

Whatever the religious or iconographic content of the Healing Dream, whether it appears to an individual in a dream or to tens of thousands in a mass vision, it seems intent upon calling attention to the relatedness of all within a dynamic Whole.

In one extraordinary and well-investigated case study in the town of Rua, Zimbabwe, in 1991, a group of several dozen children at the nearby Ariel School claimed to have seen a strange being appear out of a shining oval near their playground during recess. The various children's accounts and drawings of the fifteen-minute incident are surprisingly consistent. In the face of considerable adult skepticism, the children, aged approximately six through thirteen, steadfastly maintained, in the words of one emphatic young girl: "I don't care if others believe us or not. We know what we saw." Some of the Zimbabwean children said that the creature had imparted a message: "How the world is going to end," as one put it, "maybe because we don't look after our planet. Like the trees will go down, and there will be no air." Those thoughts appeared, she says, to be coming "from the man's eyes," which seemed to convey pictures directly into her mind.

An odd isomorphism runs through those occasions where an inhabitant of our world meets a denizen of some unknown, invisible other. Recall Sylvia's earlier comment about one of her spirit grandfathers: "When this one looks at me, I know what he knows. Not words. The only thing that's very alive is the eyes." And did not *Ishmael* author Daniel Quinn receive the same message as the children of Rua when, in his own vivid childhood dream, he encountered creatures who mourned the destruction of their world, and spoke to him "in my mind," making it clear they "needed me, and wanted to share their secrets"?

It would seem that something—from within, or without, or both—is demanding from us a relationship, an exchange, an unrenounceable kinship. It has been noted that in times of great cultural change, Plains Indian visionaries experience "strange, incomprehensible, and mysterious objects, events, and beings . . . that express the not yet known, the unseen, or the not yet visualized."[33] There is a growing belief among elders of many traditions that the earth has been so grievously wounded by our unconsciousness that the time has come to share long-guarded spiritual treasure. To them, it is we citizens of industrial civilization who look like sleepwalkers, marching somnambulently off a precipice, dragging the world down with us. In a time when science is deciphering nature's holiest codes, with unforeseeable results, what the Zuni call *Awonawilona,* the "mighty something" that endows all things with *mili,* the "breath of life," might also reveal its secrets.

Perhaps our wildest dreams are attempts to grasp this unknowable something—to know the things of this world as "the ineffable structured into images." We live surrounded by dimensions we cannot compass. The Healing Dream comes to us as the multidimensional Sphere to the dimensionally challenged Flatlander, proclaiming its patent enigma: "I am many circles in one." The late quantum physicist David Bohm once noted: "Our whole thought process is designed to keep our attention riveted on the here and now. We need this to get across the street. But consciousness is always in the unlimited depth which is beyond time and space. If you went deeply enough into the actual present, then maybe there would be no difference between this moment and the next, this place and elsewhere, or elsewhen. It is perhaps only a matter of attention."

When we pay attention, are we also changing our world, our very substance? We are extrusions of the spiritual realm into the physical—of consciousness into the ashen debris of the Big Bang. Surely that evolutionary process, which brought forth thinking, feeling creatures from stardust, still plays with us, works upon us, creating of us matter ever more endued with sentience. Will we someday enter into a more transubstantial existence—one where mind and matter exert increasing influence upon each other, and the House of Dreams becomes our dwelling place?

"It is a vast dream," Schopenhauer wrote of the universe as he saw it, "dreamed by a single being, but in such a way that all the dream characters dream, too. Hence, everything interlocks and harmonizes with everything else." The same thought was expressed with simple eloquence by a Kalahari Bushman who was asked to explain the significance of dreaming. "But you see, it is very difficult," answered the wizened emissary from time's beginning. "For always, there is a dream dreaming *us.*"

What, then, does *that* Dream want? Perhaps, someday, we all shall know.

Epilogue

I wish to enter her like a dream,
Leaving my roots here on the beach.
　　　　　　　—*Anne Sexton*

I was once asked by an editor to describe how a Healing Dream might, in his words, "help the average person be effective in their daily lives." The question flummoxed me. Big dreams are summonses from the unknown. They give voice to what we have hidden from ourselves, with all the risk and potential that implies. To gaze upon our dreams intent on a purely pragmatic meaning is to miss the admonishment of the old Hindu proverb: "When a thief looks at a saint, he sees only his pockets."

None of us asks to be confronted in the night with mysteries, oracles, and conundrums, to have something barge into our inner lives that we did not invite. When I first began to explore my dreams, I hoped for some hint whether to dart right or left, some guidance to save my skin. But my dreams rarely accommodated me. Indeed, I wondered at first if they had any meaning beyond a startling implosion of experience.

A dream will help us if we are willing to dwell for a time within its ambiguities without resolving them, to sink into its depths without always knowing when—or where—we shall surface. The ancient alchemists spoke of dissolving one's substance in the *aqua divina,* the divine water, which, says one treatise, "darkens the light, and lights the darkness." Waking consciousness must be commingled with the wisdom of the dream. To carry the power of a Healing Dream into daily life, traditional peoples would sing its song, enact its dance, paint its symbols on their faces and dwellings in order to sustain its presence in their lives and share its gift with the community at large. This was not merely decorative or "creative," but a way of making the invisible visible.

This book began as an attempt to make visible my own journey through the imaginal realm. But over the years, it grew ever more inclusive as I met many others to whom the Healing Dream had spoken in their sleep. I have been surprised how often disparate dreamers described the image of a strange fish emerging from the water, a symbol of a dream's emergence from the watery depths of the unconscious.

One striking "fish dream" was brought to me by the editor of this book. He confessed he'd had little interest in dreams before he'd unexpectedly gotten the assignment. I had even wondered if he was the right person for the task, until he sent me an E-mail prior to our first meeting: "Should I take this as a sign? Last night, I had a vivid dream that I was fishing and suddenly hooked an enormous fish. Could the fish represent your manuscript?"

I asked him for more details, and he wrote back:

I am fishing with a friend on the narrow walkway of a dock extending into the water. I take a fishing pole, throw one cast in and—boom—I have a strike! I can immediately feel that I have an enormous fish on the line, but I am nevertheless surprised at just how big it is when I pull it up onto the dock—four or five feet long, and rather wide, sort of in the shape of a flounder. It's so long and unwieldy that the ends of the fish extend beyond the edges of the dock. Feeling somewhat squeamish—it seems too strong to grab by hand, and I think it might bite me if I try to dehook it—I am hoping someone will use a net to help me control it. But the people on the dock just stand behind me. I can see I'm on my own.

I was heartened. Here was a form of the "presenting dream" that psychologists note often appears early in therapy to portend the course things will take. (Indeed, the editing process is often inadvertently therapeutic, though it's usually the writer who begins on the couch and the editor who winds up needing therapy.) It struck me that the very spirit of the book had presented itself to him. Nor could I escape the feeling that here was the Healing Dream incarnate, speaking forcefully to us both on its own behalf.

This book's scope is "rather wide." "Long and unwieldy" seemed a clear reference to the outsized, seven-hundred-page manuscript I originally submitted. To flounder, the dictionary says, means "to struggle awkwardly to move, as in deep mud," and the book's progress had been mired for months as the publishing house tried to figure out what to do with it. The book had flip-flopped from editor to editor until its pile of pages had landed, still thrashing, on my editor's desk. (No wonder he felt queasy.)

On one level, the "dock" *is* his desk. A dock receives cargo from ships that have been voyaging at sea—in this case, the authorial cargo of words and ideas, gathered on journeys far and wide. The word *haul* implies manual effort, and to "land" the book indeed required both elbow grease and midnight oil. *Haul* is a spillover word rich with multiple meanings. The process of reeling in the book was "a long haul"—many years of work punctuated by many deadline extensions. We both (if only to keep ourselves going) imagined the book to be "for the long haul" of literary longevity. (The publisher, for its part, hopes its patience will be rewarded with "a good haul.") *Haul* also means "a bundle of parallel yarns" to be bound together—a good description of a manuscript, but also of Healing Dreams themselves.

In the dream, the fish still has the hook in its mouth. "Hooked" is a colloquialism for getting caught up in an activity (my editor hopes the book will prove an addictive read, and maybe worries about "being on the hook" himself). But another nuance was revealed a week or so after he told me his dream: I happened to see a *New York Times* article that described an exhibit of avant-garde artists who, in the curator's words, "had a desire to break down the barrier between art and life."[1] The story was illustrated by a brightly colored Roy Lichtenstein painting (captioned "Scavenging from Ordinary Life," an apt comment on dreams) that depicted Donald Duck and Mickey Mouse *fishing from a dock*. In the meticulously rendered cartoon, Donald, clutching a straining pole, exclaims, "I've hooked a big one!" while Mickey suppresses a laugh. He and the viewer can see that Donald has unwittingly snagged his hook on the back of his own coat—he has caught himself! The painter lets us in on a little joke, but the Healing Dream has the last laugh: in dreamwork, it is the unseen "back side" of ourselves that we are reeling in.

When my editor finally faces the fish head-on, the dream takes on a slightly ominous tone. He was suddenly, he told me, filled with anxiety. In his dream, *the ends of the fish extend beyond the edges of the dock*. Perhaps it is not only the overlong manuscript but dreams themselves that extend beyond the edge, beyond the neatly demarcated boundaries we set. (The "ends of the fish" could be a pun on the *purposes* of the fish, which are extensive—not only my ambitions for the book but also the Healing Dream's own agenda.)

Looking up my editor's word choice to describe how big this fish is—*enormous*—I discovered that its archaic meaning was "monstrous." The word's root means "out of rule" (as in unruly) and "beyond measure" (as in unquantifiable). The Healing Dream claims to be a creature not unlike the one invoked in these lines from the biblical Book of Job:

> Canst thou draw out Leviathan with a hook?
> or his tongue with a cord which thou lettest down?
> Canst thou put a hook into his nose?
> or bore his jaw through with a thorn?

The words are uttered by a spiritual force too vast to compass through purely rational means. Job wonders if the deity that speaks to him is creative or destructive, just or unjust. (It is neither, and both.) Similarly, the purposes of the Healing Dream may not be entirely knowable. It reveals the universe as it is. It is not here to make it all better; it is here to make us more true.

My editor's dream advises us to take an attitude of some humility toward its ultimate source of power. Each literary act is an invocation: a book about dreams becomes a dream itself, not entirely containable within its covers.

My editor concluded his letter: "The dream ended (I woke up) without securing the fish." But perhaps his dream can never be "secured." He must face the unknown, as we all do, with some confusion how to proceed. He can find no easy answers. Others stand on the dock behind him, but the task of how to confront it is left entirely up to him.

What, then, should he do with his fish? Cut off its head and its tail to make it "fit"? Gut it of its vital innards; partake of it by eating it; display it as a trophy; throw it back? Or should he extend the dock? He cannot force the fish/book/dream to precisely fit his conscious purposes. Its very existence is a provocation, a challenge that demands some kind of response, yet it offers no guarantees whichever choice he makes. Perhaps *this* is why dreams do not just come out and simply tell us what we need to know: they wish us—our soul wishes us—to embark on the journey without knowing the destination. It is not given to us to arrive without ever departing. Perhaps the path, a sincere striving to understand more, *is* the goal. In the end, the task of an examined life—the task Healing Dreams set vividly before us—is ours alone to reject or embrace; which way we choose makes all the difference in the world.

Notes

Introduction

1. Dr. Allan Hobson and Dr. Robert McCarley, authors of the 1977 "activation-synthesis" model, quoted in "New Clues to Why We Dream," by Erica Goode, *New York Times,* Nov. 2, 1999, p. D1.

2. David Foulkes, *Dreaming: A Cognitive-psychological Analysis.* Hillsdale, NJ: Lawrence, Erlbaum, 1985, pp. 165–66, quoted in Harry T. Hunt, *Multiplicity of Dreams: Memory, Imagination, and Consciousness* (New Haven: Yale University Press, 1989), p. 11.

3. *Boulder Daily Camera* April 2, 1990, p. 1, and April 14, 1990 p. 1.

4. Carl Sagan quotes from a letter written to him by an anguished man: "Waves are coming from outer space somewhere—beaming through my head and transmitting thoughts, words, and images into the heads of anybody within range. . . . Images will pop into my head *that I did not put there.* . . . Dreams are not dreams anymore—they are more like Hollywood productions" (Carl Sagan, *The Demon-Haunted World: Science as a Candle in the Dark,* New York: Random House, 1996). The description fits, on the surface of it, many of the criteria for what I am calling the Healing Dream.

Chapter 1. What Is a Healing Dream?

1. Morton T. Kelsey, *God, Dreams, and Revelation: A Christian Interpretation of Dreams* (Minneapolis, MN: Augsberg Fortress, 1991), p. 33.

2. C. G. Jung, "On the Nature of Dreams" (1948), in *Dreams*, trans. R.F.C. Hull (Princeton, NJ: Princeton University Press, Bollingen Series XX, 1974), p. 76. Wrote Jung: "Even primitives distinguish between 'little' and 'big' dreams, or, as we might say, 'insignificant' and 'significant' dreams. . . . Significant dreams . . . are often remembered for a lifetime, and not infrequently prove to be the richest jewel in the treasure-house of psychic experience."

3. Joel Covitz, *Visions of the Night: A Study of Jewish Dream Interpretation* (Boston: Shambhala, 1990), p. 28.

4. Writes Howard Rheingold in his book, *They Have a Word for It:* "*Beluthahatchee* is still used, in some sections of America that were settled by the descendants of Bantu-speaking slaves, to mean a 'legendary, blissful state where all is forgiven and forgotten.'"

5. Peter Lamborn Wilson, *Shower of Stars: Dream and Book* (Brooklyn, NY: Autonomedia, 1996), pp. 154–55.

6. C. G. Jung, *Dreams*, p. 82.

7. Barbara Hannah, *Jung: His Life and Work* (Boston: Shambhala, 1991), pp. 117–18.

8. Ibid., pp. 106–11.

9. C. G. Jung, *Memories, Dreams, Reflections*, ed. Aniela Jaffé (New York: Random House/Vintage, 1965), p. 183.

10. In the Tibetan tradition, Jung might have been seen as a *terton,* or "treasure discoverer." Such people are reputed not only to be able to search out religious relics and holy books (*terma*) hidden in caves by long-departed lamas, but also to find secret texts and spiritual practices in dreams.

11. In Stephan A. Hoeller, *The Gnostic Jung and the Seven Sermons to the Dead* (Wheaton, IL: The Theosophical Publishing House, 1982), pp. 48–50.

12. Morton T. Kelsey, op. cit., pp. 255–58.

13. Ibid., p. 271.

14. Robert Johnson, *Inner Work: Using Dreams and Active Imagination for Inner Growth* (San Francisco: HarperSanFrancisco, 1989), pp. 220–21.

15. Quoted in Roger Knudson, "The Ongoing Significance of Significant Dreams II," paper presentation for International Conference of the Association for the Study of Dreams, July 6–11, 1999, University of California, Santa Cruz, p. 16.

16. Quoted in Ray Grasse, *The Waking Dream* (Wheaton, IL: Quest Books, 1996), p. 85.

17. Mary Watkins, *Waking Dreams* (Dallas, TX: Spring Publications, 1984), p. 113.

18. C. G. Jung, *Dreams*, p. 101.

19. S. Valadez, "An Interview with Ulu Temay, Huichol Shaman," *Shaman's Drum* 6 (1986):19.

20. This is, of course, not universally true. The Berti of North Africa "are not encouraged to dream and to remember their dreams," have no dream specialists, and "only rarely tell others in the morning what they dreamt about or discuss their dreams with others" (Anthony Shafton, *Dream Reader: Contemporary Approaches to the Understanding of Dreams,* Albany: SUNY Press, 1995, p. 173).

Chapter 2. What Does the Dream Want?

1. Jorge Luis Borges, *Labyrinths: Selected Stories and Other Writings* (New York: New Directions, 1964), p. 47.

2. Sigmund Freud, *The Interpretation of Dreams,* trans. James Strachey (New York: Avon Books, 1965), p. 389.

3. Cited in Robert L. van de Castle, *Our Dreaming Mind* (New York: Ballantine Books, 1994), p. 99.

4. Garma C. C. Chang, trans., *The Hundred Thousand Songs of Milarepa, Volume 2* (Boston: Shambhala Books, 1989), p. 488.

5. Sir Francis Crick and Graeme Mitchison, cited in Harry T. Hunt, *The Multiplicity of Dreams: Memory, Imagination, and Consciousness* (New Haven: Yale University Press, 1989), pp. 10–11. Hunt summarizes this standpoint as: "The dream remembered is dreaming gone wrong; and it is then the very height of nonsense to allow such material to influence one's waking life."

6. Cited in Peter Lamborn Wilson, op. cit., p. 26.

7. Robert Brier, *Ancient Egyptian Magic* (New York: Quill, 1980), pp. 214–24.

8. C. G. Jung, *Memories, Dreams, Reflections,* p. 181.

9. Mary Watkins, op. cit., p. 134.

10. Marie-Louise von Franz and Fraser Boa, eds., *The Way of the Dream* (Boston: Shambhala, 1994), pp. 15–16.

11. Jung neatly balanced the potential and challenge when he wrote: "The animal is the symbolic carrier of the self. . . . It expresses the fact that the structure of wholeness was always present, but was buried in profound unconsciousness, where it can always be found again if one is willing to risk one's skin" (C. G. Jung, *Mysterium Coniunctionis,* Princeton: Princeton University Press, Bollingen Series XX, 1977, p. 214).

12. Cited in Naomi Epel, *Writers Dreaming* (New York: Vintage Books, 1994), p. 105.

13. Lee Irwin, *Dream Seekers: Native American Visionary Traditions of the Great Plains* (Norman: University of Oklahoma Press, 1996), p. 92, citing DeMallie, *The Sixth Grandfather: Black Elk's Teachings Given to John G. Neihardt,* p. 111.

14. James Hillman, *Dream Animals* (San Francisco: Chronicle Books, 1997), pp. 4–5.

Chapter 3. The Dream of the Body

1. Sigmund Freud, *The Interpretation of Dreams,* pp. 258–59.

2. Morton T. Kelsey, op. cit., p. 262.

3. Robert L. van de Castle, *Our Dreaming Mind* (New York: Ballantine Books, 1994), pp. 362–68.

4. Peter Brown, *The Cult of the Saints* (Chicago: University of Chicago Press, 1981), p. 80.

5. Ibid.

6. Russell A. Lockhart, "Cancer in Myth and Dream," in *Dreams Are Wiser Than Men,* ed. Richard O. Russo (Berkeley: North Atlantic Books, 1987), p. 136.

7. Charles Hutzler, "Cults Boom as New Millennium Looms," Copyright 1998 The Associated Press (Internet 7/24/99).

8. For additional examples, see Frederic Meyers, "The Subliminal Consciousness," *Proceedings of the English Society for Psychical Research* 8 (1892): 375, and P. Tissie, *Les Alientes Voyageurs* (Paris: Octave Doin, 1887).

9. Jayne Gackenbach et al., *Control Your Dreams* (New York: HarperPerennial, 1990), p. 117.

10. Ibid., pp. 100–101.

11. Ibid., p. 113.

12. E. W. Kellog III, Ph.D., private communication, and "Lucid Dream Healing Experiences: Firsthand Accounts" (1996), abstract paper presented at the Association for the Study of Dreams Conference in Santa Cruz, July 6–10, 1999, p. 2.

13. Larry Dossey, M.D., *Reinventing Medicine: Beyond Mind-Body to a New Era of Healing* (San Francisco: HarperSanFrancisco, 1999), pp. 146–48. Though Dr. Dossey did not obtain the man's medical records, he told me he found him sufficiently credible in correspondence and phone calls to make the case worth publishing.

14. Dreaming is in some cultures a prerequisite to becoming a doctor. The anthropologist W. R. Merrill reports that among the Raramuri Indians of Mexico, only someone called to the healing profession by a dream (traditionally, one in which God offers pieces of paper signifying knowledge of curing) is authorized to practice. (In Anthony Shafton, *Dream Reader: Contemporary Approaches to the Understanding of Dreams*, Albany: SUNY Press, 1995, p. 178).

15. Morton T. Kelsey, op. cit., pp. 271–72.

16. Mark Pelgrin, *And a Time to Die*, ed. S. Moon et al. (Wheaton, IL: Theosophical Publishing House, 1962).

Chapter 4. Dreams of Personal Calling

1. D. Tedlock and B. Tedlock (eds.), *Teachings from the American Earth: Indian Religion and Philosophy* (New York: Liveright, 1975).

2. Harry T. Hunt, *The Multiplicity of Dreams: Memory, Imagination, and Consciousness* (New Haven: Yale University Press, 1989), p. 45.

3. W. Brugh Joy, *Avalanche: Heretical Reflections on the Dark and the Light* (New York: Ballantine Books, 1990), pp. 13–14.

4. Robert van de Castle, op. cit., p. 25.

5. C. G. Jung, *Memories, Dreams, Reflections*, pp. 13–15.

6. Daniel Quinn, *Providence: The Story of a Fifty-Year Vision Quest* (New York: Bantam, 1995), pp. 14–19.

7. Researcher David Pillemer notes that "personal event memories" tend to be neglected by psychology outside the context of trauma. He maintains that these are locked into long-term recall by "sensory images" rather than verbal narrative memory. The image and its attendant emotions "energize" the narrative constructed around it. The parallel with significant dreams is apparent (D. B. Pillemer, *Momentous Events, Vivid Memories*, Cambridge, MA: Harvard University Press, 1998, pp. 50–51 and 70–71, cited in Knudson, "The Ongoing Significance of Significant Dreams II," paper presentation for International Conference of the Association for the Study of Dreams, July 6–11, 1999, University of California, Santa Cruz).

8. Cited in Naomi Epel, op. cit.

9. Roger M. Knudson, Ph.D., "The Ongoing Significance of Significant Dreams: The Case of the Bodiless Head," *Dreaming* 9(4) (1999): 10–11.

10. Lee Irwin, op. cit., p. 161.

11. Stephanie Citron-Baggett, *The Phenomenology of the Transformative Dream*, Georgia State University (doctoral dissertation), 1988, p. 110.

12. Ibid.

13. Stephen Aizenstat, "Tending the Dream Is Tending the World," Santa Cruz, CA: 16th International Conference of the Association for the Study of Dreams, July 8, 1999.

14. Morton T. Kelsey, op. cit., p. 67.

Chapter 5. Dreaming Together

1. As in this Korean woman's dream poem, cited in Fred Jeremy Seligson's book, *Oriental Birth Dreams:* "Bathing/in a stream, alone/in the moonlight/I saw a red pepper/floating around me/Without thinking/I picked it out of the water/and woke up/Ten months later/I had a gentle/though obstinate/boy."

2. Medard Boss, *The Analysis of Dreams* (New York: Philosophical Library, 1958), pp. 177–78.

3. This woman recalls that when she was fifteen, she dreamed about a friend who had moved several states away. On the first night, she saw the girl in a backyard that was "a solid garden of flowers." The next night, "It was flowers again, only there was fog in it. And the third day, you couldn't see the flowers anymore, just her waving good-bye in the fog. Later I found out that the day after I'd had the dream, she'd died of cancer. I didn't even know she was sick."

4. Joost A. M. Merloo, *Hidden Communion: Studies in the Communication Theory of Telepathy* (New York: Garrett Publications/Helix Press, 1964), pp. 68–69.

5. Ibid., p. 11, my paraphrase.

6. Sigmund Freud, *Studies in Parapsychology* (New York: Collier Books, 1963), pp. 74–75. Freud adds that even if there were such a thing as "an undisguised and unadulterated telepathic dream," then it should not be called a dream at all, but instead "a telepathic experience in a state of sleep."

7. Joost A. M. Merloo, op. cit., p. 53.

8. C. G. Jung, *Psyche and Symbol,* ed. Violet S. de Laszlo (New York: Doubleday/Anchor Books, 1958), p. 14.

9. Stanley Krippner and Montague Ullman, "Telepathy and Dreams: A Controlled Experiment with Electro-Encephalogram-Electro-Oculogram Monitoring," *Journal of Nervous and Mental Disease* 151(1970): 394–403.

10. Arthur Schnitzler, *Dream Story,* trans. Otto P. Schinnerer (Los Angeles: Sun and Moon Press, 1995). Originally published as *Träumnovelle* (Berlin: S. Fischer Verlag, 1926).

11. In a striking instance of Jung's notion of archetypes, the dream of this unsophisticated woman is nearly identical to the lyrical dream vision of British literary figure J. B. Priestley: "Time speeded up, so that I saw generations of birds . . . flutter into life, weaken, falter, and die. Wings grew only to crumble; bodies were sleek and then, in a flash, bled and shriveled; and death struck everywhere at every second. . . . I felt sick at heart. . . . Time went faster still. . . . The birds could not show any movement, but were like an enormous plain sown with feathers. But along this plain, flickering through the bodies themselves, there now passed a sort of white flame, trembling, dancing, then hurrying on; and as soon as I saw it I knew that this flame was life itself, the very quintessence of being" (J. B. Priestley, *Man and Time,* London: Bloomsbury Books, 1964, pp. 306–7).

Chapter 6. The Dream Society

1. Erich Fromm, *The Forgotten Language* (New York: Rinehart and Co., 1951).

2. Lee Irwin, op. cit., p. 189: "Every shared dream or vision enters into the general stream of mythic discourse and helps shape the religious worldview of the community. . . . Dreams and visions are the fundamental means for social and cultural transformation."

3. Barbara Tedlock, ed., *Dreaming: Anthropological and Psychological Interpretations* (Santa Fe, NM: School of American Research Press, 1992), p. 116.

4. Peter Lamborn Wilson, op. cit., p. 158.

5. Howard Schwartz, *The Dream Assembly: Tales of Rabbi Zalman Schachter-Shalomi* (Nevada City, CA: Gateways, 1989), p. 6.

6. Psychologist G. William Domhoff, for one, believes the case is closed. In his book *The Mystique of Dreams: A Search for Utopia through Senoi Dream Theory* (Berkeley: University of California Press, 1985), he concludes (p. 96): "Kilton Stewart was a well-meaning charmer and storyteller, but in his eagerness to be a prophet, he misunderstood the Senoi and incorrectly attributed his own ideas to them."

7. Jeremy Taylor, *Where People Fly and Water Runs Uphill* (New York: Warner Books, 1992), p. 109.

8. Ibid., p. 111.

9. Matthew 25:40: "Truly I say to you, as you did it to one of the least of these my brethren, you did it to me."

10. Anthony F. C. Wallace, "Dreams and Wishes of the Soul: A Type of Psychoanalytic Theory among the Seventeenth-Century Iroquois," *American Anthropologist* 60 (1958): 236.

11. Ibid., p. 240.

12. Ibid.

13. Jeremy Taylor, op. cit., pp. 119–21.

14. Anthony Shafton, *"Black Dreamers in the United States,"* in Kelly Bulkeley, ed., *Among All These Dreamers* (Albany: SUNY Press, 1996), pp. 85–93.

15. Charlotte Beradt, *The Third Reich of Dreams*, trans. Adriane Gottwald (Chicago: Quadrangle Books, 1968), p. 62.

16. Ibid., p. 159.

17. Ibid., pp. 11–12.

18. Ibid., pp. 39–40.

19. Michael Ortiz Hill, *Dreaming the End of the World: Apocalypse as a Rite of Passage* (Dallas: Spring Publications, 1994), pp. 56–57.

20. Matthew I. Wald, "Cancer Study on 1950's A-Test Is Released," *The New York Times*, October 2, 1997, p. A11.

Chapter 7. The Invisible Community

1. James Hillman, *The Dream and the Underworld* (New York: HarperPerennial, 1979), p. 40.

2. C. G. Jung, *Memories, Dreams, Reflections*, p. 178. Referring to his own experiences, Jung adds: "It is a style I find embarrassing; it grates on my nerves, as when someone draws his nails down a plaster wall, or scrapes his knife against a plate. But since I did not know what was going on, I had no choice but to write everything down in the style selected by the unconscious itself."

3. J. M. Cohen, ed., *The Life of Saint Teresa of Avila by Herself* (New York: Penguin Books, 1987), p. 174.

4. Stephanie Citron-Baggett, op. cit., pp. 117–23.

5. Harold Bloom, *Omens of Millennium: The Gnosis of Angels, Dreams, and Resurrection* (New York: Riverhead Books, 1996), p. 87.

6. Marie-Louise von Franz, *Dreams* (Boston: Shambhala Books, 1991), p. 59.

7. Patrick Harpur, *Daimonic Reality* (New York: Arkana/Penguin, 1994), p. 42, quoting W. B. Yeats, *Mythologies* (London, 1959), p. 336.

8. Jung was eloquent about the glories and the rigors of such encounters: [The archetype] can be healing or destructive, but never indifferent. . . . It mobilizes philosophical and religious convictions in the very people who deemed themselves miles above any such fits of weakness. Often it drives with unexampled passion and remorseless logic towards its goal and draws the subject under its spell, from which despite the most desperate resistance he is unable, and finally no longer even willing, to break free, because the experience brings with it a depth and fullness of meaning. C. G. Jung, *On the Nature of the Psyche*, trans. R.F.C. Hull (Princeton, NJ: Princeton University Press, Bollingen Series XX, 1960), pp. 115–17.

9. Writes Jung: "It would be vain to try to understand the [archetypal] dream without the help of a carefully worked-out context, for it expresses itself in strange mythological forms." He adds that ordinary interpretation is not enough, for such dreams "express an eternal human problem . . . not just a disturbance of personal balance."

10. Harold Bloom, op. cit., p. 91.

11. Barbara Tedlock, op. cit., pp. 33–34.

12. Amy Tan, personal communication, 1998, and in Naomi Epel, op. cit., pp. 282–83.

Chapter 8. Binding the Wound of Time

1. Joel Covitz, op. cit., p. 54.

2. J. W. Dunne, *An Experiment with Time* (New York: The Macmillan Co., 1938), p. 7.

3. Ibid., p. 88.

4. Ibid., p. 69.

5. Freud weighs in on déjà vu with his usual reductive gusto. Speaking of déjà vu experiences of landscapes within dreams, he writes, "These places are invariably the genitals of the dreamer's mother; there is indeed no other place about which one can assert with such conviction that one has been there once before" (Sigmund Freud, *The Interpretation of Dreams*, p. 435).

6. Joost A. M. Merloo, op. cit., p. 75.

7. Morton T. Kelsey, op. cit., p. 271.

8. Anthony F. C. Wallace, "Dreams and Wishes of the Soul: A Type of Psychoanalytic Theory among the Seventeenth-Century Iroquois," *American Anthropologist* 60 (1958): 240.

9. Michael Harner, *The Way of the Shaman: A Guide to Power and Healing* (San Francisco: Harper and Row, 1980), pp. 100–101.

10. Morton Kelsey, op. cit., p. 265.

11. Harry T. Hunt, op. cit., p. 88, quoting Homer, *The Odyssey*, trans. R. Fitzgerald, pp. 370–71.

12. J. W. Dunne, op. cit., p. 50.

13. Joel Covitz, op. cit., p. 10.

14. Fred Alan Wolf, *Parallel Universes: The Search for Other Worlds* (New York: Simon and Schuster, 1988), pp. 221–22.

15. Ibid., p. 205.

16. The same insight is rendered less technologically in Marcel Duchamps's famous painting *Nude Descending a Staircase.*

17. One of the most famous cases in the parapsychological annals of "retro-cognition" was the 1901 experience of two English sightseers in France. Miss Moberley and Miss Jourdain, principal and vice principal respectively of the St. Hugh's Women's College at Oxford, were walking toward the Petit Trianon in Versailles when they saw two gardeners in grayish-green coats and tricorner hats. The place became, Miss Moberley was to later write, "intensely still." They met other people in similarly old-fashioned costumes as they walked on in silence. Only after their return to Paris did they discuss their experience, first independently committing to paper what they had seen, then spending years meticulously researching the anachronistic sights. They were finally able to date the costumes and structures to the Versailles of Marie Antoinette, including a little bridge they had passed which had since disappeared (M. L. von Franz, *Psyche and Matter* [Boston: Shambhala Books, 1992], p. 115.)

18. Tom Brown, Jr., *The Vision* (New York: Berkley Books, 1988), pp. 118–21.

19. Robert L. van de Castle, op. cit., p. 8, citing G. Gorer, *African Dances: A Book about West African Negroes* (New York: Knopf, 1935).

20. Fred Alan Wolf, op. cit., p. 203.

21. Ibid., pp. 298–99.

22. J. W. Dunne, op. cit., p. 68.

23. Fred Alan Wolf, op. cit., pp. 223–24.

24. Marie-Louise von Franz, *On Dreams and Death* (Boston: Shambhala Books, 1987), p. 150, citing C. G. Jung, *Letters,* vol. 2, p. 561.

Chapter 9. The Otherworld

1. Aldous Huxley, *The Doors of Perception and Heaven and Hell* (New York: Harper Perennial Library, 1990), pp. 96–97.

2. University of California pharmacologist J. C. Calloway hypothesized that the pineal gland, stimulated by darkness, converts serotonin into melatonin, which is converted during sleep into beta-carboline derivatives (*Brain-Mind Bulletin,* February 1989).

3. Aldous Huxley, op. cit., pp. 100–101.

4. Huxley suggests "a region of the mind, where they can use their own and other people's wishes, memories, and fancies to construct a world" (Huxley, op. cit., p. 139).

5. Henry Corbin, *Creative Imagination in the Sufism of Ibn 'Arabi,* trans. Ralph Manheim (Princeton, NJ: Princeton University Press, Bollingen Series XCI, 1969), p. 4.

6. Garma C. C. Chang, op. cit., pp. 485–86.

7. A believer would say that the dreamer had been at the foot of the heavenly throne. A non-theist might suggest that the dreamer has conflated his notions of a Supreme Being with images of, say, the Lincoln Memorial—a titanic, seated, bearded white marble figure in a templelike setting who Americans associate with universal compassion and goodness. Yet I have heard quite a few such dream-descriptions, of God as a gigantic, almost statuary being, so awesome the dreamer's only point of contact was the hem of a garment.

8. Thomas Merton, *Zen and the Birds of Appetite* (Boston: Shambhala Publications, 1968), p. 119.

9. Anon., *The Cloud of Unknowing and Other Works,* trans. Clifton Wolters (New York: Penguin Books, 1978), pp. 129–30.

10. Reynolds Price, *A Whole New Life* (New York: Atheneum Books, 1994), pp. 43–46.

11. Robert Johnson, *Balancing Heaven and Earth* (San Francisco: HarperSanFrancisco, 1998), pp. 123–25.

12. Harry T. Hunt, op. cit., p. 136, citing P. Carrington, "Dreams and Schizophrenia," *Archives of General Psychiatry* 26 (1972): 343–50.

13. John Perry, *The Far Side of Madness* (Englewood Cliffs, NJ: Prentice-Hall, Inc., 1974), p. 11.

14. Stanley Krippner, ed., *Dreamtime and Dreamwork* (Los Angeles: J. P. Tarcher, 1990), pp. 233–34, citing Freud's *The Interpretation of Dreams.*

15. Stanley Krippner, op. cit., pp. 185–93.

16. Morton T. Kelsey, op. cit., p. 138.

17. John G. Neihardt, ed., *Black Elk Speaks* (Lincoln: University of Nebraska Press, 1979), pp. 241–42.

18. Ibid., pp. 241–50.

19. In his *Asian Journals,* Thomas Merton portrays Trungpa gazing into a ritual mirror describing Shambhala's inhabitants and buildings as if he were looking at them through field glasses.

20. Sandy Johnson, *Book of Tibetan Elders* (New York: Riverhead Books, 1996), pp. 90ff.

Chapter 10. Healing the Shadow

1. In Jung's first formulation of this idea, the "shadow" was defined as any part of the personality that lay outside the sphere of consciousness.

2. Luke 15.

3. Marie-Louise von Franz with Fraser Boa, *The Way of the Dream* (Boston: Shambhala Books, 1994), p. 80.

4. Robert Louis Stevenson, *The Strange Case of Dr. Jekyll and Mr. Hyde and Other Famous Tales* (New York: Dodd, Mead & Co., 1961).

5. Robert Johnson, *Owning Your Own Shadow: Understanding the Dark Side of the Psyche* (San Francisco: HarperSanFrancisco, 1991), p. 22.

6. Garma C. C. Chang, op. cit., pp. 487–88.

7. Barbara Tedlock, *The Beautiful and the Dangerous: Encounters with the Zuni Indians* (New York: Viking, 1992), pp. 158–59.

8. Mary Watkins, op. cit., p. 147.

9. Herbert V. Guenther, *The Life and Teachings of Naropa* (Boston: Shambhala, 1995), pp. 32–37.

10. Ibid., pp. 30–31.

11. "Dream sickness or initiation ceremony," writes the famous anthropologist Mircea Eliade, "nearly always involves death and symbolic resurrection . . . [with] cutting up of the body performed in various ways (dismemberment, gashing, opening the abdomen, etc.)" (Quoted in Michael Murphy, *The Future of the Body,* Los Angeles: Jeremy P. Tarcher, 1992, p. 210).

12. Marie-Louise von Franz, *On Dreams and Death,* p. 71.

13. Personal conversation, Bataan Faigao, personal student of Chen Man-Ching, 1996.

14. Anthony Shafton, op. cit., p. 500.

15. Carl Jung, *Answer to Job,* trans. R.F.C. Hull (Princeton, NJ: Princeton University Press, Bollingen Series, 1973), pp. ix–x.

16. Harold Bloom, op. cit., p. 67.

17. James Fadiman and Robert Frager, eds., *Essential Sufism* (San Francisco: Harper-SanFrancisco, 1997), p. 86.

Chapter 11. The House of Dreams

1. Andreas Mavromatis, *Hypnagogia: The Unique State of Consciousness between Wakefulness and Sleep* (London: Routledge, 1991), frontispiece.

2. André Breton, *Manifestoes of Surrealism* (Ann Arbor: University of Michigan Press, 1969).

3. James Hall, *Sangoma* (New York: Simon and Schuster/Touchstone, 1994), p. 194.

4. Jamake Highwater, *The Primal Mind* (New York: New American Library, 1981), p. 81.

5. Ibid., p. 75.

6. Harold Bloom, op. cit., p. 95, quoting Friedrich Nietzsche, *The Dawn of Day.*

7. Mark Solms, "Dreaming and REM Sleep Are Controlled by Different Brain Mechanisms," lecture at the 16th Annual International Conference of the Association for the Study of Dreams, July 6–11, 1999, University of California at Santa Cruz.

8. Stephen LaBerge, *Lucid Dreaming* (Los Angeles: J. P. Tarcher, 1985), pp. 30–31.

9. Joel Covitz, op. cit., p. 17.

10. Diane Kennedy Pike, *Life as a Waking Dream* (New York: Riverhead Books, 1997), p. 1.

11. An ancient Pali text describes a dream practice based on conquering natural laws: "Unhindered he goes through walls and through mountains as if they were empty space. He dives into the depth of the earth and comes back again as if out of water. He walks on water without sinking as if on earth. He floats crosslegged on the air like a winged bird" (cited in I. P. Couliano, *Out of This World* (Boston: Shambhala, 1991, p. 91).

12. Chögyam Trungpa *Training the Mind and Cultivating Loving-Kindness,* ed. Judith L. Lief (Boston: Shambhala, 1993), p. 29.

13. Henry Corbin, op. cit., p. 239.

14. Ibid.

15. Michael Murphy, *The Future of the Body* (Los Angeles: Jeremy P. Tarcher, 1992), p. 98, citing Swami Nikhilananda.

16. Ibid., p. 193, citing John Robinson.

17. Ray Grasse, op. cit., p. 155.

18. Marie-Louise von Franz, *Psyche and Matter* (Boston: Shambhala, 1992), p. 272.

19. This incident might be considered an example of what Mircea Eliade, in *The Sacred and the Profane,* called a krakaphony—one of those moments when the natural world itself seems to send forth unusual signs and omens.

20. For a more thoroughgoing discussion, see Aniela Jaffé, *The Myth of Meaning* (Zurich: Daimon, 1983).

21. Andreas Mavromatis, op. cit., pp. 29–30.

22. Lee Irwin, op. cit., pp. 37–38, quoting Gene Weltfish, *The Lost Universe: The Way of Life of the Pawnee,* pp. 404–6.

23. Her experiences would doubtless have been considered less bizarre in a traditional culture. I am reminded of the words of Lakota Sioux John Fire (Lame Deer): "The real vision . . . is not a dream; it is very real. It hits you sharp and clear like an electric shock. You are wide awake and, suddenly, there is a person standing next to you who you know can't be there at all, yet you are not dreaming; your eyes are open" (John Fire and Richard Erdoes, *Lame Deer, Seeker of Visions* (New York: Simon and Schuster, 1972, p. 65).

24. Marie-Louise von Franz with Fraser Boa, op. cit., pp. 16–17.

25. Sigmund Freud, *The Interpretation of Dreams,* p. 620.

26. Mary Watkins, op. cit., p. 3.

27. Ray Grasse, op. cit., pp. 35–36, quoting C. G. Jung, "The Symbolic Life" in *Collected Works,* vol. 18 (Princeton: Princeton University Press, 1980), p. 255.

28. Lee Irwin, op. cit., p. 237.

29. Jamake Highwater, op. cit., p. 69.

30. D. M. Dooling and Paul Jordan-Smith, eds., *I Become Part of It: Sacred Dimension in Native American Life* (San Francisco: HarperSanFrancisco, 1989), p. 20.

31. Scott Thybony, field notes, May 1996; private communications with Ben Barney, Theresa Cahn-Tober, Victress Hitchcock; Michelle Boorstein, "Deity Visit to Navajos Questioned," *The Denver Post,* June 16, 1996, pp. 18f.

32. Ingo Swann, *The Great Apparitions of Mary* (New York: Crossroad, 1996), pp. 119–31.

33. Lee Irwin, op. cit., p. 46.

Epilogue

1. Edward M. Gomez, "Modern Art's Missing Link: The Jersey Scene," *The New York Times,* February 21, 1999, pp. A47–48.

Index

and synchronicity, 312, 313–14
and time, 240
and tribal cultures, 43
Jung, Franz, 22–24

Kagwahiv people, 187
Kalachakra (Tibetan ritual), 238
Karass, dreaming by, 152–54
Kasatkin, Vasily, 64, 68
Kazantzakis, Nikos, *The Last Temptation of Christ,* 295–96
Keats, John, 52
Kellog, W. K., 76
Khamtrul Rinpoche, 268–69
King, Martin Luther, Jr., 163
Konqobe, Percy Ndithembile, 126–28
Krakaphony, 346n19
Krishna, Gopi, 259–60, 261
Kubrick, Stanley, *Eyes Wide Shut,* 142–43

Lady-Smith Black Mambazo, 174
Laing, R. D., 13
Lakota culture, and dreams, 48
Lame Deer (Native American sage), 21, 347n23
Language, and dreams, 21, 47–50
"Last Night," Machado, xi
The Last Temptation of Christ (film), Kazantzakis, 295–96
Lawrence, Laura, 190–95
Lennon, John, murder of, 228
LeShan, Lawrence, 43
Lindbergh, Charles, 322
Literary approach to dream interpretation, 47–50
Living images, in dreams, 173–208
Lockhart, Russell, 117
Logic of dreams, 29
Lone Man (Teton Sioux leader), 253
Love, 134–35
dreams and, 144
Loved ones, shared dreams, 120–21
Lucid dreams, 76–77, 303–9
Luria, Isaac, 187
Lyons, Orren, 160

McGarey, Gladys, 84–85
Machado, Antonio, "Last Night," xi
Madonna, dreams of, 185–86
Maggid, 187–90
The Magic Mountain, Mann, 148
Mahakala (Tibetan deity), 293
Makabella, Claude, 205

Malraux, André, 325
Mandorla, 298
Mann, Thomas, *The Magic Mountain,* 148
The Man Who Fell to Earth (film), 12
Marpa the Translator (Tibetan sage), 325
Marriage, 146–47
Maya people, and dreams, 155
Meaning, in Healing Dreams, 38, 40
Medical practitioners, and dreams, 80–86
Medieval Christians, and precognitive dreams, 220–21
Meier, C. A., 314
Memories, Dreams, Reflections, Jung, 23
Memory, and precognition, 217–18
Mental illness, 190, 321–22
Merleau-Ponty, Maurice, 27
Merloo, Joost, 122–23, 125, 141, 218
Merrill, William, 316–17
Merton, Thomas, 111, 252
Meyers, Frederic, 76
A Midsummer Night's Dream, Shakespeare, 17
Milarepa (Tibetan saint), 42, 250, 272, 283
Mind-body connection, in dreams, 78
Miraculous healings, 78–80
Mirror world of shadow, 283–86
Myoē (Japanese Zen sage), 231, 325
Mysterium tremendum, 192, 197
Mystery of Healing Dreams, 39–40, 43–44
Myth, dreams and, 12–13

Narendra (Swami Vivekananda), 311–12
Naropa (Tibetan sage), 289–91
Native Americans
and animals, 58
and childhood dreams, 92–93
See also Indigenous peoples; Tribal societies; tribes by name
Nature
Healing Dreams and, 86–90
loss of connection with, 324
Navajo people and dream spirits, 178, 326–27
Nazi Germany, dreams in, 165–69
Negative qualities, Healing Dreams and, 272–96
The Never-Ending Story (film), 5–7
Newton, John, 104–5
New York Times, 334
Nietzsche, Friedrich, *The Dawn of Day,* 302
Nightmares, 62
Nonlocal reality, 233, 235
Nonself, dreams and, 28
Nonsense, of dreams, 29
Non-Western cultures, and dreams, 42

Tedlock, Barbara, 155
Telepathic dreams, 123–25, 128, 341n3, n6
Temiar Senoi (Malay tribe), 154–55
Temporal simultaneity, 233
Teresa of Avila, Saint, 178
Tertium (unknown factor), 314
Terton (treasure discoverer), 338n10
Thelma (*sangoma* priestess), 222
Themes in dream interpretation, 11–12
Therapy, for nightmares, 62, 63
The Third Reich of Dreams, Beradt, 165–68
Thoreau, Henry David, 297
Tibetan Buddhism, deities of, 181
Time, 238–40
    as fourth dimension, 235
    indigenous cultures and, 234
    predictive dreams and, 210–13
Titanic disaster, precognitive dreams, 232
Tracking dreams, 122–29
Traditional cultures
    and dream figures, 174
    and time, 238, 239–40
    See also Indigenous peoples; Native
        Americans; Tribal societies
Transformational changes, 111–18
Transforming power of Healing Dreams, 21, 38
Trekchö, 307–8
Tribal societies, 324–25
    contact with dream spirits, 190
    and dreams, 34–35, 149, 158–60, 315,
        338n20, 340n14
    figures in, 174–76
    interpretation of, 42–43
    precognitive, 219–20, 226–28
    dream-sharing customs, 151–52, 154–55
    shamanic training, 199
    spirit figures, 184
    and time, 239–40
    See also Indigenous peoples; Native Ameri-
        cans; Traditional cultures
Trivial events, precognitive dreams of, 232
Two guitars dream, 46–47, 49–50, 53–54

Ullman, Montague, 171
Unborn child, dream of, 119–20
Unconscious, 27
    and disease, 87
    relationship with, 22
Underworld dreams, 258, 262–63

Values, Healing Dreams and, 29
van Damm, John, 157–58
van de Castle, Robert, 212

van der Post, Laurens, 14, 160–61
    The Dream of the Grasshopper, 313
van Eeden, Frederik Willems, 303–4
Venesection, Galen, 75
Venn diagrams, 298
Visionary, life of, 269–70
Visions, 180, 342n2
Visitations, 54, 198, 204–5
    dreams in pregnancy as, 120
    Healing Dreams, 326–28
Vital, Hayim, 187
Vocation, dreams and, 105, 111–18, 256
    See also Calling in life
Voices, in Healing dreams, 177–84
Volkelt, J., 62–63
von Franz, Marie-Louise, 52, 111–12, 275,
    313, 321–22
Vonnegut, Kurt, *Cat's Cradle*, 152
Vuksinick, Louis, 258–61, 265

Waking dreams, 310–12
Waking Dreams, Watkins, 323–24
Wallace, Anthony, 159, 219
Warning dreams, 219
Warnings, dream interpretations, 11
Warts, psychosomatic disappearance of, 77
Water, dream symbolism of, 87–90
A Waterfront Community Dream Journal,
    157–58
Watkins, Mary, 51–52
    Waking Dreams, 323–24
Western civilization, and spirit world, 182, 184
Wheeler, John, 235, 237
Wholeness, sense of, 29–30, 70–72, 196–97
Wilson, Peter Lamborn, 48
Wilson, Woodrow, 284
Wise child archetype, 120
Wittgenstein, Ludwig, 303
Wolf, Fred Alan, 232–33, 235, 237–38, 240
Woodman, Marion, 18
Word-puzzles in dreams, 67
Wounded Knee massacre, 267
Wovoka (Plains Indian prophet), 160
Writers Dreaming, Gurganus, 55
Writing of dreams, 48

Yazzie, Irene, 326
Yeats, William Butler, 91, 182–83

Zieghelboim, Jacob, 279–83
Zimbabwe visitation, 329
Zohar, 219, 223, 232
Zuni Indian rituals, 284